CHILDREN IN PLAY, STORY, AND SCHOOL

Children in Play, Story, and School

Edited by

Artin Göncü

Elisa L. Klein

THE GUILFORD PRESS
New York   London

191230

© 2001 The Guilford Press
A Division of Guilford Publications, Inc.
72 Spring Street, New York, NY 10012
www.guilford.com

Printed in the United States of America

This book is printed on acid-free paper.

Last digit is print number: 9   8   7   6   5   4   3   2   1

Library of Congress Cataloging-in-Publication Data

Children in play, story, and school / edited by Artin Göncü, Elisa
    L. Klein.
        p. cm.
    Includes bibliographical references and index.
    ISBN 1-57230-577-0
    1. Play. 2. Storytelling. 3. Child development. 4. Early
childhood education—United States.   I. Göncü, Artin. II. Klein,
Elisa L.
    LB1137 .C474   2001
    372.21—dc21   2001035103

About the Editors

Artin Göncü, PhD, is a professor in the Department of Educational Psychology at the University of Illinois at Chicago (UIC). He received his doctorate in Developmental Psychology from the University of Houston. Previously, he served as coordinator of the graduate program in Early Childhood Education at UIC, as a postdoctoral research fellow at the University of Utah, and as a research associate and a preschool teacher at the Human Development Lab at the University of Houston. Dr. Göncü is a board member of the Piaget Society and the Center for Research on Child Culture at Ankara University, in Turkey. He serves on the editorial boards of *American Educational Research Journal, Early Education and Development,* and the *Bogazici University Journal of Education.* Among his publications are *Analyzing Children's Play Dialogues* (1984, edited with Frank Kessel) and *Children's Engagement in the World: Sociocultural Perspectives* (1999).

Elisa L. Klein, PhD, is an associate professor in the Department of Human Development and the Institute for Child Study at the University of Maryland at College Park, where she is currently a Lilly/Center for Teaching Excellence Fellow. She received her doctorate in Human Development and Family Studies from The Pennsylvania State University. Previously, Dr. Klein was the director of the Center for Young Children at the University of Maryland, and was a faculty member at The Ohio State University. A recent Child Development Research Fellow in the Administration on Children, Youth and Families of the U.S. Department of Health and Human Services, Dr. Klein assisted in the development of the final report for the Head Start Family Child Care Demonstration project. She has served on the editorial boards of *Early Childhood Research Quarterly* and *Early Education and Development,* and currently is an Advisory Board member to the Half the Sky Foundation, an education and philanthropic organization designed to conduct research and provide early intervention programs in public orphanages in the People's Republic of China. Among her publications are *Children and Computers* (1985) and recent articles in *Early Childhood Research Quarterly* and the *International Journal of Early Childhood Education.*

Contributors

Virginia Allhusen, PhD, Department of Psychology and Social Behavior, School of Social Ecology, University of California–Irvine, Irvine, CA

Yair Bar-Haim, PhD, Institute for Child Study, Department of Human Development, University of Maryland, College Park, MD

Anna Bondioli, PhD, Department of Philosophy, University of Pavia, Pavia, Italy

Inge Bretherton, PhD, Human Development and Family Studies, University of Wisconsin–Madison, Madison, WI

Charissa S. L. Cheah, PhD, Department of Psychology, Yale University, New Haven, CT

Alison Clarke-Stewart, PhD, Department of Psychology and Social Behavior, School of Social Ecology, University of California–Irvine, Irvine, CA

Lynn Dietrich Darling, PhD, Department of Human Development, University of Maryland, College Park, MD

Rheta DeVries, PhD, Regent's Center for Early Developmental Education, University of Northern Iowa, Cedar Falls, IA

Greta G. Fein, PhD, Department of Human Development, University of Maryland, College Park, MD

Nathan A. Fox, PhD, Department of Human Development, University of Maryland, College Park, MD

Lee Galda, PhD, Department of Curriculum and Instruction, University of Minnesota, Minneapolis, MN

Rivka Glaubman, PhD, School of Education, Bar-Ilan University, Ramat Gan, Israel

Artin Göncü, PhD, College of Education, University of Illinois at Chicago, Chicago, IL

Frits Goossens, PhD, Department of Child Psychology, Vrije University, Amsterdam, The Netherlands

Lois A. Groth, PhD, Graduate School of Education, George Mason University, Fairfax, VA

Patricia Herman, PhD, Prevent Child Abuse–Wisconsin, Madison, WI

Carollee Howes, PhD, Department of Education, University of California–Los Angeles, Los Angeles, CA

Gabi Kashi, MA, School of Education, Bar-Ilan University, Ramat Gan, Israel

Elisa L. Klein, PhD, Department of Human Development, University of Maryland, College Park, MD

Rina Koresh, MA, School of Education, Bar-Ilan University, Ramat Gan, Israel

Larry J. Nelson, PhD, School of Family Life, Brigham Young University, Provo, UT

Erin Oldham, PhD, Edmund S. Muskie School of Public Service, University of Southern Maine, Portland, ME

Michelle B. Patt, MS, College of Education, University of Illinois at Chicago, Chicago, IL

A. D. Pellegrini, PhD, Department of Educational Psychology, University of Minnesota, Minneapolis, MN

Douglas R. Powell, PhD, Department of Child and Family Studies, Purdue University, West Lafayette, IN

Kenneth H. Rubin, PhD, Department of Human Development, University of Maryland, College Park, MD

R. Keith Sawyer, PhD, Department of Education, Washington University, St. Louis, MO

Brian Sutton-Smith, PhD, Department of Human Development, University of Pennsylvania, Philadelphia, PA

Louisa B. Tarullo, EdD, Commissioner's Office on Research and Evaluation, Administration on Children, Youth, and Families, U.S. Department of Health and Human Services, Washington, DC

Contents

PART I

❧

Introduction

1

❧

Children in Play, Story, and School

A Tribute to Greta G. Fein

ARTİN GÖNCÜ
ELISA L. KLEIN

We prepared this volume to honor the contributions of Greta G. Fein to the fields of developmental psychology and early childhood education. Throughout her career, Greta's work focused on understanding and educating young children. She worked with children and their families first as a teacher and then as a researcher and policymaker. Her efforts to understand young children in her research focused on children's pretend play, storytelling, and the role of day care in children's development and education. It is these areas of work that have grown in relation to one another in Greta's career and that have guided many of us. Thus, it is these three areas of research that we celebrate in this volume.

Greta G. Fein's work on pretend play brought this activity to the attention of developmental psychologists and early educators as an important undertaking of childhood that is worthy of scientific inquiry in its own right. Most notable was her 1975 article, "Transformational Analysis of Pretending," in which she examined early pretend play as an expression of infants' developing symbolic competence. Beginning with this contribution, Greta's work expanded to include development and expression of symbolic competence during the toddler and preschool years. Based on her empirical work, Greta provided a develop-

mental model on symbolic competence presented first in her 1979 chapter and later elaborated in 1981. The components of this model such as
decontextualization, self–other relations, object substitutions, and role
adoptions have become established categories of research on children's
play. The present volume brings forth the most recent advances in conceptualizing pretend play as symbolic competence in chapters by
Bondioli, Glaubman and her collaborators, and Sutton-Smith.

More recently, Greta has incorporated communicative and affective
dimensions of children's play into her work. In this line of work, she
forcefully argued that pretend play is a free-flowing activity in its communication and affect. In her 1982 article, Greta described how children
flexibly establish communicative frames for their pretend play (Fein,
Moorin, & Enslein, 1982). Later on, in 1989, Greta "bust[ed] loose," to
borrow Sutton-Smith's term (see Chapter 7), from the traditional conceptualization of pretend play in claiming and illustrating that pretend
play is an interpretive activity in which young children master the
meaning of experiences of deep emotional significance. To do so, children use pretend play as freedom in maneuvering the nature and flow
of events as they wish. In the same article, Greta proposed a model of
how pretend play serves as a reflective activity and supported it with
the data she collected from "master players." Greta's conceptualization
of pretend play as an affective as well as a cognitive activity influenced
many scholars of pretend play and storytelling such as Sawyer, Rubin,
Bondioli, Glaubman, DeVries, Sutton-Smith, Bretherton, Pellegrini, and
Galda whose works are included in the present volume.

Greta's interest in children's communication and representation in
pretend play led her to the study of another imaginative activity in
which children express themselves freely: storytelling. She made the
connection between pretend play and storytelling for us by stating that
"symbolic play is an early developing narrative form, it may prepare
the way for other forms, such as story telling" (p. 155). In an expected
manner, Greta's work focused on aspects of narrative competence in
symbolic play. She concentrated on two aspects of narrative competence
as functioning as an actor, giving voice to story events, and as a director,
justifying and managing story events. Building on the work of Sutton-
Smith, Greta (1995) recently characterized children's storytelling in
terms of seven developmental levels. The influence of Greta's work on
storytelling is evident in this volume in the chapters by Sutton-Smith,
Herman, and Bretherton, Pellegrini and Galda, and Groth and Darling.

Greta's work in the adult–child interaction, day-care, and social
policy arenas has helped to shape the framework of critical issues in
child care for more than two decades, beginning with her landmark volume with Clarke-Stewart, *Day Care in Context* (1973). Well before the
more recent debate about the effects of day care on infants fueled by

Belsky's (1986) provocative article, Fein and Clarke-Stewart (1973) stressed the importance of research that looks at the relationships between quality of care and child outcomes. A second collaboration with Clarke-Stewart (1983) yielded a comprehensive update for the *Handbook of Child Psychology*. This piece, combined with special issues on infant day care in *Early Childhood Research Quarterly* (1988a, 1988b) edited by Greta Fein and Nathan Fox, and Greta's research on infant day care in Italy (e.g., Fein, Gariboldi, & Boni, 1993) unraveled interactions between quality of care and infant development. In all this work, Greta (1993) has been clear about the social and political context of child care, noting that "extrafamilial child care is an established social reality, one which psychological or educational research did little to bring about. Those who feed the stigma divert us from the difficult task of improving the quality and accessibility of child care for American families" (p. 390). As the chapters by Clarke-Stewart and colleagues, Howes and Oldham, Fox and Bar-Haim, Patt and Göncü, Powell, and Klein and Tarullo illustrate, Greta's commitment to advancing children's development and education is maintained by many scholars in research on attachment, teacher–child collaboration, and social policy.

Influenced by Greta G. Fein's work on play, story, and school, a community of scholars came together in this volume to make the following points. First, children express their interpretations of events spontaneously in play and storytelling in school/child-care settings, enabling researchers to have direct access to children's functioning *in situ*. Second, children express themselves directly in play, story, and school as well as indirectly, revealing important information for clinical and educational use. Third, play, story, and school allow us to focus on different psychological dimensions of development such as cognition, communication, and affect. Fourth, we share the conviction that play, story, and school are inextricably connected in the life of young Western children. Understanding children's development and education should mean studying these activities in relation to one another. Fifth and finally, play, story, and school allow us to study the development of children both when children engage in these activities, alone or with peers, parents, or other adults, enabling us to understand the contribution of different people to children's development and education.

ORGANIZATION OF THE BOOK

The three substantive sections are devoted to play, storytelling, and school and child care, respectively. The book concludes with a chapter by Greta G. Fein.

In Part II, "Children in Play," we explore how social play arises

(Sawyer; Cheah, Nelson, & Rubin), its developmental and educational significance (Cheah, Nelson, & Rubin; DeVries), and the ways in which we can promote social play in early education classrooms (Bondioli, Glaubman, Kashi, & Koresh). These chapters collectively emphasize children's play as a free-flowing activity of affective significance. In addition, consistent with the current emphasis in our field on understanding children's development in its social and cultural context (cf. Göncü, 1999), each chapter makes a concerted effort to describe social play within its context. The chapters discuss in detail social play as a function of children's partners, the play setting, and the kind of adult–child interaction and adult values that provide the framework for children's development. As a corollary to these, chapters in the first section discuss methodological considerations in studying social play.

Conceptualizing social pretend play as a free-flowing activity motivated by children's need to master experiences of affective significance has resulted in two important contributions articulated in the first section: (1) social play contributes to children's development of oral tradition and peer culture (Sawyer) as well as promoting social, cognitive, and affective competence (Cheah et al.), and social pretend play is motivated by children's own needs;therefore, using social play in an educational setting means we must follow the children's lead in the classroom (DeVries). Further, "training" programs designed to promote pretend play should take into account children's ability and desire to symbolize in making a judgment about whether an intervention is needed and, if so, where it should start. The evidence shows that when done appropriately, play(ful) interventions work effectively in diverse cultures of the world such as the United States (DeVries), Italy (Bondioli), and Israel (Glaubman et al.).

Part II opens with a contribution from Sawyer, who conceptualizes pretend play as an improvisational activity. Sawyer likens children's pretend play to adult improvisational theater and discusses the similarities between these two activities. Sawyer provides both psychological and historical analyses to show that children's social play enables children to develop a peer culture with its own oral tradition. Sawyer illustrates that social play is simultaneously an activity of the individual child and an activity of the peer group, and maintains that developmental psychology has typically conceptualized and analyzed social play from the perspective of individual children without considering the play group as a unit of analysis. Thus, Sawyer proposes the peer group as an additional unit of analysis to be considered in future work and presents data from his own research with preschool-age children to illustrate his ideas.

Consistent with Sawyer's emphasis on social play as a culture-making activity during childhood, Cheah et al. discuss the contribution of social play to children's development and warn us that nonsocial play may be a risk factor in early childhood. Cheah and collaborators discuss the classical and current developmental theories on the nature and significance of social play, present a thorough literature review on the correlates of social and non-social play forms, offer an analytic strategy, and conclude with the possible factors contributing to the development of social play. Cheah and her collaborators present data indicating that in order to understand children's behaviors we need to go beyond observable behaviors of children and look at their physiological functioning. Also, consistent with the current arguments that children's play cannot be understood without taking into account their familial and cultural background (Göncü, 1999), Cheah et al. recommend that children's play be examined in relation to parental values and cultural priorities.

The next three chapters of Part II examine play as an educational tool and discuss how to promote play in the classroom. DeVries opens her presentation with a review of prominent theories such as those of Dewey, Piaget, and Vygotsky. Using these and her own views as a base, DeVries takes a constructivist look at the use of play as an educational device in early childhood programs, and she determines that the meaning of play and its implementation vary across programs. DeVries identifies four variations. In one type of classroom, play is peripheral to learning. In another, play is disguised work. In a third, play is conceptualized as a significant social and emotional activity. And, finally, in the fourth type, play is recognized as a significant activity serving social, emotional, moral, and intellectual functions. DeVries uses teachers' conceptions of play, classroom setup and materials, and peer interaction to illustrate the differences among these four types of early childhood classrooms. After illustrating the differences across programs in the meaning and use of play, DeVries concludes that play as a descriptor of developmentally appropriate practice may have outlived its usefulness because its meaning can be easily misunderstood. To persuade educators of the value of educational play, child developmental specialists must conceptualize and describe what kinds of specific play activities contribute to children's development and knowledge.

In the first of two chapters covering two play intervention studies, Bondioli discusses the role of adult intervention in promoting pretend play in early childhood classrooms. She argues that previous intervention programs focused primarily on the effects of adult intervention without paying careful attention to the nature of the intervention. In her contribution, Bondioli presents a model of adult intervention developed on the basis of ideas drawn from the work of Wood and Vygotsky in which she argues that an effective tutor has to perform two main tasks. The first is to facilitate children's expression of symbolic meanings; and the second is to tutor in children's "zo-ped" in order to improve their play performances. Consistent with DeVries, Bondioli states that an effective tutor should remember that he or she should be both a competent and an imaginative and cooperative companion to children, and that he or she is a teacher with an educational task to accomplish, providing play intervention according to children's existing skills. Also, consistent with Sawyer, Bondioli recognizes social play as a group as well as an individual activity and illustrates that intervention programs should take into account group as well as individual children's activities. Bondioli's empirical work follows the presentation of her model, supporting her claims that adult guidance based on children's needs results in improved symbolic competence on the part of the children.

Both Bondioli's chapter and the chapter following, by Glaubman and her collaborators, argue that adult intervention should not be limited to enhancing the play of children who appear not to be functioning to their fullest potential. In their chapter, Glaubman et al. make it clear that middle- as well as low-income children can benefit from working with an adult who helps children to improve the narrative quality of their pretend play. This chapter presents a model of intervention that draws from the work of Bruner as well as Fein and espouses that children should be introduced gradually to symbolic use of objects in imaginative plots. The model involves introducing children to the realistic features and functions of objects first and then to their potential imaginative use. In the final stage of intervention, the adult helps children to construct imaginative story lines in which play use of objects is embedded. In addition, this model requires that play intervention be provided outside children's play activities, indirectly inviting children to incorporate symbolic activities into their play on their own accord rather than as a result of adult request.

In Part III, "Children in Story," we first explore the psychological origins and significance of storytelling. This effort appeared necessary in view of the fact that storytelling is a common activity of childhood although only a few early childhood educators have paid attention to it (e.g., Paley, 1981). One contribution of the present chapters to the existing literature is in their illustration that children's stories are like their pretend play insofar as stories are a type of symbolic representation where children talk about events of deep affective significance. As the chapters by Sutton-Smith, Herman and Bretherton, and Groth and Darling exemplify, children's narratives may be full of intense feelings, such as those surrounding the loss (in divorce) of a parent, and vivid imaginary creatures and events, such as poisonous mice or being in a dungeon. A second contribution especially evident in the work of Sutton-Smith is to note that children's stories become increasingly complex with age.

The chapters seek to illustrate that storytelling contributes to children's development and education. At varying degrees of explicitness, all the contributors argue that storytelling is an activity of reflection, enabling children to recognize and articulate their feelings. Herman and Bretherton also discuss the significance of storytelling as a therapeutic activity that helps children cope with stressful events. Groth and Darling, and Pellegrini and Galda, show the educational function of storytelling with a focus on the connection between storytelling and literacy. In addition, Groth and Darling state that events involved in participating in storytelling and enactment contribute to children's development of morality and autonomy.

Sutton-Smith opens his chapter with a presentation of Fein's thesis that it is critical emotional events that lead children to engage in pretend play and to tell stories. Fein's proposal that a double-layered system of representations, one for practical and one for affective knowledge, is summarized to account for how affective knowledge becomes the subject of children's play and stories during the third year of life. Afterward, Sutton-Smith seeks to establish the origins and nature of emotionality involved in pretend play and stories. Toward this end, he justifies treating pretend play and narrative and then proposes a double-layered system of his own that is in some ways parallel to Fein's. Sutton-Smith argues that pretend play and story are both orderly and disorderly, and thus paradoxical, activities. For example, pretend play can be both constructive and destructive at the same time. By drawing from recent advances in neurology, Sutton-Smith proffers an evolutionary explanation for the paradoxical nature of pretend play and narratives. Although speculative, his compelling argument is that activities such as pretend play may be children's solution to the conflict between the involuntary primary emotions that are located in amygdala and the voluntary secondary emotions that are located in the cerebral cortex. Presentation of empirical data follow this discussion and the chapter concludes with developmental functions of pretend play and narrative.

Herman and Bretherton present postdivorce children's reaction in their narratives to loss. Preschool-age children's narratives in response to a story stem presented as part of a larger battery of tests constituted the basis of Herman and Bretherton's analyses. In this procedure, the story beginning is acted out with family figures and the child is then invited to demonstrate and describe what happens next. Using Fein's work on symbolic play, among others', as a point of departure, Herman and Bretherton expected that children's narratives would reflect their reaction to their parents' divorce. Extensive qualitative analyses and the clinical interpretations based on such analyses revealed that children identified the family figures with their own parents. In an expected manner, children expressed feelings about divorce, including a wish for family reunification, sadness at the loss of fathers, and anger fathers, as well as feelings of vulnerability. In addition, children's narratives revealed significant information about their relationships with their mothers and fathers which Herman and Bretherton characterized as benevolent, malevolent, or ambivalent.

The last two chapters in Part III examine the educational functions of storytelling in schools. In the first of these chapters, Pellegrini and Galda argue that narrative language is used as a response to a highly emotional event such as conflicts with peers and breaches of conventionality. Thus, certain types of relationships such as friendships would be more conducive to narrative language than others such as acquaintances. In addition, Pellegrini and Galda discuss how different activities of children such as pretend play and structured instruction may play a role in their use of narrative language. Pellegrini and Galda report on a study in which they observed kindergarten children either in friend or in acquaintance dyads as children engaged either in pretend play or in writing activities overseen by an adult. The analyses were based on the children's production of different linguistic forms as well as the dynamics of their interactions. By drawing our attention to the complexity of their results, Pellegrini and Galda provide specific directions for future research on how children's relationships and activities contribute to their development and education.

Groth and Darling examine storytelling and its educational function in preschool classrooms. They participated in the activities of a classroom where children did not have much previous experience in storytelling, and they then served as scribes to the children, who dictated their stories. Subsequently, the children were asked to enact their stories before the entire group. An extensive database included field notes, videotapes, and children's stories. Groth and Darling's analyses begin with a description of how the children were chosen to participate in the storytelling activity, their reactions to transformations of words into print, and their conceptions of structural elements of a written story, such as its length and title. Then, the authors move on to the description of the children's enactment of their stories with a focus on casting procedure, style, and production. Based on their analyses, Groth and Darling conclude that storytelling and dictation contribute to children's development of literacy.

Part IV, "Children in School," explores children's emerging interactions in the larger world as they move into child-care and early school settings. The significance of child-care and school experiences for young children is examined through a focus on widening spheres of influence from family to school to larger societal contexts. The importance of the infant and young child's attachment formation and the effect of extended time in child care on children's social relationships is explored from three different vantage points: individual variation in the establishment of attachment relationships with primary caregivers in child care (Howes & Oldham), appropriate assessments of attachment for children who have already developed relationships with other adults (Clarke-Stewart, Allhusen, & Goossens), and predictability of lifespan theories of attachment from early assessment of attachment (Fox & Bar-Haim). The nature of teacher–child interactions in constructivist early childhood classrooms is analyzed (Patt & Göncü). Relationships between these two critical environments for children's development, the home and school, are looked at through the larger lens of policy for parent–school partnerships (Powell). Finally, the implications of our understanding of children's development along with other dimensions of quality that contribute to optimizing child-care and early education settings is discussed with respect to the formulation of social policy (Klein & Tarullo).

The emphasis on social policy issues is most timely and critical to the developmental and educational focus of the volume. With the increased interest in child care, preschool, and Head Start classrooms as the first and primary social context for learning beyond the home, an understanding of how we define quality and establish policies to ensure that all children have the opportunity for high-quality programs in the early years is essential. Recent research on the effects of low-quality programs during infancy and early childhood dramatically shows that poor or limited experiences inhibit optimal development. Decreased opportunities for play, stories, and interactions with adults and peers that are important conduits for healthy cognitive, social, and emotional development may contribute to a poor beginning to formal schooling. Indeed, America's Goals 2000 cited the need for children to enter school "ready to learn" as the number-one priority for this country's educational aspirations. Because of its emphasis on the significance of early education, this book will be of interest to scholars in the field of child care and social policy.

Clarke-Stewart and her colleagues take a close look at the validity of the Strange Situation as the primary data source in research on attachment formation of children in child care. A careful review of the history of research on infant care and attachment notes the growing consensus that few differences exist in strength of measured attachment in child-care and in non–child-care children. Clarke-Stewart and collaborators suggest that the Strange Situation may not be a fair assessment of attachment security for children in child care. They argue that the Strange Situation is a fundamentally different assessment for those who are used to repeated separations from mothers as part of their regular schedule as they enter the child-care setting, and who are consistently played with and comforted by adults other than their parents, than it is for those who are usually at home with their mothers. If separations are a routine part of children's schedule, they may react with less distress during the Strange Situation procedure. They won't seek immediate comfort and proximity with their mothers. To examine this more closely, Clarke-Stewart and colleagues developed a new measure, the California Attachment Procedure, which does not include maternal separations or interactions with strange women as does the Strange Situation. In this chapter, they report on a study in which they used both the Strange Situation and the California Attachment Procedure with a sample of toddlers. Results suggest that the Strange Situation measure itself may be the source for differences in attachment insecurity found in the child-care sample in attachment research.

Howes and Oldham examine the ways in which young children form attachment with child-care providers. Looking at toddlers who developed relationships with caregivers after initial attachment with parents, Howes and Oldham are interested in how children use their previously developed repertoire of social behaviors with new adults, and if the emergence of this new attachment relationship differs in significant ways which necessitates the use of new relationship skills. Individual variation may necessitate differential responses on the part of the caregivers. Toddlers entering new child-care settings may be fearful and avoidant, whereas others may be trusting and affectionate from the outset. Sensitive caregivers are alerted to these signals as indicative of individual variations that require personalized strategies for helping children in the formation of new attachment relationships. In the longitudinal study reported here, Howes and Oldham looked at type and intensity of attachment behaviors of toddlers at first entry to child care and then assessed attachment security 6 months later. Individual differences at entry to child care were not predictive of attachment security at 6 months. The authors caution, however, that this should not be interpreted as reason to assume that all children make this adjustment easily and without caregiver attention and support. To the contrary, the personalized support given, especially by one particular adult in settings with multiple caregivers, helped all children in this initial transition period

A third chapter, by Fox and Bar-Haim, completes the focus on attachment issues in child care and beyond. The authors look at the formation of attachment relationships during infancy and their influence on later relationships beyond. Attachment theorists have examined states of mind with regard to attachment experiences in older children and adults in an attempt to determine whether working models of attachment change over the course of the lifespan. In this chapter, Fox and Bar-Haim review recent research on lifespan conceptualizations of attachment, with particular focus on the influence family life events and nonparental caregivers (such as in child care) may have on stability of attachment behaviors over time. A lifespan model must account for any shifts in attachment that may occur as a result of the changes that occur during normal development of the child in the family and the larger world. The authors suggest that indeed stability of mental representations would be unusual given the many transitions that naturally occur throughout children's lives, and that this limits the predictability of later attachment from early working models. This in turn may place less emphasis on the "criticality" of attachment relationships during the first 12 months of life and increased focus on the shifts and transitions that are the hallmark of lifespan development.

In their chapter, Patt and Göncü examine the essential tension between constructivist principles of development and learning and teacher–child interaction in an early childhood classroom. They articulate what many constructivist teachers struggle with on a daily basis: developing the role of a facilitator and collaborator in children's constructions of activities, encouraging the development of autonomy and independent thinking, yet also efficiently running a classroom and supporting the play of young children. Patt and Göncü explore the varying conditions in the classroom that may lead constructivist teachers to provide different types and levels of guidance during particular events and report on a study of teacher–child interactions during cooking activities that confirm the flexible and complex nature of these interactions.

Powell provides a new perspective on parent–school connections in his chapter. He examines consistencies and inconsistencies in publicly espoused calls for parent–school partnerships and how these connect with or diverge from both theoretical perspectives and professional practice standards. Powell carefully describes the historical evolution of parent involvement from helpmates who supported school policy with no opportunity for input, to current views based on the assumption that parents are vital "partners" in the schooling enterprise. As the last goal of the National Educational Goals developed to guide U.S. education into the 21st century, parent–school partnerships have been incorporated into professional practice standards in early childhood education. Powell discusses the underlying theoretical perspectives in this evolution, including contributions from ecological and social interaction theory, and current approaches to professional–client relationships in the helping professions. The notion of shared decision making between families and schools, and its implications for the care and education of young children is examined in light of current and future approaches to parent–school relationships.

In the final chapter in this section, Klein and Tarullo address the emerging connections between research on child-care quality and policy and practice initiatives at the federal level in child care in the United States today. The chapter traces the advent of modern U.S. child-care policies and the influence of research on child-care quality on federal reforms. The primary focus of research on child care has been on the identification and measurement of essential indicators of quality and how these variables interact with ones that reside within the child and the family. Recent federal initiatives have targeted the quality issue as central to all research efforts, as the number of infants and young children in some form of nonparental care has rapidly increased yet the quality of child care has often been found to be poor. Klein and Tarullo provide a brief overview of the historical antecedents of modern child-care issues in this country and tie current research on child-care quality into this perspective. They conclude that although there has been a marked increase in our knowledge base on the determinants of child-care quality and its influence on children's emerging developmental competencies, changes in federal policies in child care have not kept pace with current research findings.

The final chapter, by Greta G. Fein, provides a brief summary of her own development, the events in her life that led her to devote her career to the study of young children and their well-being. She concludes with a discussion of ideas expressed in the present volume.

REFERENCES

Belsky, J. (1986). Infant day care: A cause for concern? *Zero to Three, 6,* 1–9.

Clarke-Stewart, A., & Fein, G. G. (1983). Early childhood programs. In P. H. Mussen (Series Ed.), & M. M. Haith & J. J. Campos (Vol. Eds.), *Handbook of child psychology: Vol. 2. Infancy and developmental psychobiology* (4th ed., pp. 917–999). New York: Wiley.

Fein, G. G. (1975). A transformational analysis of pretending. *Developmental Psychology, 11,* 291–296.

Fein, G. G. (1979). Play and the acquisition of symbols. In L. Katz (Ed.), *Topics in early childhood education.* Norwood, NJ: Ablex.

Fein, G. G. (1981). Pretend play: An integrative review. *Child Development, 52,* 1095–1118.

Fein, G. G. (1993). In defense of data adoration and even fetishism. *Early Childhood Research Quarterly, 8*, 387–395.

Fein, G. G. (1995). Toys and stories. In A. D. Pellegrini (Ed.), *The future of play theory* (pp. 151–164). Albany: State University of New York Press.

Fein, G. G., & Clarke-Stewart, A. (1973). *Daycare in context*. New York: Wiley.

Fein, G. G., Gariboldi, A., & Boni, R. (1993). Transitions to group care: The behavior of Italian infants and their teachers. *Early Childhood Research Quarterly, 8*, 1–4.

Fein, G. G., Moorin, E. R., & Enslein, J. (1982). Pretense and peer behavior: An intersectoral analysis. *Human Development, 25*, 392–406.

Fein, G. G., & Fox, N. (Eds.). (1988a). Infant day care, 1. *Early Childhood Research Quarterly, 3*(3).

Fein, G. G., & Fox, N. (Eds.). (1988b). Infant day care, 2. *Early Childhood Research Quarterly, 3*(4).

Göncü, A. (1999). *Children's engagement in the world: Sociocultural perspectives.* New York: Cambridge University Press.

Paley, V. (1981). *Wally's stories.* Cambridge, MA: Harvard University Press.

PART II

❧

Children in Play

2

🦋

Play as
Improvisational Rehearsal

Multiple Levels of Analysis
in Children's Play

R. KEITH SAWYER

When I became interested in pretend play in my first year of graduate school, I started my research by reading Greta G. Fein's 1981 review article in *Child Development*. This article provided an invaluable introduction to the field, as it had both breadth and depth, an integration of past work and an insightful critique. A few years later, I met Greta, just after she had reviewed my first book (Sawyer, 1997a). Her review comments were supportive, constructive, and insightful, and it was a pleasure to meet her in person. Because I study the improvisational aspects of play, I have continued to draw inspiration from Greta's critique of script models of play (Fein, 1987, 1991).

Children's sociodramatic play ranges from scripted to improvisational. At the scripted extreme, for example, children enact common event sequences from adult life, such as serving a meal; or they enact episodes from a popular animated movie. At the improvisational extreme, children combine characters, locations, and events to create a completely novel drama. Because of my interest in improvisational discourse, I have chosen to study the most improvisational episodes of sociodramatic play, and I study these group improvisations by focusing on the dramatic dialogues that children engage in—both as they enact their fantasy and as they negotiate and direct that fantasy (Sawyer, 1997a).

Like sociodramatic play, adult conversation is improvised—no one joins a conversation with a written script, and participants generally cannot predict where the conversation will go (Sawyer, 2001). In the past few years I have been studying an extremely improvisational form of adult discourse, the spontaneously created dialogues of *improvisational theater*—an alternative genre of theater in which the actors do not work from a script but instead collaboratively create their dialogue on stage (Sawyer, 1997b). Improv groups, like all theater groups, rehearse to prepare for their performances. But unlike conventional theater, the groups do not rehearse to prepare or to refine scripts. Instead, improv groups rehearse to hone the interactional, improvisational skills of the ensemble, to learn each other's rhythms, and to develop trust among the group members. Rather than learning a script, the group is learning the *process* of improvisation—how to listen to each other, how to get their heads into the odd mind-set of not thinking ahead. They're also learning to become an ensemble: how to create collaboratively with the group.

By analogy, sociodramatic play functions as a rehearsal for the improvisations of everyday adult conversation—the informal small talk that is so important to friendships, family life, and peer culture. Play is uniquely suited to this developmental function because its improvisation requires children to incorporate two influences that also operate on adult conversation: the *oral culture* and the *peer group*. Psychologists generally study sociodramatic play at an individual level of analysis, operationalizing variables for each child, and studying the development of individual children. Because most psychologists focus only on the individual child, they rarely manage to address these extra–individual influences: the preschool's oral culture and the preschool peer group.

In this chapter, I argue that a complete understanding of social development during play requires an analysis of not only the child's development but also development at these two collective levels of analysis. In sociodramatic play, development takes place on all three levels simultaneously. I provide examples that demonstrate that the group improvisations of play result in the development of the preschool class as a group and the development of the classroom's oral culture. The study of play conversation requires analysis at all three levels, because although they are interdependent, they are not reducible to each other (Sawyer, 1999). This interdependence is essential to development in any one of the levels; none of these levels can develop without the simultaneous presence of the other two. In this chapter, I focus on the two levels that are usually neglected by developmental psychologists: the oral culture and the peer group.

Oral culture is a subset of children's peer culture; it includes the texts, games, interactional patterns, scripts, and narratives that are voiced during play. Several social science disciplines—including folkloristics and linguistic anthropology—take the epistemological position that oral culture is a valid level of analysis in its own right, not requiring a reduction to psychological analyses of the individuals participating in the culture. In the first section, I provide some examples of how children's oral culture takes on a life of its own during improvisational play.

Sociodramatic play also results in development of the peer group. Children do not develop in isolation; they develop as part of social wholes—the family or the preschool class. As with any social group, repeated encounters result in a kind of group learning. In the second section, I draw on research on the life cycles of adult groups to explore how group play could result in group development.

Why can't we study all three levels by studying individual children's development? After all, preschool groups are formed of individual children, and the texts of peer culture would not exist if they were not internalized and spoken by individual children. Developmental psychologists typically proceed by assuming that everything interesting about development can be identified by studying the developmental trajectories of specific children, an assumption that has been referred to as *methodological individualism* (O'Neill, 1973).

But in fact, we cannot study oral cultures or peer groups by studying their component members, because interacting groups demonstrate the property of *emergence*—the behavior of the group is unpredictable and nonreducible to the mental states or behaviors of individual members of the group. Emergent behavior is found in many types of complex dynamical systems and is a foundational concept of much of today's computational modeling, including connectionist models of cognition and artificial-life models of social phenomena (Sawyer, 1999). When entities at one level of analysis (children) engage in complex interactions in a group, the entity at the next higher level of analysis (the peer group, the oral culture) *emerges* from those complex interactions. In complex systems, the behavior of the system is not additively predictable from the behavior of the component members (Clark, 1997; Resnick, 1994).

In a paradoxical and yet concrete way, these two higher levels of analysis—the peer group and the oral culture—take on a life of their own, and provide the context and the setting for child development. I say "paradoxical" because it is not the case that "new stuff" is mysteriously created by emergence; after all, the group is composed of individual children and nothing else. However, these two emergent levels of analysis begin to influence participants in a process that emergence theorists call *downward causation* (Sawyer, 1999); when complex systems exhibit downward causation, reductionist analysis cannot give us a complete explanation.

Emergent thinking is found in many disciplines that study complex systems—including connectionism, artificial life modeling, and complexity theory. In developmental psychology, emergent thinking is associated with socioculturalists, who argue that we cannot study development by studying individual children (see, for example, Rogoff, 1990). Socioculturalists are emergence theorists because they emphasize that these two levels of analysis—the group and the culture—cannot be reduced to analyses of individuals.

The next two sections present examples of how the improvised conversations of play result in development at the two collective levels of analysis, the peer group and the oral culture. Following these examples, I present an extended discussion of a recent study of children's play improvisations, with statistical analyses that evaluate the relative merits of reductionist and emergentist analyses of play discourse.

THE DEVELOPMENT OF ORAL CULTURE

It is the game that is played—it is irrelevant whether or not there is a subject who plays.
—HANS-GEORG GADAMER (1975, p. 93)

I have suggested that oral culture cannot be reduced to psychological study, and that the texts of oral culture must be studied as an independent level of analysis. An everyday example of oral culture that demonstrates this point is the urban myth. One classic urban myth tells the "true story" of how Neiman-Marcus charged a shopper $250 for its cookie recipe, not the $2.50 the woman had been expecting to pay. As revenge on the store for refusing to reverse this charge, she now provides the recipe for free and exhorts others to pass it along. In fact, Neiman-Marcus didn't even make a special cookie until after this myth had spread so widely that customers kept asking for "the cookie." Variants of this myth have been around for at least 50 years. The earliest documented version appears in a 1948 cookbook, describing a $25 fudge cake recipe sold by a railroad. In the 1960s, the story was told about the Waldorf-Astoria hotel's "Red Velvet Cake." In the 1970s, a similar story was told about Mrs. Fields' cookies.

The oral culture of a preschool classroom manifests the same processes in microcosm. Through the improvisational rehearsals of play, stable yet ephemeral texts of oral culture emerge, without conscious planning, design, or composition on the part of individual children. These improvisations are social, collaborative, emergent processes, and the performances that result are often different from what any single participant could have scripted. Many theater groups take advantage of this form of group creativity, using improvisation to develop scripts. For example, the British director Mike Leigh is famous for using improvisation to develop scripts and characters. Improvisation is the key to Leigh's unique directing style. During his 25-year career, Leigh has created over 20 award-winning movies, television films, and plays that begin with no script. Instead, he begins with an intuition, or a scene with a certain atmosphere, or a situation—really, just the seed of an idea.

Starting only with this seed, scenes and dialogues are worked out in close collaboration with his actors in months of rehearsals and improvisations, like a crystal forming and growing around the original seed idea. In the initial improvisations, Leigh works closely with the main actors, collaboratively creating each character's personality and his or her personal history. As the overall plot emerges from these improvisations, Leigh begins to create a rough plot outline—but he keeps it to himself.

After developing the characters, the next step is to have the actors improvise scenes that Leigh is beginning to sketch out. But the actors don't know what is "supposed" to happen in the scene, or where it fits in the overall scheme of the movie. When they are first thrust into a scene with another actor, their dialogue is as spontaneous as it would be in real life. But there is no improvisation when shooting: Leigh has written out a script and the actors memorize their lines before the final scene is filmed. Still, the actors don't know how it all fits together until they sit in the screening room and see the final edit of the film.

Why would a director use improvisation to develop a script when it takes so much longer and costs so much more than simply buying a script from a playwright? Leigh believes that improvised scenes are more true to life than any script, that improvisation can create dialogues that are more realistic than anything a playwright could invent.

Leigh's technique is not just for independent art-house films—it also forms the cornerstone of the most successful improv group, Chicago's Second City Theater, and its famous spinoff, *Saturday Night Live*. The founder, Paul Sills, convinced a group of fellow actors to try experimenting with a set of improvisational children's games that his mother had been using in preschool classrooms. Second City is still going strong in Chicago, performing every weekend on North Wells to sellout crowds of tourists and suburbanites. But in an ironic twist, Second

City, the originator of improv, no longer performs any improvisation on stage.

In fact, Second City has a strict policy that the actors will *not* perform improvisations during their shows. However, Second City continues to use improvisation during rehearsal, as a technique for developing skit ideas. If a good idea emerges during one of these improvisations, the cast collaborates to develop and refine the idea into a scripted 5-minute comedy sketch. The skits on *Saturday Night Live* often seem rooted in an improvised rehearsal, because some of these ideas have the oddball unpredictability that you see in an improv show.

The Development of Scripts through Play Improvisation

I've used an example from theater to demonstrate how group improvisation can result in the emergence of a text that then takes on a life of its own and is gradually refined into a written script. In one study of group improvisations, teachers asked a group of second- and third-graders to develop a play to perform for their parents (Baker-Sennett, Matusov, & Rogoff, 1992). But the children were not given a script, and the adults stayed in the background and did not direct the rehearsals. In this *playcrafting* assignment, children were given the same task as improvisational actors—to rehearse together, when there is no director and no script, for the final performance.

The children did remarkably well at the task and successfully performed their own plays at the end of the 1-month rehearsal period. This task is well within the abilities of 7-, 8-, and 9-year-olds. Children can work together to create a play, without being directed by an adult. Baker-Sennett et al. examined the conversational techniques that children used to negotiate their creation and found that the children frequently improvised during the rehearsals, as a kind of shorthand way of proposing new script ideas. That is, rather than explicitly propose their new idea to the other children, they start enacting and speak their proposed lines *in character*. The children were not taught to do this—these improvisational techniques emerged spontaneously among the child actors. What's more, over the course of the month of rehearsals, the percentage of time they spent improvising in character increased. As the basic form of the play fell into shape, as they became comfortable with each other and had worked out ground rules for collaboration, they could spend more time improvising—negotiating in character—rather than having to step out of character and speak as a director.

For comparison, the teachers also asked adults to help some of the groups. In these groups, the children never improvised together; instead, the adult directors made all the decisions and told the children what to do. In fact, the children were expecting the adults to do that, and consequently they sat waiting for direction. But with no adult to direct, the playcrafting task allowed the children to practice important skills that no teacher can teach—skills that can only be learned by doing. By improvising and rehearsing together, the children were learning essential conversational and social skills: how to solve problems and develop plans in group settings, how to share decision making, how to collaborate on a creative task—how to improvise.

The Development of Verbal Games through Play Improvisation

The pattern observed in the playcrafting experiment—that children begin their improvisational collaborations with more explicit metacommunication and then gradually shift to implicit, in-frame negotiation—seems to be a common pathway in the development of children's oral culture. In 1980, Susan Iwamura published a study of the verbal games created by two preschool girls as they rode to preschool every morning. Iwamura taped and transcribed their verbal games at both the beginning and the end of the school year, and she documented a development in these collaborative verbal performances that she called *ritualization*. Toward the end of the school year, once a particular game became ritualized, it had its own power to control the children—the ritual structure of the game created its own inertia, or momentum, which made it difficult for either child to modify any further.

How did these games develop? When they first emerged from unstructured interaction, these games had a lot of flexibility and room for embellishment—they did not start out ritualized right away. Iwamura documented a regular pattern to the process of ritualization. First, the girls experimented with *chains of adjacency pairs*, which gradually evolved into *routines*. These two developments were accompanied by a great deal of explicit discussion. With repetition and refinement, a routine eventually developed into a *ritualized routine*, and this final development tended to happen without much explicit discussion, almost as if the process of ritualization had a life of its own.

As with any peer group, it is tempting to analyze these verbal games as a property of the *group*—rather than arguing that they have an independent life of their own. But analysis at the group level misses a key point about children's oral culture: Once the game has been developed to a certain point, the children no longer have control over it; it begins to control them. A game that they have created, in turn, constrains their available range of creativity while they engage in it.

If we did not view the game as an independent level of analysis, we would have to analyze it as a property of the group, and this would cause us to miss the independent controlling force that the game has. The following example, from Opie and Opie's (1959) classic study of children's folklore, demonstrates how a game can sustain a life of its own, even across generations.

The Development of Playground Rhymes over Historical Time

Both of the foregoing studies were of a single group of children creating a verbal game or text through a process of improvisational collaboration. But, in both cases, one could argue that we might better understand the game by analyzing the group; after all, these games seem to be the property of a single group. To demonstrate that oral culture is an independent level of analysis, we need to do the sort of historical–anthropological analysis that is rarely conducted by developmentalists but is standard for folklorists.

A lot of children's games and rhymes are like adult folklore—like urban myths or jokes—because children don't learn their playground games from books. Games such as hopscotch are passed on for generations, in many cases without the participation of adults. And like urban myths, children's games don't have an official version—every town and every playground seems to have its own unique variation to the hopscotch game.

The English folklorists Peter and Iona Opie published their canonical survey of children's games in Britain in 1959. In one fascinating study, they focused on a single playground rhyme, which they first heard children use in 1939 and was still being used in the mid-1950s. By researching written records of children's rhymes, they were able to trace this same rhyme as far back as 1725 (see Figure 2.1).

With this playground rhyme, we see the truth of Gadamer's insight: "It is the game that is played" (p. 93). With this folklore text from children's oral culture, it is clear that its life and history are independent of any individual child and not reducible to any single child's mental representation. Even if we tried to analyze the rhyme in terms of memory, narrative development, and oral transmission, we would still need to consider the longevity of the text and how it could survive across so many generations of children. The rhyme passes on from city to city, from generation to generation, with remarkably little change. These children's parents probably did not teach them this rhyme—its transmission and reproduction most likely remained within the peer culture itself.

1725

Now he acts the *Grenadier*,
Calling for a *Pot of Beer:*
Where's his Money? He's forgot:
Get him gone, a Drunken Sot.

1774

Whoes there
A Granidier
What dye want
A Pint of Beer
Whoes there
A Granidier
What dye want
A Pint of Beer

1780

Who comes here?
    A Grenadier.
What do you want?
    A Pot of Beer.
Where is your Money?
    I've forgot.
Get you gone
    You drunken Sot.

1907

Eenty, teenty, tuppenny bun,
Pitching tatties doon the lum;
Who's there? John Blair.
What does he want? A bottle of beer.
Where's your money? I forgot.
Go downstairs, you drunken sot.

1910

Far are ye gaein'?
Across the gutter.
Fat for?
A pund o' butter.
Far's yer money?
In my pocket.
Far's yer pocket?
Clean forgot it!

1916

Rat a tat tat, who is that?
Only grandma's pussy-cat.
What do you want?
A pint of milk.
Where's your money?
In my pocket.
Where is your pocket?
I forgot it.
O you silly pussy-cat.

1939

A frog walked into a public house
And asked for a pint of beer.
Where's your money?
In my pocket.
Where's your pocket?
I forgot it.
Well, please walk out.

1943

Rat tat tat, who is that?
Only Mrs. Pussy Cat.
What do you want?
A pint of milk.
Where's your penny?
In my pocket.
Where's your pocket?
I forgot it.
Please walk out.

1950

Mickey Mouse
In a public house
Drinking pints of beer.
Where's your money?
In my pocket.
Where's your pocket?
I forgot it.
Please walk out.

FIGURE 2.1. History of a playground rhyme.

27

The children who play this game today have no idea where it came from; they learn it from their peers, and each playground group makes it their own. In my undergraduate class "Play and Development," I lead a discussion about peer cultures in which I ask the students to share playground rhymes from their childhood. They are always surprised that classmates from across the country were singing essentially the same rhymes; at the same time, they are surprised to hear the many variations. Without ever consciously thinking about it, they realize that they had always assumed these rhymes were created by a friend of theirs or a student at their own preschool.

Connections: Contemporary Play Research

These three examples demonstrate that the oral culture of children is an emergent social product, emerging as a result of the improvisational nature of play. These examples of oral culture also develop over time, demonstrating that they have a stability across play episodes. Once an oral text has emerged, it begins to constrain the children's later play improvisations, in a continuing dialectic. The existence of this dialectic has two implications: (1) that we can only understand oral culture by analyzing children's group interactions; and (2) that we cannot understand children's group interactions without also analyzing these folkloristic processes. These twin directions of influence are always present in emergent social interactions. The group collaboratively creates an emergent social product—the story, game, or rhyme—and that emergent product, in turn, constrains the future actions of the group.

The sociologist Bill Corsaro (1985) has analyzed the independence of peer culture, focusing on the "interactional routines" of the preschool classroom. His analyses also demonstrate that these patterns, although collaboratively improvised, have a life of their own. These oral texts often become so ritualized that they can seem like a script, and this is one of the insights of the application of script theory to children's play (Nelson & Gruendel, 1979). However, as Fein (1991) pointed out, the script metaphor underemphasizes the creativity that children display in appropriating and embellishing the patterns. Although many games and rhymes have a structure that constrains children's creativity, they are never simply repeating a script verbatim. Children always appropriate (Rogoff, 1990) or embellish (Corsaro, 1985) these patterns, making them their own. Although the stability and independent development of these oral texts limit the extent of the process, it is never a straightjacket; the game is never played the same way twice.

This raises many issues for studies of both play and oral culture—what kinds of texts allow for more or less creativity? What is the relative role in development of ritualized versus improvisational games? What kind of creativity is required to perform a ritualized game, and is it different from the improvisational creativity required by free dramatic play?

GROUP LEARNING IN CHILDREN'S PLAY

In the foregoing discussion, I presented several examples of the emergence and development of the texts of oral culture. In sociodramatic play, these texts evolve and emerge, and by participating in these oral texts, children learn and develop as individuals. However, none of these texts were "authored" by an individual child; in each case, the text emerged through a group improvisational process. The creator of an oral culture is not an individual; it is the peer group, and sometimes a series of peer groups, over historical time. Now we turn to a consideration of how the preschool peer group can be viewed as another independent level of analysis.

At the same time that each child is learning social skills, the entire preschool classroom is learning as a group—in a sense, learning to be an ensemble, learning shared play themes and inside jokes that even their parents might not hear about. We can use the analogy with adult improvisational theater to help us understand how children's play contributes to group development. Improv groups do not rehearse to get better at performing a script, nor do they rehearse for the benefit of each individual actor. Instead, the function of their rehearsal is to help the group develop as an ensemble. Even if the group is an effective, well-rehearsed ensemble, one of the members could join another group and be horribly out of sync. The rehearsals do not make the group better because they are making each of the members better; rather, the group is getting better through *group learning*.

Few development specialists have studied a child's peer group as an independent level of analysis. But several organizational researchers have studied how groups develop over time, what is sometimes called the *life cycle* of groups. The development of a group has often been neglected by those who study intergroup communication—including most social psychologists—because the vast majority of these experiments use groups of students brought together just for the experiment, with no history and no time to develop (Frey, 1994). Another problem with group communication research is that it has focused on problem-solving task groups, thus ignoring informally formed social groups such as those of a preschool classroom. These informal groups are much more likely to depend on communication to create and maintain the group and its sense of identity, to socialize new members, and to enact changes in group processes (Frey, 1994).

Organizational researchers focus on the life cycle of groups for eminently practical reasons. Most complex tasks in the world are too much for a single person, and group projects are universal in modern organizations. When the goal is to understand how best to get something done in a large organization, the perspective is naturally to look to the group, not to the individuals in it. Another reason for analyzing the group as an independent level of analysis is that most organizations experience turnover, with employees leaving and new employees joining. In some industries, turnover is so high that in 5 years a group may have all new members. The only thing that remains constant is the group itself—its structure, its goals, its own idiosyncratic organizational culture, its oral history, its relations with all the other groups in the organization.

These studies of adult groups demonstrate that task-focused groups develop along predictable life cycles, regardless of the members of the group or the tasks that they are assigned. The identification of these universal developmental patterns demonstrates the value of considering the group as an independent level of analysis. Perhaps the canonical model of group development is Tuckman's (Tuckman, 1965; Tuckman & Jensen, 1977). Tuckman's 1965 article was a review of about 50 studies of therapy groups, training groups, natural groups, and laboratory groups. Tuckman's model proposed five stages, the first three involving group formation and the last two relating to group maintenance and eventual termination (Hartley, 1997): *exploration, evaluation, consensus, performance*, and *adjournment*. With nontask groups, the three group formation stages tend to occupy most of the group's history; task-focused groups tend to rush through these stages and spend the majority of their time in the *performance* stage. A children's preschool classroom is a "nontask" group; at the beginning of the school year, children are forming groups and are in the *exploration* and *evaluation* stages, while they begin to form expectations of each other and a rudimentary group identity. A month or two into the school year, children's peer groups move into the *consensus* stage, where group cohesion has emerged. Although adult task groups tend to pass quickly through this stage and into the *performance* stage, children's play groups remain in this stage indefinitely. Studies of adult task groups have found that improvisational communication is most central at the *consensus* stage, so it is not surprising that improvisation plays such an important role in preschool peer interaction.

As we saw with the Opie and Opie's nursery rhyme, the texts of oral culture can outlast any one group, although as each group participates in these texts, the text is modified slightly. This example demonstrates that the oral culture of a group is independent of the group itself. Some recent organizational research has also begun to consider not only the life cycle of the group but also the development of the organizational culture of the group. Like preschool classrooms, adult groups develop their own oral traditions, folklore, and interaction norms. These remain more or less stable, even with turnover in the group. Wheelan et al. (1994) suggested that developmental phases can be identified by the presence or absence of *content themes* in group conversations. Their method involves analyzing extended group conversations to determine what is being discussed. Over time, major themes emerge. Wheelan et al. argue that themes emerge as a result of developmental processes that are inherent in any group. Contrary to earlier theories that argued either that group leaders initiate themes or that vocal members of the group initiate them, Wheelan et al. found that leaders and vocal group members had little influence on these processes. Instead, the development of this "oral culture" was the result of an emergent, collective process.

There are many distinct small groups in a single classroom of 24 children. In my yearlong ethnography (Sawyer, 1997a), I identified four well-defined and extremely stable play groups (pp. 68–72). These groups are nontask groups, and they are self-organizing and self-maintaining. Consequently, communication and negotiation are perhaps more important than in most small groups. Everything about the group emerges through group communication, because nothing is specified in advance—no task, no procedures, no communication norms, no status relations. Nonetheless, just like adult work groups, the preschool play group has its own identity and maintains continuity even as different children move in and out of the group.

Wheelan et al. (1994) also found that there were similar group development patterns across different group types, and that the developmental processes of individual groups were similar to the developmental processes of the total organization containing those groups: The parts reflect the whole, in a phenomenon that they refer to as *mirroring*. In mirroring, group discussions became more alike over time in their thematic content. In a preschool classroom, where several distinct groups play in close proximity, we might find similar "mirroring," with play themes migrating from group to group. In fact, I documented several cases of this migration (Sawyer, 1997a). In some cases, themes are carried by a child that relocates from one group to another, but in other cases, the groups are so near each other that they simply overhear play talk in the nearby group and seamlessly weave these themes into their own play improvisation.

These examples from group communication research demonstrate that the group can be fruitfully studied as an independent level of analysis. Group development displays general patterns and stage sequences that are worthy of study in their own right. Although these researchers have focused on adult task groups, this research makes several predictions about children's play groups that tend to be correct, suggesting that developmental research could benefit from a study of the group level of analysis.

A CASE STUDY: LEVELS OF ANALYSIS IN PLAY IMPROVISATION

In recent empirical work, I have been exploring different levels of analysis in children's play. I have been particularly interested in demonstrating empirically that peer group and oral culture phenomena cannot be studied by reducing them to individual child variables. In this study, I analyzed children's play dialogue at two levels of analysis—the oral culture level, and the individual child level—with the goal of demonstrating that phenomena at the oral culture level could not, even in theory, be explained by reduction to any variables associated with the participating children.

My analyses focused on the *metacommunicative strategies* that children used to collaboratively negotiate the play frame. I analyzed a two-turn sequence where the first child proposed an elaboration or change to the play frame, and the second child responded to that proposal, either agreeing or disagreeing with it. My hypothesis was that these *improvisational sequences* mediated the emergence of children's oral culture. To determine the viability of reduction to the child level of analysis, I also aggregated information from all the improvisational sequences that a given child participated in, to derive each child's *interactional profile*: a collection of all child variables that could possibly be used to predict verbal behavior in a play negotiation sequence.

For each improvisational sequence, I coded both the proposal and the response on two metacommunicative strategy variables: *frame* and *explicitness* (see Sawyer, 2000, for additional detail). The frame variable coded whether the child was speaking as a play character or had stepped out of character to speak in a director's voice. The explicitness variable coded the directness of the child: whether the child's turn, by explicitly stating its purpose, left fewer options available to the partner. My analyses focused on the strategy used by the responder; there were variables at two levels of analysis that might have predicted the responder's strategy use. First, at the child level of analysis, the responding child's interactional profile might predict the response strategy in this particular instance. Second, at the conversational level of analysis, the strategy of the proposer might predict the response strategy.

As one would expect, the relationship between the response strategy and the interactional profile of the responding child was statistically significant; each child has an overall interactional tendency that partly predicts his or her behavior in a given interaction. But I also found statistical significance, and even stronger effect sizes, at the conversational level of analysis: Responders tended to use the same strategy as was used by the proposer. This is consistent with intersubjectivity research more generally, which has repeatedly found that interactants tend to mirror the immediately prior action of their partner (e.g., Göncü & Kessel, 1988).

On those occasions when responders do not use the same strategy, their strategy is predicted by whether they accept or reject the proposal. If they are accepting the proposal, they use a more in-frame and more implicit strategy than the proposal; if they are rejecting it, they use a more out-of-frame and more explicit strategy. This suggests that an intersubjectively shared frame enables implicit and in-frame strategies. When a child accepts a proposal, that child can then build on the dramatic frame just proposed; this shared dramatic frame makes it easier for a child to successfully construct a more implicit and more in-frame strategy. However, if a child rejects a proposal, he cannot rely on a shared frame to disambiguate his utterance, forcing him to become more out of frame and explicit.

To determine whether the conversational level contributed predictive value above and beyond the child level, I conducted two linear regression analyses with the response strategies as the outcome variable and with two predictor variables: the proposal strategy, and the child's interactional profile.

Table 2.1 reports the results of four linear regression models, two for each of the two strategy variables. The pattern of findings is similar for both strategy variables, frame and explicitness. In both cases, the first model used only the child-level variable—the child's interactional profile—and the second model added in the conversational-level variable—the proposal frame or explicitness.

With both strategy variables, the effect size of the conversation level is much greater than the child level. For example, with the frame strategy Model 2, the conversational-level variable had seven times the effect size (β) of the child-level variable. Compared to Model 1—with only the child level variable—Model 2 predicted 6 times the variance (R^2).

These analyses demonstrate effects at the conversational level of analysis that cannot be reduced to analyses of individual children.

**TABLE 2.1. Relative Influence on Response Strategy
of Child Level and Conversational Level**

	β	R^2	p
Frame strategy			
Model 1: child level	.353	.124	.0001
Model 2: child level + conversational level	.108 (child) .752 (conv.)	.630	.0001
Explicitness strategy			
Model 1: child level	.216	.045	.0001
Model 2: child level + conversational level	.182 (child) .412 (conv.)	.215	.0001

These two-turn sequences are similar to the initial stages of Iwamura's verbal games: the chains of adjacency pairs that are the early roots of what later become ritualized games. These improvisational sequences are microexamples of children's oral culture; they are emergent social products, and they seem not to be amenable to reductionist analysis of the participating children.

CONCLUSION

The processes by which work is accomplished, by which people are transformed from novices into experts, and by which work practices evolve are all the same processes.
—EDWIN HUTCHINS (1995, p. 351)

Hutchins's analysis of navigational work teams demonstrated that development occurred on two levels simultaneously: While the work gets done, the participants develop in ability, and the team's work practices—their "oral culture"—develop as well. By analogy, in the preschool classroom, while play (work) is being done, children are learning, and the oral culture of the classroom is developing. In addition, the group as a social entity develops on its own parallel trajectory. In improvisational play, all three developments are happening at the same time, in the same activity.

The theme of this chapter—that development specialists can incorporate multiple levels of analysis by focusing on individual conversational encounters—is a guiding principle of much sociocultural research (Rogoff, 1990). I have emphasized development at two emergent levels of analysis in this chapter: the development of the stories, games, and rhymes of children's oral culture and the development of the peer groups of a preschool classroom. Over time, each child's development occurs in parallel with development at these two emergent levels.

Psychologists have discovered that pretend play helps children to form their personalities and develop their social skills. Pretend play is essential for the normal development of a wide range of social, cognitive, and language skills. Psychologists attribute this to the fact that children's play is incredibly creative and improvisational (Sawyer, 1997a). The essence of adult conversation is also creative improvisation, and in play, children rehearse the ability to improvise—within a group, and within the texts of an oral culture. These are the same skills that children will need in primary school, as they develop friends and social groups by participating in creating conversations. Children at play are learning something much more important than facts and technical skills: They are rehearsing for the improvisations of everyday life. Play is important *because* it is unscripted—it allows the child to practice improvisation with oral texts, within an evolving peer group. Children need to improvise with others, because the conversations they will have as adults are also creatively, collaboratively improvised (Sawyer, 2001).

Once again, an analogy with improv theater is helpful. Some improv groups get to a point where they really click together; they have an ineffable ensemble feel that attunes them to one another. When one of these actors leaves and joins another group, he or she will not perform as well right away, because part of what he or she has "learned" is embedded in the group dynamic of the first group and is specific to that context. Nonetheless, the actor has learned something that is transferable to the new group—has probably become a better actor and is better able to follow the second group's learning process.

This analogy demonstrates that two kinds of learning are always happening in parallel: group learning that cannot be transferred to another context and also individual learning, which is transferable to other contexts. When a child spends a year in a preschool classroom, that group becomes attuned to each other like an improv group. When children graduate to kindergarten, they are starting over again with a new group. But the children have learned something in preschool that makes them more developmentally advanced and prepares them for kindergarten. How can we characterize the cognitive learning that takes place, in tandem with and in the context of the group learning that is undeniably going on?

This question has, for the most part, not been addressed by child development specialists. To risk being overly simplistic, the field is split between individualistic psychologists who study how individual children develop, without taking groups and culture into account, and sociocultural psychologists, who study groups and culture in development but often do not extend their analyses to individual children. Consequently, we do not have many studies that examine both parallel developments simultaneously and how they contribute to each other. At times, each group avoids the issue by denying the importance of the other's perspective: Individualists say, "We're concerned about child development that is generalizable and transferable, the context doesn't interest us," and socioculturalists say, "Nothing can be meaningfully identified as being inside the child's head, knowledge is embedded in systems of cultural and group practices."

In a recent interview, Marian Radke-Yarrow (Cairns, 1998) said that the "unfinished business" of developmental research is "in investigating the connectedness among the many levels and facets of behavior in its contexts." Particularly in group behavior such as sociodramatic play, these levels of analysis are unavoidably intertwined, because development occurs at three levels of analysis simultaneously; the child's learning is only a part of the story. When we see the 200-year history of a nursery rhyme, it becomes obvious that a child-level analysis cannot explain everything that goes on in children's play. Once we acknowledge that development and change occur at these three levels simultaneously, it forces us to study children's play in a more interdisciplinary way; we can no longer proceed in the conventional psychological fashion, by operationalizing variables at the child level of analysis and conducting statistical studies in which the independent units of analysis are individual children.

I have drawn inspiration from Greta G. Fein's work because she has never limited her perspective to a reductionist focus on individual children. This breadth is demonstrated by the scope of this volume: Part III focuses on storytelling, which edges into the realm of folklorists and anthropologists; Part IV focuses on day care, touching on the concerns of sociology, family studies, and education. Not many developmentalists can claim such a broad influence on the field.

REFERENCES

Baker-Sennett, J., Matusov, E., & Rogoff, B. (1992). Sociocultural processes of creative planning in children's playcrafting. In P. Light & G. Butterworth (Eds.), Context and cognition: Ways of learning and knowing (pp. 93–114). Hillsdale, NJ: Erlbaum.

Cairns, R. (1998). The development of a researcher and a discipline: Interview with Marian Radke-Yarrow. SRCD Newsletter, 41(2), 1–6.

Clark, A. (1997). *Being there: Putting brain, body, and world together again.* Cambridge, MA: MIT Press.

Corsaro, W. A. (1985). *Friendship and peer culture in the early years.* Norwood, NJ: Ablex.

Fein, G. G. (1981). Pretend play in childhood: An integrative review. *Child Development, 52,* 1095–1118.

Fein, G. G. (1987). Pretend play: Creativity and consciousness. In D. Gorlitz & J. F. Wohlwill (Eds.), *Curiosity, imagination, and play: On the development of spontaneous cognitive and motivational processes* (pp. 281–304). Hillsdale, NJ: Erlbaum.

Fein, G. G. (1991). Bloodsuckers, blisters, cooked babies, and other curiosities: Affective themes in pretense. In F. S. Kessel, M. H. Bornstein, & A. J. Sameroff (Eds.), *Contemporary constructions of the child: Essays in honor of William Kessen* (pp. 143–157). Hillsdale, NJ: Erlbaum.

Frey, L. R. (1994). Introduction: The call of the field: Studying communication in natural groups. In L. R. Frey (Ed.), *Group communication in context: Studies of natural groups* (pp. ix–xiv). Hillsdale, NJ: Erlbaum.

Gadamer, H.-G. (1975). *Truth and method.* New York: Seabury Press.

Göncü, A., & Kessel, F. S. (1988). Preschooler's collaborative construction in planning and maintaining imaginative play. *International Journal of Behavioral Development, 11,* 327–344.

Hartley, P. (1997). *Group communication.* New York: Routledge.

Hutchins, E. (1995). *Cognition in the wild.* Cambridge, MA: MIT Press.

Iwamura, S. G. (1980). *The verbal games of preschool children.* New York: St. Martin's Press.

Nelson, K., & Gruendel, J. M. (1979). At morning it's lunchtime: A scriptal view of children's dialogues. *Discourse Processes, 2,* 73–94.

O'Neill, J. (Ed.). (1973). *Modes of individualism and collectivism.* New York: St. Martin's Press.

Opie, P., & Opie, I. (1959). *The lore and language of schoolchildren.* New York: Oxford University Press.

Resnick, M. (1994). *Turtles, termites, and traffic jams: Explorations in massively parallel microworlds.* Cambridge, MA: MIT Press.

Rogoff, B. (1990). *Apprenticeship in thinking: Cognitive development in social context.* New York: Oxford University Press.

Sawyer, R. K. (1997a). *Pretend play as improvisation: Conversation in the preschool classroom.* Norwood, NJ: Erlbaum.

Sawyer, R. K. (1997b). Improvisational theater: An ethnotheory of conversational practice. In R. K. Sawyer (Ed.), *Creativity in performance* (pp. 171–193). Greenwich, CT: Ablex.

Sawyer, R. K. (1999). The emergence of creativity. *Philosophical Psychology, 12*(4), 447–469.

Sawyer, R. K. (2000). *Levels of analysis in pretend play discourse: Metacommunication in conversational routines.* Unpublished manuscript.

Sawyer, R. K. (2001). *Creating conversations: Improvisation in everyday discourse.* Cresskill, NJ: Hampton Press.

Tuckman, B. W. (1965). Developmental sequence in small groups. *Psychological Bulletin, 63,* 384–389.

Tuckman, B. W., & Jensen, M. A. (1977). Stages in small group development revisited. *Group and Organizational Studies, 2,* 419–427.

Wheelan, S. A., McKeage, R. L., Verdi, A. F., Abraham, M., Krasick, C., & Johnston, F. (1994). Communication and developmental patterns in a system of interacting groups. In L. R. Frey (Ed.), *Group communication in context: Studies of natural groups* (pp. 153–178). Hillsdale, NJ: Erlbaum.

3

*

Nonsocial Play as a
Risk Factor in Social
and Emotional Development

CHARISSA S. L. CHEAH
LARRY J. NELSON
KENNETH H. RUBIN

We begin this chapter on a personal note. A little more than 20 years ago, when the two "senior" authors of this chapter were merely children, the third author (Rubin) met Greta G. Fein at a Roundtable on Children's Play at the University of Minnesota. At the time, Fein was arguing that play represents a mirror into the child's mind; that it reflects child's competence and development. Rubin agreed entirely; in fact, it was at this meeting that he issued a challenge to the scholars in attendance. They believed that play was *more* than simply a reflection of the child's current cognitive and social-cognitive developmental status, and he challenged them not just to say it but to "prove" it. It was relayed to Rubin, well after the meeting, that the forcefulness of this confrontation took many in the audience by surprise. The prevailing view was that play *produced* development, that it was an evocative milieu within which children learned this, that, or the other, and Rubin did not argue against this position. But, though reasonable on the surface, it could not just be accepted, without proof.

Shortly after this meeting, Rubin was asked by Mavis Hetherington to contribute the chapter on play to the soon to be published *Handbook of Child Psychology* (1983). Rubin accepted this invitation, as it suggests rather strongly that one's work and thoughts on a given topic are actually appreciated. Such an invitation, however, requires that the author write a book-length chapter on a wide-ranging topic of substance. And, from a personal perspective, the feelings associated with such an invitation include not only pride and satisfaction, but also worry and fear! Being one who studies affect regulation, it is understood that it is commonplace for those who are subjected to *dysregulation* to respond in a way that will alleviate the upset. In this regard, author Rubin decided to call his friend Greta Fein to invite her to share the honor and angst associated with being a *Handbook* author.

The product, coauthored with Brian Vandenberg, stands now as an oft-cited chapter in which play was not simply described, vis-à-vis developmental theory and trajectories, but also defined as a psychological phenomenon (Rubin, Fein, & Vandenberg, 1983). The collaborative project was, in most respects, joyful. It was a real-life reflection of how peer co-construction serves as a developmental "mover and shaker" for it produced a book-length product and it established not only a professional but also a personal relationship between coauthors Fein and Rubin. More than a decade later, an opportunity developed for Rubin to leave the comforts of Canada and move to the greater Washington, DC, area. Knowledge that Greta Fein would be a departmental colleague served as one of the significant factors that made the move across the border not only tempting but also comforting. And so, this chapter is dedicated to Greta Fein . . . a co-writer, collaborator, and friend.

Children spend much of their youthful energy engaged in play. Indeed, play, in its various forms, is a serious business—not only for the active participants but also for students of the phenomenon. To many researchers, play is viewed as a generative force in children's social, emotional, and cognitive development (see Fromberg & Bergen, 1998; Rubin et al., 1983; Saracho & Spodek, 1998). The extent to which children engage in play with others is of added developmental significance. In light of the complexity and developmental significance of children's play, and especially play with peers, it seems important to examine whether children who fail to engage others in social play are at risk for negative consequences.

The goal of this chapter is to examine the significance of social play in normative development and the harmful consequences of nonsocial play. Specifically, we review research which has examined (1) the prevalence of social and nonsocial behaviors in early childhood, (2) individual and developmental differences in the expression of particular types of these behaviors, (3) those constructs or phenomena that predict, are correlated with, and are the putative consequences of particular forms of playful endeavor, and (4) various methods used to assess these behaviors.

SOCIAL AND NONSOCIAL PLAY

Given the focus of this chapter, we begin by outlining the role of social play in child development. In doing so, we admit to deviation from the norm in our defining that which we are labeling "play." That is, rather than viewing play in much the same manner as described by Rubin et al. (1983) in their chapter on "Play" for the *Handbook of Child Psychology*, we focus on the social and nonsocial contexts within which particular play behaviors may occur. Thus, the primary focus of our discussion centers on "social play" and/or the lack thereof. When observing children at play, a variety of structural *components* of play and levels of *social participation* can be seen. Both the structural components and the levels of social participation represent defining features of social play.

STRUCTURAL COMPONENTS OF PLAY

Prior to discussing the social contexts of play, we first outline the structural components of play. The structural approach to the understanding and classification of children's play behaviors is drawn largely from the writings of Piaget (1962) in his book *Play, Dreams, and Imitation in Childhood*. In this volume, Piaget described a taxonomic model for the development of children's games. He distinguished three main types of ludic activities characterizing children's games—namely, practice games, symbolic games, and games with rules. As well, he suggested that constructive games constituted "the transition from all three to adapted behaviors" (p. 110).

These structural categories of play were subsequently refined by Smilansky. Smilansky (1968) suggested that the child moves naturally from one "stage" of play to the next "in keeping with his biological development" (p. 5). The stages Smilansky described included the following:

1. *Functional activities*, in which the same movements are repeated with or without objects. Children appear to engage in functional activities solely to gain pleasure from the performance of the behavior itself.
2. *Constructive activities*, which involve the building or creating of something. Behavior is sustained by constructive goals.

3. *Dramatic play*, in which there is some involvement of nonliterality—a symbolic transformation and production of decontextualized behaviors. Dramatic, or pretend play, allows the child to be many things at once; children can be themselves, actors, observers, and participators in a symbolic exercise.
4. *Games with rules*, in which there is spontaneous acceptance of a division of labor, prearranged rules, and the adjustment to these rules.

According to Smilansky (1968), these four types of play develop in a relatively fixed sequence, with functional play appearing first in infancy and games with rules last at about 6 or 7 years of age. It has been suggested that moving from functional play to exploration and finally to constructive and dramatic play may allow the young child an opportunity to answer, in sequence, two important questions about objects. That is, opportunities to manipulate objects in a functional–sensorimotor fashion and to explore these objects may answer the question, "What do these things do?" (Hutt, 1970). Once the object-derived question has been answered, the child may pose the self-derived question, "What can I do with these things? " The answers come in the forms of exploratory/constructive and dramatic activities.

Social Participation

Children not only choose the types of play activities in which to engage but also whether or not to participate with others in those activities. Perhaps the best known taxonomic description of the social contexts within which children play is drawn from the early research of Parten (1932). In her classic study, Parten described six categories of social participation. The first four categories comprised *non*social or *semi*-social play activities, including (definitions are taken from Rubin's [1993a] version of the Play Observation Scale):

1. *Unoccupied behavior*—the demonstrated marked absence of focus or intent.
2. *Onlooker behavior*—the observation of others' activities without attempting to join peers in play.
3. *Solitary play*—playing apart from the other children at a distance greater than 3 feet, or with his or her back to other children. During solitary play, the child plays with toys that are different from those the other children are using. The focal child is centered on his or her own activity, and pays little or no attention to others in the area.

4. *Parallel play*—the child plays independently; however, the activity often, though not necessarily, brings him or her within three feet of other children. The child plays *beside*, or in the company of, other children but not *with* his or her companions.

Parten (1932) also defined two categories of socially interactive play.

5. *Associative play*—the child interacts with other children and may be using similar materials; however, there is no real cooperation or division of labor.
6. *Cooperative play*—a group activity organized for the purpose of carrying out some plan of action or attaining some goal. Play partners coordinate their behaviors and take particular roles in pursuit of the common goal. In studies postdating the 1970s, both associative and cooperative play have been combined as *social play* for purposes of obtaining adequate interobserver reliability (e.g., Rubin, Maioni, & Hornung, 1976; Rubin, Watson, & Jambor, 1978).

THE DEVELOPMENTAL SIGNIFICANCE OF SOCIAL PLAY

Theoretical Perspectives

In development, both the structural and social aspects of play have significance for children. Thus, having provided a definition of both the structural components and distinctions in social play, we can now address the issue of its developmental significance. For young children, social play provides an important and unique context within which cognitive and social skills may be acquired and practiced (Goldman, 1998).

Piaget and Play

To Piaget (1962), play represented the functional invariant, assimilation, in its purest form. While assimilating, children incorporate events, objects, or situations into existing ways of thinking. Thus, as "pure assimilation," social play was not considered an avenue to cognitive growth but rather a reflection of the child's present level of cognitive development.

According to Piaget, it was through the "functional exercise" of practice play that (e.g., clapping hands) that children came to acquire and hone the basic motor skills inherent in their everyday activities. In contrast with practice play, during which actions are exercised and elaborated for their functional value, symbolic play (i.e., pretense) allowed the exercise of actions for their representational value. Games with rules necessarily incorporate social coordination and a basic understanding of social relationships. In the case of games, rules and regulations are imposed by the group, and the overriding structure results from collective organization.

Piaget not only believed that the structural components of play were developmentally important but that the *social* aspects of play were significant facilitators of developmental change. For example, he believed that interpersonal conflict naturally resulted from social interaction. Interpersonal conflict incurs developmental change because differences in opinion provoke cognitive disequilibria that are sufficiently discomforting so as to elicit attempts at resolution through the exchange of ideas, thoughts and beliefs, and negotiation. As a result, children experience sociocognitive gains. In sum, play allows children to engage their physical and social surroundings in an attempt to find out how these environments "work."

Mead and Peer Play

Mead (1934) stressed the significance of playful peer interaction for the development of the self-system. He believed that children developed notions about the self through the behaviors directed at them, proactively and reactively, by their peers. Thus, exchanges among peers, in the contexts of cooperation, competition, conflict, and friendly discussion allowed the child to gain an understanding of the self as both subject and object. In this regard, Mead proposed that peer interactions such as play with others were an important factor not only in the evolution of social perspective-taking skills but also in the development of the self-system.

Other Theories of Play

Finally, other theoretical accounts have focused on the cognitive, linguistic, and emotional advances promoted by children's play. For example, cognitive theorists have demonstrated the role that social play, particularly pretend play, has in the development of a theory of mind about others (e.g., Astington, Harris, & Olson, 1988; Lillard, 1998). A child's theory of mind is the understanding that other people have mental states (e.g., feelings, desires, beliefs, and intentions) and that these states underlie and help to explain their behavior (Sigelman, 1999). This understanding about one's own mental states (i.e., mind) and those of others takes the form of a theory in that it makes certain ontological distinctions, has a causal–explanatory framework, and defines its constructs vis-à-vis other constructs in the theory (Wellman, 1990). As children explore their social and physical world through social play, they encounter new information that leads them to revise their "theories." In particular, pretend play with others provides opportunities to build and expand mental representations by requiring pretenders to (1) negotiate (e.g., decide the topic of and roles within the pretend play), (2) reconcile conflicting views, (3) take on different perspectives (e.g., the role of the character being played), and (4) act out emotional situations (Lillard, 1998). Thus, play presents the setting for children to expand their understanding of their own mental states and those of others.

Play allows the individual to explore new combinations of behaviors and ideas within a psychologically safe milieu. Through play, children develop behavioral "prototypes" that may be used subsequently in more "serious" contexts. Children's play fosters creativity and flexibility (e.g., Bruner, 1972).

Linguists have proposed ways in which play may help children perfect newly acquired language skills and increase conscious awareness of linguistic rules. Play provides a superior context within which children may gain valuable language practice as they experiment with the meaning, structure, and function of language. For example, children may use old words in unique ways when they need to describe something, or they may invent new word forms as they subconsciously begin to learn about past tense and plurals. Children eventually learn the exceptions to these rules, but through playing with different forms, they begin to better understand how language works (Garvey, 1974). Play conversations also work to improve communication skills. These skills, in turn, are important components of many of the developmental acquisitions attained during childhood, particularly narrative representation, social cognition, intersubjectivity, and fantasy play (Sawyer, 1997).

Sawyer (1997) has proposed an improvisational model of children's interactions during play, which allows for the conceptualization of how children act strategically during turn taking in an interactional sequence. The play episode allows for the opportunity for innovation, while at the same time provides rules and constraints vis-à-vis the prior flow of the play drama. Göncü (1993a, 1993b) has suggested that the improvisational processes typical of social pretend play are critical to the development of intersubjectivity (i.e., two participants arriving at a mutual understanding). These processes prepare children for an ever increasingly complex social life within which a variety of interactional contexts exist that range from more ritualized and structured to more improvisational. (Sawyer, 1996).

Finally, Fein (1989) has suggested that children pretend in an effort to reconstruct and gain mastery over emotionally arousing experiences. When children come to realize that others have similar emotional regulatory needs and that others (peers) share with them similar emotion-arousing experiences, they begin to direct their pretense activities to peers. Just as with other skills discussed previously, by engaging in pretend play with others, children are able to practice regulatory skills. For example, children are able to learn how to keep play interactions at an affectively tolerable level so that the interchange does not become so emotionally intense that play is disrupted or so emotionally low in intensity that play ceases due to boredom. Thus, play provides a "safe" milieu in which a child can experience emotions and practice regulatory skills.

In summary, many theorists have posited that social play provides a setting within which children may explore their physical and social worlds. In turn, this exploration promotes cognitive, language, social, and emotional mastery. Further, through the repeated social interaction afforded by play, children learn important lessons about themselves as well as others.

Empirical Support

Researchers have provided strong support for the theoretical perspectives noted earlier. For example, with regard to cognitive development, Pepler (1982) found that children (3- to 5-year-olds) who engaged frequently in sociodramatic and constructive play performed better on tests of intelligence than did their agemates who were more inclined to play in a sensorimotor fashion, in which the actions were engaged in for the sensations they produced. Similarly, it has been reported that training children to engage in sociodramatic (group make-believe) play improves children's IQ scores, and the effects are relatively long lasting (Smith, Dalgleish, & Herzmark, 1981). In general, sociodramatic play appears to be an important factor contributing to the development of (1) oral language and vocabulary (see Shore, 1998, for a review); (2) story production, story comprehension, communication of meaning, and the development of literacy (Christie, 1991, 1998; Roskos & Neuman, 1998) and subsequent reading and writing achievement (Galda, Pellegrini, & Cox, 1989); (3) the ability to do tasks of mental representation (Youngblade & Dunn, 1995); and (4) mathematical thinking (see Jarrell, 1998).

Insofar as social development is concerned, results from various studies indicate that sociodramatic play among preschoolers is associated with interpersonal problem-solving skills, social competence, and perspective-taking skills (Doyle & Connolly, 1989; see Nourot, 1998). Further, preschoolers who engage in more interactive/cooperative play, versus noninteractive play, are better liked by their peers (Ladd & Price, 1993).

During middle childhood, pretend play allows children to reveal to peers their secrets, emotions, ambitions, and intentions (Rubin & Coplan, 1994). Consequently, it is no wonder that sociodramatic play in the company of peers is considered a "marker" of social competence in early and middle childhood (e.g., Howes, 1988).

It should be noted that many of the empirical studies described previously that suggest the developmental significance of play are correlational in nature. There has been, however, a fair amount of experimental research that directly examines the developmental significance of play. Of particular importance are studies in which play training methods have been studied. The play training method involves systematically coaching children to engage in greater amounts of sociodramatic play. Manipulation of play behaviors can be associated with future measures of social skills to determine whether increases in play behaviors contribute to social or cognitive competence. In studies of this kind, concerted attempts to encourage social pretend play have led to increases in children's sociodramatic play with peers (e.g., Smilansky, 1968). In addition, children coached in fantasy play do indeed show improvements in perspective taking, social problem solving, and group cooperation (Rosen, 1974; Saltz & Johnson, 1974; Smith & Syddall, 1978).

Using play training methods, researchers have found that play is related not only to interpersonal social skills but to cognitive advances as well. For example, Vukelich (1995) examined the effects of exposure to print and interaction with a more knowledgeable other on kindergarten children's environmental print knowledge. Three school classes were randomly assigned exposure to (1) print during play in print-enriched settings; (2) print and functional experiences with a more knowledgeable other during play in print-enriched settings; and (3) play in nonenriched settings. Prior to and following 3 weeks of play in each setting, ability to read the environmental print appropriate to each setting was assessed in context with words embedded in their supporting context and out of context with words written on a list. Results indicated that exposure to the print and functional experiences with a more knowledgeable other around this print significantly influenced the children's ability to read environmental print on both reading tasks, especially in a play setting.

In another study, Williamson (1992) examined the effects of play training on story comprehension among older primary children who were identified as poor comprehenders. Recall ability was assessed before and after play training and revealed that the reenactment of stories for subgroups of older primary children was effective in facilitating story comprehension.

The foregoing examples represent just a few supportive arguments for the developmental significance of social play. In general, these experimental studies suggest that play is a powerful precursor to children's social and cognitive developmental progress and a useful tool in intervention. Given such research support, there is reason for concern for children who do not engage in this growth-promoting behavior. We turn now to a discussion of nonsocial play, including its various forms, meanings, and consequences.

NONSOCIAL PLAY IN CHILDHOOD

If social interaction or social participation is advantageous for children (e.g., Piaget, 1962), it appears logical to assume that the lack of social interaction should prove troublesome. Recently, this latter belief has become mainstream among those who have suggested that shy or socially withdrawn children are "at risk" for later maladaptation. In fact, it is now widely accepted that children who consistently experience an impoverished quality of peer interaction during the early and middle childhood years may be "at risk" for later social and emotional problems in adolescence and adulthood. These problems include school dropout, delinquency, aggression, depression, low self-esteem, and loneliness (see Rubin, Bukowski, & Parker, 1998, for a review).

But what precisely happens when children spend their time alone? Researchers have traditionally not distinguished between the variety of behaviors that children can display when playing alone when in social groupings with peers. For the most part, the terms "behavioral solitude," "social withdrawal," and "nonsocial play" have been used interchangeably to connote a wide variety of underlying mechanisms. However, recent research has revealed the importance of identifying qualitatively different types of nonsocial behavior.

The Multiple Forms of Nonsocial Play Behaviors

In the early 1980s, Rubin (1982) distinguished between two clusters of solitary behaviors in which children may engage; he labeled these solitary–passive and solitary–active behaviors. Solitary–passive behavior comprises the quiescent exploration of objects and/or constructive activity while playing alone. Solitary–active behavior is characterized by repeated actions with or without objects for the pure physical sensation (sensorimotor) and/or by solitary dramatizing (i.e., pretend play in solitude). Put in terms of the previously described work of Piaget (1962) and Smilansky (1968), the former construct comprises constructive or exploratory activity; the latter comprises sensorimotor or functional play while alone. Importantly, "alone" in the foregoing definitions means playing in solitude when among peers (such as in a classroom or on a playground).

Coplan, Rubin, Fox, Calkins, and Stewart (1994) described a third cluster of solitary behaviors, *reticence*, consisting of prolonged looking at the partner without accompanying play (onlooking behavior) and being unoccupied. Various studies have been conducted to examine the predictors, correlates, and consequences of these three forms of nonsocial behavior.

The Different "Meanings" of Nonsocial Play

With the identification of the three foregoing forms of solitude, researchers began to ask the question: Is the frequent display of all forms of nonsocial play in early childhood "necessarily evil" (Rubin, 1982)? It has long been believed that the frequent production of solitary behavior, while in the presence of peers, reflects developmental immaturity; a deficiency in social skills; an inability to regulate fearful, wary emotions; and/or other aspects of psychological maladaptation (e.g., Barnes, 1971; Parten, 1932). It is now rather clear that nonsocial play is a complex and multidimensional construct. Recent advances in the study of social withdrawal have produced a literature suggesting that different expressional forms of solitude carry with them different psychological meanings (see Rubin & Stewart, 1996, for an extensive review). Moreover, as we discuss later, these underlying psychological mechanisms appear to change as a function of age.

Solitary–Passive Behavior

In early childhood, solitary–passive behavior is associated positively with (1) competent problem solving whilst alone or in cooperative tasks with peers, (2) peer acceptance, and (3) indices of emotion regulation (e.g., Rubin, Coplan, Fox, & Calkins, 1995). In addition, such behavior is reinforced positively by teachers and parents as well as by peers. Preschool children who frequently engage in solitary–passive play (e.g., doing puzzles or artwork, building blocks, or reading) appear to be object-oriented rather than people-oriented. These children excel at

object-oriented tasks, are more task persistent, and have a higher attention span. On the other hand, they perform poorly during people-oriented social tasks (e.g., "show and tell" during small group time)
(Coplan & Rubin, 1998b). Generally, then, solitary–passive play among
preschoolers is not associated with indices of maladaptation.

In attempting to provide an etiological explanation for children's
frequent production of solitary–passive play, researchers have mentioned the possibility that the children who engage in high frequencies
of this activity are relatively disinterested in social engagement and
have low approach and low avoidance motivations (Asendorpf, 1991,
Rubin & Asendorpf, 1993). To the extent that such an explanation
would not be suggestive of high-risk status for "solitary–passive" children, it is not surprising that Rubin, Coplan, et al. (1995) recently reported that nonsociable but emotionally regulated children were more
likely to display solitary–passive behavior when engaged in solitary activities as compared to any other form of nonsocial behavior.

It has been suggested that solitary–constructive and solitary–exploratory play are encouraged by preschool teachers because they
maintain order in the class and closely approximate the kinds of behavior generally occurring in elementary school classrooms.

Solitary–Active Behavior

Solitary–active behavior, when produced in a social group, is characterized by repeated sensorimotor actions with or without objects in which
the focus of the actions is the physical sensation that results and/or by
dramatizing in solitude. It is important to distinguish solitary–active
behavior from two other types of dramatic play: (1) dramatic play when
the child is alone (i.e., not in the company of peers) and (2) sociodramatic play in the presence of peers. The former is quite normal for
young children, and the latter, as discussed previously, is a marker of
social competence (e.g., Howes & Matheson, 1992).

The extremely low frequency of occurrence of this form of play
makes it difficult to study without the use of extensive observational
periods. However, its infrequent enactment makes this form of play a
highly salient and noticeable form of in-class behavior; as such, it is regarded by peers and teachers alike as rather peculiar. The cluster of behaviors comprising solitary–active play has been associated with indices of (1) impulsivity among preschoolers (Coplan et al., 1994; Rubin,
1982), (2) peer rejection from as early as the preschool years, and (3)
externalizing problems (in particular aggressiveness) and immaturity
throughout the childhood years (Coplan & Rubin, 1998; Rubin, 1982).
Thus, solitary–active behavior, although nonsocial in nature, appears to

be associated with externalizing, as opposed to internalizing problems, in childhood. High frequencies of solitary–functional (sensorimotor) and solitary–dramatic play in preschoolers are negatively related to observations of positive peer interactions and the receipt of social initiations from peers (Rubin, 1982). Even in midchildhood, solitary–active behavior remains significantly associated with teacher and peer derived indices of aggression (Rubin & Mills, 1988).

Rubin, LeMare, and Lollis (1990) have suggested that whereas some children may voluntarily withdraw from peer interaction, others may, in fact, be actively isolated by the peer group. This may be the case for those children who engage in a high frequency of solitary–active behaviors. Ameliorative action would thus be appropriate when it is noted that a child's activities are dominated by this form of nonsocial activity.

Reticent Behavior

The third cluster of solitary behaviors, "reticence," may be identified by the frequent production of prolonged watching of other children without accompanying play (onlooking) or being unoccupied (Asendorpf, 1991; Coplan et al., 1994). Reticent behavior is believed to reflect social fear and anxiety in a social context; preschool-age children who are often reticent are thought to experience what has been termed a social "approach–avoidance" conflict (Asendorpf, 1991). That is, while desirous of peer interaction (high approach motivation), these children find that entering social situations elicits feelings of anxiety and the development of a powerful need to avoid interaction (high avoidance motivation).

It is normal for most children to experience this conflict, to some extent, in the presence of unfamiliar peers. The resolution of this conflict usually involves the movement from onlooking to hovering near the social interactors of interest to parallel play and then finally to social interchange (Bakeman & Brownlee, 1980). However, children who are extremely inhibited in the presence of unfamiliar peers do not make this progression, and because of their felt anxiety, they display prolonged onlooking of other peers without accompanying play and/or unoccupied behaviors. For example, Coplan et al. (1994) found a significant relation between reticent behavior and hovering in 4-year-olds. Reticence was also associated with overt indications of anxiety (e.g., crying and automanipulatives such as digit sucking and hair pulling) as well as maternal ratings of shyness (Coplan & Rubin, 1998b). Further, reticence is highly stable across situations.

For example, children who are reticent during free play also display high frequencies of onlooking and unoccupied behaviors during situations requiring task completion or self-presentation. As well, there is a higher incidence of internalizing problems reported for children who exhibit a high frequency of reticent behavior both in the laboratory (Schmidt et al., 1997) and in preschool classroom (Coplan & Rubin, 1998a) free-play settings.

REPRESENTATIVE METHODS OF ASSESSING SOCIAL AND NONSOCIAL PLAY

In the attempt to study children's behaviors including social and nonsocial play, researchers have relied on several sources of information concerning the nature of these behaviors, including direct behavioral observations, teachers, and children's peers. In the section that follows, we present several of these methods as well as the advantages and disadvantages associated with their use.

Observational Taxonomies

Observational techniques involve the systematic recording of children's play behaviors. There are several advantages of observational techniques. First, the behaviors observed are "face valid." Second, "blinded" observers reduce biases in the coding process. That is, coders are not influenced by their past knowledge of a child's behaviors. Third, coders can be trained to observe and record very specific and detailed behaviors.

Disadvantages include the following: (1) Observational assessments are both time- and labor-intensive, (2) children may behave in an atypical manners when aware that they are being observed, (3) observers are typically exposed only to restricted samples of behavior that are gathered during limited time intervals in limited contexts, and (4) infrequently occurring but salient events such as disruptive behavior may be missed between time-sampling intervals. Despite these weaknesses, the breadth and depth of behavior that can be observed without problems of bias, recall, and accuracy make observational techniques particularly useful. Furthermore, wireless transmission systems, hidden cameras with running video logs, and other methodological advances in both time- and event-sampling techniques have increased the "generalizibility" of direct observational techniques.

Several observational coding schemes currently exist designed to assess social play and its related constructs (Bergen, 1987; Fewell &

Glick, 1998; Pellegrini, 1998). The social aspects of children's play have been investigated using time sampling (e.g., Ladd & Price, 1986, 1993; Rubin, 1989), event samples (e.g., Pettit & Harrist, 1993), and scan samples (e.g., McNeilly-Choque, Hart, Robinson, Nelson, & Olsen, 1996). These coding schemes have been employed to observe social play in the classroom (e.g., Rubin, 1982; Rubin & Maioni, 1975; Rubin et al., 1976; 1978), on the playground (e.g., Pellegrini, 1995), and in the home with adults (e.g., Pettit & Bates, 1990). In our work, we have made frequent use of the Play Observation Scale (POS; Rubin, 1989). This measure is described in greater detail below as an example of an observational taxonomy used in the study of play.

The Play Observation Scale

The POS (Rubin, 1993a) is an observational taxonomy designed to assess the structural components of children's play nested within social participation categories. Accordingly, the POS employs a time-sampling methodology within which 10-second segments are coded for both social participation (e.g., solitary, parallel, and group) and the cognitive quality of children's play (e.g., functional–sensorimotor, constructive, and dramatic). Several additional free-play behaviors are assessed, including instances of unoccupied behavior, onlooking, exploration, peer conversation, anxious behaviors, hovering, transitional behavior, rough-and-tumble play, and aggression.

The use of the POS in our laboratory (e.g., Fox et al., 1995; Rubin, Coplan, et al., 1995) and in many others (e.g., Guralnick, Conner, Hammond, Gottman, & Kinnish, 1996; Minnett, Clark, & Wilson, 1994; Tout, de Haan, Campbell, & Gunnar, 1998) has allowed for a clearer understanding not only of children's social play behaviors but also of developmental (e.g., Rubin, 1982), contextual (e.g., Einslein & Fein, 1981), sex (e.g., Johnson & Ershler, 1981; Moller, Hymel, & Rubin, 1992), and temperamental (e.g., Coplan & Rubin, 1998b) differences. Further, numerous studies have been conducted in which correlates of the various POS categories of play have been examined (e.g., Hymel, Rubin, Rowden, & LeMare, 1990). Recently, the POS has been used extensively in studies of children with disabilities and disorders (e.g., Guralnick et al., 1996; Minnett et al., 1994).

Outside Source Assessments

Outside source assessment procedures involve asking "expert" informants, such as peers, parents, and teachers, to rate or nominate children's social participatory inclinations. There are several general advantages to using paper-and-pencil rating scales or nomination techniques. To begin with, outside source assessment is comparatively quick and inexpensive. As well, parents, classmates, and teachers have the potential to observe children in many different circumstances and for long periods; thus, they can make inferences about specific children's "everyday" behaviors. The following are more specific advantages, as well as disadvantages, associated with each respective informant.

Teacher Measures

Researchers often ask teachers to rate the frequency with which children engage in particular behaviors. There are numerous advantages associated with using teachers as informants. First, as noted previously, because teachers are not members of peer-group networks and see behaviors in a variety of school contexts, they are in a better position to provide objective information about specific children's "everyday" behaviors (Coie & Dodge, 1988). Second, the collection of teacher data is comparatively quick and inexpensive. Finally, in special relation to the study of nonsocial behaviors, teachers, compared to young children's peer ratings, may be more adept and accurate at identifying children who engage in less salient behaviors such as withdrawal (e.g., Ladd & Mars, 1986; Younger, Schwartzman, & Ledingham, 1985).

Despite these advantages, it may well be that teachers do not always perceive behavior in the same ways that peers and neutral observers do. For instance, in light of possible child behavior changes over the course of a school year, teachers may retain early-year perceptions of a child's behavior and thus may not be totally accurate in their assessments. Teachers are also likely to be less accurate in estimating frequencies or rates of behavior when compared with observers. Finally, potential confounds may exist in teacher ratings due to gender or relational biases (cf. Ladd & Profilet, 1996; Coie, Dodge, & Kupersmidt, 1990; Rubin, Coplan, Nelson, Cheah, & Lagace-Seguin, 1998).

It should be noted that there are few, if any, teacher measures that directly assess children's social play. One exception is the Preschool Play Behavior Scale (Coplan & Rubin, 1998a). This measure was designed specifically to assess social play, solitary–passive behaviors, reticent behaviors, rough-and-tumble play, and solitary–active behaviors. Using behavioral observations to support the construct validity of the measure and parental and teacher ratings to establish the psychometric properties, Coplan and Rubin demonstrated that this teacher report measure has the potential to be an important accompaniment and/or replacement for more time-consuming behavioral observations.

Peer Behavior Nominations

In peer nomination procedures, children are asked to designate peers who engage in specific behaviors (e.g., "Who plays by themselves a lot of the time?") (e.g., Crick & Grotpeter, 1995). The strength of peer ratings of behavior is that children's perceptions of others' behavior is measured directly without being filtered through the eyes of adult teachers or observers. Because children react to others based on their interpretations of behavior (whether accurate or not), child representations of others are critical for the social adjustment of peers in the group at large.

As with teacher ratings, this approach is not without limitations. Disadvantages include (1) differences in children's abilities to recall descriptions of various behaviors, including social withdrawn behavior; (2) biases in children's interpretation of social behavior caused by existing group reputations of peers being judged; and (3) biases in attention and recall that may be a function of children's gender-role stereotypes (see Younger, Schneider, & Daniels, 1991). These concerns are highlighted for preschool- and kindergarten-age children. As Hymel (1983) has cogently pointed out, young children's friendships tend to fluctuate frequently as a function of reactions to specific events (e.g., fighting over a toy) or moods, resulting in on-again, off-again associations with peers. As a result, daily perceptions of other children's behavior may vary as a function of most recent experiences with a peer.

Parents

Parents see their children's behaviors in a variety of contexts; thus, they are in a position to provide a wide range of information. Further, parents may be more adept than peers at identifying a wide range of behaviors, including less salient behavior such as social withdrawal. However, parents (1) often describe their children in a positive light, in an attempt to (2) portray themselves in a socially desirable manner, and (3) are influenced by their perceptions of what their child's behavior is in comparison to what they would like it to be.

In summary, there are unique advantages and disadvantages associated with the use of parents, peers, teachers, and observers, respectively, as informants. It should be noted that one of the most pervasive problems with each of the informants discussed earlier is the lack of many existing rating scale measures designed to directly assess social play. One notable exception discussed previously is the Preschool Play Behavior Scale (Coplan & Rubin, 1998a). Future work should be aimed at creating other measures, including parent rating scales and peer nomination techniques, designed specifically for the assessment of children's play behaviors.

NORMATIVE DEVELOPMENTAL PATTERNS OF SOCIAL AND NONSOCIAL PLAY

In developing the now familiar social participation categories noted earlier, Parten (1932) concluded that the typical 3-year-old was a solitary or parallel player, whereas the 5-year-old spent much more time being socially engaged. A closer examination of the literature has revealed a more complex set of conclusions (e.g., Barnes, 1971; Rubin et al., 1978).

In contrast to toddlerhood, it is during the preschool period that social play becomes much more prominent. There is a substantial increase in the frequency of social contacts, and interactive events become longer, more elaborated, and more varied (Eckerman, Whatley, & Kutz, 1975; Holmberg, 1980). As well, preschoolers tend to play with a wider range of playmates than do toddlers (e.g., Howes, 1983).

Rubin et al. (1978) reported that preschoolers (4-year-olds) engage in significantly more unoccupied, onlooker, and solitary play and in less group (i.e., associative or cooperative) play than kindergarten children (5-year-olds). Developmental changes in the play of preschoolers were characterized by an increasing cognitive maturity of their solitary, parallel, and group interactive activities (e.g., Rubin et al., 1978). Thus, although the relative frequency of functional (sensorimotor) play was found to be greater among preschool-age children than among kindergartners, the relative incidence of the more mature forms of play (i.e., dramatic play and games with rules) was greater among kindergartners. The most frequently observed behavior during this 2-year age period was constructive play; solitary–sensorimotor behaviors became increasing rare from preschool to kindergarten. More recent research has demonstrated that both the relative frequency and complexity of constructive activity continues to increase from the preschool to middle childhood period (Johnson, 1998).

Finally, kindergarten children have been observed to engage in more parallel–constructive, parallel–dramatic, and group–dramatic play than preschoolers. In addition, there is evidence of a decrease in the proportion of time spent in solitary–functional and parallel–functional play (Rubin et al., 1978).

From early to middle childhood, the two forms of play activities that increase in prominence are sociodramatic play and games with rules. In early childhood, social pretense serves to support and promote emotional and social development; it is especially significant in allowing children to find a niche within their relevant peer group. For older primary-grade children, collaborative pretense continues to serve these purposes and becomes especially important in the establishment and maintenance of intimate peer friendships (Howes & Matheson, 1992).

Thus, it has been established that the social interactive activities of children become increasingly frequent and complex with age. However, not only do the social interactive activities change with age, but the meanings of these activities, particularly socially withdrawn behaviors, change over time. Asendorpf (1993) has proposed, and found in studies of dyadic interaction, that with increasing age beyond the preschool years, reticent behavior gradually merges with solitary–passive behavior to yield a single construct of social withdrawal. According to Asendorpf, this increased statistical association between previously unassociated constructs represent the attempt of reticent children to cope constructively with their fearfulness and uncertainty by "losing themselves" in nonsocial play with objects (Asendorpf, 1991).

Asendorpf's (1991, 1993) notions about the changing meaning of solitary behaviors coincide with Younger and colleagues' data-driven reports that with increasing age, withdrawn behaviors become more salient to the peer group (Younger, Gentile, & Burgess, 1993). It is also known that perceived deviation from age-normative social behavior is associated with the establishment of negative peer reputations. Thus, it has been suggested that the psychological meaning of passive–solitude changes, reflecting psychological uncertainty, negative self-appraisals, and insecurity in one's relationships.

In partial support for these conjectures, we recently reported that at age 7, children who were identified as both highly emotionally dysregulated and dispositionally unsociable displayed as much solitary–passive behavior as those unsociable children who were not emotionally dysregulated (Rubin, Kennedy, Cheah, & Fox, 1999). This finding supports the conjecture that at 7 years of age, emotionally dysregulated–unsociable children may have learned to mask their social anxieties by engaging in object-centered, quiescent, and solitary behaviors. Importantly, those children identified as emotionally dysregulated but sociable demonstrated behaviors much like their 4-year-old counterparts (Rubin, Coplan, et al., 1995); they engaged in more disruptive behavior and rough-and-tumble play and were rated by their mothers as having more externalizing difficulties than did sociable children who were able to regulate their emotions.

It is also the case that researchers have found nonspecific indices of social withdrawal in middle childhood (i.e., measures that aggregate observed reticence and solitary–passive behavior) to be associated with indices of internalizing problems (e.g., Hymel et al., 1990; Rubin, Hymel, & Mills, 1989).

In summary, it seems clear that different forms of social and nonsocial play have different psychological "meanings." Moreover, the meanings of these behaviors change somewhat with age.

ORIGINS OF SOCIAL AND NONSOCIAL PLAY

Given the contemporaneous and long-term significance of social and nonsocial play, it would appear important to ask questions about their origins. It seems plausible to suggest that dispositional factors that are inherent to the individual child (such as temperament or personality) may influence the quality of children's play. Usually such dispositional factors are considered to be biological based and have a quality that is internal to the child. It seems equally plausible that variability in the quality of children's play may be a function of parent–child relationships, as well as of their parent's socialization beliefs and behaviors. Finally, the interactive effects of temperament and parenting take place within a cultural context that may govern the meanings and production of play behaviors. In the following section we review dispositional, parenting, and cultural factors that may influence children's social and nonsocial play.

Dispositional Factors

In keeping with a dispositional explanation for the frequent demonstration of reticent behavior, Fox and colleagues have shown that infants who display a pattern of stable right frontal electroencephalographic (EEG) asymmetry (a biological disposition) are subsequently more fearful, anxious, compliant, and behaviorally inhibited as toddlers, as compared with other infants (Fox & Calkins, 1993; Schmidt & Fox, 1996). With preschoolers, it has been found that children who exhibit relatively high frequencies of social interaction and positive affect during free play exhibit greater relative left frontal EEG activation; alternatively, children who display high frequencies of reticence demonstrate greater right frontal EEG activation, suggesting that resting frontal asymmetry may be a marker for certain temperamental dispositions (Fox et al., 1995). These data are consistent with recent findings linking individual differences in the pattern of frontal EEG activation asymmetry to the expression of positive and negative affect (Fox, Schmidt, Calkins, Rubin, & Coplan, 1996).

For example, Fox et al. (1996) found that preschoolers who were highly *sociable* in same-age, same-gender play quartets and who exhibited greater relative *right* frontal EEG asymmetry were more likely to exhibit *externalizing* problems than *sociable* children who exhibited greater relative *left* frontal EEG asymmetry. Shy children who were *reticent* in the play quartet and exhibited greater relative *right* frontal EEG asymmetry, however, were more likely to exhibit *internalizing* problems than shy children who exhibited *left* frontal EEG asymmetry. These findings suggest that the pattern of frontal EEG asymmetry in combination with social behavioral styles during play is a significant predictor of maladaptive behavior problems during the preschool period.

Schmidt et al. (1997) recently found a positive relation between cortisol production in saliva and the demonstration of extremely inhibited behavior. Still more recently, Tout, de Haan, Campbell, and Gunnar (1998) found a significant relation between social behavior and cortisol activity for boys but not for girls. For boys, externalizing behavior was positively associated with cortisol reactivity whereas internalizing behavior (of which POS recorded reticence was a marker) was negatively associated with median cortisol levels. Surprisingly, median cortisol levels rose from morning to afternoon, a pattern opposite to that of the typical circadian rhythm of cortisol. This rise in cortisol over the day was positively correlated with internalizing behaviors for boys.

Taken together, these findings suggest that preschoolers who display reticent behaviors have an underlying dispositional or biological "makeup" that may evoke feelings of dysregulated social anxiety when in social company. These feelings of anxiety, in turn, may preclude children from participating in play with others.

Parenting

Through parent–child interaction, children learn directly and indirectly how to engage in various forms of play, including how they pretend (Haight, 1998). For example, after engaging in pretend activities with their mothers, children integrate their mothers' pretend talk into their play (Haight & Miller, 1992). Parents also influence the play of their children by virtue of the types of relationships they form with them. For example, the parent–child relationship may provide a secure base from which children can explore their physical and social surroundings. Preschoolers who have a history of a secure attachment relationship with their mothers are more likely, than their agemates who are classified as "insecurely attached" to demonstrate social initiations and competent social interactions in peer play (e.g., Booth, Rose-Krasnor, McKinnon, & Rubin, 1994).

Further, parents who exhibit behaviors characterized as involved, warm, and appropriately controlling tend to have children who are observed to engage in more cooperative play, whereas parents who are low in warmth, high in control, and frequently use power-assertive disciplinary strategies have children who are more nonsocial in their play (e.g., Hart, DeWolf, & Burts, 1993). After identifying, via observations, children who were highly withdrawn and average in social adaptation, Rubin and Mills (1990) found that mothers of withdrawn children were more likely than mothers of average children to believe that social skills should best be taught in a directive manner and that maladaptive behaviors should be responded to in a high-powered, coercive fashion. These mothers were also more likely than mothers of average children to indicate that they would feel guilty and embarrassed by displays of maladaptive behavior, and they attributed these behaviors to dispositional factors.

Finally, parents influence children's play through their role as social "directors." That is, they supervise, mediate, and arrange play opportunities for their children. Ladd and Golter (1988) reported that mothers who arranged child–peer engagements had preschoolers who (1) had a larger number of playmates, (2) had more consistent play companions in their informal nonschool networks, and (3) were better liked by their peers. Mothers who initiated peer activities were likely to have children who spent more time playing in peers' homes; this latter variable was associated with peer acceptance (Ladd, Hart, Wadsworth, & Golter, 1988). Finally, maternal tendencies to mediate (i.e., facilitate and scaffold) peer activities are related to child sociability during play (Hart et al., 1998). From these findings, it would appear as if the parents' provision of opportunities for peer interaction and play help empower their children with the abilities to initiate and manage their own peer interactions.

In summary, differences in observed play behaviors of children are related to various aspects of the parent–child relationship, including parent–child interaction, parent–child attachment, parenting beliefs, styles, and behaviors.

Consequences of Nonsocial Play

As discussed previously, social withdrawal has been found to be contemporaneously associated with several negative factors, including peer rejection, loneliness, internalizing disorders, and negative self-worth (e.g., Coplan & Rubin, 1998b). However, the only longitudinal data extant pertaining to the long-term risk status of socially withdrawn, wary, reticent children stem from a handful of studies. For example, Rubin and colleagues followed forward a group of children from age 5 years to age 15 years. They reported that passive withdrawal at 5 and 7 years of age predicted self-reported feelings of depression, loneliness, and negative self-worth and teacher ratings of anxiety at age 11 years (Hymel et al., 1990; Rubin & Mills, 1988). In turn, social withdrawal at age 11 years predicted self-reports of loneliness, depression, negative self-evaluations of social competence, feelings of not belonging to a peer group that could be counted on for social support, and parental assessments of internalizing problems at age 15 years (Rubin, 1993b; Rubin, Chen, McDougall, Bowker, & McKinnon, 1995).

These latter findings have been augmented in recent reports from other studies. For example, Renshaw and Brown (1993) found that passive withdrawal at ages 9 to 12 years predicted loneliness assessed 1 year later. Morison and Masten (1991) have indicated that children perceived by peers as withdrawn and isolated in middle childhood were more likely to think negatively of their social competencies and relationships in adolescence.

In summary, children who do not interact with their peers, including during play, appear to be at risk for contemporaneous difficulties and long-term maladaptive outcomes. Specifically, studies indicate that social withdrawal may be a risk factor for the development of internalizing problems.

Culture

What we know about the developmental significance of social and nonsocial play is constrained by the cultures in which we study these phenomena. Most, if not all, of the studies described thus far have been specific to Western cultures. We know little about the developmental progression of social and nonsocial play and its significance in non-Western cultures. Emerging data, however, give us reason to believe that culture plays a significant role in the expression of social and/or nonsocial play.

One obstacle in cross-cultural research is the potential bias inherent in the methods of assessment. For example, despite the recent surge in cross-cultural research, most studies have used "Western" questionnaires to assess "Westernized" beliefs, norms, and behaviors. Cross-cultural researchers have questioned the wisdom of using the Western social science play literature to understand the meanings of child behavior in other subcultures and cultural settings (see, e.g., Roopnarine & Carter, 1992; Soto & Negron, 1994; see Roopnarine, Johnson, & Hooper, 1994, for a review). Importantly, few researchers have attempted to make direct, cross-cultural comparisons of behaviors using observational techniques. Using behavioral observations would minimize many social conventional biases found in questionnaire and rating scale data.

Pan (1994) conducted an observational study to explore Taiwanese children's play behaviors and found that the variety of cognitive and social play behaviors displayed by Chinese children do not deviate significantly from those of children in Western cultures, at least with regard to the behaviors described in an early version of the POS. However, most of the children in the study were homogeneous in terms of middle-class socioeconomic status. In addition to the structural similarities or differences of the types of children's social play across cultures, the size of play groups may differ. For example, in contrast to U.S. children, Marquesan children in Polynesia almost never play alone or even in dyads (Martini, 1994). These children spent the majority of their play time in groups of 3 to 6 children, and in even larger groups of 7 to 10 children.

Relatedly, of particular cross-cultural interest are behaviors, including play, which may be considered "normal" in one culture but "deviant" in another. For example, as we have shown, in Western cultures, passive, reticent behavior is viewed negatively by parents and peers alike. Yet in China, children are encouraged to be dependent, cautious, self-restrained, and behaviorally inhibited (Ho, 1986). Such behaviors are considered indices of accomplishment, mastery, and maturity (King & Bond, 1985). Similarly, shy, reticent, and quiet children are described as well behaved. Indeed, socially reticent behavior is praised and encouraged (Ho, 1986). In support of these cultural notions, Chen et al. (1998) found that observed child inhibition, at age 2 years was associated positively with mothers' punishment orientation and negatively with mothers' acceptance and encouragement of achievement in a Canadian sample; however, the relations were in the opposite direction in a Chinese sample. That is, child inhibition was associated positively with mother's warm and accepting attitudes and negatively with rejection and punishment orientation. These results indicate possible different adaptational meanings of behavioral inhibition across the two cultures, which may result in developmental differences in observed child behaviors. Indeed, socially inhibited behavior in China is positively associated with competent, prosocial behavior and with peer acceptance in childhood (Chen, Rubin, & Li, 1995; Chen, Rubin, & Sun, 1992).

While researchers have focused on latitudinal differences between Western (i.e., individualistic) versus Eastern (i.e., pluralistic) cultures, there may also be longitude differences in thinking and behaving. For example, most researchers who study adaptive and maladaptive behaviors from a cross-cultural perspective believe that the "meanings" of prosocial and aggressive behavior are *similar* in Chinese and Western cultures (Ho, 1986). In fact, in both cultures, sociability and cooperation in children are positively valued and encouraged whereas aggression is negatively perceived and prohibited (e.g., Chen & Rubin, 1992).

There has been less research exploring the "meanings" of these behaviors in cultures varying in longitude. Although most of the work that has been done has focused on aggression rather than sociability, a look at these findings reveals why we cannot simply assume that the "meanings" of these behaviors are universal. For example, in some "southern" cultures, it has been suggested that aggression is viewed somewhat more positively than in Eastern and Western cultures. In one study of Israeli boys, aggressiveness as rated by peers was associated positively with sociability and leadership (Krispin, Sternberg, & Lamb, 1992). Similarly, in southern Italy, aggression has become increasingly accepted as a means to negotiate exchanges with others. Further, Corsaro and Rizzo (1990) found that Italian preschoolers engaged in more disputes than did their U.S. counterparts. Relatedly, Casiglia, LoCoco, and Zapulla (1998) reported that children viewed by peers as aggressive were also viewed as social leaders. Although there has been little work examining possible differences in the "meanings" of social and/or nonsocial play, this work on aggression demonstrates the need for future work in this area.

Taken together, the foregoing findings suggest strongly that the cultural milieu and societal values may encourage or inhibit demonstrations of highly sociable or highly unsociable behavior. In studying intercultural and cultural variations in children's play, we can better recognize the unique cultural properties that are reflected in children's activities (Cooney & Sha, 1999; Roopnarine, Lasker, Sacks, & Stores, 1998).

SUMMARY AND CONCLUSION

In this chapter, we have examined the constructs of children's social and nonsocial play. In particular, we have discussed the developmental significance of social play and the potential risks associated with certain forms of nonsocial play. We reported that social play was associated with positive markers of both social (e.g., interpersonal problem-solving skills, perspective-taking skills, and group cooperation) and cognitive (e.g., reading and comprehension skills) competence. Similarly, solitary–passive behaviors were associated positively with competent problem solving, emotion regulation, and task persistence. Conversely, we outlined the numerous risk factors associated with other types of nonsocial play. For example, children who display social reticence experience internalizing problems and peer rejection, whereas children who display solitary–active behaviors tend to experience externalizing disorders and peer rejection.

Next we examined the advantages and disadvantages of various methods used to study children's interactions and play. In particular, we focused on behavioral observational methods of assessment used in the study of normative development, as well as causes, correlates, and consequences of individual differences in young children's social and nonsocial play. Finally, we discussed the origins of individual and group variability found in social and nonsocial play, including dispositional factors, parental influences, and cultural contexts. The research presented suggests that cultural milieus and societal values create a framework within which these different behaviors may be evaluated.

It is apparent that play is an important context within which children come to understand their interpersonal and intrapersonal worlds. By studying play, we begin to understand the developmental significance, both positive and negative, of social and nonsocial activity in the lives of children.

REFERENCES

Asendorpf, J. (1991). Development of inhibited children's coping with unfamiliarity. *Child* Development, 62, 1460–1474.

Asendorpf, J. (1993). Beyond temperament: A two-factor coping model of the development of inhibition during childhood. In K. H. Rubin & J. Asendorpf (Eds.), *Social withdrawal, inhibition, and shyness in childhood* (pp. 265–290). Hillsdale, NJ: Erlbaum.

Astington, J. W., Harris, P. L., & Olson, D. R. (Eds.). (1988). *Developing theories of mind.* New York: Cambridge University Press.

Bakeman, R., & Brownlee, J. R. (1980). The strategic use of parallel play: A sequential analysis. *Child Development, 51,* 873–878.

Barnes, K. E. (1971). Preschool play norms: A replication. *Developmental Psychology, 5,* 99–103.

Bergen, D. (1987). Stages of play development. In D. Bergen (Ed.), *Play as a medium for learning and development* (pp. 49–66). Portsmouth, NH: Heinemann.

Booth, C. L., Rose-Krasnor, L., McKinnon, J., & Rubin, K. H. (1994). Predicting social adjustment in middle childhood: The role of preschool attachment security and maternal style. *Social Development, 3,* 189–204.

Bruner, J. S. (1972). The nature and uses of immaturity. *American Psychologist, 27,* 687–708.

Casiglia, A. C., LoCoco, A., & Zapulla, A. (1998). Aspects of social reputation and peer relationships in Italian children: A cross-cultural perspective. *Developmental Psychology, 34,* 723–730.

Chen, X., Hastings, P. D., Rubin, K. H., Chen, H., Cen, G., & Stewart, S. L. (1998). Child-rearing attitudes and behavioral inhibition in Chinese and Canadian toddlers: A cross-cultural study. *Developmental Psychology, 34,* 677–686.

Chen, X., & Rubin, K. H. (1992). Correlates of peer acceptance in a Chinese sample of six-year-olds. *International Journal of Behavioral Development, 15*(2), 259–273.

Chen, X., Rubin, K. H., & Li, B. (1995). Social and school adjustment of shy and aggressive children in China. *Development and Psychopathology, 7,* 337–349.

Chen, X., Rubin, K. H., & Sun, Y. (1992). Social reputation and peer relationships in Chinese and Canadian children: A cross-cultural study. *Child Development, 63,* 1336–1343.

Christie, J. F. (1991). *Play and early literacy development.* Albany: State University of New York Press.

Christie, J. F. (1998). Play: A medium for literacy development. In D. P. Fromberg & D. Bergen (Eds.), *Play from birth to twelve and beyond: Contexts, perspectives and meanings* (pp. 50–55). New York: Garland.

Coie, J. D., & Dodge, K. A. (1988). Multiple sources of data on social behavior and social status in the school: A cross-age comparison. *Child Development, 59,* 815–829.

Coie, J. D., Dodge, K. A., & Kupersmidt, J. B. (1990). Peer group behavior and social status. In S. R. Asher & J. D. Coie (Eds.), *Peer rejection in childhood* (pp. 17–59). New York: Cambridge University Press.

Cooney, M. H., & Sha, J. (1999). Play in the Day of Qiaoqiao: A Chinese perspective. *Child Study Journal, 29,* 97–111.

Coplan, R. J., & Rubin, K. H. (1998a). Exploring and assessing nonsocial play in the preschool: The development and validation of the preschool play behavior scale. *Social Development, 7,* 72–91.

Coplan, R. J., & Rubin, K. H. (1998b). Social play. In D. P. Fromberg & D. Bergen (Eds.), *Play from birth to twelve and beyond: Contexts, perspectives and meanings* (pp. 368–377). New York: Garland.

Coplan, R. J., Rubin, K. H., Fox, N. A., Calkins, S. D., & Stewart, S. L. (1994). Being alone, playing alone, and acting alone: Distinguishing among reticence, and passive– and active–solitude in young children. *Child Development, 65,* 129–138.

Corsaro, W. A., & Rizzo, T. A. (1990). *Conflict talk.* New York: Cambridge University Press.

Crick, N., & Grotpeter, J., (1995). Relational aggression, gender, and social-psychological adjustment. *Child Development, 66,* 710–722.

Doyle, A. B., & Connolly, J. (1989). Negotiation and enactment in social pretend play: Relations to social acceptance and social cognition. *Early Childhood Research Quarterly, 4,* 289–302.

Eckerman, C. O., Whatley, J. L., & Kutz, S. L. (1975). Growth of social play with peers during the second year of life. *Developmental Psychology, 11,* 32–49.

Einslein, J., & Fein, G. G. (1981). Temporal and cross-situational stability of children's social and play behavior. *Developmental Psychology, 17,* 760–761.

Fein, G. G. (1989). Mind, meaning and affect: Proposals for a theory of pretense. *Developmental Review, 9,* 345–363.

Fewell, R., & Glick, M. (1998). The role of play in assessment. In D. P. Fromberg & D. Bergen (Eds.), *Play from birth to twelve and beyond: Contexts, perspectives and meanings* (pp. 201–207). New York: Garland.

Fox, N. A., & Calkins, S. D. (1993). Pathways to aggression and social withdrawal: Interactions among temperament, attachment, and regulation. In K. H. Rubin & J. Asendorpf (Eds.), *Social withdrawal, inhibition, and shyness in childhood* (pp. 81–100). Hillsdale, NJ: Erlbaum.

Fox, N. A, Rubin, K. H., Calkins, S. D., Marshall, T. R., Coplan, R. J., Porges, S. W., Long, J. M., & Stewart, S. (1995). Frontal activation asymmetry and social competence at four years of age. *Child Development, 66,* 1770–1784.

Fox, N. A., Schmidt, L. A., Calkins, S. D., Rubin, K. H., & Coplan, R. J. (1996). The role of frontal activation in the regulation and dysregulation of social behavior during the preschool years. *Development & Psychopathology, 8,* 89–102.

Fromberg, D. P., & Bergen, D. (1998). *Play from birth to twelve and beyond: Contexts, perspectives and meanings.* New York: Garland.

Galda, L., Pellegrini, A., & Cox, S. (1989). Preschoolers' emergent literacy: A short-term longitudinal study. *Research in the Teaching of English, 23,* 292–310.

Garvey, C. (1974). Some properties of social play. *Merrill-Palmer Quarterly, 20,* 263–180.

Goldman, L. (1998). *Child's play: Myths, mimesis, and make-believe.* New York: Oxford.

Göncü, A. (1993a). Development of intersubjectivity in the dyadic play of preschoolers. *Early Childhood Research Quarterly, 8,* 99–116.

Göncü, A. (1993b). Development of intersubjectivity in social pretend play. *Human Development, 36,* 185–198.

Guralnick, M. J., Conner, R. T., Hammond, M. A., Gottman, J. M., & Kinnish, K. (1996). The peer relations of preschool children with communication disorders. *Child Development, 67,* 471–489.

Haight, W. (1998). Adult direct and indirect influences on play. In D. P. Fromberg & D. Bergen (Eds.), *Play from birth to twelve and beyond: Contexts, perspectives and meanings* (pp. 259–265). New York: Garland.

Haight, W., & Miller, P. (1992). The development of everyday pretend play: A longitudinal study of mothers' participation. *Merrill-Palmer Quarterly, 38,* 331–349.

Hart, C. H., DeWolf, M., & Burts, D. C. (1993). Parental disciplinary strategies and preschoolers' play behavior in playground settings. In C. H. Hart (Ed.), *Children on playgrounds: Research perspectives and applications. SUNY series, children's play in society* (pp. 271–313). Albany: State University of New York Press.

Hart, C. H., Yang, C., Nelson, D. A., Jin, S., Bazarskaya, & Nelson, L. (1998). Peer contact patterns, parenting practices, and preschoolers' social competence in China, Russia, and the United States. In P. T. Slee & K. Rigby (Eds.), *Children's peer relations* (pp. 3–30). London: Routledge.

Hetherington, E. M. (Ed.). (1983). *Handbook of child psychology: Vol. 4. Socialization, personality, and social development.* New York: Wiley.

Ho, D. Y. F. (1986). Chinese patterns of socialization: A critical review. In M. H. Bond (Ed.), *The psychology of Chinese people* (pp. 1–37). New York: Oxford University Press.

Holmberg, M. C. (1980). The development of social exchange patterns from 12 to 42 months. *Child Development, 51,* 618–626.

Howes, C. (1983). Patterns of friendship. *Child Development, 54,* 1041–1053.

Howes, C. (1988). Peer interaction in young children. *Monographs for the Society for Research in Child Development, 53*(1), 1–94.

Howes, C., & Matheson, C. C. (1992). Sequences in the development of competent play with peers: Social and social pretend play. *Developmental Psychology, 28,* 961–974.

Hutt, C. (1970). Specific and diverse exploration. In H. Reese & L. Lipsitt (Eds.), *Advances in child development and behavior.* New York: Academic Press.

Hymel, S. (1983). Preschool children's peer relations: Issues in sociometric assessment. *Merrill–Palmer Quarterly, 29* 237–260.

Hymel, S., Rubin, K. H., Rowden, L., & LeMare, L. (1990). A longitudinal study of sociometric status in middle and late childhood. *Child Development, 61,* 2004–2121.

Jarrell, R. (1998). Play and its influence on the development of young children's mathematical thinking. In D. P. Fromberg & D. Bergen (Eds.), *Play from birth to twelve and beyond: Contexts, perspectives and meanings* (pp. 56–67). New York: Garland.

Johnson, J. E. (1998). Play development from ages four to eight. In D. P. Fromberg & D. Bergen (Eds.), *Play from birth to twelve and beyond: Contexts, perspectives, and meanings* (pp. 146–153). New York: Garland.

Johnson, J. E., & Ershler, J. (1981). Developmental trends in preschool play as a function of classroom program and child gender. *Child Development, 52,* 995–1004.

King, A. Y. C., & Bond, M. H. (1985). The Confucian paradigm of man: A sociological view. In W. S. Teng & D. Y. H. Wu (Eds.), *Chinese culture and mental health.* New York: Academic Press.

Krispin, O., Sternberg, K. J., & Lamb, M. E. (1992). The dimensions of peer evaluation in Israel: A cross-cultural perspective. *International Journal of Behavioral Development, 159,* 299–314.

Ladd, G. W., & Golter, B. (1988). Parents' management of preschoolers' peer relations: Is it related to children's social competence? *Developmental Psychology, 24,* 109–117.

Ladd, G. W., Hart, C. H., Wadsworth, E. M., & Golter, B. S. (1988). Preschoolers' peer networks in nonschool settings: Relationship to family characteristics and school adjustment. In S. Salzinger, J. Antrobus, & M. Hammer (Eds.), *Social networks of children, adolescents, and college students* (pp. 61–92). Hillsdale, NJ: Erlbaum.

Ladd, G. W., & Mars, K. T. (1986). Reliability and validity of preschoolers' perception of peer behavior. *Journal of Clinical Child Psychology, 15,* 16–25.

Ladd, G. W., & Price, J. M. (1986). Promoting children's cognitive and social competence: The relation between parents' perceptions of task difficulty and children's perceived and actual competence. *Child Development, 57* 446–460.

Ladd, G. W., & Price, J. M. (1993). Play styles of peer-accepted and peer-rejected children on the playground. In C. H. Hart (Ed.), *Children on the playgrounds: Research perspectives and applications* (pp. 130–161). Albany: State University of New York Press.

Ladd, G. W., & Profilet, S. M. (1996). The child behavior scale: A teacher report measure of young children's aggressive, withdrawn, and prosocial behaviors. *Developmental Psychology, 32,* 1008–1024.

Lillard, A. S. (1998). Playing with a theory of mind. In O. N. Saracho, & B. Spodek (Eds.), *Multiple perspectives on play in early childhood education* (pp. 11–33). Albany: State University of New York Press.

Martini, M. (1994). Peer interactions in Polynesia: A view from the Marquesas. In J. L. Roopnarine, J. E. Johnson, & F. H. Hooper (Eds.), *Children's play in diverse cultures.* Albany: State University of New York Press.

McNeilly-Choque, M. K., Hart, C. H., Robinson, C. C., Nelson, L. J., & Olsen, S. F. (1996). Overt and relational aggression on the playground: Correspondence among different informants. *Journal of Research in Childhood Education, 11,* 47–67.

Mead, G. H. (1934). *Mind, self, and society.* Chicago: University of Chicago Press.

Minnett, A., Clark, K., & Wilson, G. (1994). Play behaviors and communication between deaf and hard of hearing children and their hearing peers in an integrated preschool. *American Annals of the Deaf, 139,* 420–430.

Moller, L., Hymel, S., & Rubin, K. H. (1992). Sex typing in play and popularity in middle childhood. *Sex Roles, 26,* 331–353.

Morison, P., & Masten, A. S. (1991). Peer reputation in middle childhood as a predictor of adaptation in adolescence: A seven year follow-up. *Child Development, 62,* 991–1007.

Nourot, P. M. (1998). Sociodramatic play: Pretending together. In D. P. Fromberg & D. Bergen (Eds.), *Play from birth to twelve and beyond: Contexts, perspectives and meanings* (pp. 378–391). New York: Garland.

Pan, H. L. W. (1994). Children's play in Taiwan. In J. L. Roopnarine, J. E. Johnson, & F. H. Hooper (Eds.), *Children's play in diverse cultures.* Albany: State University of New York Press.

Parten, M. B. (1932). Social participation among preschool children. *Journal of Abnormal Psychology, 27,* 243–269.

Pellegrini, A. D. (1995). *The developmental and educational roles of children's playground behavior.* Albany: State University of New York Press.

Pellegrini, A. D. (1998). Rough-and-tumble play from childhood through adolescence: Differing perspectives. In D. P. Fromberg & D. Bergen (Eds.), *Play from birth to twelve and beyond: Contexts, perspectives and meanings* (pp. 401–408). New York: Garland.

Pepler, D. J. (1982). Play and divergent thinking. In D. J. Pepler & K. H. Rubin (Eds.), *The play of children: Research and theory.* Basel, Switzerland: Kargen AG.

Pettit, G. S., & Bates, J. E. (1990). Describing family interaction patterns in early childhood: A "social events" perspective. *Journal of Applied Developmental Psychology, 11*, 395–418.

Pettit, G. S., & Harrist, A. W. (1993). Children's aggressive ad socially unskilled playground behaviors with peers: Origins in early family relations. In C. H. Hart (Ed.), *Children on the playgrounds: Research perspectives and applications* (pp. 240–270). Albany: State University of New York Press.

Piaget, J. (1962). *Play, dreams, and imitation in childhood.* New York: Norton.

Renshaw, P. D., & Brown, P. J., (1993). Loneliness in middle childhood: Concurrent and longitudinal predictors. *Child Development, 64*, 1271–1284.

Roopnarine, J. L., & Carter, B. (1992a). The cultural context of socialization: A much ignored issue. In J. Roopnarine & D. B. Carter (Eds.), *Parent–child socialization in diverse cultures* (pp. 245–251). Norwood, NJ: Ablex.

Roopnarine, J., Johnson, J., & Hooper (1994). *Children's play in diverse cultures.* Albany: State University of New York Press.

Roopnarine, J. L., Lasker, J., Sacks, M., & Stores, M. (1998). The cultural contexts of children's play. In O. N. Saracho & B. Spodek (Eds.), *Multiple perspectives on play in early childhood education* (pp. 194–219). Albany: State University of New York Press.

Rosen, C. (1974). The effects of sociodramatic play on problem-solving behavior among culturally disadvantaged preschool children. *Child Development, 45*, 920–927.

Roskos, K., & Neuman, S. B. (1998). Play as an opportunity for literacy. In O. N. Saracho, & B. Spodek (Eds.), *Multiple perspectives on play in early childhood education.* (pp. 100–115). Albany: State University of New York Press.

Rubin, K. H. (1982). Nonsocial play in preschoolers: Necessarily evil? *Child Development, 53*, 651–657.

Rubin, K. H. (1993a). *The Play Observation Scale (POS).* Unpublished manuscript, University of Waterloo.

Rubin, K. H. (1993b). The Waterloo Longitudinal Project: Correlates and consequences of social withdrawal from childhood to adolescence. In K. H. Rubin & J. B. Asendorpf (Eds.), *Social withdrawal, inhibition, and shyness in childhood* (pp. 291–314). Hillsdale, NJ: Erlbaum.

Rubin, K. H., & Asendorpf, J. (1993). Social withdrawal, inhibition, and shyness in childhood: Conceptual and definitional issues. In K. H. Rubin & J. Asendorpf (Eds.), *Social withdrawal, inhibition, and shyness in children* (pp. 3–17). Hillsdale, NJ: Erlbaum.

Rubin, K. H., Bukowski, W., & Parker, J. (1998). Peer interactions, relationships, and groups. In N. Eisenberg (Ed.), *Handbook of child psychology (5th ed.): Social, emotional, and personality development* (pp. 619–700). New York: Wiley.

Rubin, K. H., Chen, X., McDougall, P., Bowker, A., & McKinnon, J. (1995). The Waterloo Longitudinal Project: Predicting internalizing and externalizing problems in adolescence. *Developmental Psychology, 7*, 751–764.

Rubin, K. H., Coplan, C., Nelson, L. J., Cheah, C., & Lagace-Seguin, D. G. (1999). Peer relationships in childhood. In M. A. Bornstein & M. E. Lamb (Eds.), *Developmental psychology: An advanced textbook* (pp. 451–502). Hillsdale, NJ: Erlbaum.

Rubin, K. H., & Coplan, R. J. (1994). Play: Developmental stages, functions, and educational support. In T. Husen & T. Postwaite (Eds.), *The international encyclopedia of education* (2nd ed., vol. 8, pp. 4536–4542). New York: Elsevier.

Rubin, K. H., Coplan, R. J., Fox, N. A., & Calkins, S. D. (1995). Emotionality, emotion regulation, and preschoolers' social adaptation. *Development and Psychopathology, 7*, 49–62.

Rubin, K. H., Fein, G., & Vandenberg, B. (1983). Play. In E. M. Hetherington (Ed.), *Handbook of child psychology: Vol. 4. Socialization, personality, and social development.* New York: Wiley.

Rubin, K. H., Hymel, S., & Mills, R. S. L. (1989). Sociability and social withdrawal in childhood: Stability and outcomes. *Journal of Personality, 57*, 238–255.

Rubin, K. H., Kennedy, A., Cheah, C. S. L., & Fox, N. A. (1999). *Emotion regulation, dysregulation and sociability at 7 years of age.* Manuscript in preparation.

Rubin, K. H., LeMare L. J., & Lollis, S. (1990). Social withdrawal in childhood: Developmental pathways to rejection. In S. R. Asher & J. D. Coie (Eds.) *Peer rejection in childhood* (pp. 217–249). New York: Cambridge University Press.

Rubin, K. H., & Maioni, T. L. (1975). Play preference and its relationship to egocentrism, popularity and classification skills in preschoolers. *Merrill–Palmer Quarterly, 21* 171–179.

Rubin, K. H., Maioni, T. L., & Hornung, M. (1976). Free play behaviors in middle and lower class preschoolers: Parten and Piaget revisited. *Child Development, 47*, 414–419.

Rubin, K. H., & Mills, R. S. L. (1988). The many faces of social isolation in childhood. *Journal of Consulting and Clinical Psychology, 6*, 916–924.

Rubin, K. H., & Mills, R. S. L. (1990). Maternal beliefs about adaptive and maladaptive social behaviors in normal, aggressive, and withdrawn preschoolers. *Journal of Abnormal Child Psychology, 18*, 419–435.

Rubin, K. H., & Stewart, S. L. (1996). Social withdrawal. In E. Mash & R. Barkley (Eds.), *Child psychopathology* (pp. 277–307). New York: Guilford Press.

Rubin, K. H., Watson, K., & Jambor, T. (1978). Free-play behaviors in preschool and kindergarten children. *Child Development, 49*, 534–536.

Saltz, E., & Johnson, J. (1974). Training for thematic-fantasy play in culturally disadvantaged children: Preliminary results. *Journal of Educational Psychology, 66*, 623–630.

Saracho, O. N., & Spodek, B. (1998), *Multiple perspectives on play in early childhood education.* Albany: State University of New York Press.

Sawyer, R. K. (1996). The semiotics of improvisation: The pragmatics of musical and verbal performance. *Semiotica, 108*, 269–306.

Sawyer, R. K. (1997). *Pretend play as improvisation. Conversations in the preschool classroom.* Mahwah, NJ: Erlbaum.

Scarsia, L. (1966). *A ciascuno il suo* [To each his own]. Torino, Italy: Einaudi.

Schmidt, L. A., & Fox, N. A. (1996). Left frontal EEG activation in the development of toddler's sociability. *Brain and Cognition, 32*, 243–246.

Schmidt, L. A., Fox, N. A., Rubin, K. H., Sternberg, E. M., Gold, P. W., Smith, C. C., & Schulkin, J. (1997). Behavioral and neuroendocrine responses in shy children. *Developmental Psychobiology, 30*, 127–140.

Shore, C. (1998). Play and language: Individual differences as evidence of development and style. In D. P. Fromberg & D. Bergen (Eds.), *Play from birth to twelve and beyond: Contexts, perspectives and meanings* (pp. 165–174). New York: Garland.

Sigelman, C. K. (1999). *Life-span human development* (3rd ed.). Pacific Grove, CA: Brooks/Cole.

Smilansky, S. (1968). *The effects of sociodramatic play on disadvantaged preschool children.* New York: Wiley.

Smith, P. K., Dagleish, M., & Herzmark, G. (1981). A comparison of the effects of fantasy play tutoring and skills tutoring in nursery classes. *International Journal of Behavioral Development, 4,* 421–441.

Smith, P., & Syddall, S. (1978). Play and non-play tutoring in preschool children: Is it play or tutoring that matters? *British Journal of Educational Psychology, 48,* 315–325.

Soto, L., & Negron, L. (1994). Mainland Puerto Rican children. In J. L. Roopnarine, J. Johnson, & F. Hooper (Eds.), *Children's play in diverse cultures* (pp. 104–122). Albany: State University of New York Press.

Tout, K., de Haan, M., Campbell, E. K., & Gunnar, M .R. (1998). Social behavior correlates of cortisol activity in child care: Gender differences and time-of-day effects. *Child Development, 69,* 1247–1262.

Vukelich, C. (1995). Effects of play intervention on young children's reading of environmental print. *Early Childhood Research Quarterly, 9,* 153–170.

Wellman, H. M. (1990). *The child's theory of mind.* Cambridge, MA: Bradford Books/MIT Press.

Williamson, P. A. (1992). The effects of play training on the story comprehension of upper primary children. *Journal of Research in Childhood Education, 4,* 130–134.

Youngblade, L. M., & Dunn, J. (1995). Individual differences in young children's pretend play with mother and sibling: Links to relationships and understanding of other people's feelings and beliefs. *Child Development, 66,* 1472–1492.

Younger, A., Gentile, C., & Burgess, K. (1993). Children's perceptions of social withdrawal: Changes across age. In K. H. Rubin & J. Asendorpf (Eds.), *Social withdrawal, inhibition, and shyness in childhood* (pp. 215–235). Hillsdale, NJ: Erlbaum.

Younger, A. J., Schneider, B. H., & Daniels, T. (1991). Aggression and social withdrawal as viewed by children's peers: Conceptual issues in assessment and implications for intervention. *Journal of Psychiatry and Neuroscience, 16,* 139–145.

Younger, A. J., Schwartzman, A. E., & Ledingham, J. E. (1985). Age-related changes in children's perceptions of aggression and withdrawal in their peers. *Developmental Psychology, 21,* 70–75.

4

❧

Transforming the "Play-Oriented Curriculum" and Work in Constructivist Early Education

RHETA DeVRIES

I first met Greta G. Fein in 1979 when I was a candidate for a faculty position at the Merrill–Palmer Institute. The book *Day Care in Context* by Greta and Alison Clarke-Stewart was a model for me as I embarked on directing a school. Similarly, Greta's work on play was groundbreaking and provided a beacon to researchers in that arena. At Merrill-Palmer and subsequently I have been impressed with the ways in which Greta mentored graduate students in supportive, nurturing, and yet challenging ways. Again, another model. Equally important, I count myself lucky to be one of those enjoying Greta's friendship.

The work of Greta Fein, celebrated in this book, has sensitized us to the many advantages of play for children's development. She (Fein & Rivkin, 1986) has also brought to our attention the fact that while play has traditionally characterized preschool and much kindergarten education, critics have viewed it as aimless. Rubin, Fein, and Vandenberg (1983) remind us that "The Puritan ethic dichotomized work and play," viewing work as "an extension of God's work" and seeing play as "the province of the devil" (pp. 697–698). They note that although this idea is

72

less pronounced now it still "contributes to the relative disregard of play as an important topic for study" (Rubin et al., 1983, p. 698).

The National Association for the Education of Young Children has defended the value of play for children's development and education in a series of position statements (Bredekamp, 1987; Bredekamp & Copple, 1997; Bredekamp & Rosegrant, 1992, 1995). This highly influential organization has advocated developmentally appropriate practice (DAP) and, referring to Fein and Rivkin (1986), has stated that "child initiated, teacher-supported play is an essential component of developmentally appropriate practice" (Bredekamp & Copple, 1997).

Reading, writing, and arithmetic (academics) are often associated with "work"—serious business having nothing to do with play. The play-oriented approach of DAP was originally conceptualized as a reaction to inappropriate programs of work emphasizing "teacher-directed instruction in narrowly defined academic skills" (Bredekamp, 1987, p. iv). One result of this was that many teachers then dispensed entirely with academics and interpreted DAP as unstructured free play without much intellectually challenging content. Many teachers who are trying to implement DAP justify their emphasis on play to the exclusion of work by stating that play is the child's work.

With the widespread acceptance of DAP as the definition of the best early education, the advocacy of play has become commonplace. Yet many teachers do not really understand and/or accept the developmentally appropriate approach with its emphasis on play as the best early education. Consequently, teachers assimilate the idea of play into their own beliefs and understandings about what education should be. The practical results as I describe them here are often classroom experiences that depart in significant ways from DAP. The problem as I see it is that teachers often interpret the idea of "play-oriented curriculum" in a variety of ways and express these interpretations in a wide variety of often contradictory classroom practices—all of which they label "play." The result is agreement at the level of rhetoric but disagreement at the practical level of children's experiences in classrooms. It is with a desire to foster more focused dialogue on what it is desirable for children to experience in high-quality early education that I write this chapter.

As Fein (1981) and her colleagues have shown, multiple theories and definitions of play, often contrasted with work, have been put forth by researchers and theorists. However, in this chapter, I focus on how *teachers* define and understand the idea of a play-oriented curriculum, especially as this understanding is reflected in the kinds of activities they provide for children and in the various ways they intervene in children's play and work.

In what follows, I first present an overview of the constructivist perspective that guides my reflections throughout this chapter. Second, I discuss early childhood teachers' views of play and work in early education. Third, I describe four interpretations of a "play-oriented curriculum" in kindergarten classes whose teachers consider their programs to be "developmentally appropriate" and discuss these from a constructivist perspective.

A CONSTRUCTIVIST PERSPECTIVE

In this chapter, I take a constructivist perspective inspired especially by the research and theory of Jean Piaget and his colleagues. With regard to play and work in early education, key constructivist ideas involve relations between play and work, the importance of the social context of play and work, and the teacher's role in promoting children's reasoning and acquisition of knowledge. These are discussed below.

Relations between Play and Work

To reflect further on the role of play and work in early education, let us consider the views of Piaget, Dewey, and Vygotsky. Piaget (1945/1962) talked about four forms of play and how these contribute to children's development. In the first, exercise or practice play, what is already known is repeated for pleasure. In the second, symbolic play or pretense, children enact ideas they are not yet able to express verbally or think about without symbols. Pretense (such as making a doll drink imaginary soup) is thus useful to the child when "interior thought is not as yet sufficiently precise and mobile" and when "logico-verbal thought is still too inadequate and vague" (Piaget, 1945/1962, p. 155). In the third, games with rules (such as Marbles, Hopscotch, and Hide-and-Seek), are play in which "competition is controlled by collective discipline, with a code of honour and fair play" (Piaget, 1945/1962, p. 168). The fourth is constructional play (such as building a car with wheels that turn or a realistic model of a boat).

Piaget presented play as something necessary and useful for the young child's development of later operational intelligence. For Piaget, the capacity to work is not opposed to play and imposed on the child by adult instruction but develops out of the play interest. That is, Piaget (1945/1962) saw symbolic play becoming more and more reflective of reality, developing "in the direction of constructive activity or work" (p. 112). For example, a child who pretends that a piece of wood is a boat may later really make a boat replica. Thus, out of symbolic play emerges the fourth category of play, constructional play. Piaget and

Inhelder (1966/1969) noted that play may be "initially imbued with play symbolism but tend later to constitute genuine adaptations (mechanical constructions, etc.) or solutions to problems and intelligent creations" (p. 59). Piaget (1945/1962) explained that "Constructional play ... occup[ies] ... a position half-way between play and intelligent work" (p. 113). Addressing the educational issue directly, Piaget (1969/1970) wrote: "In the course of its own internal development, the play of small children is gradually transformed into adapted constructions requiring an ever-increasing amount of what is in effect work, to such an extent that in the infant classes of an active school every kind of spontaneous transition may be observed between play and work" (p. 157). Some of what is called "play" might be considered "work" in that it is not always pleasurable and may require intense effort and involve initial failure. However, as Dewey (1933) pointed out, young children do not divide activities into utilitarian "work" and "play." Rather, "whatever appeals to them at all appeals directly on its own account" (p. 215). Dewey (1916/1966) commented: "From a very early age, however, there is no distinction of exclusive periods of play activity and work activity, but only one of emphasis. There are definite results which even young children desire, and try to bring to pass" (p. 203). Dewey (1933) saw play as important because in pretending with dolls, trains, blocks, etc., children "are living ... in the large world of meanings, natural and social, evoked by these things" (p. 219). Further, according to Dewey (1933), "mental play is open-mindedness," "free mental play involves seriousness, the earnest following of the development of subject matter," and "pure interest in truth coincides with love of the free play of thought in inquiry" (pp. 286–287). From this perspective, it is possible "to be playful and serious at the same time, and it defines the ideal mental condition" (Dewey, 1933, p. 286).

For Vygotsky (1933/1967), play is "the leading source of development in preschool years" (p. 6), arising from unrealizable desires that are realized in imagination. It is different from work in that the child is unconscious of the motives underlying play. Vygotsky viewed play as involving an imaginary situation. Unlike Piaget, Vygotsky made no distinction between pretense and games with rules as, in his view, pretense involves obeying the rules for behavior of the role enacted, and a game with rules turns into an imaginary situation in the sense that rules rule out certain actual possibilities for action. He gave the example of chess as a game in which pieces can only move in specified ways. Vygotsky (1933/1967) commented: "The development from an overt imaginary situation and covert rules to games with overt rules and a covert imaginary situation outlines the evolution of children's play from one pole to the other" (p. 10). Vygotsky referred to Piaget's work on moral rules and concurred with the conception of the two moralities (external and internal) in the child. Vygotsky (1933/1967) concluded that the child "has an entirely different attitude to rules which he makes up himself" (p. 11). Carrying this idea further, Vygotsky argued that in play a child is liberated from external situational constraints and begins to act independently of these. He stated: "Play is converted to internal processes at school age, going over to internal speech, logical memory, and abstract thought" (Vygotsky, 1933/1967, p. 13). For Vygotsky, the child's creation of imaginary situations is "a means of developing abstract thought" (p. 17). Preschool play turns at school age into a rule-based attitude toward school instruction and work. The essence of play is the creation of a new relationship between "situations in thought and real situations" (p. 17).

In light of observations by Piaget, Dewey, and Vygotsky, play no longer appears trivial but is seen as crucial for children's development and learning. Evolution in forms of play reflects developmental advances and deserves to be valued. Play is useful to children as they try to understand the world in which they live. Piaget and Dewey not only provide educators with a strong rationale for the value of play as well as work in early education but lead us to appreciate work that evolves from play. This work is interesting to the "workers," engages them in reflecting on meaning, brings consciousness of purpose, leads to search for means of realization, and moves toward coherence in thought. Exploration and experimentation with new objects is often referred to as play but may actually be considered work because the child adapts to the reactions of objects by constructing new relationships. Thus, we should expect to see all kinds of play and work in children's activities in developmentally appropriate and constructivist classrooms.

The Importance of the Social Context

The social context of play and work is critical because of its implications for children's development and learning. Elsewhere (DeVries & Zan, 1994), I have argued that the first principle of constructivist education is to create a cooperative sociomoral atmosphere in which mutual respect is continually practiced. By "sociomoral atmosphere," I refer to the entire network of interpersonal relations in a classroom. These pervade every aspect of the child's experience in school and profoundly influence social, moral, intellectual, personality, and emotional development. Every classroom has a sociomoral atmosphere that may be viewed along a continuum from coercion to cooperation. The rationale for this principle is drawn from Piaget's writings (e.g., Piaget, 1932/1965) in which he described the kind of interpersonal relations necessary for optimal moral and intellectual development. He defined two types of morality corresponding to two types of adult–child relations, one that promotes children's development and one that retards it. These are briefly outlined next.

Two Types of Morality

The first type of morality is a morality of obedience. Piaget called this "heteronomous" morality. The word "heteronomous" comes from roots meaning following rules made by others. Therefore, the individual who is heteronomously moral follows moral rules given by others out of obedience to an authority who has coercive power. Heteronomous morality is conformity to external rules that are simply accepted and followed without question.

The second type of morality is autonomous. The word "autonomous" comes from roots meaning self-regulation. The individual who is autonomously moral follows moral rules of the self. Such rules are self-constructed, self-regulating principles. The individual who is autonomously moral follows internal convictions about the necessity of respect for persons in relationships with others.

Two Types of Adult–Child Relationships

The first type of adult–child relationship, corresponding to heteronomous morality, is one of coercion or constraint in which the adult prescribes what the child must do by giving ready-made rules and instructions for behavior. In this relation, respect is a one-way affair. That is, the child is expected to respect the adult, and the adult uses authority to socialize and instruct the child. The adult controls the child's behavior. In this sociomoral context, the child's reason for behaving is thus outside his or her own reasoning and system of personal interests and values. Piaget called this type of relation "heteronomous." Heteronomy can range on a continuum from hostile and punitive to genuine loving control.

While in adult–child relations heteronomy is often appropriate and sometimes unavoidable, well-meaning adults often feel that it is their responsibility to manage every detail of children's behavior. Unfortunately, when children are governed continually by the values, beliefs, and ideas of others, they practice a submission (if not rebellion) that can lead to mindless conformity in both moral and intellectual life. Piaget warned that coercion socializes only the surface of behavior and actually reinforces the child's tendency to rely on regulation by others. Intellectually, the heavily coerced child may react with a passive orientation to the ideas of others, an unquestioning and uncritical attitude, and low

motivation to think, satisfied instead with parroting rote-memory answers.

Piaget contrasted the heteronomous adult–child relationship with a
second type, corresponding to a morality of autonomy, that is characterized by mutual respect and cooperation. The adult returns children's
respect by giving them the possibility to regulate their behavior voluntarily. Piaget argued that it is only by refraining from exercising unnecessary authority that the adult opens the way for children to develop
minds capable of thinking independently and creatively and to develop
moral feelings and convictions that take into account the best interests
of all parties. Mutual respect means that the constructivist teacher considers the child's point of view and encourages the child to consider
others' points of view. Dewey (1916/1966) also discussed the issue of
unnecessary adult control of children and advocated active cooperation
with children to help them find meaningful purposes in work.

While cooperation is a social interaction in which individuals regard themselves as equals, obviously children and adults are not
equals. However, when the adult is able to respect the child as a person
with a right to exercise his or her own will, one can speak about a certain psychological equality in the relationship. This is not to suggest, of
course, that children have complete freedom because such freedom is
inconsistent with moral relations with others (see DeVries & Edmiaston,
1999, for further discussion of this point).

Respecting children leads to considering their points of view by of-
fering opportunities for play and work that interest them and appeal to
their purposes. Inappropriate academic work and authoritarian management disrespect children by failing to consider their points of view.

The Teacher's Role in Relation to Children's Reasoning and Acquisition of Knowledge

Some teachers believe they should refrain from intervening in children's play. Unfortunately, some of Vygotsky's followers believe that
Piaget's theory implies that the "social environment . . . refrains from interfering with natural development" (Berk & Winsler, 1995, p. 103), and
that therefore people, and particularly adults, are "of secondary importance, while the objects and the child's actions on objects are of primary
importance" (Bodrova & Leong, 1996, p. 28). In contrast to these views,
those taking a constructivist perspective in fact endeavor to intervene in
a variety of ways to facilitate children's development and increase their
knowledge and intelligence.

Elsewhere (DeVries & Kohlberg, 1987/1990; DeVries & Zan, 1994;

Kamii & DeVries, 1978/1993; Kamii & DeVries, 1980), my colleagues and I have addressed in some detail the constructivist teacher's role in promoting children's moral and intellectual reasoning. Briefly, this involves the following considerations. First, the teacher must learn how to appeal to children's interests by observing what children do spontaneously, proposing enticing activities, soliciting children's ideas about what they want to learn, and providing ample opportunities for children to make choices and exercise autonomy. Second, the teacher must choose content that challenges children by focusing experiences on big ideas that allow in-depth study and by providing activities and materials appropriate to a wide range of developmental levels. Third, the teacher must understand children's reasoning and recognize the value of wrong ideas in the construction of knowledge. Fourth, the teacher must teach in terms of the kind of knowledge involved (directly teaching arbitrary conventional knowledge that can be known only through social transmission, encouraging children to act on objects when physical knowledge is involved, and encouraging children to create logicomathematical relationships when knowledge is logical).[1] Fifth, the constructivist teacher actively intervenes to promote children's reasoning by providing counterexamples when children construct wrong ideas about the physical world, finding out what children honestly think, inspiring children's purposes, engaging children in explaining to other children, enriching children's efforts with suggestions, and sometimes modeling a higher level of reasoning. Certain questions are avoided such as "why" questions and closed-ended questions. The constructivist teacher recognizes that it is possible to inhibit children's reasoning through giving indiscriminate praise, negating children's ideas, putting a child on the spot, threatening a child or making a child angry or defensive, rushing ahead without waiting for the child to reflect, and solving problems for children. Sixth, the constructivist teacher provides adequate time for children's investigations and in-depth engagement.

Let us now turn briefly to research on teachers' views of play.

RESEARCH ON TEACHERS' VIEWS OF PLAY AND WORK IN EARLY EDUCATION

It is important to understand teachers' views of play because these determine children's classroom experiences. Research on teachers' views of play shows that teachers use the word "play" in a number of ways, in contrast to work. Cuffaro (1995) asserts that teachers use the play label to:

- Distinguish between teacher-directed and child-initiated activities (the former being work, the latter play);
- Refer to the activities of an area (house play, outdoor play, water play);
- Describe activity that by the adult's standards does not seem goal-directed or purposeful ("they're just playing");
- Describe a child's or children's activity that seems to have some element of narrative within it that has been initiated by the participant(s) (commonly referred to as dramatic play);
- Refer to the social make-up of the activity or to a developmental stage (solitary, parallel, cooperative, group play). (p. 79)

Similarly, Romero (1991) studied two teachers' notions of work and play and reported that these teachers saw play as characterized by choice, interest, fun, creativity, lack of adult supervision and control, and lack of stress. They also talked about children's transgressions of classroom norms as "just play" (p. 124). However, for Romero's teachers, work and play were not entirely separate categories. Aerobics is fun but it can be difficult. These teachers saw play as a preparation for work.

King (1979) interviewed four kindergarten teachers on their definitions of play and work. These teachers believed that some academic work in the form of games and many art activities were examples of play.

I asked 45 experienced early childhood teachers in a summer institute to respond in writing to the open-ended questions, "What is your definition of play?" and "What are specific examples of play?" They were also invited if they wished to write how they thought others defined play. Definitions ranged from the comprehensive statement that play is "activity that is intrinsically motivated, self-initiated, pleasurable, fun, open-ended, involves creative thinking, imagination, is freely chosen, interesting, and involves experimentation" to the contrasting view that "play is an instruction time when skills can be taught (in centers) in a way in which children understand." Half the respondents said play is for learning. One-third said it is fun, that it is experimentation/exploration/discovery and/or that it is child choice. About one-fifth mentioned interaction, socialization, creativity, child initiation/direction, and/or the child's work.

Specific activities regarded as play included pretend play, block building, sand and water, music and dancing, games, outdoor play, art, manipulatives, physical-knowledge activities, books and writing, gardening, and the computer. Teachers wrote that they thought other teachers and sometimes parents think that play in school is:

- Nonacademic, nonlearning time, and only valued as recess or leisure activity.
- Just having fun.
- A waste of time, pointless, just "goofing off," something students can do at home.
- A time-filler, what kids do when teachers want a break from direct instruction.
- Time for social skill development.
- Purposeless and should be suppressed.

Closely allied to teachers' views of play is how teachers understand developmentally appropriate practice. Cole's (1996) study of five kindergarten teachers identifying themselves as developmentally appropriate showed that they believed children should "be happy" and "have fun" in school (p. 17). One teacher declared, "As long as it's fun it's developmentally appropriate" (Cole, 1996, p. 17). However, classroom observations showed that children's experiences in these classrooms varied from self-chosen (often collaborative) activity in which the teacher frequently played alongside to self-chosen exploration free from adult intervention to teacher-directed science "experiments" and math problem solving to large group rote repetition. Despite the consensus at the level of rhetoric among early educators about the value of play, this consensus often breaks down when we look at classroom practices.

With the foregoing background in mind, let us now turn to a conceptualization of four interpretations of "play-oriented curriculum."

FOUR INTERPRETATIONS OF "PLAY-ORIENTED CURRICULUM" AND WORK[2]

I focus here on what we mean when we talk about the importance of play at the level of classroom practice. In the course of observing preschool and early primary classrooms, I have been struck by the wildly diverging range of practices flying the flag of developmentally appropriate or constructivist education. Let us consider four classroom types in which children have different experiences with play and work. While I describe the broad scope of activities in these classrooms, I focus on how center time[3] is implemented. Teachers in these four types of classrooms have different understandings of how to incorporate play and work in early education.

Classroom Type A: Play is peripheral to learning and academic work.

Classroom Type B: Play is disguised academic work.

Classroom Type C: Play is integrated with social and emotional developmental goals.

Classroom Type D: Play and work are integrated with social, emotional, moral, and intellectual developmental goals.

Although the descriptions to follow of these classroom types are based on numerous classroom observations, to protect teacher identity the types are composites and are not descriptions of any single, particular classroom. Although many classrooms are "pure" examples of each type, it is also possible to find many other classrooms that are mixtures of these types. Descriptions deal with materials and activities and the teacher's role in promoting reasoning. In addition, I provide a critique of each from my constructivist perspective.

Classroom Types A and B

In Classroom Types A and B, the emphasis is on academics. These types are rooted in the history of elementary education where the mainly academic goals are focused on the acquisition of correct subject-matter knowledge. This traditional approach reflects a behaviorist view of knowledge and learning as resulting from the direct transmission of information coming from outside the individual to the inside through the senses.

Classroom Type A: Play Is Peripheral to Learning and Academic Work

In Classroom Type A, the emphasis on academic work leaves little room for play, and play is not integrated with academics. Type A teachers either do not have a well-grounded developmental perspective or they are required by administrative policy to teach in a behaviorist way, with a focus on drill and practice, reward and punishment. In fact, Teacher A's school district usually emphasizes performance on standardized tests as the only acceptable evidence of children's achievement, and he or she feels there is little choice about how to teach.

Materials and Activities. Children in Type A classrooms spend almost the entire day in a steady stream of academic work, though they leave the classroom to go to physical education, art, music, or library. For example, one might observe children being drilled on the color names of paper circles, time on a clock face, the number of cents in pictured coins, or letter sounds. They might recite the days of the week and the months of the year. They do a lot of worksheets on letter sounds and addition algorithms as they sit at their desks. When children line up to go to the bathroom, the teacher might hold up a letter card for the person at the head of the line to identify. If correct, the child goes down the hall to the bathroom. If incorrect, the child goes to the end of the line. Art activities are teacher-directed, sequenced lessons that instruct children on how to create identical products such as rabbits with cotton tails. The result is a "factory" atmosphere in which children produce products such as worksheets and crafts that depend on teacher direction.

Center time is reserved for the last 20 or 30 minutes of the day as a reward to children who have finished their work. During this period

- They build with blocks.
- They play with toy cars and trucks.
- They dress dolls and engage in pretend play.

Lesson plans in Type A classrooms typically label this as "self-selected free play," and these are not considered educational activities. Limited materials offer children few choices, and competition is sometimes keen for the scarce materials provided.

The Teacher's Role. The teacher's relation to children is generally authoritarian in Type A classrooms. She is the boss, makes all the rules, and expects children to be submissive. For example, in one class lesson on "s," when a child says "Ssss" when not asked to do so, the teacher might say, "How many times do I have to tell you not to talk unless I tell you to?" After intense work on "s," children are told to get out their pencils. This signal of a transition leads them to stretch and whisper a bit. The teacher then begins counting menacingly, "1, 2, 3, 4, 5," and immediate quiet ensues.

The teacher's involvement with the children during this free playtime is limited to monitoring children's behavior and disciplining children in conflicts by forcing them to leave their play and sit at their desks.

Commentary and Critique from a Constructivist Perspective. Several years ago, a teacher new to our constructivist program observed that the difference between what we were doing and what she saw in most classrooms was that we did not have "free play." She commented that "free play" in early education meant that the teacher is free from teaching responsibility while children are free from adult interference to do what they want. Wien (1995) describes some teachers who understand developmentally appropriate practice to mean that child choice belongs only to free play, reflecting a view of practice as "deeply split into two compartments or conflicting spheres held in tandem as separate frameworks for conducting practice" (p. 106). The teachers in Type A classrooms seem to take this view. Type A teachers view play and academics as two entirely different sorts of activities and see no role for teachers in children's play. Play is barely acknowledged as having any place in school, and it is considered useful only to give children a refreshing break from work and to motivate them to get work done. It is notable that the centers in this type of classroom are usually crowded against the walls in the least space possible, with most classroom space taken up by individual desks and chairs. Play is truly peripheral in Type A classrooms—literally and figuratively.

Although children may have some choice of activities during free play in Type A classrooms, they do not have enough time to develop and pursue in depth the complex problems that can arise when children go beyond superficial use of materials, especially when teachers ask the kinds of questions that lead children into enriched exploration and experimentation. Such investigations are not facilitated by the Type A teacher who provides no materials that lend themselves to experimentation and who takes no interest in what the children are doing unless conflict or misbehavior occurs. Teacher Type A's understanding of the teacher's role in children's play in DAP is that a responsible teacher must simply monitor and control children's behavior. Wien (1995) has called this "teacher dominion," in contrast to "developmentally appropriate" (pp. 8–9) relations with children.

I have observed that inadequate resources in both materials and time often result in an unfriendly and destructive competitive attitude among the children who vie for the opportunity to play with scarce materials.

Unfortunately, too many teachers (or their administrators), especially in early primary grades, believe that a period of free play after academic work is an acceptable compromise between academics and developmentally appropriate practice. Such a compromise distorts the idea of play-oriented developmentally appropriate education. Peripheral use of play impersonates educational use of play.

The problem with play and work in Type A classrooms is not so much a problem with objectives as with how to promote the objectives. Constructivist teachers have many of the same objectives but approach them in different ways. For example, to learn about coin values, children in a Type D classroom might play a Piggy Bank card game (Ed-U Cards, 1965; Kamii & DeVries, 1980) in which children use cards with pictures of 1, 2, 3, 4, or 5 pennies and a nickel to figure out which combinations make 5 cents.[4] In this game, children do a lot more reasoning and spend much more time actively thinking about coin values than in teacher-directed drills. Math games and math problems arising from everyday life and discussed among children are more powerful ways of teaching number and arithmetic than drills and worksheets (see Kamii, 1982, 1985, 1989, 1993). Color names are more easily learned in the context of conversation during art and other activities in which children are more personally invested in working with colors. The "s" sound is more solidly learned as children listen to a book about a silly snake and discuss the words in the story as well as names of children in the class that begin with this letter.

I would also like to add here that considerable research has shown that when children are rewarded for doing something, they devalue it and lose any interest they might have had in it (see review in Kohn, 1993). The use of play as a reward for completing academic work thus defeats a teacher's (or parent's) hope of motivating children to learn academics.

From a constructivist perspective, children in Type A classrooms do not have adequate opportunities to interact with each other or to engage their reasoning in activities in which they want to figure out how to do something. We do not see a community in which children engage with others to pursue meaningful purposes. The children are clearly acting in terms of the teacher's interests, not their own. Coercion keeps children at what Dewey might call stultifying tasks.

Classroom Type B: Play Is Disguised Academic Exercises

In Classroom Type B, children also work on academics, but these are disguised by the use of colorful materials intended to appeal to children's interests. Instead of using worksheets, the teacher offers workbook content in a format that allows children to be more active. This format is more appropriate for young children than the academics in Classroom Type A. However, although the teacher thinks of these activities as play, children do not share this view.

Materials and Activities. Children in Type B kindergarten classrooms spend some time in large-group activities such as listening to stories and watching informational videos like one on farm animals. In contrast to center time in Type A classrooms, their center time activities are integrated with academic goals. Children typically do not have free choice but are assigned and follow some kind of daily or weekly rotation though the following types of centers:

Classification/math

- They match paper cutouts of flowers and flowerpots by putting together those of the same color.
- They count the number of watermelon "seeds" to match the numeral on a watermelon card.
- They put cut-out, numbered bees in numerical order.
- They make graphs of the number of pink, yellow, and blue cutout flowers placed on a table by the teacher.

Literacy

- They match the halves of paper butterflies, one half with an upper-case letter and the other with its lower-case letter.
- They cut out the four sections of a sheet of paper and put schematic drawings of a story in an arbitrary predetermined order.

Fine motor/art

- They cut out "petals" outlined by the teacher on construction paper for precut flower stems.
- They glue tufts of tissue paper flowers on precut, construction paper "trees."
- They paint at an easel where the teacher has outlined on the paper a butterfly shape.

Children are allowed to use the woodworking, colored rice, Legos, puppet theater, or housekeeping centers only in the beginning of the year when the teacher feels children need a transition into work.

The Teacher's Role. The teacher intervenes little except to instruct children on how to do the activities and usually remains rather disengaged. She mainly observes as children obediently do assigned tasks and checks their work from time to time to correct errors. After about 30 minutes, the teacher sings a clean-up song, and children put materials away in order to go to a "special" (physical education, music, art, or library) outside the classroom.

Commentary and Critique from a Constructivist Perspective. Teacher Type B, like Teacher Type A, places priority on academics as the goal. However, in an attempt to introduce an element of play, the teacher sugarcoats academic exercises with cute materials presumed to appeal to

children. The problem with Type B activities is not with trying to provide appealing materials.[6] The problem is that the appeal is superficial
when the materials disguise a basically uninteresting exercise. Such an
activity does not inspire children's real interest in their own purposes.
They are doing the activity only because the teacher wants them to.
When focused on producing right answers and specified products in
these tasks, children in Type B classrooms know that they are not playing. Often, such tasks unnecessarily make something dull out of content
that children would in more authentic contexts find extremely interesting. Dewey (1913/1975) criticized efforts to "make things interesting"
when he stated that "It reduces method in instruction to more or less external and artificial devices for dressing up the unrelated materials, so
that they will get some hold on attention" (p. 23). Dewey argued for a
more authentic approach in which the child sees the connection of new
material to what the child already values. In one instance in a Type B
classroom, a teacher was perplexed when she reported that "children
complained that they didn't have anything to do!" The teacher seemed
to be asking, "Weren't the children active? Weren't they engaged in
'hands-on' activities? Hadn't I provided thematic centers as recommended by early educators?" In my view, the thinly disguised work
does not fool children into thinking that what they are doing is meaningful. From their point of view, it is not play.[7] It is no wonder that the
children in Classroom B feel they have nothing to do! What they mean
is, "We don't have anything we *want* to do. Csikszentmihalyi (1975)
comments on the striking phenomenon of children—and adults—who
"complain that 'there is nothing to do' when they are surrounded by in-
numerable stimuli" (p. 204). He accounts for this in terms of deprivation of the kinds of activities that so capture complete absorption that
the sense of time is lost.

In Type B classrooms, children are able to move around more than
in Type A classrooms. However, they do not choose but are assigned to
activities. Research by Apple and King (1977) shows that if the teacher
requires children to engage in an activity, children tend to think of it as
work and undesirable, even if the content is something they would enjoy if freely chosen. As noted by Jackson (1968), King (1979), and Wing
(1995), children are not fooled by work presented by teachers as play.

"Play" in Classroom Type B is mainly a combination of trivial arts
and crafts and thinly disguised work (or, rather, as Dewey would probably say, labor) that requires little thought. These would be better characterized as "tasks" rather than "activities," especially in light of the fact
that children are required to do them.[8] Cutting out petals for the flower
stem is "busy work" in the sense that no challenge is involved, and no
apparent use is to be made of these materials later. Although gluing tis-

sue paper requires a certain technique of twisting the eraser end of a pencil to create tufts, this also seems to present no difficulty or challenge. Sequencing the drawings is arbitrary when the "correct" sequence is not the only one a child might imagine. The matching (colors and letters) and counting and ordering (numerals) tasks might be termed "tests" in the sense that the teacher wants to know if the child knows the answers. Or perhaps the teacher thinks of these as practice. However, in these tasks one cannot practice what one does not already know, and if one knows it, practice is not necessary. How much more effective it is, for example, to teach number by engaging children in a game of High Card[9] in which they not only think about numerical seriation but reason to compare the relative values of numbers. Art, story reading, personal writing, and group games provide better contexts in which children construct knowledge of colors, number, and written language.

The value of graphing is attenuated by the teacher's arbitrary decision about what children are to graph and by the lack of genuine need or purpose for the graphs. How much more effective it is in a Type D kindergarten where children create a graph of magnetic name cards every morning to indicate lunch choices. The useful result is the daily attendance and lunch count.

In Classroom Type B, children are fed mainly a diet of trivia and "busy work" that neither appeals to their personal interests and purposes nor challenges them to figure out how to do something. "Stultifying tasks" might also describe many of children's activities in this classroom. They have little more opportunity than do children in Type A classrooms to interact with other children or to engage in meaningful, purposeful activities that promote reasoning. Although coercion may be more masked, children still feel its presence and experience little autonomy.

Classroom Types C and D

In contrast to the focus on academics in Classroom Types A and B, Classroom Types C and D share the goal of development. These have roots in the early history of American early education. What I call the "child-development tradition" was begun in 1919 with the opening of The Play School in New York City by Lucy Sprague Mitchell (Antler, 1987) and Caroline Pratt (1948/1970). This school, later evolving into the Bank Street School, was also influenced by John Dewey and psychodynamic theory that led to an emphasis on emotional and social development. Techniques were developed to foster self-initiated play in activities permitting the child's release of unconscious feelings and working out of psychological inner conflicts (see Biber, Gilkeson, &

Winsor, 1959; DeVries & Kohlberg, 1987/1990; Weber, 1969, 1984). The most fundamental concern was to facilitate the play and social interaction of the child in a way that would promote ego strength or positive mental health. Curriculum stressed self-selected, self-directed activities in centers of interest (e.g., housekeeping, blocks, sand, water, art, books, puzzles, science, and woodworking). Although Dewey's influence led to a commitment to the stimulation of thinking, up to the late 1950s the emphasis on emotional development was dominant or better elaborated than the emphasis on intellectual development. According to Spodek (1977), the teacher's role up until the early 1960s was noninterventionist: "The noninterventionist view held that the teacher's role was to provide a stimulating, attractive environment in which young children could play. The teacher would then step aside and let children play without adult interference. The teacher was supposed to support development, not intervene in the processes" (p. 7). Concerns with promoting the school success of disadvantaged children in the 1960s and 1970s led to a new stress on cognitive and linguistic competencies. However, when trying to facilitate children's learning and intellectual development, child-development teachers often reflected behaviorist theory and practices without realizing this contradiction with their emotional and social theory and practices (e.g., see DeVries & Kohlberg, 1987/1990, Chap. 10, on Bank Street Theory and Practice). An appreciation of Jean Piaget's research and developmental theory led to efforts to change the child development approach, especially in its cognitive aspects, in order to bring it more in line with this new perspective (see DeVries & Kohlberg, 1987/1990, Chap. 3, on Piagetian Programs for a critique of approaches based on Piaget's theory).

Classroom Type C: Play Is Integrated with Social and Emotional Developmental Goals

In Type C classrooms, teachers view play as mainly for social and emotional development, and work is deemphasized if included at all. What is described here for Classroom Type C is a "watered-down" version of a child development approach such as Bank Street. Play in these classrooms fits the general image of what a developmentally appropriate classroom should look like. Many early childhood teachers have progressed to this level in their ability to foster children's development through play.

Activities and Materials. Children in Type C kindergarten classrooms can choose to play alone or together and move freely among the following kinds of center activities:

Sensory

- They pat and roll pink Play-Doh.
- They smell small jars containing a lemon, onion, and other things and learn that the nose is to smell with.
- Using funnels, they pour water into different containers, empty them, and wash a doll.

Literacy

- They look at books in the library area.
- They listen to stories read by the teacher or on audiotape, write or draw stories, and dictate stories to an adult.
- They write however they wish at the writing table.

Construction

- They build structures with blocks.
- They build with Legos.

Pretend

- They wear dress-up clothes and pretend to cook and eat dinner and feed the baby in the housekeeping center.

Art

- They paint at the easel.

Cooking

- They help the teacher make muffins by pouring ingredients as the teacher directs. Each child who is observing gets a chance to stir. They help to fill the muffin cups and go with the teacher to put them in the oven.

Classification

- They sort plastic bears by color.

Science

- They watch steam from a kettle and learn that water evaporates into the air; they watch as the flame of a candle is extinguished when a glass is placed over the candle, and learn that fire needs air to burn.

The Teacher's Role. Teachers in Type C classrooms vary widely on the degree to which they take a controlling role in relation to children.

Many are warm and nurturing, but many are sometimes arbitrarily controlling (and thus at least mildly authoritarian). They provide many of the types of activities recommended as developmentally appropriate, but the teacher's role at center time is limited to that of observer, director, materials manager, and order keeper. Frequently, he or she more or less leaves children to play by themselves until a problem arises. Except for the occasional reprimand, Teacher Type C is usually relaxed and pleasant with children, although in some Type C classrooms, the teacher may sometimes be emotionally disengaged. The teacher spends center time observing, directing the cooking activity, and reminding children to put materials away when they are finished. Posted rules are made by the teacher and given to children. When conflict over the use of objects occurs, a typical response is, "If you can't share nicely, I'll put it up and nobody can play with it." Children are exhorted to share.

Commentary and Critique from a Constructivist Perspective. Children in Type C classrooms undoubtedly gain a great deal from many of their activities. In fact, Teacher Type C has moved far beyond Types A and B in providing developmentally appropriate activities for children. An approach emphasizing social and emotional aspects of play may be a necessary step on the way to implementing play in more comprehensive ways. Yet many Type C teachers often hear people criticize their programs as "just play." How can Type C teachers improve the value of play and integrate work in their programs? My purpose is to show how educators can improve the value of these classroom activities and, by doing so, address the concerns of critics who see little value in the play they observe in Type C classrooms.

Whether an activity is Type C or Type D depends on the ways in which children are able to engage in it. In assessing the value of an activity for children's development and learning, the teacher must consider the developmental levels of children. Some of the activities (such as Play-Doh) described in Classroom Type C are high in value for 2-, 3-, and even some 4- and 5-year-olds but are not challenging to older or more advanced children. Some activities (such as pretend play, blocks, writing, and book reading) are appropriate and beneficial for both younger and older children because the materials lend themselves to use at a range of developmental levels. No matter what else children experience in a classroom, these activities, given adequate time, are rich in developmental possibilities that are not limited to social and emotional benefits.

Although the activities in Type C classrooms do promote child choice and engage children's interests and purposes, many are below children's capabilities. They fail to challenge children to figure out solutions to new problems and develop new ways of thinking. Many of the activities underestimate what children could do with more challenging or complex materials and situations. For example, most 5-year-olds who have been in preschool are old hands at Play-Doh, and it offers few new possibilities. Mixing Play-Doh for younger children to use might confront children with the need to think about the relative effects of adding more flour and more water. However, this, too, may be too simple for older children unless they are given a recipe with pictures to "read" and are encouraged to experiment, perhaps even to develop their own recipes. Challenges may also be created by introducing many different modeling materials and implements. Children can work to create particular effects, experiment with different kinds of modeling substances, study sculptures made by artists, and collaborate with others on projects such as making a sculpture museum.

The water play can be dramatically transformed into more challenging investigation and experimentation with the provision of different materials and interventions that encourage children to figure out how to create new effects with water (see the description for Classroom Type D and the section that follows on the Type D teacher's role in relation to children's reasoning and acquisition of knowledge).

Pretend play is valuable for children's construction of representations and their further development of symbolic thought. It can be expanded and enriched by engaging children in deciding whether they want to change their house center to another pretend context (flower shop, restaurant, grocery store, etc.), preparing the materials they will need, and discussing how to use them. Pretend centers can provide opportunities for writing (writing names of flowers and prices, menus, etc.), calculation of bills and using number to figure out how to make change with pretend money, and organizing their respective roles, thus exercising and developing literacy, numeracy, representational ability, and symbolic thought.

Cooking can be turned over to children by providing recipe books illustrated to aid reading (see Kamii & DeVries, 1978/1993; University of Illinois Child Care Center, 1985) and by supporting children's autonomy and cooperation as they take turns and work together in pairs to make snack for the class. This experience is far more educational than observing the teacher do most of the food preparation.

Sorting bears is another example of disguised, purposeless work (except when a child invents the idea of sorting on his or her own). Many teachers think they are teaching classification through such sorting activities. However, this kind of sorting involves simple groupings of subclasses and does not require thinking about relations between superordinate and subordinate classes, the hallmark of classification.[10] Although most kindergarten children are not yet capable of hierarchical classification of subordinate classes into a superordinate class, they can profit from the use of materials in which hierarchies can be made. With this as the long-term goal, more open-ended activities to promote thinking about class relations are much better than simple sorting for the sake of sorting. For example, card games such as Making Families and Go Fish (Kamii & DeVries, 1980) involve classificatory reasoning that young children can do even before they are capable of the class inclusion necessary for true classification. Children must think about making sets of two, three, or four cards that are alike in some way but not identical (e.g., four sheep, ducks, dogs, and horses of blue, red, white, and yellow). In such games, children are motivated by their interest to think again and again about class membership by constructing similarities and differences in the course of playing the game. Such intellectual activity is more likely to promote the construction of class relations than simple sorting for the sake of sorting. As Piaget pointed out: "The child can certainly be interested in seriating for the sake of seriating, and classifying for the sake of classifying, etc., when the occasion presents itself. However, on the whole it is when he has events or phenomena to explain or goals to reach in an intriguing situation that operations are the most exercised" (Piaget & Garcia, 1971/1974, p. 26). The challenge for teachers is to figure out how to select events and phenomena that will intrigue children and lead to development of reasoning.

When subject-matter content is included, Type C teachers sometimes take a behaviorist approach to teaching. For example, many Type C teachers, like Montessori, believe that children learn by absorption through their senses and by association. In the activity in which children smell different objects, the assumption is that children will associate the smell with the object. In contrast, Type D constructivist teachers view sensory activities as guided and organized by the intelligence. That is, when the child actively reasons about sensory experiences, what is known comes from the organizing intelligence and not from perception alone (see Piaget, 1961/1969). Instead of explaining how a child learns what a lemon smells like by passive association, Type D teachers understand this to be a process of active assimilation in which the child uses intelligence to interpret sensory experiences. This type of classroom activity is not helpful to older preschool and kindergarten children because they already know how these objects smell. In this case, the content is too easy. Moreover, it is closed-ended and cannot go any further.

Other examples of a behaviorist approach to selecting science activities are found in the planned observations of a steaming kettle and the extinguishing of a candle. In these activities, children are expected to learn that water evaporates and that fire needs air (or oxygen) to burn. The problem with these activities is that children cannot observe the physical interactions causing these phenomena. Because they cannot understand these events, they can at best only parrot what the adult says. Most likely, the events will be regarded as incomprehensible "magic." These are examples of content that is impossible for young children to understand. From the constructivist perspective, trying to teach such subject matter not only fails to teach the contents but also has a possible harmful effect. When children have to try to understand too much content that is beyond them, they may lose confidence in their abilities to learn or "tune out" to school entirely.

Type C teachers generally underestimate children's capacity for reasoning in work and play. They seem to believe that it is enough to let children engage in what from a constructivist perspective is low-level play.

Classroom Type D: Play and Work Are Integrated with Social, Emotional, Moral, and Intellectual Development

Type D teachers represent the ideal constructivist teacher. They extend their developmental goals beyond social and emotional development to include a conscious focus on moral and intellectual development as well. Constructivist teachers expand the Type C notions about social and emotional development by conceptualizing the development of personality and the child's hierarchy of personal values as constructions the child elaborates in the course of everyday experiences (see DeVries, 1997; Piaget, 1954/1981, 1928–1964/1995). They include the specifically moral and intellectual development of children as important aims.

Materials and Activities. Type D constructivists engage children in making rules to live by and some decisions about life in the classroom, ask what children want to learn about, center the curriculum around children's interests, and engage children in social and moral discussions of issues that arise in the classroom and issues that are found in children's literature. Compare the classrooms described previously with a Type D classroom in which kindergarten children engage in the following typical activities (both work and play) according to their free choice during center time. In addition to a number of activities found in Type C classrooms (such as block building and play with other construction toys, reading books, and using standard art materials that are always available), they use the following types of centers.

Group games

- They play the classification game, Guess Who, in which they have to conceptualize and pose yes–no questions to a partner, eliminate possibilities, respond to the other's questions, and try to guess the identity of a mystery card.[11]

- They play the Cover Up game in which players roll a die to determine how many of the squares to fill on their 12-square card.
- They play the card game Making Families to try to figure out what card to ask for in order to make sets where hierarchical categories (such as sheep) are composed of four subclasses (different colors).

Pretend

- They make a shoe store in the pretend area and pretend to buy and sell shoes, write price signs, receipts, and answer the telephone.
- Using a wolf puppet and a red sweater for a hood, they cooperate to act out *Little Red Riding Hood* for other children in the library corner.

Physical knowledge/cooking/art

- Two children negotiate how to follow a written and illustrated recipe to make something for the class snack.
- They experiment at the water table with a variety of transparent plastic glasses that have small, medium, and large holes drilled into sides and/or bottoms. The teacher on a later day provides a pegboard on a stand over the water table (with legs removed so it sits on the floor, and metal cup holders that hook into the pegboard) so children can arrange glasses and more easily observe the results of draining.

Math/spatial reasoning

- They work with pattern blocks and tangrams, using Cuisinaire's plastic shape frames (see Sales & Sales, 1994, 1995). Once a frame is filled, it can be lifted to leave the block design on the table, and then reused to create the same shape with different blocks (each pattern block shape comes in only one color).
- Individual children survey the others and make graphs on something the surveyor wants to know (such as what are the favorite TV programs of the class members).

Literacy

- They write in personal journals at the writing table, writing (or pretending to write) stories which they illustrate, or making a list of things they did over the weekend, or dictating a story for the teacher to write down.

In all activities, children engage in conflict resolution with the teacher's help or by themselves. Many of the activities extend over several days or even weeks.

The Teacher's Role. The teacher not only observes but also engages with children in activities, wondering aloud and posing questions to promote reasoning (e.g., "I wonder why the water stays in that glass [with side hole only]," or "Do you think you can get the water to flow from one to another and then another and another?"). Sometimes she takes part in a game as a player alongside children. As children work with the shape frames and blocks, the teacher asks such questions as the following: "Do you think you can make that shape with other colors?" "Could you make it all yellow?" "Would that work?"

Conflicts occur, and the teacher intervenes to facilitate children's resolutions and self-regulation, emphasizing that the conflict is theirs and they must figure out what to do. He or she helps children listen to each other and makes sure all agree to a resolution (see DeVries & Zan, 1994, for other principles of teaching in conflict situations). For example, during a game of Cover Up played by two 4-year-old girls and the teacher, a problem arises with regard to the order of turns. Both girls think they are next, and there is a long impasse during which the teacher refrains from settling the problem and asks again and again what they can do to solve the problem, making it clear that responsibility for a solution belongs to the children. Finally, one girl suggests they each take a die and roll them at the same time! This is what they do. Later, the teacher confided that she was astonished and pleased with their solution, one that would never have occurred to her, illustrating how children's solutions to their conflicts are often different and work better (because the children feel ownership of the solution) than what teachers might suggest. In another Type D classroom, a child complains that another called him a name. The teacher responds, "Have you told him how you feel about that? What can you say to him?" and the child goes away to assert his feelings and, if not satisfied, returns to ask the teacher's help in communicating.

Recognizing that group games could, if too easy, fall into the category of mere entertainment, Teacher Type D selects games he or she expects to offer intellectual challenges and observes to see whether, in fact, children's reasoning is challenged. If a game turns out to be too easy or too difficult, the teacher learns that it does not offer educational possibilities for his or her children and either retires the game or modifies it.

The teacher promotes literacy development by integrating the need to read and write throughout many activities in print-rich classrooms. For example, each game has a set of written rules, and the teacher makes a "big deal" out of reading the rules to find out how to play the game. In the shoe store, they have opportunities to read and write. They read class rules as they illustrate them. Children have to read recipes in order to find out how to make snack. Like Type C teachers, Teacher Type D reads stories aloud, encourages children to write or draw stories of their own, and takes down children's dictated stories, developing their appreciation for literature and writing. While reenacting a story they know well, the teacher facilitates children's consolidation of their knowledge of sequential temporal events and their knowledge of "story," an important component of literacy. The teacher encourages children to engage in a variety of writing activities so that children come to conceive of themselves as writers.

The Type D teacher promotes children's reasoning about number by providing materials involving number in group games and pretend play and by conducting discussions of everyday issues involving number. For example, when children make the "logical error of addition" in a path game by counting as "1" the last space on which they landed on the previous move (rather than going forward on the count of "1"), the teacher provides a die with four 1s, a 2, and a 3 so that children will have many experiences of confronting the unsatisfying situation in which they count "1" and go nowhere! At a certain point in their development, children feel something is wrong. Such a feeling of internal conflict is the beginning of a feeling of logical necessity that eventually leads to self-correction of this error.[12] In making a snack, children must calculate, for example, how many crackers to spread if everyone is to get two. If they had six balls when they went outdoors and only four when they are ready to come inside, the teacher encourages children to think how many they need to look for.

In physical-knowledge activities (see Kamii & DeVries, 1978/1993) such as the water draining and cooking, the teacher provides opportunities for children to construct knowledge about the world of objects, making comments and asking questions to draw children's attention to its many spatial and causal problems. She hopes children will be inspired to find their own purposes as they pursue questions that interest them. In the water activity, the Type D teacher views the child not as "just playing" but as making progress in constructing knowledge about the properties of water and its containers, even constructing greater intelligence with increased capability to reason. In cooking, the teacher encourages children to think about irreversible physical changes (e.g., what happens when flour is mixed with a liquid). With pattern blocks and tangram frames, the teacher encourages children to construct relations of equivalence by encouraging children to discover, for example, that two triangles make a parallelogram.

Commentary from a Constructivist Perspective.   In the course of trying to show how to improve the activities in Classroom Types A, B, and C, I have shared a lot of the Type D constructivist approach and perspective. Readers will therefore not be surprised to read that two characteristics emphasized in Type D classrooms are often missing in Type C (as well as Types A and B) classrooms. First is the conscious work of Type D teachers to create a certain kind of sociomoral atmosphere (discussed later in the section on the social context) in which the teacher respects children and takes their perspective into account. Some, perhaps many, Type C classrooms are characterized by a positive interpersonal dynamic but do not reflect a conscious effort to cooperate with children. Second is the constructivist focused effort to facilitate children's intellectual development by microanalyzing children's thinking in activities and by providing materials and suggestions that lead children into play and work with more complex materials and situations.

Let us consider in more detail the rationales for activities provided in Type D classrooms. Group games are much in evidence in Type D classrooms where the teacher views this play as important for children's social and moral as well as intellectual development (see Kamii & DeVries, 1980; DeVries & Kohlberg, 1987/1990). In these competitive games, children must cooperate with each other to agree on rules, abide by them, and accept their consequences, in order to play. Thus the teacher's emphasis is on cooperation as overarching and including the competition. As issues of fairness arise, the teacher helps children think about these moral problems in their lives.

In the Guess Who and Making Families games, children have the opportunity to use classificatory reasoning to think about classes and their relations. In Making Families, the problem is a matter of thinking of the superordinate category of sheep with its subordinate subclasses of colors. The child has to think of one subclass (such as the red sheep) that is missing from his or her hand (and thus not observable at that moment). In Guess Who, the problem is even more complicated and challenging for 4- and 5-year-olds because of the difficulty of turning affirmations into negations. Piaget (1974/1980) showed that negations are especially difficult. For example, if the partner says "Yes" to the question, "Does your person wear glasses?" it is necessary to turn the affirmation into a negation and think, "I have to push this one down because he does *not* wear glasses," and to perform the action of negating or eliminating the faces *without* glasses. In this game, children are motivated to use more mobile thinking in order to master this "mind twister."

In the less challenging game of Cover Up, there is no opportunity for strategy, but children who have had little experience with games can become committed to the reciprocity of turn taking and think about number. Continued assessment of one's standing in the game can involve thinking about the number of spaces yet to be filled, comparing the number filled on one's card with that of the opponent, and thinking what would be the ideal number to roll on the next turn. Children in the example had to invent a fair solution to their conflict over who would be first. A constructivist teacher views conflict resolution as part of the curriculum because these kinds of moral experiences promote the perspective taking necessary for interpersonal understanding and moral development.

As noted in the description of Type C classrooms, pretend play exercises and develops children's literacy, representational ability, and symbolic thought. Acting out a story helps children become reflective about the parts of a story and the motives and feelings of its characters. These experiences also contribute to children's interpersonal understanding.

As children prepare a snack, they are challenged to cooperate by negotiating what each partner will do, to "read" the recipe or its pictures (which the teacher read to them before they started), and to follow the directions.

Children have possibilities to develop their reasoning in the water activity by constructing causal relationships and correspondences among the sizes of holes, sizes of streams, and positions of holes in order to make various waterfall/fountain arrangements.

Pattern block and tangram frames challenge children's spatial reasoning as they try to figure out how to fill the same shape in several ways with different colors/shapes.

Journal writing provides an opportunity for children not only to communicate with pictures and words but also to reflect on the pleasures and sorrows of their lives and thus construct a more differentiated personality and system of values. Art also offers children another way to communicate with various media and frequently provides opportunities to construct physical- and logicomathematical knowledge. For example, creating paper sculptures faces children with the problem of how best to attach the end of a paper strip firmly to the base (with paste, glue, staple, etc.) and with the spatial problems in arranging strips in relation to each other. In the case of illustrating their rulebook, children have the opportunity to take further ownership of the rules they made to regulate their relationships in the classroom, thus promoting moral development of a system of values.

Making graphs involves solving the logicomathematical problem of the unit of measurement (e.g., using a cube or inch-square on a paper to represent each child) and offers children the opportunity to take a scientific approach to finding answers to their own questions.

All these self-chosen activities offer children in Type D constructivist classrooms the opportunity to exercise autonomy as they pursue
their interests, create their own purposes, and pursue intriguing questions raised by themselves or the teacher, and to exercise reasoning to
figure out how to accomplish various personal goals. In all interactions
with children, the Type D teacher respects children and cooperates with
them, minimizing the exercise of unnecessary coercion (see DeVries &
Zan, 1994, for discussion of how the teacher accomplishes this).

The constructivist Type D teacher also includes academic goals in
planning activities, but these are embedded in the context of play and
work in which children find personal interest and value. Play merges
into work as children develop a seriousness of purpose and desire to
create high-quality work characteristic of older children and adults
whom they admire.

CONCLUSION

The National Association for the Education of Young Children (NAEYC)
has taken a courageous stand in support of DAP as the standard in
early education from birth through third grade. The NAEYC position
statements advocating a play-oriented approach have had enormous influence, especially in communicating the inappropriateness of "teacher-
directed instruction in narrowly defined academic skills" (Bredekamp,
1987, p. iv). The NAEYC's descriptions of appropriate practices have
gone a long way toward creating an attitude of acceptance of these
among preschool and elementary administrators and teachers. Unfortunately, however, research on teachers' definitions of play and how they
carry out DAP reveals a lack of consensus about its practical implementation. This may be due, in part, to the fact that while the position statements attempt to give examples of DAP, they are limited in their description of specific practices. Thus readers are left to interpret (and
misinterpret) how general ideas are reflected in practices.

The NAEYC's advocacy of a play-oriented approach results in a
public-relations problem. The problem with play is that it is seen by
many critics as aimless or trivial activity that falls short of educational
justification. In my view, this perception is too often a reality. The play
that often occurs in classrooms is, in fact, activity below children's competency levels that does not deserve to be called educational experience.

The description of four practical interpretations of what a play-oriented curriculum is dramatizes the vastly different classroom experiences offered to children under the flag of DAP. In Classroom Type A,
play is viewed as peripheral to learning and academic work, and its ed-

ucators seem to believe that a short period of free play after a day of academic work is an acceptable compromise between academics and DAP. In Classroom Type B, what is called play is really academic exercises disguised with colorful materials, and its educators seem to believe that what in my view is really trivial "busy work" is meeting DAP guidelines. In contrast to Classroom Types A and B where academics are the goals, Classroom Types C and D take development as their goal. In the Type C classroom we see what is usually thought of as DAP, a program where social and emotional goals are integrated in center-based play that is a mixture of activities rich in developmental possibilities and activities that are low level in terms of intellectual challenge. Type D constructivist classsrooms go beyond Type C by adding challenging intellectual and moral goals in both play and work. A special effort is made in constructivist Type D classrooms to create a cooperative sociomoral atmosphere that fosters children's social and moral development by engaging them in rule making, decision making, conflict resolution, and social and moral discussions. Unlike teachers in Classroom Types A, B, and C, teachers in Type D classrooms intervene to promote children's reasoning and construction of knowledge. Type D activities not found in the other types include group games that are justified in terms of specific moral and cognitive challenges, and physical-knowledge activities involving movement and changes in objects that offer unique possibilities for the development of reasoning and knowledge. Much of what children do in constructivist classrooms is, in fact, work, or is moving toward work. That is, activities often involve seriousness of purpose, great effort, exploration and experimentation that is not always successful, sometimes frustration, and adaptation in figuring out something new in knowledge and reasoning.

Unfortunately, the NAEYC's criticism of inappropriate work has had the effect of giving all work a bad name in early education. Perhaps it is time to resurrect the idea of work and talk about appropriate work in early education.

In critiquing the activities in Classroom Types A, B, and C, I have tried to show how many of the same objectives may be realized by an alternative constructivist approach that retains the valuable characteristics of play and also offers more educational justification by its emphasis on reasoning and the construction of knowledge and intelligence.

Where do we go from here? We must continue to uphold the value of play while being clearer about the *kinds* of play and work we advocate. These must be justified in terms of its specific value for children's learning and development. We must not limit our programs to play but also encourage children to pursue purposes and activities that are more properly called "work," maintaining, however, the criterion of children's interest. We must distinguish between inappropriate work and appropriate work. In our definitions of high-quality early education, we must include a clear description of the teacher who establishes a cooperative (rather than authoritarian) relationship with children, creates a cooperative sociomoral atmosphere in the classroom culture, and intervenes to promote children's reasoning and construction of knowledge. With greater clarity and specificity in our advocacy of play and work, we can overcome the objections to play that are so often raised by parents, school administrators, and the public.

NOTES

1. This principle is based on Piaget's (e.g., 1964, 1969/1970) distinction between two types of psychological experience. Physical experience consists of action on objects and leads to physical knowledge of objects themselves (e.g., knowledge that an object rolls when pushed). Logicomathematical experience is the individual's introduction of characteristics the object does not have (e.g., the number of objects, and similarities and differences among objects are relationships created in the mind of the knower). A third type of knowledge, arbitrary conventional knowledge, is created by agreement among people (e.g, names of objects and dates of holidays) (see DeVries & Kohlberg, 1987/1990, for further discussion).

2. These are my own interpretations (with which others may not agree) based on observation of many preschool and early primary classrooms from Mexico and the United States to Australia, Japan, Thailand, and Korea.

3. Center time is a period when children engage in a variety of activities at the same time. One center may be a table where children do art activities, and another might be the pretend area with child-size replicas of a stove, refrigerator, and so on.

4. Thirty cards are dealt in a facedown pile for each player. Players take turns turning over one card at a time. If the first card is 5 pennies or a nickel, the player puts the card in his or her "bank" (a container of some sort). If it shows any other number, the player discards the card in the middle of the table, face up. The next player who turns up a card that does not show 5 cents looks among the discarded cards and tries to find a combination of cards that total 5 cents. When children master these combinations, cards can be added, with the goal of making 10 or 25 cents.

5. These developmentally appropriate large-group activities are also found in Classroom Types C and D.

6. Teacher Types C and D also try to provide appealing materials that will interest children.

7. Fein and Wiltz (in press; also Apple & King, 1977; Gupton & Cooney, 1997; King, 1979) have pointed out that it is important to consider children's perceptions of whether an activity is play or not.

8. I see "tasks" as situations in which the child does something because of the teacher's interest, to oblige the adult. "Activities," in contrast, are situations in which the child's interest and personal purpose are dominant.

9. High Card, also known as War (Kamii & DeVries, 1980), is played with regular playing cards but with face cards removed. All cards are dealt in a facedown pile for each player. Then players simultaneously turn up the top cards from their piles. The player who turns up the card that is more takes both cards. When there is a tie, each player turns over the next card, and the person who turns up the larger number takes all four cards. The winner is the person who collects all (or, alternatively, most) cards.

10. Piaget (1941/1952) defined classification as a system of inclusions and discussed the development of the logic of classification as hierarchical inclusion of subordinate classes in a superordinate class. For example, the class of "flowers" may be composed of "roses" and "tulips." If there are more roses than tulips, young children respond to the question, "Are there more flowers or more roses?" by saying there are more roses than flowers. This indicates the inability to think about the roses as both a separate class and a part of the class of flowers.

11. In this game, each player has a large plastic frame with 20 small frames attached in rows, each frame containing a different cardboard face. The small frames may be flipped up or down so the face is or is not visible to the player using that frame. Two players facing each other cannot see the other's cardboard faces (one set backed in red, the other in blue). The set of 20 faces (that can be arranged in different order on the large frame) in one frame is identical to those of the other (although the same face may occupy different positions in the two frames). A third set of yellow-backed cardboard faces is placed face down. Each player chooses one face card from this pile and places it in a niche at the front of the frame. The object of the game is to guess the identity of the other's mystery face. To figure out who the other's yellow character is, players take turns asking yes–no questions such as, "Does your person wear glasses?" With the clue in the answer, the player then either leaves up all faces wearing glasses or eliminates them by putting them all face down. If all questions are answered correctly, the last remaining face should be the identity of the other's yellow card.

12. As they begin to have a feeling of logical contradiction in this situation, children often stumble and "stutter" in their count, saying, "1," but not going anywhere, then "1," and hesitatingly moving the marker forward.

REFERENCES

Antler, J. (1987). *Lucy Sprague Mitchell: The making of a modern woman*. New Haven: Yale University Press.

Apple, M., & King, N. (1977). What do schools teach? *Curriculum Inquiry, 6*(4), 341–357.

Berk, L, & Winsler, A. (1995). *Scaffolding children's learning: Vygotsky and early childhood education*. Washington, DC: National Association for the Education of Young Children.

Biber, B., Gilkeson, E., & Winsor, C. (1959, April). Basic approaches to mental health: Teacher education at Bank Street College. *Personnel and Guidance Journal*.

Bodrova, E., & Leong, D. (1996). *Tools of the mind: The Vygotskian approach to early childhood education*. Englewood Cliffs, NJ: Prentice-Hall.

Bredekamp, S. (1987). *Developmentally appropriate practice in early childhood programs serving children from birth through age 8*. Washington, DC: National Association for the Education of Young Children.

Bredekamp, S., & Copple, C. (1997). *Developmentally appropriate practice in early childhood programs*. Washington, DC: National Association for the Education of Young Children.

Bredekamp, S., & Rosegrant, T. (Eds.). (1992). *Reaching potentials: Appropriate curriculum and assessment for young children* (vol. 1). Washington, DC: National Association for the Education of Young Children.

Bredekamp, S., & Rosegrant, T. (Eds.). (1995). *Reaching potentials: Transforming early childhood curriculum and assessment* (vol. 2). Washington, DC: National Association for the Education of Young Children.

Cole, M. (1996). *"As long as it's fun it's developmentally appropriate": An exploration of the educational ideology of five kindergarten teachers*. Paper presented at the annual meeting of the Mid-Western Educational Research Association, October, Chicago.

Csikszentmihalyi, M. (1975). *Beyond boredom and anxiety*. San Francisco: Jossey-Bass.

Cuffaro, H. (1995). *Experimenting with the world: John Dewey and the early childhood classroom*. New York: Teachers College Press.

DeVries, R. (1997). Piaget's social theory. *Educational Researcher*,

DeVries, R., & Edmiaston, R. (1999). Misconceptions about constructivist education. *The Constructivist, 13*(1), 12–19.

DeVries, R., & Kohlberg, L. (1990). *Constructivist early education: Overview and comparison with other programs*. Washington, DC: National Association for the Education of Young Children. (Original work published 1987 by Longman)

DeVries, R., & Zan, B. (1994). *Moral classrooms, moral children: Creating a constructivist classroom atmosphere*. New York: Teachers College Press.

Dewey, J. (1933). *How we think: A restatement of the relation of reflective thinking to the educative process*. Lexington, MA: Heath.

Dewey, J. (1966). *Democracy and education*. New York: Free Press. (Original work published 1916)

Dewey, J. (1975). *Interest and effort in education*. Edwardsville: Southern Illinois University Press. (Original work published 1913)

Ed-U-Cards. (1965). *Piggy Bank*. New York: Author.

Fein, G. (1981). Pretend play in childhood: An integrative review. *Child Development, 52*(4), 1094–1118.

Fein, G., & Clarke-Stewart, A. (1973). *Day care in context*. New York: Wiley.

Fein, G., & Rivkin, M. (Eds.). (1986). *The child at play: Review of research, Volume 4*.

Washington, DC: National Association for the Education of Young Children.

Fein, G., & Wiltz, N. (1998). Play: As children see it. In D. Fromberg & D. Bergen (Eds.), *Play from birth to twelve: Contexts, perspectives, and meanings* (pp. 37–49). New York: Garland.

Gupton, P., & Cooney, M. (1997). *Children's perceptions of play: A qualitative study.* Unpublished manuscript.

Jackson, P. (1968). *Life in classrooms.* New York: Holt.

Kamii, C. (1982). *Number in preschool and kindergarten.* Washington, DC: National Association for the Education of Young Children.

Kamii, C. (1985). *Young children reinvent arithmetic.* New York: Teachers College Press.

Kamii, C. (1989). *Young children continue to reinvent arithmetic: Second grade.* New York: Teachers College Press.

Kamii, C. (1993). *Young children continue to reinvent arithmetic: Third grade.* New York: Teachers College Press.

Kamii, C., & DeVries, R. (1980). *Group games in early education: Implications of Piaget's theory.* Washington, DC: National Association for the Education of Young Children.

Kamii, C., & DeVries, R. (1993). *Physical knowledge in preschool education: Implications of Piaget's theory.* New York: Teachers College Press. (Original work published 1978)

King, N. (1979). Play: The kindergarten perspective. *The Elementary School Journal, 80*(2), 81–87.

Kohn, A. (1993). *Punished by rewards: The trouble with gold stars, incentive plans, A's, praise, and other bribes.* New York: Houghton Mifflin.

Piaget, J. (1952). *The child's conception of number.* London: Routledge & Kegan Paul. (Original work published 1941)

Piaget, J. (1962). *Play, dreams, and imitation: Formation of the symbol. (Original work published 1945)*

Piaget, J. (1964). Development and learning. In R. Ripple & V. Rockcastle (Eds.), *Piaget rediscovered: A report of the conference on cognitive studies and curriculum development* (pp. 7–20). Ithaca, NY: Cornell University Press.

Piaget, J. (1965). *The moral judgment of the child.* New York: Free Press. (Original work published 1932)

Piaget, J. (1969). *The mechanisms of perception.* New York: Basic Books. (Original work published 1961)

Piaget, J. (1969/1970). *Science of education and the psychology of the child.* New York: Viking Compass. (Original work published

Piaget, J. (1980). *Experiments in contradiction.* Chicago: University of Chicago Press. (Original work published 1974)

Piaget, J. (1981). *Intelligence and affectivity: Their relation during child development.* Palo Alto, CA: Annual Reviews. (Original work published 1954)

Piaget, J. (1995). *Sociological studies.* New York: Routledge. (Original work published 1928–1964)

Piaget, J., & Garcia, R. (1974). Physico-geometric explanations and analyses. In J.

Piaget, *Understanding causality*. New York: Norton. (Original work published 1971)

Piaget, J., & Inhelder, B. (1969). *The psychology of the child*. New York: Basic Books. (Original work published 1966)

Pratt, C. (1970). *I learn from children*. New York: New York: Cornerstone Library. (Original work published 1948 by Simon & Schuster)

Romero, M. (1991). Work and play in the nursery school. In L. Weiss, P. Altbach, G. Kelly, & H. Petrie (Eds.), *Critical perspectives on early childhood education* (pp. 119–138). Albany: State University of New York Press.

Rubin, K., Fein, G., & Vandenberg, B. (1983). Play. In P. Mussen (Ed.), *Handbook of child psychology, Vol. IV, Socialization, personality, and social development* (pp. 693–774), New York: Wiley.

Sales, C., & Sales, J. (1994). *Using pattern block frames*. White Plains, NY: Cuisenaire.

Sales, C., & Sales, J. (1995). *Using tangram frames*. White Plains, NY: Cuisenaire.

Spodek, B. (1977). What constitute worthwhile educational experiences for young children? In B. Spodek (Ed.) *Teaching Practices: Reexaming assumptions* (pp. 5–20), Washington, DC: National Association for the Education of Young Children.

University of Illinois Child Care Center. (1985). *I made it myself: A cookbook for young children*. Chicago: University of Illinois at Chicago.

Vygotsky, L. (1967). Play and its role in the mental development of the child. *Soviet Psychology, 5*, 6–18. (Original work published 1933)

Weber, E. (1969). *The kindergarten: Its encounter with educational thought in America*. New York: Teachers College Press.

Weber, E. (1984). *Ideas influencing early childhood education: A theoretical analysis*. New York: Teachers College Press.

Wein, C. (1995). *Developmentally appropriate practice in "real life": Stories of teacher practical knowledge*. New York: Teachers College Press.

Wing, L. (1995). Play is not the work of the child: Young children's perceptions of work and play. *Early Childhood Research Quarterly, 10*(2), 223–247.

5

The Adult as a Tutor in Fostering Children's Symbolic Play

ANNA BONDIOLI

There is now solid research evidence and a theoretical basis in support of the idea that pretend play is a medium for the growth of cognitive, creative, and socioemotional skills that will be useful in a school environment. As a result, an increasing number of researchers in the area of early childhood education consider play as the core of the preschool curriculum and recommend that teachers actively promote children's symbolic skills (Klugman & Smilansky, 1990; Rivkin, 1986).

Two lines of research support the contribution of adults to children's play: studies on mother–child play and the "training studies." The former illustrates the importance of the adult's role in fostering and developing children's pretend activity in the home environment (Howes, Unger, & Matheson, 1992; O'Connell & Bretherton, 1984; Sachs, 1980; Slade, 1987). The latter demonstrates the strong influence of the adult intervention on the play behaviors of disadvantaged children in preschool settings (for reviews, see Fein, 1981; Smilansky & Shefatya, 1990). Both areas of research find theoretical support in Vygotsky's concept of zone of proximal development, which refers to the phase of development in which a child has only partially mastered a task but can participate in its execution with the assistance and supervision of a more capable partner (Rogoff, 1990; Vygotsky, 1978). Adult–child interaction during play sessions may help children to foster and exercise their play skills not yet completely mastered or developed.

In view of Vygotsky's hypothesis and the results of studies on adult–child play, it is plausible to argue that development of play skills is not solely a result of maturation but also a result of proper adult intervention. Thus, all children, not only the disadvantaged ones, need adult assistance to become expert players—that is, to develop the wide range of cognitive and social skills that are a part of the most advanced forms of pretend play. Encouraging pretend play activity may be one of the most important activities in early childhood education, particularly for young children whose pretend play skills are just emerging.

Despite this insight, however, the play of young children is not held as a high priority in educational settings, as is their academic achievement. As Smilansky (1990) underlines, although classrooms frequently have "the tools" for play, sociodramatic play is not usually supported in those educational environments. Smilansky and other authors (e.g., Bowman, 1990; Johnson & Ershler, 1982; Saltz & Saltz, 1986) emphasize the importance of appropriate adult intervention in fostering make-believe play, and hope that educators will increase their professional skills in order to provide adequate support for children's play activities.

As a result of not considering play a valuable activity, scholars have not paid attention to the question, "What is appropriate adult intervention?" In fact, there is not much agreement among scholars about the way in which an intervention should be developed in order to promote children's symbolic skills. Some researchers consider adult modeling the most effective medium (Fein, 1975; Fenson & Ramsay, 1981); some underline the importance of the adult's verbal play interaction (Sachs, 1980); others suggest that adult intervention must be characterized by a divergent and nonobtrusive form of play participation (Shmulker, 1981).

Another important question considered in the literature but left unresolved relates to how to establish bridges between children's existing pretend play ability and the play level proposed by the adult. Beizer and Howes (1992) offered three models to describe the ways in which adults support children's pretend play at home. These are the "zone of proximal development" model, the "smorgasbord" model, and the "scaffolding" model. In the first model, adults verbally suggest and/or model pretend play at levels beyond the child's independent play capacity, eliciting levels of pretend play higher than what children are able to do on their own (Belsky & Most, 1984; Fiese, 1989; Fenson, Kagan, Kearsley, & Zelazo, 1984; Fenson et al. 1976, Watson and Fisher, 1977. In the second model, as in the first, the adult makes direct suggestions to guide children's symbolic play but children, rather than adults, are considered responsible for selecting suggestions that fit for their zone of proximal development (cf. O'Connell & Bretherton, 1984). In the scaffolding model, adults modify their input in response to the changing developmental capacities of infants and toddlers, and provide structure for interaction and support for the child's efforts (e.g., Fiese, 1989, 1990, Kavanaugh, Whittington, & Cerbone, 1983; Sachs, 1980). Beizer and Howes conclude that all of these models provide support for Vygotsky's claim that more experienced partners guide the development of children's pretend play, but they do not offer evidence about the efficacy of these models.

Consistent with Beizer and Howes's interpretation, the training studies support Vygotsky's hypothesis about the importance of the adult in eliciting higher levels of play from children. However, the training studies also offer only limited insights about the characteristics of the adult's intervention that are responsible for children's play gains because they are focused more on the effects of the interventions (outputs) rather than on the treatments themselves.

There are two difficulties involved in elaborating an intervention model that indicates how to interact and play with a group of children in order to promote their symbolic skills. The first difficulty relates to the elusive quality of play and pretense (Fein, 1978). In play, means are more important than goals, process than product; play is an open-ended activity. So, the adult who interacts with children to enhance their play must therefore be playful. The adult must recognize that play is a divergent and not a convergent enterprise and, thus, must act accordingly.

In elaborating the elusive quality of pretend play, Fein (1987) claims that pretense is characterized by a system of triple divergent relations. These are the relations between pretense and the immediate environment, between pretense and child's actual experience, and, finally, among pretend events. In pretend play, an object is used as if it were another, a person behaves as if he or she were another, and the immediate time and place are treated as if they were otherwise and elsewhere (*referential freedom*); the child paraphrases and transforms his or her own experience (*denotative license*), and the sequences that emerge have a nonlinear recursive quality (*sequential uncertainty*). Furthermore pretense serves *affective functions* such as regulation and modulation of emotions. Children use pretend play to express aspects of their experiences that they find either intriguing or disturbing. Thus, the adults must respect the features of nonliterality, as-ifness, and vivid emotional quality that characterize children's pretend play.

The second difficulty relates to the developmental nature of play and pretense behaviors, which become increasingly articulated and refined with children's age. A model of adult intervention must take into account how an adult can help children become expert players on the basis of children's developmental level.

In this chapter, I present a model that indicates how to interact and play with a group of children in order to foster their symbolic skills. The model is articulated in terms of two submodels: a tutorial model and a scaffolding model. These two submodels are combined to design and implement interventions aiming to promote the symbolic play of a group of children. The tutorial model indicates the strategies the adult can use to solicit, maintain, and develop pretend play by respecting the qualities of this important childhood activity. The scaffolding model takes into account the developmental nature of pretend play and makes use of the tutorial strategies in order to make children's play increasingly advanced. The tutorial model aims to sustain pretense; the scaffolding model aims to promote it. The model is illustrated in the following pages by examples derived from studies that document the effects of adult/children play experiences.

THE TUTORIAL MODEL

This model was developed based on the work of Wood, Bruner, and Ross (1976). The adult functions delineated in a problem-solving context were adapted to the characteristics of pretend play. Wood et al., identified six functions of the tutor in the "scaffolding" process: recruitment, marking critical features, direction maintenance, reduction in degrees of freedom, frustration control, and demonstration or modeling. *Recruitment* refers to the tutor's enlisting the child's interest in and adherence to the requirements of the task. *Marking critical features* consists of the tutor's underlining certain relevant features of the shared task. *Direction maintenance* refers to the expert partner's keeping the child in pursuit of a particular objective by keeping the child both "in the field" and motivated. *Reduction in degrees of freedom* means that the adult must simplify the task, fill in the blanks, and let the learner perfect the subroutines that he or she can manage. *Frustration control* refers to the tutor's support for the child at times of difficulty. *Demonstration* or *modeling* consists of the tutor's modeling a solution to a task, imitating in an idealized form an attempted solution tried by the tutee. These functions proved to be effective when the task proposed to the child was cognitive and convergent. Now I try to indicate and illustrate by examples[1] how they can be tuned to the special characteristics of symbolic play, whose nature is divergent and affective.

Recruitment

Play is a spontaneous and a self-motivated activity. It does not seem necessary to induce children to participate. Therefore, the first tutorial function of the model must be formulated in a "negative" form, as something the tutor should not do: The tutor must not introduce a play activity by interrupting the spontaneity of what children are doing. In contrast, the tutor must try to be a part of an ongoing play activity. In the beginning, an adult's participation should take the form of being an empathic observation of children's behavior. The tutor's subsequent verbal communications and play acts should be in line with the symbolic contents of children's play and well matched to the affective meanings expressed by them.

The intervention should be child centered and nonobtrusive. That is, the adult should not impose his or her ideas but follow and sustain those of children. The mirror or echo communication[2] seems to be an effective strategy to accomplish the first function. It consists in putting in words the play action of a child or in repeating his or her play statement in a tone that marks the emotional quality of the contents expressed. Here is an example:

Example 1

The caregiver approaches Silvia (35 months) who has laid a doll down in the cradle.

SILVIA: He is tired (*showing the doll to the caregiver*).

CAREGIVER: Is the baby tired?

SILVIA: He went to see Granny

CAREGIVER: Ah, Silvia's baby went to see Granny!

SILVIA: (*Approaches the cradle and takes the doll in her arms.*)

CAREGIVER: Oh, Silvia's baby has waked!

SILVIA: (*Lays down the doll on the table and caresses him.*)

With her mirror interventions, the caregiver helps Silvia develop and represent an autonomously chosen affective theme (baby caregiving) without adding new play ideas but only reflecting and clarifying those of the little girl's.

Marking Critical Features

This process underlines pretense as a transformational activity in which something represents the meaning of something else. By observing children at play or by playing with them, the tutor stresses the transformations or fictional features of pretense in order to help children develop and enrich their play ideas. In the previous example, for instance, following Silvia's initial idea, the tutor interprets Silvia's gestures and responds to her verbalizations by remarking that the doll must be considered a living being, and that Silvia herself is the "mother." So the adult underlines two of the most important features of pretense: the attribution of living qualities to inanimate objects and the role adoption.

Marking critical features also means to interpret and communicate the emotional value of a pretend situation. In this case the tutor's mirror behavior does not concern the content but the affective meaning of a pretend activity, as in the following example:

Example 2

Three children are playing with some hair-grips. Mattia brings the hair-grips to the caregiver.

CHIARA: Look at these big teeth! (*showing the open hair-grip which looks like a toothed mouth*).

MATTIA: Look, a crocodile, it eats, it's a crocodile!

RICCARDO: You've seen, this is a shark! (*Opens the hair-grip and points it at the caregiver pretending to eat her.*)

CAREGIVER: It's very dangerous!

MATTIA: (*Takes another hair-grip.*) This is another crocodile, two crocodiles (*opening another hair-grip*). Look out, be careful, I'm going to eat you up. Yum, yum!

By presenting herself as frightened by the dangerous creature animated by the children, the caregiver legitimates the symbolic transformations proposed by Mattia and Riccardo (the hair-grip as a crocodile or a shark) and remarks the nonliteral use of objects.

In the following example in which the adult admits the possibility that a child can have three mothers, she underlines that in pretend play it is possible to contradict likelihood and reasonableness:

Example 3

Upon children's request, the adult personifies a baby. She lies down on a little folding bed and says, Who is my mother?" Three children reply, "Me, me, me. . . . " The adult says, "OK, I've got three mothers, but you must take care of me, mustn't you?"

By accepting the three children's proposals the tutor meets children's need to play the role of "a person who gives care," indirectly remarking that a pretend world can be ruled by laws different from those of the real world.

With more experienced players the tutor may teach children that a pretend situation has its own rules which must be respected, as in the following example. The tutor remarks that it is necessary to reverse in front of a sudden imaginary wall; if a dog appears on the road, it is necessary to drive carefully, and one must not get out of a car if it is going at full speed:

Example 4

The adult and some children are sitting on a sofa that they pretend it is a car. They pretend to go on a trip to see their grandmothers.

IVAN: (*Pretends to drive making the noise of an engine.*) Vroomm, vroom.

ADULT: Attention! He's driving! Vroom! (*Makes the noise of an engine and wavers on the sofa pretending the bends.*)

IVAN: There's the wall!

ADULT: The wall? And then do turn! Reverse ... look, reverse, there, then we can start. (*pointing at a point in the room*)

LAURA: There's a dog! (*pointing at a point in the room*)

ADULT: Where?

LAURA: It is wagging its tail!

ADULT: (to Ivan) Mind you don't run it over!

LUCILLA: I'm going to see if it is dead! (*Gets out of the sofa.*)

ADULT: Where are you going? You must be careful because if the car runs fast you get hurt!

LUCILLA: (*Sits down on the sofa again.*)

Direction Maintenance

What characterizes pretend play are digression and wandering and ambiguity and incompleteness. Therefore, instead of trying to direct this unstructured activity, the tutor must help children develop their own ideas about play and integrate them. In the case of play, direction maintenance as a tutorial function must be reformulated as the development function.

This function can be carried out by two particular strategies: the "open question" and the "introduction or thematic enrichment," introduction of new ideas congruent with those previously expressed by the children. The open-question strategy aims to help children express play ideas not yet completely formulated or developed; the introduction strategy suggests new cues to children in order to enrich or complete their play. Combined with the "echo or mirror communication," the two strategies often permit play to take off or a play project to be carried out, as in the following example:

Example 5

ADULT: *(to the group)* Then, what are we playing at? [Open question]

IVAN: At pistols.

ADULT: At pistols? [Echo communication] Let's play at pistols! And what are we playing at with pistols? [Open question]

IVAN: At firing!

ADULT: At firing? [Echo communication]

GIADA: At firing at a wolf!

ADULT: Is the wolf arriving? [Echo communication]

GIADA: Yes, it is!

ADULT: Then if the wolf arrives we must hide! Let's hide behind here. [Introduction] *(Goes behind the sofa and all the children follow her.)* And now what can we do with the pistols? [Open question]

LAURA: Let's shoot!

ADULT: Shoot? [Echo communication]

LAURA: Yes, let's shoot! ... Bang, bang! *(pretending to shoot with a hair dryer beyond the sofa)*

ADULT: Bang, bang! [Echo communication] *(pretending to shoot using her hand as a pistol)*

The tutor has a maieutic role: he or she approaches play with and attitude of curiosity and tolerance for uncertainty; the tutor is aware that he or she does not have a right to decide *a priori* the content, the roles, and the course of symbolic activity. He or she must pay attention to "what happens and when it happens" and stimulate children to develop play scripts or themes by themselves.

With children who play alone without verbalizing their play ideas, the maieutic function can be carried out in a more direct way, with the tutor's interpretation of the child's play action expressed with an interrogative voice inflection, as in the following example:

Example 6

CHIARA: (*putting some small sticks in a basket*) I put the radio there, I put the . . .

CAREGIVER: What are you doing? [Open question]

CHIARA: (*Doesn't answer and continues to put the small sticks in.*)

CAREGIVER: (*to Chiara and the group*) She's making an animal, in my opinion. [Interpretation]

CHIARA: I'm making an animal, I'm making an elephant!

CAREGIVER: An elephant! [Echo communication] And where's that elephant going? [Open question]

CHIARA: To the town of the Garagoi.

CAREGIVER: To the town of . . . ?

CHIARA: Of the Garagoi.

CAREGIVER: Of the Garagoi! [Echo communication]

In the following example, the caregiver's verbal interventions aiming to get Chiara to express and clarify her play ideas solicit the participation of other children who were spectators.

MASSIMO: (*Was playing with a rope; approaches the caregiver.*) Where's the elephant?

CAREGIVER: (*pointing at the construction made by Chiara with the small sticks*) It's there. Chiara's making it!" [Echo communication] (*Plays ball and pretends that there is an elephant to involve Massimo.*) She has said she's making an elephant going to the town of the Garagoi." [Summarizing echo communication]

The caregiver's interest in Chiara's symbolic play attracts Mattia's attention. Mattia, who was playing with a rope, approaches the caregiver and the other children. A small group is now attentive to Chiara's play.

CAREGIVER: (*to Chiara*): What is it going to do in the town of the Garagoi? [Open question]

CHIARA: It is going to do its needs in the potty!

CAREGIVER: But are there any big potties? [Interpretation]

CHIARA: No, small!

CAREGIVER: But then is that elephant small or big? [Open question]
CHIARA: Small.

Reduction in Degrees of Freedom

Reduction in degrees of freedom in pretend play requires that the tutor undertake the most difficult tasks such as the creation and the maintenance of a shared play frame, the development of a narrative plot, and consideration of new ideas which can expand and enrich the course of play and permit the less experienced players to participate. Considering that pretend play in educational contexts takes place in a group situation and that the different partners do not have the same symbolic play skill and experience, the tutor must adopt the role of a democratic leader to let each player participate according to his or her capacity. The preceding examples 1, 4, and 5 illustrate this function. In example 1, the adult's echo communications offer Silvia support, which permit the girl to develop her play ideas and act accordingly. In example 4, the adult also takes the role of a speaker who, stressing and commenting on the children's play cues, gives a substantial character to the pretend situation and contributes to maintain the play focus. In example 5, a play theme emerges from the single player's contributions by means of the adult's verbal interventions that clarify each child's proposals and integrate them in a play project.

Frustration Control

Children from 2 to 3 years of age are rarely able to cooperate in developing a shared pretend situation (cf. Göncü, 1993). Each child elaborates a play project of his or her own and often fails to negotiate it with his or her play partners. Conflicts and quarrels arise. As a result, shared play activity does not often develop. However, as we have seen, the tutor can contribute to the development of group play by reducing the degree of freedom, helping children elaborate their own ideas and integrate them in a common script. Thus, frustration deriving from the failure to solve interpersonal conflicts can be reduced.

Controlling frustration has an additional positive effect that involves arousal modulation, as a result of which a playful climate for the activity and the involvement of participants are maintained. To control frustration, the adult has to empathize with the emotional meanings children express in their play by paraphrasing such meanings in a form that can elicit a common play. In the following example, we see how addressing Riccardo's feelings results in his engagement in the activity.

Example 7

Lara, with a book in her hand, approaches Veronica and, making a roar and pointing at a doll, shows her the image of a lion.

CAREGIVER: (*in an excited tone*) A lion! Oh, the baby is afraid of the lion, let's run away soon! (*Takes refuge in a sheltered corner of the room. All the children follow her; they stay close to her.*) We've left the baby with the lion, come on, we must save him otherwise the lion will eat him!

VERONICA: (*Fetches the doll and brings it into the corner, then she begins to run around the room.*)

CAREGIVER: Come along, quick! The lion is running after us, let's run away with Veronica! (*Begins to run followed by the children. After running for a while she says:*) Let's get under the cover! Let's take refuge upon a tree! (*Followed by all the children she mounts a big cube.*)

Lara, Veronica and Sharon embrace their caregiver pretending to be afraid. Riccardo watches puzzled.

CAREGIVER: (*to Riccardo*) Riccardo, can you see the lion? Where's the lion?

RICCARDO: (*pointing to a corner of the section*) There.

The adult recruits the children, proposing to them Lara's sketchy play ideas in a narrative form and interpreting their affective content: the fear of a helpless creature threatened by an aggressive wild animal. With her second intervention the adult acknowledges Veronica's contribution, expressing it in a more socialized narrative form in line with the emotional meaning included in the first theme: If a lion is wandering around, it is necessary to run away and hide. The tutor's empathy with the affective core of symbolic play, that is, with the dramatic representation of a dangerous situation, gives a "reality" to the imaginary lion, which appears to Riccardo terribly vivid.

Demonstration or Modeling

Modeling should be aimed at showing children a wide range of play activities such as how to do symbolic substitutions, to take and attribute roles, to create imaginary situations, to communicate "in and about play," and to cooperate with peers in performing a shared play script. Modeling does not concern play contents or ideas but only the way in which the ideas are represented.

It is important that modeling function should be self-consciously performed by the tutor and tuned up to children's capacity. The model indirectly offers patterns of symbolic play behaviors that children can imitate. As Wood et al claim, the tutor's modeling is really an idealization of the tutee's already expressed idea. The following example is an illustration of both modeling and the entire range of the tutoring functions.

Example 8a

Riccardo covers himself with a sheet, Chiara imitates him. The caregiver lifts the blue sheet under which Chiara was hidden.

CAREGIVER: Who is down here? Who's beneath this wave? (*approaching Riccardo*) Who's beneath another wave?

RICCARDO: (*Laughs and then uncovers himself.*)

CAREGIVER: (*Laying the sheet on the floor*) Look, it looks like the sea! I'm going for a bathe in the sea!

The caregiver recruits both Riccardo and Chiara by proposing to them a symbolic substitution—the blue curtain as a sea wave; then she suggests a play idea in accord with it. As we see in the following lines, two children follow the modeled proposal.

Example 8b

CHIARA: (*Plunges into the sheet and pretends to swim.*)

MATTIA: (*giving the caregiver a green sheet*) This is another sea!

Then the tutor tries to recruit other children, proposing a play script that can potentially involve the whole group.

Example 8c

CAREGIVER: Oh, this is another green sea, then, let's lay it here and let's make another sea! Who's coming with me to have a quick dip in the sea?

RICCARDO: Me!

Riccardo, Mattia, and Massimo plunge into the sheets.

After having created a group activity through her interventions, the tutor now maintains it by actively playing with the children.

Example 8d

CAREGIVER: Let's swim a bit! Well done! Bravos! (*Pretends to swim.*)

RATTIA: A dive! (*Jumps on the sheet.*)

CAREGIVER: A dive! Massimo, come and dive into this wave!

The children go on swimming and diving on the sheets.

Then (see example 8e) the caregiver modulates arousal by suggesting a pretend danger, aiming to support children's involvement and to encourage them to expand pretend play. In so doing, she also brings to children's attention one of the critical features of the pretend situation: the symbolic substitution (the sheet as a sea wave).

Example 8e

CAREGIVER: (*Takes a tulle and moves it upon the children's heads.*) Look out! There's a high wave which submerges these children! (in a low voice) I can hear, I can hear, I seem to hear that someone is arriving . . .

MATTIA: (*shouting*) A shark!

In the ensuing conversation, the tutor outlines a narrative script (if we are pursued by a shark we must seek refuge in a boat) by empathizing with the affective meaning of Mattia's proposal of an imaginary wild fish—a shark. Later on, the script is further developed by the child who, using a featherduster as a weapon, plays the role of a shark-killer hero.

Example 8f

CAREGIVER: (*in a fright*) Oh! Then, let's go on a raft, we need a boat, something . . .

MATTIA: I'll attack it! (*Hits the featherduster hard on the floor.*)

CAREGIVER: (*screaming*) Did you kill it?

MATTIA: Yes, I did.

RICCARDO: We need a boat! (*Resumes the caregiver's idea.*)

CAREGIVER: But we haven't a boat here!

MASSIMO: Oh, we haven't!

RICCARDO: We have got a boat!

CAREGIVER: Where's the boat?

RICCARDO: (*Looks around.*)

RATTIA: The boat is here. I've found it! (*Brings a cushion to the caregiver.*)

The particular strategies used by the caregiver to develop the play script are paying attention to and acknowledging the play cues of the individual children as well as soliciting the group to find out a solution to the problem without proposing it by herself ("but we haven't a boat here!"; "Where's the boat?"). By doing so, she succeeds in recruiting the other children who now appear to be involved in the pretend situation.

Example 8g

CAREGIVER: Here's the boat, we've found it! [The caregiver's echo communication concentrates the attention of the group on Mattia's solution.]

The caregiver puts the cushion among the sheets and Chiara sits down upon it at once. Riccardo takes another cushion to the caregiver.

RICCARDO: Here's my boat! (*Putting his cushion near the other, then he sits down on it*)

[By recognizing Mattia's idea, the caregiver makes the mates adopt it; the situation gets shared.]

In sum, the play interaction of the tutor aims to develop group play by soliciting new contributions from the children, by acknowledging each of children's proposals, by integrating single play cues in a narrative script, and by modulating arousal for the involvement of the entire group. Finally, in the course of her engagement in play, the tutor provides children with examples of different pretend phenomena.

THE SCAFFOLDING MODEL

The tutoring model provides a description of the functions performed by the adult in consideration of the principal characteristics of symbolic play, such as spontaneity, nonliterality, divergence, as-ifness, and its affective quality. Thus, the tutoring model helps us determine the appropriateness of the adult's intervention. However, we also need to indicate how a tutor can enhance children's symbolic skills and control the effectiveness of his or her intervention. To do so requires identification of symbolic play skills that must be fostered on the basis of a developmental model as well as a determination of how to match children's existing symbolic capacity and what they need to learn. Next I summarize a scaffolding model developed to address these issues as it also includes the tutoring model (cf. Bondioli, 1996). In the following paragraphs, I first outline a developmental model which guides the adult intervention and then illustrate how an adult can identify the "zo-ped" of a group of children and plan a scaffolding intervention. I conclude after having summarized my program of research.

The Developmental Model

Our model includes discussion of five developmental lines concerning different skills necessary to perform symbolic play. They are decontextualization, decentration, integration, execution control, and social competence (see Fein, 1978). Decontextualization refers to the increasing ability of the child to use objects, identities, and situations in a manner that is detached from the immediate environment. For example, with regard to the objects, the child initially uses them prototypically (e.g., a spoon to stir), then he or she makes symbolic substitutions (e.g., a block as an iron), then the child pretends that an imaginary object exists (e.g., child pretends to drink from a cup that does not exist).

Decentration refers to the increasing ability of the child to move from self-referenced actions (e.g., pretend feeding of self) to other-referenced actions (e.g., pretend feeding of doll), adoption of roles (e.g., becoming Superman), and reciprocal role attributions (e.g., taking and assigning roles).

Integration refers to the increasing capacity of the child to enact an ordered sequence of pretend play, following a script or a narrative theme. In the beginning, the child enacts only a single scheme (e.g., only one pretend action), then he or she repeats it, changing the recipient (e.g., the child pretends to feed the doll and then him- or herself), afterward he or she can combine play actions in a sequence (e.g., the child takes a pan and puts it on the cooking range and takes a lid and puts it on the pan). Later the child represents an episode involving a sequence of actions (e.g., the child pretends to go shopping in a supermarket and behaves accordingly). At last, he or she can add a narrative quality to his or her play representing an episode with an initial problematic situation, a sequence of actions aiming at the solution of the problem, and an ending.

Executive control refers to the increasing capacity of the child to use speech in play in increasingly less egocentric way. For example, initially a child says "an injection . . . I'm making an injection" as she feeds a doll, and later on her language gains a social quality when the child enacts a role and speaks for the character as well. Thus, executive control evolves from egocentric to social verbalization and from language in play to language about play.

The last developmental line the tutor considers in assisting children to become expert players is children's social competence. This refers to the increasing capacity of the children to share pretend activity with their playmates. This developmental line goes from solitary play to parallel play and then to associative and cooperative play.

The Research: Working in the Zone of Proximal Development

As stated previously, to provide assistance that would be meaningful for children, the tutor needs to take into account the "zo-ped" of individual children. In addition, based on my observations that children's peer groups have an identity of their own, I propose that the tutor take into account the group's zone of proximal development of the group as well (Bondioli & Savio, 1994a, 1994b). Toward this end, we set up a scale to identify the actual and proximal development of individual children and the play groups, the Rating Scale of Children's Ludic–Symbolic Skills, called the SVALSI in Italian (Bondioli & Savio, 1994a). It is composed of five subscales, corresponding to the previously mentioned five developmental lines. Each subscale includes one or more areas whose items are graduated from low to high levels on the basis of the research literature on the development of symbolic play. Table 5.1 illustrates the subscales, the areas, and the items of the scale.

By observing children playing spontaneously in a setting arranged with props aiming to elicit pretend play, it is possible to check the level of each child's capacities as shown in his or her play behaviors. We assume that a child's play behaviors appearing only once or a few times represent the zone of skills the subject is acquiring (the "zo-ped") whereas the most frequent play behaviors constitute the zone of fully mastered skills, the zone of actual development. For instance, if a child adopts a role only once during the play session or is not able to behave accordingly, we suppose that such behaviors represent play levels that need practice in order to be fully mastered. We elaborate the group's zo-ped in a similar way. The zone of proximal development would concern the highest play levels shown by the most experienced children in the group; the zone of current skills would concern the competence levels present in the group, especially shown by the children who represent the low and middle levels.

TABLE 5.1. Subscales, Areas, and Items of the SVALSI

Subscale 1: Decontextualization (Deco)

Level	Object as instrument area	Identity area	Situation area
1	Prototypical object (PO)	Functional identity (FI)	Prototypical situation (PS)
2	Substitute object (SO)	Realistic identity (RI)	Realistic situation (RS)
3	Imaginary object (IO)	Fantastic/imaginary identity (II)	Imaginary situation (IS)

Subscale 2: Decentration (Dece)

Level	Role area	Object as an agent area
1	Self-referenced action (SA)	
2	Other-referenced action (OA)	Other as a passive recipient (Opr)
3	Role adoption (Rad)	Other as an active recipient (Oar)
4	Role attribution (Rat)	Other as agent (Oa)
5	Reciprocal roles (RR)	Partner as other (Pa)

	Subscale 3: Integration (Inte)	Subscale 4: Execution control (ExCo)	Subscale 5: Social competence (SoCo)
Level	Script area	Speech area	Partnership area
1	Single scheme (SS)	Egocentric speech in play (Ein)	Solitary play (SOL)
2	Single scheme variation (SV)	Egocentric speech about play (Eout)	Imitative play (IMI)
3	Multischeme combination (MC)	Social speech in play (Sin)	Associative play (ASS)
4	Narratives (NA)	Social speech about play (Sout)	Couple cooperative play (COU)
5	Problem narrative (PA)	Social play framing (Sfr)	Group cooperative play (GRO)

Note. In each area the items are presented in a progressive way corresponding to different developmental levels, for example, Prototypical object (PO) corresponds to the first level of the decontextualization of objects, substitute object (SO) to the second, imaginary object (IO) to the third. For further information about the items of the scale and the scores that can be obtained by it see Bondioli and Savio (1994a, 1994b). Deco, decontextualization; Dece, decentration; Inte, integration; ExCo, execution control; SoCo, social competence.

Figure 5.1 is an example of a group play profile obtained assigning to each child the mean scores in the different subscales of the SVALSI. Profiles A and D show the range of the competence levels of the group: The former represents the highest scores obtained by a child in the group, and the latter represents the lowest ones; profiles B and C corre-

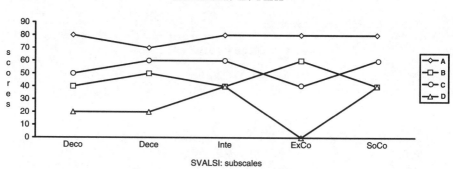

FIGURE 5.1. Competence profiles in a play group of four children. See footnote to Table 5.1 for an explanation of abbreviations.

spond to intermediate levels. Note that integration and social competence are the dimensions that exhibit the least developmental variability in the group. The greatest variability concerns execution control. Thus, to establish homogeneity in this play group and to help children achieve the most advanced forms of social play, we planned an intervention aiming to foster the least skilful children's integration and social competence. After having ensured that these competencies have been consolidated at the level shown by the most experienced players, we worked on children's ability to use language in sharing symbolic play.

In the first study reported here, we illustrated how pretend play levels of children, as assessed by the SVALSI, increased as a result of adult intervention. Initially, children were observed for half an hour playing in the play corner of their day-care center. The adult participated only as an observer. Then, in the intervention phase, the adult participated in children's play for 3 consecutive days. The length of each intervention session was about half an hour. A group of five day-care children from 17 to 21 months old participated in the study (cf. Giovannoni, 1997). Table 5.2 indicates, for each child, the levels of his or her actual symbolic skills (in regular type) and those of their proximal development (in italics).

The table indicates, for each child, both the areas in which play developed during the course of the experience and the play areas that showed no change. For instance, Laura (cf. Table 5.2) showed no gains in decentration (e.g., other-referenced actions) and execution control (i.e., she did not use language in her pretend play). On the other hand, she showed an improvement in the area of social competence. Although her most common form of social play remained imitative, which can there-

TABLE 5.2. Children's Play Gains as a Result of Adult Intervention

	Deco	Dece	Inte	ExCo	SoCo
Laura (17 months)					
Pretest	PO-FI	OA	SS *MC*		IMI
I Encounter	PO-FI *SO*	OA	SS *MC*		IMI *ASS*
II Encounter	PO-FI *IO*	OA	SS *SV*		IMI *ASS*
Alessia (21 months)					
Pretest	PO-FI	OA	SS *MC*		IMI
I Encounter	PO-FI	OA	SS *SV*	Sin	IMI-ASS
II Encounter	PO-FI *IO*	OA	SS *SV*	Sin *Sout*	ASS
III Encounter	PO-FI *IO*	OA	SS *MC*	Sin	IMI-ASS
Clara (21 months)					
Pretest	PO-FI	OA	SS *MC*	IMI	
I Encounter	PO-FI	OA	SS *SV*	Sin	IMI-ASS
II Encounter	PO-FI *IO*	OA	SS *SV*	Sin *Sout*	ASS
III Encounter	PO-FI *IO*	OA	SS *MC*	Sin	IMI-ASS
Alessandra (21 months)					
Pretest	PO-FI *SO*	OA	SS *MC*		IMI
I Encounter	PO-FI	OA	SS		SOL
II Encounter	PO-FI *IO*	OA	SS *SV*		IMI *ASS*
III Encounter	PO-FI	OA	SS		ASS
Luca (21 months)					
Pretest	PO-FI *SO*	OA	SS *MC*	Ein *Eout*	SOL
I Encounter	PO-FI	OA	SS *SV*	Sin *Sout*	
II Encounter	Absent	Absent	Absent	Absent	Absent
III Encounter	Absent	Absent	Absent	Absent	Absent

Note. In this table and in Table 5.3, the abbreviations refer to the items of the SVALSI (see Table 5.1) corresponding to different developmental levels (e.g., PO, prototypical object; SO, substitute object). For each child the levels of their actual symbolic skills are indicated in regular type; those of their proximal development are indicated in italics.

fore be considered her actual level of competence, the interaction with the adult sometimes allowed her also to perform associative play forms. For example, at one point the adult, pretending to be a "lady," combed her own hair in front of the mirror. In turn, Laura took the comb from the caregiver's hands and began to comb the adult's hair. Then, the adult acknowledged by saying: "Ah, you are combing my hair, thank you!" Also, in the decontextualization area, Laura improved her actual level of competence, normally characterized by the prototypical use of objects and the enacting of functional roles, by making occasional object substitutions and pretending with imaginary objects. For example, the adult put a clothespin in a pot to cook it, pretending that it was a sausage. Laura got near her, took the "clothespin sausage," and put it in her mouth pretending to eat it. When the adult asked her if it was done, Laura answered by saying "no" and put the "sausage" in the pot again. Although these play behaviors rarely appeared in Laura's initial play, they appeared in connection with the adult's interventions and solicitations. Thus, they can be considered representative of levels of competence not yet consolidated and are indicated in the table in italics.

When we move onto the examination of the entire group's gains (see Table 5.2), we see that four children increased their play levels in the area of social competence. Besides Laura, Alessia, and Clara, whose most common levels of competence were imitative play in the pretest, progressively developed more social behaviors, often showing episodes of associative play with the adult and their playmates. Also, Alessandra's social play started with imitative play behaviors but became totally associative in the last session.

Three children, Alessia, Clara, and Luca, increased their play levels in the area of execution control. In every case, the children's gains concerned the transition from the use of social language "in play" to the use of language to communicate about play. In every case, however, this improvement needed to be consolidated in the future in that the social verbalizations about play appeared only occasionally and were less spread in the group.

Some gains in the area of decontextualization also appeared for four children. They consisted in adding symbolic substitutions and imaginary objects to their more prototypical acts of decontextualization.

In addition to considering children's gains, we used the SVALSI to assess the adult's play behavior in order to measure the degree to which the intervention was geared toward the children's actual versus proximal zone of development. Table 5.3 shows the data concerning the adult's play. The adult's intervention appeared to be perfectly suitable for the group's zo-ped in the areas of execution control and social competence:

TABLE 5.3. The Assessment of the Adult's Intervention

	Deco	Dece	Inte	ExCo	SoCo
I Encounter	PO-FI *IO*	OA	MC	Sin-Sout	ASS
II Encounter	IO-FI *RI-RS*	OA *Rad-Rat*	MC *NA*	Sin-Sout *Sfr*	ASS
III Encounter	IO-FI *RS*	OA *Rat*	MC	Sin *Sout*	ASS

her most frequent level of play matches the most advanced levels of the children's play. When the children's actual zone of development in the area of social competence was represented by imitative play, the adult's play was prevailingly associative. The adult often commented on the children's play actions and was quick in participating in their play initiatives. In so doing, she modeled associative play, a more advanced level of social play than the one in which the children were able to participate.

Also, the adult's use of language was an attempt to solicit verbal expressions from the children. She always communicated "in play" and often also "about play" to demonstrate how language can be used to share a play project or to maintain a shared play plot.

In certain areas we found some actions of the adult to be beyond children's zo-ped. For example, in decontextualization, when the adult proposed to transform the actual area of play into a hairdresser salon, none of the children accepted her invitation. Also, in the area of integration, when the adult proposed a script and suggested the group enact it, the children did not react positively; it was as if they did not understand the adult's request. Further, in decentration, when the adult proposed a role play, the children did not join in. In general, however, the results of the first study supported our claim that when the adult's scaffolding is sensitive to children's developing needs, children benefit from the assistance provided by adults in reaching more advanced levels of functioning in pretend play. This interpretation gains greater currency if we take into account the fact that the adult tutor did not have advanced knowledge of children's play abilities and that her assessment was based on her ongoing observations during her interactions with the children.

Scaffolding effects were also examined in a quasi-experimental study (Bondioli & Savio, 1994b) where performance in three conditions were compared: peer play, scaffolding by an adult, and not-play. Fifteen children (age range: 31 to 43 months) of a nursery school class were randomly assigned to three groups. Each group was videotaped for 30 minutes while playing spontaneously in a school corner furnished for pretend play, and each child's symbolic play skill was assessed by the SVALSI. On the basis of their pretest scores, the children were assigned to five competence levels: (1) low level, (2) low–middle level, (3) middle level, (4) high–middle level, and (5) high level. Three groups were then formed with each group including five children, one from each level, so that the resulting groups were equally heterogeneous. (Each group included children at different levels of competence.) Each group was randomly assigned to one of the three conditions.[3]

1. *Peer play.* The five children of the first group took part in 13 consecutive meetings (except on weekends) of 30 minutes each in the

same play space and with the same materials used during the pretest. The children had the possibility of freely interacting with one another using the materials at their disposal. The adult was present as an observer.

2. *Play scaffolding by a tutor.* The five children of the second group also took part in 13 consecutive meetings characterized by the gradual adult participation. In the first phase, the first three meetings, the children played freely without adult intervention. In the second phase, the next seven successive meetings, the adult actively participated in the play of children using the tutorial functions as she deemed appropriate. The third phase, the last three meetings, was similar to the first.

3. *Control group.* Unlike the first two groups, the third group did not have the opportunity to play in a structured situation even though the children took advantage of the play occasions offered during the school day. They were simply pretested and posttested at the same time as the treatment groups.

In the posttest the values of H (the estimator of the Kruskal Wallis test) indicated significant differences among the groups, $p(H > 4.618)$ $< .1$. An analysis of the average scores of the three groups indicated that children in the adult–tutor condition benefited from the treatment more than children in the peer play condition did. In both conditions, however, children whose play levels were low or low-to-middle benefited from the treatment the most.

The analysis of the adult's intervention, carried out by applying to her play behaviors the categories of the SVALSI, showed that the adult played in a way that was fine-tuned to the children's zo-ped. By considering the limits of the least competent partner's zone of proximal development, she proposed situations that consolidated children's potential and actual skills.

In conclusion, to foster children's pretend play abilities, a tutor has to perform two main tasks. First he or she has to facilitate children's expression of symbolic meanings in creating a shared play frame (tutoring task). Second he or she has to act in children's zo-ped in order to improve their play performances (scaffolding task). With regard to the tutoring task, the adult has to respect and promote the distinctive traits of pretending, such as denotative license, referential freedom, affective meaning, and shared symbolism. This means that he or she not only has to be a competent player (imaginative and cooperative) but also has to keep in mind that the adult has an educational task to accomplish. With regard to the scaffolding task, the adult has to observe children's existing skills and increase his or her pretend play interventions in full consideration of such skills. These tasks and attitudes should be counted among the professional skills of a good day-care center or nursery-school teacher contributing to early childhood development.

NOTES

1. The examples are derived from the transcripts of videotaped observations collected in numerous Italian day-care centers and nursery schools.

2. The mirror or echo communication is a strategy inspired by the work of psychotherapist Carl Rogers (Raskin & Rogers, 1989). It is used in the relationship approach to play therapy (Axline, 1969; Guerney, 1983, 1984; Moustakas, 1973; for a review, see Hughes, 1991, Chap. 10). The therapist strives to create an atmosphere of total acceptance. He or she is nondirective and attempts to communicate a feeling of warmth, openness, and respect. An important principle of this approach is that the therapist recognizes the child's feelings and attempts to reflect them back to the child. The reflection of children's feelings, as they are expressed in words, gestures, or the symbolic meaning of the play, is intended to help them to gain insight into those feelings.

3. The equivalency of the groups was proved by applying the Kruskal–Wallis test of monovalent variance for ranks.

REFERENCES

Axline, V. (1969). *Play therapy* (rev. ed.). New York: Ballantine.

Beizer, L., & Howes, C. (1992). Mothers and toddlers: Partners in early symbolic play: Illustrative study. In C. Howes, O. Unger, & C. C. Matheson, *The collaborative construction of pretend: Social pretend play functions* (pp. 25–43). Albany: State University of New York Press.

Belsky, J., & Most, R. (1984). From exploration to play: A cross-sectional study of infant free play behavior. *Developmental Psychology, 17*, 630–639.

Bondioli, A. (1996). *Gioco e educazione*. Milano: Franco Angeli.

Bondioli, A., & Savio, D. (1994a). *Osservare il gioco di finzione: una scala di valutazione delle abilità ludico-simboliche infantili (SVALSI)*. Bergamo: Junior.

Bondioli, A., & Savio, D. (1994b). Play training as an action in children's zone of proximal development. *Scientia Paedagogica Experimentalis, 31*(1), 45–68.

Bowman, B. (1990). Play in teacher education: The United States perspective. In E. Klugman & S. Smilansky (Eds.), *Children's play and learning* (pp. 97–101). New York and London: Teachers College, Columbia University Press.

Fein, G. G. (1975). A transformational analysis of pretending. *Developmental Psychology, 11*, 291–296.

Fein, G. G. (1978). Play revisited. In E. Lamb (Ed.), *Social and personality development* (pp. 70–90). New York: Holt, Rinehart & Winston.

Fein, G. G. (1981). Pretend play in childhood: An integrative review. *Child Development, 52*, 1095–1118.

Fein, G. G. (1987). Pretend play: Creativity and consciousness. In D. Gorlitz & J. F. Wohlwill (Eds.), *Curiosity, imagination and play* (pp. 283–304). Hillsdale, NJ: Erlbaum.

Fenson, L. (1984). Developmental trends for action and speech in pretend play. In I. Bretherton (Ed.), *Symbolic play* (pp. 249–270). New York: Academic Press.

Fenson, L., Kagan, J., Kearsley, R. B., & Zelazo, P. R. (1976). The developmental progression of manipulative play in the first two years. *Child Development, 47*, 232–235.

Fenson, L., & Ramsay, D. (1981). Effects of modeling action sequences on the play of twelve-, fifteen-, and nineteen-month-old children. *Child Development, 52*, 1028–1036.

Fiese, B. H. (1989, April). *Creating the zone of proximal development: Lesson from the study of symbolic play.* Paper presented at the biennial meeting at the Society for Research in Child Development.

Fiese, B. H. (1990). Playful relationships: A contextual analysis of mother–toddler interaction and symbolic play. *Child Development, 61*, 1648–1656.

Giovannoni, F. (1997). *Giocare con i bambini al nido: Un'esperienza di promozione delle abilità ludico-simboliche infantili.* Unpublished doctoral thesis, University of Pavia.

Göncü, A. (1993). Development of intersubjectivity in social pretend play. *Human Development, 36*, 185–198.

Guerney, L. (1983). Client-centered (non-directive) play therapy. In C. Schaefer & K. O'Connor (Eds.), *Handbook of play therapy.* New York: Wiley.

Guerney, L. (1984). Play therapy in counseling settings. In T. D. Yawkey & A. D. Pellegrini (Eds.), *Child's play: Developmental and applied* (pp. 291–322). Hillsdale, NJ: Erlbaum.

Howes, C., Unger, O., & Matheson, C. C. (1992). *The collaborative construction of pretend: Social pretend play functions* New York: State University of New York Press.

Hughes, F. P. (1991). *Children, play, and development.* Boston, London, Toronto: Allyn & Bacon.

Johnson, J. E., & Ershler, J. (1982). Curricular effects on the play of preschoolers. In D. J. Pepler & K. H. Rubin (Eds.), *The play of children: Current theory and research* (pp. 130–144). Basel: Karger.

Kavanaugh, R. D., Whittington, S., & Cerbone, M. J. (1983). Mothers' use of fantasy in speech to young children. *Journal of Child Language, 1*, 163–183.

Klugman, E., & Smilansky, S. (Eds.). (1990). *Children's play and learning.* New York and London: Teachers College, Columbia University Press.

Moustakas, C. (1973). *Children in play therapy* (rev. ed.). New York: Aronson.

O'Connell, B., & Bretherton, I. (1984). Toddlers' play, alone and with mother: The role of maternal guidance. In I. Bretherton (Ed.), *Symbolic play* (pp. 337–368). Orlando, FL: Academic Press.

Raskin, N. J., & Rogers, C. R. (1989). Person-centered therapy. In R. D. Corsini & D. Wedding (Eds.), *Current psychotherapies* (4th ed., pp. 155–194). Itasca, IL: Peacock.

Rivkin, M. S. (1986). The teacher's place in children's play. In G. Fein & M. Rivkin (Eds.), *The young child at play* (pp. 213–217). Washington, DC: NAEYC.

Rogers, C. R. (1945). The nondirective method as a technique for social research. *American Journal of Sociology, 19,* 279–283.

Rogoff, B. (1990). *Apprenticeship on thinking.* New York: Oxford University Press.

Sachs, J. (1980). The role of adult–child play in language development. In K. H. Rubin (Ed.), *Children's play* (pp. 33–47). San Francisco: Jossey-Bass.

Saltz, R., & Saltz, E. (1986). Pretend play and its outcomes. In G. Fein & M. Rivkin (Eds.), *The young child at play* (pp. 155–173). Washington, DC: NAEYC.

Shmulker, D. (1981). Mother–child interaction and its relationship to the predisposition of imaginative play. *Genetic Psychology Monographs, 104,* 215–235.

Slade, A. (1987). A longitudinal study of maternal involvement in symbolic play during the toddler period. *Child Development, 58,* 367–375.

Smilansky, S. (1990). Sociodramatic play: Its relevance to behavior and achievement in school. In E. Klugman & S. Smilansky (Eds.), *Children's play and learning* (pp. 18–42). New York and London: Teachers College, Columbia University Press.

Smilansky, S., & Shefatya, L. (1990). *Facilitating play: A medium for promoting cognitive, socio-emotional and academic development in young children.* Gaithersburg, MD: Psychosocial and Educational Publications.

Vygotsky, L. S. (1978), *Mind in society: The development of higher psychological processes.* Cambridge, MA: Harvard University Press.

Watson, M., & Fisher, K. (1977). A developmental sequence of agent use in late infancy. *Child Development, 48,* 828–836.

Wood, D., Bruner, J. S., & Ross, G. (1976). The role of tutoring in problem solving. *Journal of Child Psychology and Psychiatry, 17,* 89–100.

6

🍎

Facilitating the Narrative
Quality of Sociodramatic Play

RIVKA GLAUBMAN
GABI KASHI
RINA KORESH

We met Greta G. Fein personally in Israel, at the beginning of the 1990s, when she came as an invited guest to Tel-Aviv and Bar-Ilan universities. As we listened to Greta's lectures and talked with her, we admired her as a person and as a scientist. From then on, we cooperated in doing research on pretend play and children's narratives, using Greta's theoretical ideas and research tools. Working with Greta was an exceptional intellectual experience, always exciting and inspiring. Greta Fein remains for us always an authority from whom we can learn about children's play and narratives.

The large number of publications on pretend play and its facilitation pertain to children's cognitive, emotional, and social development. However, reference to the narrative aspect of children's play is still sparse. The premise of the present work is that the narrative quality of pretend play, especially its imaginative character, is responsible for the developmental functions of play, and therefore it should be a major focus of play research. In the following pages, we argue for a narrative approach to the study of sociodramatic play focusing on the imaginative aspect, discuss an intervention that is consistent with our approach, and describe an illustrative study. We begin our presentation with a conceptualization of children's pretend play as a kind of narrative, discuss the contribution of object use in play to the construction of play narratives, and the need for these ideas to be incorporated into play interventions. Afterward, we move on to the detailed description of intervention phases along with other methodological considerations and our results. We conclude with the implications of our findings.

THE NARRATIVE ASPECT OF CHILD DEVELOPMENT AND PRETEND PLAY

In the last few decades, cognitive psychology in general and the field of cognitive development in particular came to recognize the importance of the narrative mode of thinking. The human mind builds narratives that describe and organize both the "inner" and the "outer" world in which the person lives and acts. The most prominent advocate of this approach is Bruner (1986, 1990, 1996), although reference to narrative can also be found in the area of research that examines "theory of mind" (e.g., Flavell, 1992; Perner & Astington, 1992; Sabbagh & Callanan, 1998; Woolley, 1995; Woolley & Wellman, 1993).

Bruner's approach to the narrative is one of the two major approaches that influenced the work reported in this chapter. Bruner (1986, 1990, 1996) posits the narrative as a symbolic schema through which a person interprets the world. Narrative typifies human (or human-like) intentions and actions, their conditions and consequences (Bruner, 1986). Thus, narrative or story is a condensation of life that can be interpreted only as a structural coherent whole unit.

Consistent with Bruner's view, child psychologists claim that narratives reflect the nature of young children's minds with regard to cognition, memory, and affect (Chafe, 1990; Scarlett & Wolf, 1979). Narratives are based on a child's personal experiences rather than on a logical or categorical ability to organize thoughts—as was emphasized by psychologists such as Piaget and Vygotsky (Astington & Gopnik, 1991; Bruner, 1986, 1990; Olson, 1990; Sutton-Smith, 1986). The child forms narratives in order to create meaning (Westby, 1986), hence narrative structure appears early in the life of human infant, even before language emerges, and "determines the order of priority in which grammatical forms are mastered by the young child" (Bruner, 1990, p. 77). Therefore, it is plausible to expect that further development, as expressed in the child's pretend play, will emerge in narrative forms.

The striking similarity between structural aspects of pretend play and the narratives (Bretherton, 1989; Galda, 1984; Gardner, 1980; Pellegrini, 1985; Wolf & Grollman 1982; Wolf, Rygh, & Altshuler, 1984) motivates adopting a narrative approach to pretend play (Eckler & Weininger, 1989). The narrative's basic features are clearly identified in pretend play, especially in highly scripted protocols (Pellegrini, 1985). These are described as sequential structure and dramatic quality in a composite made up of an actor, an action, a goal, a scene, an instrument, and a trouble or problem (Bruner, 1990; also see chapters by Sutton-Smith and Pellegrini & Galda, this volume).

The second theory that influenced our work is a theory of pretend play developed by Fein (1987, 1989), who describes pretend play as a reflective, interpretive–expressive system "designed to manipulate representations of emotionally consequential aspects of living" (Fein, 1987, p. 302). Fein claims that the symbolic structures that define the content and sequences of play can explain the origins of the bizarre and fantastic ideas represented in play and the effect of such representations on the affective domain of development (Fein, 1987, 1989).

Bruner's and Fein's ideas, which were independently developed, have four common elements that call for integrating them into one conceptual framework in justifying adopting a narrative approach to the study of pretend play. One common element refers to imagination as a central component that enables the narrative or pretend play production and is the basis for explaining its quality. A second common idea Fein and Bruner share is the dramatic quality that characterizes both the narrative and the pretend play.

A third common element in the theories of Fein and Bruner is in their conceptualization of the functioning of the human mind in constructing pretend and narrative. Both Fein and Bruner explain the mental movements from the realistic to the imaginative, each in a different yet resembling mode. With regard to play, Fein (1989) explains this as acting within two levels of the mind. One mind serves the child's development of empirical knowledge base by representations of the immediate reality and experience. The second mind serves to detach these representations from objective reality, making them meta-representations and, thus, permitting the child to understand pretense as a different kind of mental phenomenon. Ultimately, such understanding enables children to work through their emotions and develop mastery over them (Ariel, 1984; Fein, 1989; Leslie, 1987).

With regard to narrative, Bruner (1990) suggests the "dual landscape" feature of the mind. In the narrative, one landscape refers to the reality context of the story and its development, whereas the other deals with the interpretations of things and their inner meaning to both the narrator and the audience. "It deals with the stuff of human action and human intentionality . . . the world of beliefs, desires, and hope" (Bruner, 1990, p. 52).

Finally, a fourth common element of Fein's and Bruner's theories refers to the basic human need for meaning making of their world, which they do through communication in social and cultural contexts. Meaning making occurs in play through negotiations among children as they try to reach shared understanding (Fein, 1989; Giffin, 1984), and in narrative it occurs as individuals try to interpret events as structural and coherent wholes (Bruner, 1996).

Noteworthy is both authors' claim that communicative clarity is not the aim in the activity of sharing meaning. Rather, the central idea shared by the participants in play and in narrative is ambiguity (in play) or uncertainty (in narrative) in communication. Ambiguity and uncertainty permit a variety of public or private interpretations as well as opportunities to revise in the joint effort to construct substantive imaginative experiences (Sutton-Smith, 1997).

These shared ideas between Fein and Bruner lend support to our thesis that the same conceptual framework can be used in understanding how the child constructs meanings and the role of imagination in meaning construction. This conceptual framework embraces the child's cognitive, affective, and communicative development that occurs in real and imaginative contexts (Sutton-Smith, 1997)—development that is constructed in narrative forms and is expressed in stories and pretend play. As we discuss in detail in the methods section, our conceptualization of story and pretend play as activities of similar psychological and structural nature influenced the adaptation of measures in assessing pretend play that have not been used in previous training studies.

NARRATIVE, IMAGINATION, AND PLAY OBJECTS

Sociodramatic play and narrative share the elements summarized previously. However, sociodramatic play differs from narrative in two important ways. First, by definition sociodramatic play, which is our present focus, always occurs at least with two children, and second, it evolves around play objects (Elgas, Klein, Kantor, & Fernie, 1988; Hughes, 1987; McLoyd, 1980; Pellegrini, 1991). The relations of these features to narrative construction in play are discussed in the next section.

In sociodramatic play, children construct cognitive and emotive meanings through continual communicative and metacommunicative negotiations (Bateson, 1956; Bretherton, 1984, 1989; Giffin, 1984; Göncü, 1993a, 1993b). Children construct meaning in the form of common play narratives, and they do so by mutual negotiations. Each player brings to the activity an individualistic inner meaning, constructed in the person's unique contexts and experiences (Bretherton, 1984, 1989; Schank

& Ableson, 1977). As the joint activity takes place, children seek to integrate their individual experiences in the attempt to establish a joint action plan as they may simultaneously hold onto their idiosyncratic meaning (Fein, 1989, p. 354; Schank & Ableson, 1977).

The second feature of sociodramatic play—that is, object use in play and its contribution to narrative construction—was our central concern in the intervention reported in this chapter. As pretense evolves with real or replica objects, players first need to agree on the meaning and use of these realistic objects. Upon this agreement, children build an "as if" reality of their own. They need to do so in order to activate imagination that enables the departure from the real and the transmission of "inner" meaning. The nonreal–imaginative "as if" sphere of play affords the child an opportunity to overcome constraints of time, locale, and actual play objects that dominate reality (Weininger, 1986). Children's ability to distance themselves from the real environment influences the level of play (Johnson, Christie, & Yawkey, 1987) and the construction of imaginative narratives.

Children's use of objects in constructing their representations has been characterized as two hierarchic transformations: object and ideational (Göncü & Kessel, 1988; Matthews, 1977; McLoyd, 1980; Pellegrini, 1991). Object transformations are functionally related to real objects (e.g., a stick becomes a horse). Ideational transformations are ostensibly free from real objects present in the play environment (e.g., pretending to be a witch).

Children are expected to use more ideational transformations as they develop (i.e., distance themselves from the play environment in constructing imaginative activities). Low standards of play were typified in studies of object transformations, where the immediate properties of toys, objects, and props were central in children's play, dictating children's associations and actions. In contrast, when children use ideational transformations, children's play reaches dimensions such as decontextualization where objects are used in the service of children's preplanned plot (Johnson et al., 1987; Shefatya, 1990; Smilansky, 1968; Smilansky & Shefatya, 1990). Thus, children can act symbolically on a fantastic level of play only when they are free from the associative connotations of the objects, toys, and props of the immediate environment and of their physical features (Piaget, 1962; Smith, Gore, & Vollstedt, 1986). Such use of ideational transformations is possible through the use of imaginative, secondary, mental processes (Fein, 1987, 1989; Frijda, 1988). In our view, this ability of the child to free him- or herself from the domination of the actual object and to activate imagination to construct narrative is the heart of pretend play.

PLAY INTERVENTIONS, IMAGINATION, AND THE NARRATIVE

Studies of pretend play reveal that children differ in their play competence. Some are superplayers (Fein, 1987, 1989), some play ordinarily, and others play rather dull narratives or hardly play at all. Some researchers claim that the latter come mostly—but not always—from lower socioeconomic status (SES) groups. Their play is lacking in quality and in quantity of basic sociodramatic play categories, and they demonstrate low use of play objects (Johnson et al., 1987; Shefatya, 1990; Smilansky, 1968; Smilansky & Shefatya, 1990). Other researchers oppose this notion, claiming that the gaps found are not indicative of the subjects' disadvantage but are an artifact of the studies' methodological and conceptual shortcomings (Göncü, 1999; McLoyd, 1982; Schwartzman, 1978). Others claim that variability in children's play performance is a result of development. For instance, at 3 years children's stories are dependent on actual objects, props, and body movements, whereas at 5 years words and images take the place of objects and activities (Scarlett & Wolf, 1979). Still others argue that a high level of play depends on adequate prior training (Martinez, Cheyney, & Teale, 1991).

Observations performed in various Israeli kindergarten classes and nursery schools indicated that play was becoming extinct and only a few children were occupying the home, kitchen, or sick bay/infirmary play areas. Most of the play scripts of those who were playing were dull and repetitive, showing the same roles and actions day after day and using play objects mainly at the level of object transformations. Kindergarten children were busy most of their time with "learning" tasks, which left little time for free play. Elkind (1990) complains about the same trend in other Western societies that emphasize academic achievement. Thus, it seemed that we had to intervene not only to facilitate children's narratives through imaginative use of objects at the ideational level of transformations but to reintroduce pretend play and its appreciation to kindergarten teachers.

In view of these considerations, we have examined the previous interventions with the purpose of drawing from them in constructing our own intervention program. In general, we found that previous interventions did not attend to facilitation of imagination or narrative. For one group of interventions the purpose was to built on imitative role play and widening repertoires of children's knowledge base (Smilansky, 1968; Smilansky & Shefatya, 1990; Wood, McMahon, & Cranstoun, 1980; Woodward, 1984). A second group of interventions used adults to mediate between children and their reality experiences (Johnson et al., 1987). A third group of interventions provided a theme and suitable materials for play (Dansky, 1980; Smith & Syddall, 1978) or encouraged children to reenact roles of thematic fantasy tales (Saltz, Dixon, & Johnson, 1977; Williamson & Silvern, 1991). In a fourth group of interventions, children made up their own stories (DeMille, 1973; Freyberg, 1973) or combined both methods of reenacting roles of thematic fantasy tales and making up their own stories (Singer & Singer, 1977; Udwin, 1983). Only in this fourth group of studies did intervention focus on the narrative aspects of children's play. However, similar to other intervention efforts, these studies did not support children's free and imaginative use of objects as a result of the fact that adults introduced and directed the narratives. Therefore, we devised an intervention with the emphasis of gradually increasing the imaginative use of play objects within the context of a spontaneous social interaction.

The twofold aims of the study were to test the hypothesis that improving the imaginative power of children by using a specific intervention will produce a better narrative quality and quantity of sociodramatic play and to understand the structure and complexity of sociodramatic play as a negotiated narrative. The results relating to the first purpose (i.e., the effect of the intervention on the narrative) are reported here. The results pertaining to the second purpose are presented only partially, as they relate to the narrative. It was hypothesized that intervention aimed to enhance the imaginative power of children of both low- and medium-SES background would improve their sociodramatic play narratives in quantity and quality.

METHOD

Sample

Participants were 349 children, attending 16 kindergarten classes in four towns of two central districts of Israel. Average age was 66 months old (range 56–72). Of the 349 children, 174 were low-SES and 175 medium-SES. The kindergarten classes were randomly divided into an experimental group (receiving intervention) and a control group (receiving enrichment sessions). No differences were found in SES and verbal IQ (Peabody Picture Vocabulary Test—Revised; PPVT-R) between the experimental and control groups. An interaction was found between SES and IQ across groups, showing that children in lower SES were also lower in their IQ than middle-SES children.

Measures

The measures presented here were used to analyze children's pretend play plots derived from our naturalistic observations. We conducted observations at each kindergarten three times before the intervention started to form a baseline, and three times after the intervention ended, to measure children's progress. Each observation included one plot of the playing group. A total of 96 play plots were observed, half of these comprised the baseline and the remaining half comprised the post-intervention observations. Observations of all play plots were both tape-recorded and recorded in writing. Children's speech and actions, descriptions of play objects and props, and their usage were included in the written recordings. Each session was transcribed, combining data from both sources. Some plots were videotaped for purposes of teacher education and reliability analyses. All scripts had to pass two basic preset threshold standards in order to enter the analysis: Smilansky's (Smilansky & Shefatya, 1990) definition of sociodramatic play (all six components) and Howes's (1980) highest two features of social play interaction. Only those plots meeting these criteria were included in the analysis. All play scripts were analyzed double-blinded by three scorers. Interscorer reliability of scoring for each measure was found high between each pair of the three scorers (range of $r = .80$ to $r = 1.00$). Cronbach coefficient alpha was also found high (in the range of $\alpha = .88$ to $\alpha = .95$).

Consistent with the theoretical background adopted in the study, our measures pertain to (1) the narrative quality and (2) the level of imaginative object use.

Narrative Quality

Narrative quality[1] is defined by its organization of form (Applebee, 1978; Pellegrini, 1985; Wolf & Grollman, 1982), complexity of structure (Eckler & Weininger, 1989; Glaubman, 1992; Kroll & Anson, 1984; Mandler, 1984; Mandler & Johnson, 1977; Rumelhart, 1977), and level of content (Bruner, 1990; Fein, 1989). Thus, the narrative quality consisted of three subscales corresponding to organization, complexity and content of narrative.

1. Organization of Form (OoF) (Applebee, 1978) is a 6-point scale of organization and structure of the narrative from low—collection of disconnected events—to high—well-organized coherent narrative.

2. Complexity of Pretense Play Plot (CoPPP) (Glaubman, 1992) is a 14-subscale measure with four sections: organization of ideas and thoughts (five subscales), flexibility and complexity (four subscales), originality and innovation (three subscales), and fluency (two subscales).[2]

3. Ordinariness–Exceptional–Fantasy Scale (OEFS) (Fein, 1989) is a 5-point scale measuring the level of content of pretend plots, from mundane to fantastic.

Imagination

Imagination was measured by a protocol called Level of Imaginative Object Use (LIOU) (Glaubman, 1992; Johnson et al., 1987; Smilansky & Shefatyah, 1990). This protocol consists of three subscales, each yielding a score of 1 (low) to 5 (high) points.

1. The first subscale measures the reality level of the *objects* used, from lowest, real concrete (i.e., drinking from real cup and saucer) to substitution (i.e., drinking from an empty playing block), and to imagined nonexisting "as–if" "objects" (i.e., drinking from an imagined cup).

2. The second subscale measures the *activity* level of usage. On the lower level is associative activity (a child talks on the present phone; another, by the mirror, wears lady's dress and shoes, etc.). At the higher level is preplanned imagined activity (a child playing a king puts a pretend crown on his head, telling his playmates to watch, while the queen orders her servant to decorate the throne (an empty space).

3. The third subscale measures contingency of the *play ideas* to the actual objects in the play area. At the lower level ideas are contingent to the objects (pretending to cook when seeing a pot on the kitchen oven; being sick at the sick bay). At the highest, ideas are fully ideational (pretending to watch a movie on a blank wall, telling a girl standing there that she is blocking their sight).

Statistical Controls and Related Measures

We were concerned about identifying the effect of the intervention apart from other potentially effective aspects of children's lives. Children's SES and IQ were found in prior studies as effecting their quality of pretend play (Johnson et al., 1987; Shefatya, 1990; Smilansky, 1968; Smilansky & Shefatya, 1990). In addition, to make certain that our intervention was responsible for the results, not children's creativity (which shares some characteristics with imagination) or their teacher's prior experience, it seemed necessary to control for these variables. Consequently, we collected data about four variables, planning to use them as covariates. These were (1) SES, as measured by Rand (1975); (2) verbal intelligence, as measured by the PPVT-R (Dunn & Dunn, 1981); (3) creativity, as measured by the Alternative Uses Test (Guilford, 1959); and (4) teacher's experience, as measured by years of teaching experience.

Procedure

Intervention continued for 3 months. The kindergarten teachers determined the experimental and control groups with the assistance of the researchers. Intervention sessions were integrated into the regular class teaching activities and conducted in small groups of children, with six to eight meetings per small group and eight sessions with the whole class. All teachers were instructed to avoid any adult intervention in the natural course of play (unless children's safety was at stake). All teachers, experimental as well as control, were advised to set in the daily schedule at least three-quarters of an hour for children's free play in the play areas and to place all intervention objects among the other objects in the play areas.

Meetings with Teachers and Enrichment in the Control Group

The researchers met with all 16 teachers of both experimental and control groups in five general meetings. In the first three joint meetings, discussions included general knowledge about play and play interventions, emphasizing especially the importance of sociodramatic play. The fourth meeting was held toward the end of the intervention period, and the main subject of discussion was the narrative. The fifth meeting was held toward the end of the study to report the results to the teachers. In between meetings, the researchers visited the classes to control for equal conditions (of teacher attention, playtime, play opportunities, and quantity and quality of play objects in the play areas), collect data, and observe the teacher's interventions and demonstrate or give extra guidance when needed.

In addition to these five meetings, three additional meetings were held with the experimental group's teachers, aimed for reciprocal learning and clarifying of the specific intervention guidelines, using videotaped sessions and a visit to one of the kindergartens for demonstration. Two additional meetings were held with the control group's teachers, discussing the importance and benefits of play, the various methods of play intervention, how to read play scripts, ideas of play enrichment, and so on. Work with control group teachers also included a visit to the demonstration center.

Because the control group teachers participated in some of the meetings, they also learned about the various aspects of children's sociodramatic play, including analysis of a pretend play episode for its narrative quality. Thus, they received the same information and basic knowledge as the experimental group teachers. The differences between experimental and control groups were, therefore, only in the training in the specific intervention that the experimental group teachers received. The control group teachers were generally advised to encourage children's play but did not receive any specific directions in the way they should intervene to facilitate it. This was left for their consideration.

The Intervention Program in the Experimental Group

The intervention consisted of four stages leading to imaginative use of play objects. In constructing the intervention, we adhered to the following guidelines:

1. We instructed the teachers to intervene only in out-of-play situations, in short and intensive episodes (20-minute sessions). They were asked never to intervene in children's in-play sessions.
2. All activities were aimed at encouraging children's spontaneity and minimizing the role of the adult during children's play activities. Teachers were to observe the play areas and to follow natural play developments for further interventions.
3. The intervention was gradual and took place in a stage-by-stage fashion. It evolved from working with a small group of children to working with the whole group and giving children the opportunity to develop their play ideas while negotiating with others. When needed, the teacher used one to one intervention, recommending the involvement of superplayers who were more advanced in their imagination than the children included in the intervention (Fein, 1987).

Stage 1: Enacting with Familiar Objects

This stage was performed with one familiar object at a time. After establishing full familiarity with an object (a cup, a torch) by passing it from one child to another and commenting on its features, the children dramatized the use of the object, with only assisting cues from the teacher. The purpose at this stage was to assist the children to develop full-blown ideas of their own choice. The cues referred to participating "people" (e.g., child, mother, and grandfather) who jointly carry out "actions" (eating, traveling) in various settings (e.g., kitchen and garden), possibly adding more people and objects when needed. It was important that a few children played together to create a joint idea (e.g., grandfather comes for a visit, and the family is eating dinner together) and each of them played a different role of their own choice. Children, in turn, negotiated among themselves the ideas, roles, and actions in their ensuing activities. The children were required to construct a logical ending of the session when they wanted to stop, without cutting short their ongoing activity (e.g., parting from the grandfather who is going back to his own house).

Stage 2: Enacting with Multiple and Substitution Objects

This stage was performed alternatively with two types of objects: The first group had a few familiar but unrelated objects (e.g., comb and plate or teddy bear, fork, and hat). The second group were obscure objects with which the children were not familiar (e.g., a plastic circle, a tree twig, or part of broken toy). The purpose of this stage was to further develop children's ability to dramatize by negotiating around increasingly complex objects. The teacher assisted the children with cues only when necessary, encouraging them to discuss among themselves what should be done next. As in the first stage, here and in following stages cues referred to "people" who jointly carry out "actions" in various situations, possibly adding more people and objects when needed and possibly referring to props (e.g., box as table or cloth as garment). Each activity involved more than one child interacting with other participants who jointly created situations. Here, too, children were required to construct a logical ending of the session when they wanted to stop the event, without cutting short their ongoing activity. It was the teacher's responsibility to see to it that her involvement diminished as the children's fluency increased, before moving on to the next stage.

Stage 3: Enacting with Imaginative "Objects"

The purpose of this stage was to free the children from depending on concrete objects to develop a narrated drama. The initiating "object" is completely imaginative (e.g., an imaginative pumpkin in an empty box and a butterfly "held" in a closed empty palm). There is nothing concrete to refer to, but the children play as if they were actors performing actions in certain settings with the "objects" present, adding more "objects" as needed. The supposed "object" may be introduced by the teacher or by any child who wishes to do so. Additional objects introduced along the plot may be real, substitute, or imaginative. It is essential that all ideas are initiated by the children (taking the pumpkin to a picnic ground, cooking it on fire, etc.).

Stage 4: Complicating the Plot Structure

When children were successful in developing fluent ideas around objects (real, substitute or imaginative), the teacher introduced the last stage, with the purpose of developing the quality element of the narrated drama, the "plot complexity." While the children enacted something of their initiative, she interrupted the course of events by saying such things as "Oh, what has happened . . . ," or "all of a sudden something came across . . . ," or "Oh, what an accident," or "Listen, the phone is ringing," and so on. The children took the cue and reacted to it, introducing a complexity to their acting.

Within each stage, the teachers were free to use different strategies in enhancing children's play with the purpose of keeping children interested and initiating. The teacher tried to keep children away from rote repetition that might lead to boredom and disinterest. Teachers' strategies involved introducing ideas about use of an object, a role (who are you?), a locality (where are you?), an action (what are you doing?), a picture that the teacher or the children observed in a book or a painting, or even the beginning of an imaginative story.

RESULTS

The total number of plots (*n*) was 96. Each plot transcript was divided into separate sequentially numbered lines of speech (e.g., "Boy: Let's play tennis, Daddy") or action units ("Mom: *as if she is eating ice cream*"). Analyses of the plots were based on these speech and action units (see the example in the appendix).

All measures were analyzed by the Statistical Analysis System package for the computer. MANCOVA (Multivariate Analysis of Covariance) of all measures revealed significant differences in the pretest for SES background of the participants. Thus, the intervention effects between experimental and control groups were separately computed for low- and medium-SES background groups. (All means and standard deviations were computed as Z-scores.) Table 6.1 presents means, standard deviations, and significance of all narrative measures in a three-way factorial design of 2 SES (low- and medium) × 2 Intervention (experimental and control) × 2 Time (pre- and postintervention) with Time being the repeated measure. Covariance was computed to control for IQ (PPVT-R), Creativity, and teacher's experience, in both pre- and posttests.

Results are also presented in Figure 6.1 for each of the measures as follows: (a) Level of Imaginative Object Use; (b) Organization of Narrative Form; (c) Complexity of Plot in Pretense Play; (d) Ordinariness–Exceptional–Fantasy Scale of Contents.

No differences were found between experimental and control groups in any measure except for complexity of play plot during the pretest. As reported in Table 6.1 and in the figures, results clearly indicate that intervention had an overall effect. In addition, we found interaction effects of time by intervention in each of the measures, pointing to the significant effect of the intervention on each of the abilities measured, as compared with baseline scores. However, it should be noted that the large standard deviations in posttest scores indicate that intervention may have not been equally beneficial for all children.[3]

With regard to SES, both low- and medium-SES experimental

TABLE 6.1. Means, Standard Deviations, and Analysis of Covariance (ANCOVA) of Narrative Measures

	Low SES				Medium SES			
	Control		Experimental		Control		Experimental	
Measures	Pre	Post	Pre	Post	Pre	Post	Pre	Post
Object use								
M	−.89	−.67	−.67	1.90	.95	.61	1.12	3.24
SD	.38	.45	.67	1.0	.78	.53	1.17	1.0
Organization								
M	−.78	−.91	−.90	1.57	.79	.79	.92	4.04
SD	.45	.00	.00	1.41	.45	1.56	.90	1.46
Complexity								
M	−.60	−.71	−.88	.31	.24	.12	−.20	2.21
SD	.17	.16	.18	.76	.34	.47	.29	.60
Content								
M	−.40	−.52	−1.00	.78	.79	.79	.79	2.10
SD	.74	.70	.00	.65	.89	1.24	.89	.82

Note. The analyses are based on Z-scores because of different ranges of the various measures. Full statistics for the analyses are available from Rivka Glaubman. The number of plots observed is 96, but analyzed for 48 in the repeated-measures ANCOVA. All p's for interaction < .001.

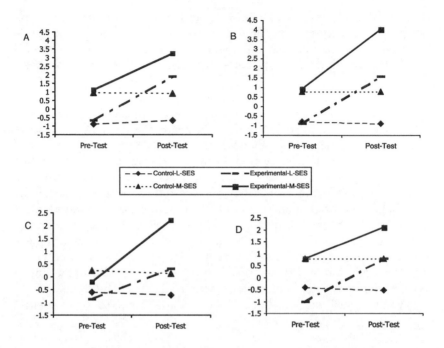

FIGURE 6.1. Pre- and postmean scores for narrative measures. The number of plots = 96. (A) Imaginative Level of Object Use; (B) Organization of Form; (C) Complexity of Plot; (D) Ordinariness–Fantasy of Content

groups progressed significantly from pre- to posttest as a result of the intervention, although the lower-SES children were lower in all measures as compared to their medium-SES counterparts in both experimental and control groups. However, the low-SES children in the intervention group gained greater imaginative and narrative scores than their peers in the medium-SES control group who had a better head start, as may be seen from the baseline scores. In contrast, the performance of low- and medium-SES children in the control group did not change either in imaginative object use or in any of the play narrative measures.

Although both lower-SES as well as medium-SES children in the experimental group improved as a result of the intervention, the gap between them varied in the different measures. In two of the measures, the LIOU and Ordinariness–Fantasy Scale of Contents, the gaps between the experimental medium- and low-SES groups narrowed in time. The Time by SES interaction on these two measures can be seen in Table 6.1 and in Figures 6.1a and 6.1d. In contrast, on the measure of

Complexity of Plot, the gap between the different SES experimental groups widened in time. A triple interaction of Time by Intervention by SES on this measure points to this gap ($F(7,40) = 9.8$; $p < .001$). This may be seen more clearly in Figure 6.1c. Finally, on Organization of Form, the gap between the two groups remained the same over time.

With regard to the effects of covariates, no interactions were found between narrative measures and the three covariant variables, namely, Verbal IQ, creativity, or teacher's experience. The only relation that we found between any two covariates was a correlation between verbal IQ and creativity, and this was correlated with the LIOU in the post-intervention phase. However, these relations held for children both in the experimental and control groups, indicating that neither intelligence nor creativity contributed directly to the effects of the intervention in either group.

With regard to the connections between imaginative object use and narrative, we found significant correlations between measures of imaginative object use and all narrative measures ($r = .69$ to $r = .73$, $p < .001$). This supports our prediction. In addition, we found that narrative measures were also found highly interrelated ($r = .60$ to $r = .71$, $p < .001$). However, in comparison, intercorrelations of the same measures with communicative measures of language and communication were found of relatively weaker connection ($r = .45$ to $r = .56$, $p < .001$). Correlations between scales were found higher in postintervention than in pre-intervention ($r = .68$ to $r = .82$, $p < .001$).

In summary, in support of our expectation, the intervention facilitated imaginative power of children of both low- and medium-SES background and produced a better narrative quality and quantity of sociodramatic play. Although there was a gap between the low- and medium-SES children along the study, the lower-SES children gained greater imaginative and narrative scores than did their peers in the medium-SES control group and closed all gaps with them in all measures of narrative and imagination.

DISCUSSION

The present study aimed to examine the effect of empowering kindergarten children's imaginative object use on the narrative quality of sociodramatic play plots. The hypothesis was that intervention designed to improve children's imaginative power of object use incorporated into the kindergarten activities outside the frame of play would be effective in enhancing their in-play imaginative object use and narrative quality of sociodramatic play.

Overall results supported the hypothesis of the study. Children in the experimental, as compared to control group, from both low- and medium-SES background improved their sociodramatic play, imaginative object use, and narrative scores following the intervention. These results with additional findings are discussed next in relation to two major issues. First, we discuss the issue of sociodramatic play as narrative and the role of empowering imagination in relation to its narrative quality; second, we discuss the effects of personal and social variables, such as social class, creativity, and intelligence, on the quality of the play narrative.

Imagination and Narrative in Pretend Play

As hypothesized, imagination in play, as measured by imaginative object use, was highly connected with all narrative measures. Imaginative level of object use improved only in the experimental and not in the control group, and as a result, changes in the narrative level of the plots were found over time only for the former. The results substantiated the claim of Shoben (1980), Egan (1988), Singer and Singer (1990), and Udwin (1983) about "imagination as a means of growth" (Shoben, 1980, p. 21). Training conducted outside the classroom play setting was proven again to produce increments in classroom play setting as a result of an increased capability for spontaneous play (see review by Fein, 1981). Our findings are consistent with the results of previous studies in which intervention was introduced within the framework of play or thematic-story enactment (Christie, 1986; Freyberg, 1973; Singer & Singer, 1990; Udwin, 1983).

Our finding that the improvement in children's play was caused by our intervention rather than simply by time enables us to proffer the interpretation that the intervention had given children the opportunity to activate their "second mind" (Fein, 1989) and develop their ability for metarepresentation (Leslie, 1987) by decoupling objects from their real daily associative meanings. For example, the improvement in the scale of content sustained Fein's argument (1987) in showing that children were able to free themselves from the constraints of their immediate locale and time (Fein, 1987, 1989; Frijda, 1988). These findings show that the more able the children are with their imaginative power, the freer they become to enact their ideas on the fantasy level of content.

The development of decontextualized behavior uncoupled from real-world events is reflected in the orientation of pretense toward substitutional and imaginative objects (Fine, 1987; Johnson et al., 1987; Smilansky & Shefatya, 1990) or ideational transformations (McLoyd, 1980; Pellegrini, 1991). Yet, what characterizes pretend play as narrative is the capability of acting concurrently in dual-landscape contexts, on both levels of the mind—the daily reality and the interpretative imaginary (Bruner, 1990; Fein, 1989). This is necessary to enable children's negotiation with their peers for meaning making in the imaginary world. Indeed, the intervention allowed such negotiations to take place, leading to longer and more elaborate play scripts (Bruner, 1986, 1990; Westby, 1986).

We argued that to analyze pretend play plots as narratives it is necessary to use several measures, each covering a different feature of the narrative. Building on the previous studies that measured a relatively limited features of narrative (e.g., Eckler & Weininger, 1989; Roskos, 1988), the present study provides a thorough measure of narrative quality through its organization of form (Applebee, 1978), complexity of the plot (Glaubman, 1992), and ordinariness level of content (Fein, 1989). We feel that our measures fill the gap in the literature noted by Westby (1986). Our approach of focusing on different features of narratives allowed us to better understand children's functioning in the imaginative realm. For example, the complexity of plot revealed information beyond the formal structure of pretend narratives in addition to being highly correlated with the story grammar. The complexity measure covers multiple aspects of plot: its organization of ideas and thoughts, flexibility and complexity, originality and innovation, and fluency.

The various measures of the play narrative in the present study were found to be highly correlated. This pattern of correlations has two implications relating to the structure and to the construct of the measures. With regard to the structure, the correlation pattern supports our argument that the measures test different aspects of the same domain, corroborating Bruner's (1986) claim that the narrative can be interpreted only as a structural coherent whole unit, which is an integrated compound of its components. Additional support for this claim can be found in the emerging picture of the intervention effects on different narrative measures, each of which shows a similar trend of improvement as a result of intervention.

With regard to construct, the intercorrelations demonstrate higher correlations between measures that are conceptually connected (e.g., imagination, narrative form, structure, and content) and lower correlations between measures whose relations with one another are not theoretically elaborated (e.g., language and communication with imagination and narrative). This pattern supports the construct validity of the scales measuring narrative and the connection between imagination and narrative, according to the convergent and discriminant validation procedures suggested by Campbell and Fiske (1959).

To sum up, imaginative abilities of children and the narrative structures of their pretend play could be improved by an intervention.

However, we should note that such intervention might apply differentially to different children. As the children's scores increased following intervention, the standard deviations of their scores increased too. This suggests that some children were not affected by the intervention as much as others. Further studies should follow more closely play improvement of particular children, trying to identify the specific factors responsible for individual differences in the development of play quality.

Imagination, Narrative, and Background Variables

We turn now to the second issue of possible effects of other variables on the intervention results. SES of children was manifested as the most salient variable in this study. SES has been found to be a major source of effect on the level of pretend play (Fein, 1981; Shefatyah, 1990; Smilansky, 1968; Smilansky & Shefatyah, 1990). The differences that were found between SES levels in the present study, particularly in the baseline measures, are in accord with the previous findings. Improvement of dull sociodramatic play has been proven possible through intervention, as found also in other studies of children of low-SES background (see reviews in Johnson et al., 1987; Rubin, Fein, & Vandenberg, 1983; Shefatyah, 1990; Smilansky & Shefatyah, 1990).

The present study is unique in that it involved the same method of intervention for both medium- and low-SES-level kindergartens. Plots of the experimental group have improved significantly and positive effects were obtained as readily with lower-class as well as with middle-class children. The most intriguing results were that the experimental low-SES group obtained scores similar to or even surpassed those of the medium-SES control group children. The present findings are consistent with the findings of another study (Glaubman, 2000). In that study, we conducted the same intervention along two school years (preschool and kindergarten) and demonstrated even greater improvement of low-SES children's play as compared with the 1 year of intervention reported in this chapter. These results support the claim of Göncü (1999), McLoyd (1982), and Schwartzman (1978) that the findings of relatively low levels of imaginative play by low-SES children are not indicative of children's disadvantage but are an artifact of the studies' methodological and conceptual shortcomings. In the present study we saw that a proper treatment (i.e., the intervention) enables these children to overcome the barriers imposed on them by their social class and to play as imaginatively as their middle-class counterparts.

The achievements resulting from the study's special intervention did not relate to children's IQ, creativity, or the teacher's experience. Although creativity and IQ were found as significantly connected with the imaginative object use in the posttest, no interaction was found between these variables and any of the other measures. We tested children for creativity because of the claims that the narrative (Bruner, 1990) and pretend play are an interpretive–expressive system representing aspects of living (Fein, 1987) and are connected with the creative processes (Bretherton, 1984). Yet, as was revealed in the present study, neither IQ nor creativity had a direct effect on any of the measures.

An interesting finding was that the teacher's experience had no effect on any of the results. This means that young as well as veteran teachers can perform this rather simple and clear method of intervention successfully. It is worth mentioning that after the study ended, the kindergarten teachers who participated in the study incorporated, on their own initiative, the intervention procedure as a routine activity in their classrooms and found it to be a useful teaching method.

In conclusion, the intervention designed for raising the level of imagination in children's use of objects outside the frame of play was found to be effective. The intervention promoted higher imaginative use of play objects and better quality play narratives as measured by their structure, complexity, and level of contents. Following the intervention, play narratives of the experimental group, of both lower- and medium-SES children, improved in quality in regard to all measures. As such it may be useful for facilitating the developmental functions of play.

The present research has implications for both future research and early childhood education. With regard to the former, the instruments offered in the present research can be expanded to study other properties of pretend play narratives and their correlates. The implication of the present study for early childhood educators is that letting children play freely is not enough. The present study has substantiated Westby's (1986) claim that improving the level of narrative needs deliberate education of teachers in effective intervention methods. It has also substantiated the claim that raising the level of imagination is a crucial component in improving the quality of narrative in pretend play. The study has offered a specific strategy of intervention that proved to be easily accessible to all teachers. It emphasized that play intervention need not take place during actual play situations and that systematically improving children's imaginative use with object training is an effective means for improving the quality of their sociodramatic play narrative. Thus it offers an effective intervention for play improvement without interference in play spontaneity.

NOTES

1. Excluding here the component of social negotiation qualifier of play narrative (Fein, 1989; Williamson & Silvern, 1991).

2. The CoPPP scale was highly validated on the Story Grammar (Eckler & Weininger, 1989; Mandler & Johnson, 1977; Rumelhart, 1977), a measure widely accepted for measuring the cognitive structure of narratives ($r = .81$, $p < .001$).

3. The mere growing up and accumulating kindergarten experience rather than the intervention had an effect only on the Ordinariness–Exceptional–Fantasy scale of contents. This was indicated by the significant results of Time in this scale.

APPENDIX. AN EXCERPT
OF A PLAY-PLOT PREPARED FOR ANALYSIS

Group: Low SES
Place: At the home area   Time: Postintervention

1. MOM: Dani, collect all the things, honey, we are going to the beach.
2. DAD: (*Collects bags and all sorts of circles in a handbag.*)
3. DAD: (*to a boy*) Do you want to be our son? We are going to the beach.
4. BOY: Yes, come to the beach.
5. BOY: Let's play tennis, Daddy.
6. MOM: (*as if she is eating ice cream; they play as-if tennis*)
7. DAD: No! Hold it the other way 'round. Turn the racket over so the side that sticks out is up [as-if racket].
8. MOM (*In the meantime pretends to swim on the carpet.*)
9. BOY: Daddy, Daddy, I want you to buy me sun glasses and fruit. I'm going to buy some fruit.
10. (*Going to the grocery corner, where there is another boy as shopkeeper*)
11. BOY: How much is the fruit? (*Gives him a circle and takes plastic fruit.*)
12. BOY: I've come back. What are you going to do Daddy, diving?
   .
   .
   .
20. DAD: Yes! Look! (*Shows him the newspaper.*) Maybe it's a journey to Shefayim? (*They pretend to be reading together.*)
21. DAD: OK, Mommy, lunch! (*Takes out from the bag.*)
22. DAD: Yanir, come and eat lunch, we are leaving soon.
23. BOY: I'm coming, Dad.
24. SHOPKEEPER: (*approaching*) I have a sun tan cream if you want, and I also have Popsicles in my shop.
25. SHOPKEEPER: Come on, come and buy from me.

REFERENCES

Applebee, A. N. (1978). *The child's concept of story.* Chicago: University of Chicago Press.

Ariel, S. (1984). Locutions and illocutions. *Journal of Pragmatics, 8,* 221–240.

Astington, J. A., & Gopnik, A. (1991). Theoretical explanations of children's understanding of the mind. *British Journal of Developmental Psychology, 9,* 7–31.

Bateson, G. (1956). The message "This is play." In B. Schaffner (Ed.), *Group processes: Transactions of the second conference* (pp. 145–241). New York: Josiah Macy Jr. Foundation. Reprinted in R. E. Herron & B. Sutton-Smith (Eds.), *Child's play.* New York: Wiley.

Bretherton, I. (1984). Representing the social world in symbolic play: Reality and fantasy. In I. Bretherton (Ed.), *Symbolic play: The development of social understanding* (pp. 3–41). Orlando, FL: Academic Press.

Bretherton, I. (1989). Pretense: The form and function of make-believe play. *Developmental Review, 9*(4), 383–401.

Bruner, J. S. (1986). *Actual minds, possible worlds.* Cambridge, MA: Harvard University Press.

Bruner, J. (1990). *Acts of meaning.* Cambridge, MA: Harvard University Press.

Bruner, J. (1996). *The culture of education.* Cambridge, MA: Harvard University Press.

Campbell, D. T., & Fiske, D. W. (1959). Convergent and discriminant validation by the multitrait–multimethod matrix. *Psychological Bulletin, 56*(2), 81–105.

Chafe, W. (1990). Some things that narratives tell us about the mind. In B. K. Britton & A. D. Pellegrini (Eds.), *Narrative thought and narrative language* (pp. 79–98). Hillsdale, NJ: Erlbaum.

Christie, J. F. (1986). Training of Symbolic play. In P. K. Smith (Ed.), *Children's play: Research developments and practical applications* (pp. 57–66). New York: Gordon & Breach.

Dansky, J. L. (1980). Cognitive consequences of sociodramatic play and exploration training for economically disadvantaged preschoolers. *Journal of Child Psychology and Psychiatry, 20,* 47–58.

DeMille, R. (1973). *Put your mother on the ceiling: Children's imagination games.* New York: Viking.

Dunn, L., & Dunn, L. N. (1981). *PPVT-R—Peabody Picture Vocabulary Test—Revised.* Circle Pines, MN: American Guidance Service, Inc.

Eckler, J. A., & Weininger, O. (1989). Structural parallels between play and narratives. *Developmental Psychology, 25*(5), 736–743.

Egan, K. (1988). *Primary understanding: Education in early childhood.* New York: Routledge.

Elgas, P. M., Klein, E., Kantor, R., & Fernie, D. E. (1988). Play and the per culture: Play styles and object use. *Journal of Research in Childhood Education 3*(2), 142–153.

Elkind, D. (1990). Too much, too soon. In E. Klugman, & S. Smilansky (Eds.),

Children's play and learning, perspectives and policy implications (pp. 3–17). New York: Teachers College Press.

Fein, G. G. (1981). Pretend play in childhood: An integrative review. *Child Development, 52,* 1095–1118.

Fein, G. G. (1987). Pretend play: Creativity and consciousness. In D. Gorlitz & J. F. Wohlwill (Eds.), *Curiosity, imagination, and play: On the development of spontaneous cognitive and motivational processes* (pp. 282–304). Hillsdale, NJ: Erlbaum.

Fein, G. G. (1989). Mind, meaning and affect: Proposals for a theory of pretense. *Developmental Review, 9,* 345–363.

Flavell, J. H. (1992). Perspectives on perspective taking. In H. Beilin & P. Pufall (Eds.), *Piaget's theory: Prospects and possibilities* (pp. 107–139). Hillsdale, NJ: Erlbaum.

Freyberg, J. T. (1973). Increasing the imaginative play of urban disadvantaged kindergarten children through systematic training. In J. L. Singer (Ed.), *The child's world of make-believe* (pp. 129–154). New York: Academic Press.

Frijda, N. H. (1988). The laws of emotion. *American Psychologist, 43,* 349–358.

Galda, L. A. (1984). Narrative competence: Play, story telling and story comprehension. The development of oral and written language in social contents. In A. D. Pellegrini & T. D. Yawkey (Eds.), *Play language and stories* (pp. 105–117). Norwood, NJ: Ablex.

Gardner, H. (1980). Children's literary development: The realms of metaphors and stories. In P. McGhee & A. Chapman (Eds.), *Children's humor* (pp. 91–118). New York: Wiley.

Giffin, H. (1984). The coordination of meaning in the creation of a shared make-believe reality. In I. Bretherton (Ed.), *Symbolic play: The development of social understanding* (pp. 73–100). New York: Academic Press.

Glaubman, R. (1992, July). Sociodramatic play—the negotiated narrative. Paper presented at the Binational Science Foundation Summer Workshop, Wheelock College, Boston.

Glaubman, R. (2000). *Long-term imaginative facilitating of sociodramatic play: Effects on children's narrative- and social competence.* Manuscript in preparation.

Göncü, A. (1993a). Development of intersubjectivity in social pretend play. *Human Development, 36,* 185–198.

Göncü, A. (1993b). Development of intersubjectivity in the dyadic play of preschoolers. *Early Childhood Research Quarterly, 8*(1), 99–116.

Göncü, A. (1999). *Children's engagement in the world: Sociocultural perspectives.* New York: Cambridge University Press.

Göncü, A., & Kessel, F. (1988). Preschoolers' collaborative construction in planning and maintaining imaginative play. *International Journal of Behavioural Development, 11*(3), 327–344.

Guilford, J. P. (1959). *Personality.* New York: McGraw-Hill.

Howes, C. (1980). Peer play scale as index of complexity of peer interaction. *Developmental Psychology, 16,* 371–372.

Hughes, M. (1987). The relationship between symbolic and manipulative (object) play. In D. Gorlitz & J. F. Wohlwill (Eds.), *Curiosity, imagination, and play* (pp. 245–257). Hillsdale, NJ: Erlbaum.

Johnson, J. E., Christie, J. F., & Yawkey, T. D. (1987). *Play and early childhood development*. Glenview, IL: Scott, Foresman.

Kroll, B. M., & Anson, C. M. (1984). Analysing structure in children's fictional narratives. In H. Cowie (Ed.), *The development of children's imaginative writing* (pp. 153–183). London & Canberra: Croom Helm.

Leslie, A. M. (1987). Pretense and representations: The origin of "Theory of Mind." *Psychological Review, 4,* 412–426.

Mandler, J. M., & Johnson, N. C. (1977). Remembrance of things parsed: Story structure and recall. *Cognitive Psychology, 9,* 11–151.

Mandler, J. S. (1984). *Stories, scripts and scenes: Aspects of schema story.* Hillsdale, NJ: Erlbaum.

Martinez, M., Cheyney, M., & Teale, W. H. (1991). Classroom literature activities and kindergarten's dramatic story reenactment. In J. F. Christie (Ed.), *Play and early literacy development* (pp. 119–140). New York: State University of New York Press.

Matthews, W. S. (1977). Modes of transformation in the initiation of fantasy play. *Developmental Psychology, 13,* 212–216.

McLoyd, V. (1980). Verbally expressed modes of transformation in the fantasy and play of black preschool children. *Child Development, 51,* 1133–1139.

McLoyd, V. (1982). Social class differences in sociodramatic play: A critical review. *Developmental Review, 2*(1), 1–30.

Olson, D. R. (1990). Thinking about narrative. In B. K. Britton & A. D. Pellegrini (Eds.), *Narrative thought and narrative language* (pp. 99–111). Hillsdale, NJ: Erlbaum.

Pellegrini, A. D. (1985). The narrative organisation of children's fantasy play: The effects of age and play context. *Educational Psychology, 5*(1), 17–25.

Pellegrini, A. D. (1991). *Applied child study: A developmental approach* (2nd ed.). Hillsdale, NJ: Erlbaum.

Perner, J., & Astington, J. W. (1992). The child's understanding of mental representation. In H. Beilin & P. Pufall (Eds.), *Piaget's theory: Prospects and possibilities* (pp. 141–160). Hillsdale, NJ: Erlbaum.

Piaget, J. (1962). *Play dreams and imitation in childhood.* New York: Norton.

Rand, Y. (1975). *Dependance a l'egard du champ et culturelle.* Paris: Centre National de ka Recherche Scientifique.

Roskos, K. (1988). Literacy at work in play. *Reading Teacher, 41*(6), 562–567.

Rubin, K. H., Fein, G. G., & Vandenberg, B. (1983). Play. In P. H. Mussen, & E. M. Hetherington (Eds.), *Handbook of child psychology. Vol. 4. Socialization, personality and social development* (4th ed., pp. 694–774). New York: Wiley.

Rumelhart, D. (1977). Understanding and summarizing brief stories. In D. Laberge & S. J. Samuels (Eds.), *Basic processes in reading: Perception and comprehension* (pp. 265–303). Hillsdale, NJ: Erlbaum.

Sabbagh, M. A., & Callanan, M. A. (1998). Metarepresentation in action: 3–, 4–, and 5–year-olds' developing theories of mind in parent–child conversations. *Developmental Psychology, 34*(3), 491–502.

Saltz, E., Dixon, D., & Johnson, J. (1977). Training disadvantaged preschoolers on various fantasy activities: Effects on cognitive functioning and impulse control. *Child Development, 48,* 367–380.

Scarlett, W. G., & Wolf, D. (1979). When it's only make-believe: The construction of a boundary between fantasy and reality in storytelling. In E. Winner & H. Gardner (Eds.), *Fact, fiction and fantasy in childhood* (pp. 29–40). San Francisco: Jossey-Bass.

Schank, R. C., & Ableson, R. P. (1977). *Scripts, plans, goals and understanding.* Hillsdale, NJ: Erlbaum.

Schwartzman, H. B. (1978). *Transformations: The anthropology of children's play.* New York: Plenum.

Shefatya, L. (1990). Socioeconomic status and ethnic differences in sociodramatic play: Theoretical and practical implications. In E. Klugman, & S. Smilansky (Eds.), *Children's play and learning, perspectives and policy implications* (pp. 137–155). New York: Teachers College Press.

Shoben, E. J., Jr. (1980). The imagination as a means of growth. In J. E. Shorr, G. E. Sobel, P. Robin, & J. A. Connella (Eds.), *Imagery, its many dimensions and applications* (pp. 21–33). New York & London: Plenum.

Singer, D. G., & Singer, J. L. (1977). *Partners in play: A step-by-step guide to imaginative play in children.* New York: Harper & Row.

Singer, D. G., & Singer, J. L. (1990). *The house of make-believe: Play and the developing imagination.* Cambridge, MA: Harvard University Press.

Smilansky, S. (1968). *The effects of sociodramatic play on disadvantaged preschool children.* New York: Wiley.

Smilansky, S., & Shefatya, L. (1990). *Facilitating play: A medium for promoting cognitive, socioemotional and academic development in young children.* Gaithersburg, ND: Psychological and Educational Press.

Smith, P. K., Gore, M. T., & Vollstedt, R. (1986). Play in young children, problems of definition, categorization and measurement. In P. K. Smith (Ed.), *Children's play: Research development and practical applications* (pp. 39–57). New York: Gordon & Breach.

Smith, P. K., & Syddall, S. (1978). Play and non-play tutoring in preschool children: Is it play or tutoring which matters? *British Journal of Educational Psychology, 48,* 315–325.

Sutton-Smith, B. (1986). The development of fictional narrative performances. *Topics in Language Disorders, 7*(1), 1–10.

Sutton-Smith, B. (1997). *The ambiguity of play.* Cambridge, MA: Harvard University Press.

Udwin, O. (1983). Imaginative play training as an intervention method with institutionalized preschool children. *British Journal of Educational Psychology, 53*(1), 32–39.

Weininger, O. (1986). "What if" and "as if": Imagination and pretend play in early childhood. *International Journal of Early Childhood, 18*(1), 22–29.

Westby, C. E. (1986). Foreword (Issue Ed.). *Topics in Language Disorders, 7*(1), iv–vi.

Williamson, P. A., & Silvern, S. B. (1991). "You can't be Grandma: You're a boy": Events within the thematic fantasy play context which contribute to story comprehension. *Early Childhood Research Quarterly, 7,* 75–93.

Wolf, D., & Grollman, S. H. (1982). Ways of playing: Individual differences in imaginative style. In D. J. Pepler & K. H. Rubin (Eds.), *The play of children: Current theory and research*. Basel, Switzerland: Karger.

Wolf, P. D., Rygh. J., & Altshuler, J. (1984). Agency and experience: Actions and states in play narratives. In I. Bretherton (Ed.), *Symbolic play: The development of social understanding* (pp. 195–217). New York: Academic Press.

Wood, D., McMahon, L., & Cranstoun, Y. (1980). *Working with under fives*. Ypsilanti, MI: High/Scope Press.

Woodward, C. (1984). Guidelines for facilitating sociodramatic play. *Childhood Education, 60*, 172–177.

Woolley, J. D. (1995). The fictional mind: Young children's understanding of imagination, pretense, and dreams. *Developmental Review, 15*, 172–211.

Woolley, J. D., & Wellman, H. M. (1993). Origin and truth: Young children's understanding of imaginary mental representations. *Child Development, 64*, 1–17.

PART III

❧

Children in Story

7

Emotional Breaches in Play and Narrative

BRIAN SUTTON-SMITH

I first got to know Greta G. Fein through a series of play-centered collo-
quia at various psychology conferences over a number of years in the
1970s in association with Jerome L. Singer and Katherine Garvey. I
loved the way she could get delighted by ideas. Particularly if she
sensed a contrary possibility, you could feel her busting "in" all over.
Her mode was a nonbelligerent but excitedly incisive, "Yes/But," and
always well humored. She is one of the few I have known who are out-
standing on the three major grounds of understanding early childhood
educational practice, doing very clever and relevant experiments, and
constantly searching to reshape the theoretical paradigms within which
she is working. For me, her experiments on stereotypical or creative
play with toys and her recent experiment on toys and stories are clas-
sics. Most important, I respect her willingness to bust loose from the
idealization of play that has been central to the folk wisdom of early
childhood academia. Although it is nice to have good feelings about
children's play, it is not always a good way to know how important that
play is to children.

The present chapter derives in part from the centrality Greta gave
to the emotional aspects of play in her article "Pretend Play: Creativity
and Consciousness" (1987; Fein & Kinney, 1994). This was a study of 15
master players from 15 different classrooms whose pretend play she
found to be characterized by referential freedom, denotative license, af-

fective relationships, sequential uncertainty, and self-mirroring. (Also see Chapter 5 by Bondioli, Chapter 6 by Glaubman et al., and Chapter 8 by Herman and Bretherton, this volume, for a discussion of affective theory.) The focus here is on what she said about the affective relationships in that study which was that "pretense is charged with feelings as intense as those characteristic of attachment and it expresses thoughts as intricate as those conveyed in language" (Fein, 1987, p. 282).

> Although divergent thinking is characterized by novel and original associations, most theorists exclude bizarre or inappropriate associations from their definitions of novelty and originality. In pretend play, however, there is often ludicrous distortion, exaggeration, and extravagance, at times bordering on the bizarre. At the same time, the distortion, exaggeration and extravagance reveal a considerable degree of force. Although psychoanalytic theory offers the only extant affective interpretation of pretense . . . research within this perspective has been limited to the notion of carthasis. In contrast, cognitive theorists have all but ignored the affective side of pretense. (Fein, 1987, p. 291)

These affective representations are not scripts about everyday life, but rather "the [children] are . . . playing with representations of their own affective knowledge . . . I am proposing a double-layered system of representations, one for practical knowledge and another for affective knowledge. This double layered system emerges during the third year of life as pretend sequences become increasingly marked by nonstereotyped, personal inventions" (Fein, 1987, p. 300). In what follows, another double-layered system is introduced that makes some, but not complete, parallels with that presented here by Fein.

In a more recent article on narrative, Fein (1995) applies the same attitude about the critical role of emotion in play interpretation and applies it to children's story making. She says, "Children's knowledge of ordinary events may be important in their daily conduct but for storytelling or other narrative processes, it is their emotional meaning that makes events memorable and tellable" (p. 161). Her research shows that when children are stimulated to tell emotionally exciting stories (socalled breach stories) they work on a higher structural level, tell more stories, and introduce more extreme emotionality (villainy) in the plots (cf. Chapter 8 by Herman and Bretherton and Chapter 9 by Pellegrini and Galda, this volume).

It is the aim of this chapter, following Fein, to search further for the origins and nature of the emotionality involved in play and in stories. Treating the two together instead of separately has many justifications. Stewart (1978) says:

The work of fictions and the work of play both involve: (1) a reframing of messages; (2) a manipulation of contexts, that is, a decontextualization and a reconextualization; (3) a set of procedures for interpretation that may or may not pertain to the everyday world; (4) metacommunication; (5) reflexivity (and therefore); (6) paradox; (7) representation; and (8) the "not really true"and/or the "not really here and now," that is, a domain other than the everyday life domain. (p. 36)

What needs to be added, though not further studied here, is that in children's own imaginative practice of play, the two elements, play and narrative, are usually conjoined and often also allied with rituals, games, and dramatizations. Their ludic construction of reality is a complexity that our concepts of separate symbolic forms do not always fully engage (Kelly-Byrne & Sutton-Smith, 1983). In what follows, there is a pursuit of the paradoxical emotional nature of both play and narrative in an evolutionary as well as a contemporary perspective.

PLAY AS ORDER OR DISORDER

A preliminary route to demonstrating the paradoxical nature of play and narrative, and of emotional life, is to show that play theorists themselves have found themselves tending to describe play either in orderly terms or in disorderly terms. Allowing for the fact that there maybe ambiguity in some of these cases as to the category of placement, here are examples of these divided persuasions: First, *play as an orderly process* is assumed by most psychologists of this century apparently because they have endeavored to rationalize play as a useful socialization process. One interpretation might be that in order to surmount the older notions of play as a waste of time, they have had to show that it is a form of useful work in child development. All the following concepts are meant to indicate that play is a useful growth process. These play concepts view play as exploration (Berlyne), assimilation (Piaget), imagination (Singer), symbolism (Bretherton), playfulness (Barnett), the proximal zone of development (Vygotsky), mastery (Erikson), affect regulation (McDonald), relaxation (Patrick), intrinsic motivation (Rubin), flow (Csikzsentmihalyi), positive emotion (Lewis), autotelia and paratelia (Kerr), agentivity (Bruner), effectance (White), stress reduction (Bekoff), symbolic interaction (G. H. Mead), bonding (Harlow), surplus energy (Schiller), practice (Groos), and learning (Thorndike).

If the focus is shifted from childhood and psychology to other disciplines such as the humanities, sociology, anthropology, history, folklore, and biology, there are often quite different basic concepts about play. This is indicated, for example, by the following writers who find play often to be a *disorderly* emotional process but who are not particularly concerned with child growth. Names they give such play are grotesque realism (Bakhtin); anarchic power (Spariosu); deep play (Geertz); inversion (Babcock); dark play (Schechner); unsinn-wahnsinn (McMahon); nonsense (Stewart); panoply of tropes (Fernandez); play as disorderly, fragmentary, reversive (Fagen); the play of signifiers (Derrida); a dialectic of safety and risk (Myers); dissidence (Scott); transgressive (Stallybrass); stylized behavior (Abrahams); performance (Bauman); carnival (Falassi); ecstatic actions (Fink); fools (Fox); tricksters (Hughes); primordial negatives (Burke); willfulness (Nietzsche); desire (Hans); subjunctivity (Vaihinger); quirky variability (Gould); and exaggeration and galumphing (Miller).[1]

There are a few psychologists also who could be listed on this disorderly side of the issue. Most obvious are the depth psychologists. Their terms include play as transitional objects (Winnicott), wishful thinking and abreaction (Freud), carthasis (Menninger), and compensation (Peller). Academic psychologists of this ilk include the notion that play is instinctive (McDougall), recapitulatory (Hall), improvisational (Sawyer), divergent thinking (Lieberman), antidote (Elkind), unrealistic optimism (Bjorkland), and play as existential (Vandenberg).

PLAY AS PARADOXICAL

If the position is taken that both sets of theory content, orderly or disorderly, are probably taking hold of contrary parts of the epistemological ludic elephant, then it might perhaps be concluded that any adequate theory of play should include both of these fundamental aspects. And, in a sense this has already been done by a subsample of major play theorists who have labeled play as full of apparent contradictions. By this they mean that all play harbors contrary activities and that that is its central character. The forerunner was Gregory Bateson (1972), who viewed play as a paradox involving contradictions between reality and irreality. (The playful nip connotes a bite, but not what a bite connotes.) Others have suggested that play's paradox can also lie in the contrast between the safety that the play is supposed to ensure and the actual risks that are taken in the required performances that confront the player (Myers, in press). Although play is supposed to be just a pretense, there is quite a record of injuries associated with play and there are even types of play in which such dangers are actually included as part of the game, as in extreme gambling, Everest mountain climbing, and the eXtreme games displayed on the television station ESPN. Again, by contrast, there are those who find the play's paradox derives from the implicit contradiction between the individual's own private play fantasies and the dominating mythic fantasies of the larger culture (Goldman, 1998; Handelman, 1992). For others the paradox lies rather in the internal ludic conflicts between sense and nonsense, "Are you serious or are you just fooling" (Stewart, 1978), or even between nonsense and utter nonsense, attention to which was first called by Bakhtin (1984). In these cases it turns out that what was seen as nonsense (e.g., imitating a band using kitchen utensils as in medieval German carnivals) on closer inspection turns out to be actually a parody of such a performance because no one is really trying seriously to imitate the background music (McMahon, 1999).

My own early persuasion to call play a paradox or a dialectic (Sutton-Smith, 1978a, 1978b) between order and disorder arose from the study of games, with their two sides, their conflicting oppositions, and their resolutions. But, in particular, the key inspiration for this insight came from watching a number of 4- and 5-year-old girls attempting to play the singing game "Ring around the Roses," in which holding hands they all sang the words: "A ring around the roses, / A pocket full of posies, / Atishoo, atishoo / We all fall down" (Sutton-Smith, 1959). It was obvious that it was difficult for them to get their hands together and sing the words together and dance around as they did so. And, indeed, it was quite an achievement for all to arrive at the final point and to fall down on the ground at the same time that they were laughing heartily. It took a nose for order to be able to arrive at such a climax of disorder. It is indeed, perhaps, quite a paradox to use order for the sake of disorder. As Miller (1973) puts it astutely: "Play ... deals with the borderline between being in control and being out of control, but in play being in control is the frame within which you may safely be out of control" (p. 46; see also Miller, 1974). But whatever the immediate interpretation of these paradoxes, the important question they give rise to is why they exist in the first place. Why should play involve these binary elements? Why should play be a hunting ground for paradoxes?

A PARADOX OF EMOTIONS

Recent writing in neurology makes it possible for the first time to hypothetically reframe Bateson's brilliant thoughts about play's metacommunicative evolutionary and paradoxical function in neurological terms. The major source here is Antonio R. Damasio's book *Descartes' Error* (1994), in which he speaks of the mind's primary and secondary emotions that accompany different kinds of reflexiveness and consciousness from the very beginning of species evolution. He talks of primary emotions as being inherited from the reptiles and located in the archaic part of the brain known as the amygdala, which fires off without any conscious control in times of emergency. In reptiles and fish whose survival depends on constantly scanning for predators, this is their main brain system. In present times these emotions still occur for us when we are suddenly startled or threatened and our hearts beat faster, or we tremble or we perspire, or we are enraged at suffering a painful loss, or alternatively we are suddenly overwhelmed by feelings of surprise, triumph or joy, or love. With the coming of the mammals about 65 million years ago, however, a secondary system of emotions located in the cortex developed and these introduced consciousness and cautiousness into emotional life. Contemporary neural analyses show, however, that the involuntary archaic source of emotions still dominates the two directional pathways between the amygdala and the cerebral cortex (LeDoux, 1996).

What is exciting in terms of the present quest for the role of emotions in the play and stories of children is that play also appears about the same time on the evolutionary scene as the mammalian development of these secondary more voluntary emotions. What this suggests, though quite speculatively, is that play may well have originated in the brain as one way of integrating the two emotional systems. It is possible to view play as a solution to the paradox of the conflict between the involuntary and voluntary systems of emotional release. The fact that all players are performers, however, implies that these reconciliation's of the two kinds of emotion in play can occur because in play all actions are dramatically stylized, exaggerated, and carried on like actors on a stage (see Stewart, 1978). It is feasible that the intent of this ludic system, as instigated by the secondary emotional system, is to control the character of the emotions (Damasio, 1994, p. 155). It is noticeable, however, that most forms of play (celebrations, contests, explorations, performances, playfulness, and mind play (Sutton-Smith, in press), when satisfactory, find a place for the more involuntary forms of emotional release within the play itself such as wild excitement, the exaltations of victory, the shouting and screaming on behalf of one's team, the license to dance and laugh loudly in celebrations, the shrieking hilarity which can be a response to a favorite comedian, or the shrieking adulation which may be a response to a rock musical group, and finally the tearful release that occurs when the events represented stir the participants to sadness. In play, there appears to be a balance between the two systems. There are the routines, rules, and rituals that exercise sober control over the course of the play, and there are also the play-induced excitements as already mentioned. The latter extremities are still typically kept within play boundaries so that victory or loss does not lead to the extremities of actual attacks or actual suicide, though it has to be noted that the system sometimes breaks down and leads back to the realities of hooliganism and destruction. It might be said that play is a model for a kind of civilization which is basically an attempt to live such a secondary emotional life without too much direct joy, surprise, fear, disgust, sadness, or rage, though without thereby also neglecting the ability to react effectively with feeling and rapidity in times of emergency, and without also losing the ability to shriek with triumph, surprise, and happiness in moments which do not do injury to others. Play seems to be an attempt to avoid getting out of control while providing access to the vigor and vitality of the more extreme largely involuntary kinds of emotions. Thus, play apparently gives performative access to the fundamental "liveliness" of primary emotions without generally having to pay for the costs that might occur when these things are indulged in normally. Or, to put it as Bateson did earlier, this is why play is both directly about the reality of the "nip" and indirectly about the reality of the "bite."

Still it needs to be emphasized that although the foregoing prefatory material has conjoined the concepts of order, rationality, and voluntary control and made them sound like what Damasio would call secondary emotions, and has contrarily conjoined the concepts of disorder, irrationality, and involuntary control, and made them sound like his primary emotions; these conflations of meaning are misleading. The major emotional difference is between emotions that are involuntary or voluntary. The involuntary primary emotions, because they occur outside the subject's control, may well feel irrational and disorderly. But that is not necessarily the case. A rapid and effective but automatic response to a threatened danger is neither irrational nor disorderly. Contrarily, a well-thought-out plan to execute one's enemies as a result of racial anger voluntarily undertaken is hardly rational or orderly in the best sense. What is being dealt with here are emotions which suddenly erupt within one involuntarily or are initiated by one voluntarily. The emotions being served by either system are not in themselves different emotions. In both cases they are such emotional categories as happiness, sadness, anger and fear, disgust and surprise, and love and shame (Goleman, 1995). Play is a device that allows both of these kinds of feelings to occur to the participants. By joining the play forms, the players are choosing to get involved in various kinds of emotion (happiness, sadness, anger, fear, etc.), but at the same time they know beforehand that the desired emotions may erupt within themselves as the play proceeds (the exaltation of victory, the despair of defeat, etc.). Play combines both possibilities, voluntary and involuntary, though it is not surprising that given our general preference for civilized order we are inclined to believe that the more involuntary events are the more primitive, irrational, and disorderly. As shown, they need not be.

Again the desire to include both these positive and negative involuntary and voluntary emotions in play strongly suggests that to do so for 65 million years means that they are reinforcing to the players, animals or human. Perhaps the ability to engineer and yet enjoy these staged automatic emotions imparts a greater vitality to those who do so than they could normally experience without the associated dangers that go with such emotions. What this all also means is that despite their contribution to the vitality of our lives, there maybe a deeply primordial quality especially to the involuntary affects which are sought out with such pleasure but yet controlled in these stylized realms. Irony suggests that play could be discussed in these terms as partly a kind of ever continuing recapitulation of the emotions of ourselves as once upon a time a more reptilian species. In these terms, efforts to idealize such play make a great sense when discussing mental health and emotional illness but probably not when efforts are made to turn play into some kind of idealized form. Play may simulate being wicked, masterful, brilliant, beastly, arrogant, egocentric, macho, manic, or terrified. It can be great fun and most persons seem to need a great deal of it one way or another, either directly or vicariously. But the essential paradox of play in the present account is the universal balancing of the primary by the secondary emotions.

It might added that the Freudian alternative interpretation for this material could be that all that is being said here is about "regression in the service of the ego." It is suggested, however, that the present formulation is better expressed as a cognitive progression in the service of the primary affects, or, wryly, an ego in the service of regression. It is probable that Fein would avoid both these paradigmatic alternatives and be satisfied to take up the evidences of the integration of such primary emotions as being different in each individual case and as not requiring such overall paradigms as are suggested here. What she would agree with, however, is that the undercurrent of primary emotions is central to the nature of play and narrative.

THE EMOTIONAL SYSTEM AS A GENRE OF RECAPITULATION?

The classic recapitulation theories foster the view that individuals in their development (ontogeny) go through similar stages to those gone through biologically by earlier species (phylogeny) (Gould, 1977; Ruse,

1996). There has been little scientific support for this formulation, but what can be admired about it is the fairly realistic sense that early scholars such as Gulick, Stanley Hall, and Spencer and others had about the somewhat primary emotional or "primitive" character of a great deal of human play (Ellis, 1973). This primitivity is well captured in children's play in the last century by the works of Gomme (1894) and in this century by Iona and Peter Opie (1959) and Sutton-Smith (1959, 1981) and captured also for adults in many of the historical accounts of play (Bakhtin, 1984; Huizinga, 1949; Spariosu, 1989). In short, play continues today, as in earlier times, to encapsulate ludically something of the automaticity of the primary emotional life and something of the apparent rationality of the secondary emotional processes. In that lies its vitality and perhaps also its "intrinsic" motivation. It might be speculated biologically (though with as yet little solid evidence) that play recapitulates, in its own surprising form, the mammal binary emotional crisis. As neurologist Edelman (1992) might say, in these earlier times play became a brain-initiated neural map that allowed for the mollified expression of the primary reflexive emotions by fictionalizing them and by metacommunicating that fact. In this fictional conception, in general, but not always, the secondary emotional system and the primary emotional system are both victorious. More important, it becomes possible today to distinguish between the kinds of play fictions which are more resonant of the primary emotions and the kind which are alternatively more directly expressive of the character of the secondary emotional system, although both are always mutually involved to some degree. Finally, if the most basic and universal structure of play is thus primarily reflective of this dualistic internal emotional system, and if this has been carried on this way for perhaps some 65 million years, it is not surprising that it has been so difficult for us moderns, committed as we are typically to the civilizing secondary system of emotions, to adequately comprehend play's partly contrarious involuntary character.

As a recapitulation in part of primordialism, this theory of play and evolution also raises some skepticism about the relatively total idealizing of play that goes on in much modern child-play theory and increasingly in adult-play theory (Sutton-Smith & Kelly-Byrne, 1984; Sutton-Smith, Mechling, Johnson, & McMahon, 1995). Play may look indeed as if it is a high priority for the modern playful life of the imagination, but it is seldom, therefore, always an activity of any great delicacy, and there are plenty of driven or "dark" or primary emotional theatric contents of play as well as some more clearly chosen or secondary forms. Naturally every civilized person would wish to increase the amount of participation in the latter, but as is clear from the foregoing play examples, the evidence seems to say that the fruits of play (self-revitalization, etc.) are most likely only when there is some accompanying vicarious participation in the primary emotional scenarios.

PLAY AND NARRATIVE

The introduction showed that from her empirical work, Fein came to think of children's stories from about 3 years of age at their best as reflecting the same primary disorderly affective life that is a preoccupation within play. Whereas such disorderly affective play is protected from "reality" by play's being set aside as a secondary emotional virtual reality, in story making the same protection is provided by the story being set aside as a secondary emotional literary reality. In the one case the child is sequestered in a play space and in the other sequestered in a literary space. What has been characteristic of the 20th-century academic attitude to children's stories, however, is that the major analytic emphasis has been on the cognitive secondary not on the primary emotions. Thus most of the work of psychologists on children's narratives in the 1970s and 1980s was based on linear grammatical or script models (Mandler, 1984; Peterson & McCabe, 1983), in its way paralleling the similar interests in play as a controlling cognitive phenomenon rather than a ludic phenomenon, as illustrated in the foregoing points on "rational" play. In all these cases the interpretation of the broader role of narrative for children in culture remains dominantly conservative. This rhetorical posture is often taken even while the investigator is also recounting that the stories include such stimulants for disorderly primary emotional elements as foolish tales about animals, bogeymen, and the supernatural as well as jokes and dramatic gestures. In these confusions of both secondary and primary emotional information about narrative there is typically little indication of what the foolishness of the tale is supposed to be uniquely about. Sometimes the disorderly excesses are given some kind of socialization function, such as the tenuous thesis that they contribute to the learning of reversible cognitive operations. But more likely it is said that these noncanonical tales are just a form of fun making and play. But seeing the interpreters have no theory of what play is, using it as an explanation simply trivializes the function.

What is most important about children's stories, from the present point of view, is that they show children's preoccupation with both the primary and secondary emotional issues (Abrams & Sutton-Smith, 1977; Sutton-Smith, 1975, 1983, 1986, 1995; Botvin & Sutton-Smith, 1976; Sutton-Smith, Botvin, & Mahoney, 1976). Primary emotional elements are known within narrative theorizing as noncanonical, the breach, the trouble, the conflictful, or the Dionysian. Even Propp (1968), the most archetypal of folklore structural analysts of folk tales, counted as his most basic categories those of villainy versus villainy nullified and lack versus lack liquidated. And Bruner (1996), in his most recent account of the nine universals of narrative, counts one as: *the centrality of trouble*. He says, "Stories pivot on breached norms. That much is already clear. That places 'trouble' at the hub of narrative realities. Stories worth telling and worth constructing are typically born in trouble" (p. 142). In my own study of story making by children, stories taken from 50, 2- to 10-year-old New York City children in 1973–1975, practically all the 500 stories I collected hinged on such breach events. Here is one example from each of the storytellers' last of their stories told to us over several years. In most of them the breach element is obvious. They are fully recorded in *The Folkstories of Children* (Sutton-Smith, 1981).

> *2 years*: "A broke car / a fire in the house / a boy watched TV / the mother went out / a giant monkey story / the mother went out / cowboys fight."
>
> *3 years*: "The joker wants to kill him / all chasing each other / the earthquake started / there was a monster /he had a swollen gland / the girl jumped on the ceiling."
>
> *4 years*: "The mouse was for supper / King Kong fell in the water / there was a skeleton town."
>
> *5 years*: "The fastest tortoise / the doggy who ran away / hunting a bear / picking flowers / about a fart in Fartland / messy child pigs whose parents moved out."
>
> *6 years*: "The book with a missing color / the frog who swallowed a worm / stoopid whoopid and the airplane / how muffin got lost / Tasha and the 10 tigers / the dog has puppies who have puppies, who have puppies."
>
> *7 years*: "Freaky goes to the bathroom / he sneaked in the garden / he was very very sick / the mice were poisonous / the school pets would eat them up / Nixon's cavity prone teeth."
>
> *8 years*: "They got so weak they died / it was impossible to defeat the superior force / we are the final game of the season / Heidi didn't like the city / he ran to her crying / he pushed me down on the floor."
>
> *9 years*: "He saw a big monster / I woke up and I was my teacher / I turned into my brother / I ate some awful dog food / the food was all covered with ants / she would always write on her pants."
>
> *10 years*: "He lived miserably even after listening to the Beach Boys / they wanted to start a rock group / the lady had three fat tits / somethings gone wrong on jupiter / the death of the father / Henry the tick got out of the toilet."

The issue is whether these breach elements are only a dramatic technicality, a way to attract an audience attention or rather also to have something more fundamental to do with the primary emotional character of human life. It is noticeable that the need for the noncanonical, or "trouble," category is also true of adult-play life. The largest categories of adult play are those of fantasy, gambling losses, sports conflicts, festival intemperances, and comedic absurdities, all of which, in turn, give rise to all kinds of upside-downness, nonsense, inversions, costumes, masks, humor, struggles in the mud, falls from grace, clowns, tricksters, comedians, obscenities, and theatric absurdities. As Hall (1999) has said recently, "It is one of the paradoxes of our age that we have created entire economies around activating this fear system under safe conditions in the form of theme park rides and Stephen King novels and films which have us on the edge of our seats" (p. 45)[2]

CONCLUSION

The aim of this chapter has been to check out whether there might be any basis for Fein's sensitivity to the importance of "breach" emotional elements in both children's play and stories. If there is any truth to the recapitulatory bivalent emotional construction presented here, there is indeed solid evolutionary grounding for her expectations.

In conclusion the following points need to be emphasized:

1. In practically all these cases of children or adults at story or play, what is established first is an orderly secondary emotional situation (the playground, the theater, the book reading, etc.). This involves participant or audience activities as being within defined times and spaces and this gives an ambience of security to all of the simulations of risk and unpredictability that are to come. But once the order has been established and can be reestablished at any time, then, metaphorically speaking, the reptiles are let in the door and the readers are perhaps revitalized by doing so. The emotional revitalization of play or story according to this account is due probably to this keeping in simulated touch with the automatic involuntary emotions that continue within us.

2. Although it is most probable that all of these ludic primary and secondary emotional scenarios in which we participate in these many different ways give rise to useful positive transfer effects into our ordinary lives (most obviously of course if the player is a professional athlete, humorist, actor, film director, artist, etc.), that is clearly not their major intent. Rather, the incessant recapitulation and sequestration of primary emotions (ids, amygdala functions, irrationalities, "reptiles") is

more like a prayer than a utilitarian function. Play is a domain for mapping a virtual synthesis of the primary release of emotions and the secondary control of emotions. Participation in it, as it were, "recapitulates" an antideluvian evolutionary struggle and in so doing raises the participants culturally to a greater sense of the vitality of this resonance in all of our antideluvial lives.

The potential transfer effects, however, do need some elaboration. The divergences of this ludic and narrative behavior from conventional norms strongly suggests the probability of the emergence in play and story of an array of "novel repertoires" (Sutton-Smith, 1968), some of which may ultimately transfer to other useful functions a concept named elsewhere as "adaptive potentiation" (Sutton-Smith, 1975) and more recently as "adaptive variability" (Sutton-Smith, 1997). Although there has been much effort to see play as a form of flexibility and that may indeed be one of the skills that are potentiated by play, it is more parsimonious to see these play and story products as simply random forms of pleasurable variability (Bruner, 1972; Fagen, 1981). Presumably this original variability, and particularly the lability of play and story, makes them ultimately available for transfer to multiple other functional uses.

3. As a further point, and having suggested play as a universal dualistic use of the two systems of emotion, like many other hypotheses this one is confronted with the undoubted differences in amounts and varieties of play in different cultures (Gaskins & Göncü, 1988). There are cultures in which play is relatively disregarded because children must participate in chores and apprenticeships and it might be supposed that in such places, play would not exist so frequently as a solvent for the child population's own emotional conflicts but that these would be dealt with in more realistic or authoritarian adult terms (Miracle, 1977). There are yet other cultures in which there is early intrusion in children's play and narrative, including the socialization of that play in terms of the dominant cultural myths with little scope for deviation or for alternative playful improvisation (Scollon & Scollon, 1979). Here again one would suppose that there is less scope for alternative play behavior and more working out of the emotional conflicts in adult terms. The most obvious differences in play are found between modern societies which treat the imagination within an individualistic literary paradigm and other more ancient societies which treat it within a rhetorical oral paradigm (Goldman, 1998; Sutton-Smith & Heath, 1981) But this is all unfortunately as yet speculation because no cross-cultural studies have been done of the way in which play in varying cultures is an alternative form for emotional mollifications.

NOTES

1. To save space, the citations for these theoretical concepts and their bibliographical references are not included here. They can be found in *The Ambiguity of Play* (Sutton-Smith, 1997, pp. 218–220, 233–271).

2. I suppose it would not be fair in reflexive terms if I did not admit that in the books I have written for children (Sutton-Smith, 1950, 1961, 1976), I have shown such a strong preference for "breach" elements that some of them were banned from the New Zealand school journals at one point in my early history as a school teacher. Perhaps, therefore, the emotional recapitulation of this present account is my own burden rather than that of evolution. Naturally, I think of this admitted reflexivity as more of a personal joke than a vitiation of the hypothesis of play as a tertiary emotion presented here, but such a report, at least, puts the readers in a better position to make up their own minds (Sutton-Smith, 1994). Sheehan (1999) indeed has used an account of my children's books as a part of the symbolism of the difference between the tolerance for children's stories written by the English, the Americans and the Australasians.

REFERENCES

Abrams, D., & Sutton-Smith, B. (1977). The development of the Trickster figure in children's narratives. *Journal of American Folklore, 90*, 29–48.

Bakhtin, M. M. (1984). *Rabelais and his world*. Bloomington: Indiana University Press.

Bateson, G. (1972). *Steps to an ecology of mind*. New York: Ballantine.

Botvin, G., & Sutton-Smith, B. (1977). The development of structural complexity in children's fantasy narratives. *Developmental Psychology, 13*, 377–388.

Bruner, J. S. (1972). The nature and uses of immaturity. *American Psychologist, 27*, 686–708.

Bruner, J. S. (1996). *The culture of education*. Cambridge, MA: Harvard University Press.

Damasio,. A. R. (1994). *Descartes' error: Emotion, reason, and the human brain*. New York: Grossett/Putnam.

Edelman, G. M. (1992). *Bright air, brilliant fire*. New York: Basic Books.

Ellis, M. J. (1973). *Why people play*. Englewood Cliffs, NJ: Prentice-Hall.

Fagen, R. (1981). *Animal play behavior*. New York: Oxford University Press.

Fein, G. G. (1987). Pretend play: Creativity and consciousness. In D. Gorlitz & J.Wohlwill (Eds.), *Curiosity, imagination and play* (pp. 282–304). Hillsdale, NJ: Erlbaum.

Fein, G. G. (1995). Toys and stories. In A.D. Pellegrini (Ed.), *The future of play theory* (pp. 151–164). Albany: State University of New York Press.

Fein G. G., & Kinney, P. (1994). He's a nice alligator: observations on the affective organization of pretense. In A. Slade & D. Wolf (Eds.), *Children at play: Clinical and developmental studies of play* (pp. 188–205). New York: Oxford University Press.

Gaskins, S., & Göncü, A. (1988). Children's play as representation and imagination: The case of Piaget and Vygotsky. *Quarterly Newspaper of the Laboratory of Comparative Human Cognition, 10*(4), 104–107.

Goldman, L. R. (1998). *Child's play, myths, mimesis and make believe.* Oxford: Berg.

Goleman, S. (1995). *Emotional intelligence.* New York: Bantam.

Gomme, A. B. (1894). *The traditional games of England, Scotland and Ireland.* London: Constable.

Gould, S. J. (1977). *Ontogeny and phylogeny.* Cambridge, MA: Harvard University Press.

Hall, S. J. (1999, August 13). The anatomy of fear. *New York Times,* Section 6, pp. 42–47, 69–72, 88–91.

Handelman, D. (1992). Passages of play: Paradox and process. *Play and Culture, 5,* 1–19.

Huizinga, J. (1949). *Homo ludens: A study of the play element in culture.* Boston: Beacon Press.

Kelly-Byrne, D., & Sutton-Smith, B. (1983). Narrative as social science.*Quarterly Newsletter of the Laboratory of Comparative Human Cognition, 5*(4), 79–83.

LeDoux, J. (1996). *The emotional brain.* New York: Simon and Schuster.

Mandler, J. M. (1984). *Stories, scripts and scenes: aspects of schema theory* . Hillsdale, NJ: Erlbaum.

McMahon, F. F. (1999). "Playing with play": Germany's carnival as aesthetic nonsense. In S. Reifel (Ed.), *Play and culture studies: Vol. 2. Play contexts revisited* (pp. 177–190). Stamford, CT: Ablex.

Miller, S. (1973). Ends, means, and galumphing: Some leitmotifs of play. *American Anthropologist, 75*(1), 87–98.

Miller, S. (1974). The playful, the crazy, and the nature of pretense. *Rice University Studies, 60*(3), 31–51.

Miracle, A. W. (1977). Some functions of Aymara games and play. In P. Stevens (Ed.), *Studies in the anthropology of play* (pp. 98–104). West Point, NY: Leisure Press.

Myers, D. (in press). Play and paradox: How to build a semiotic machine. In S. Reifel (Ed.), *Play and culture studies: Vol. 3. Theory in context and out.*

Opie, I., & Opie, P. (1959). *The lore and language of school children.* New York: Oxford University Press.

Peterson, C., & McCabe, A. (1983). *Three ways of looking at a child's narrative.* New York: Plenum Press.

Propp, V. (1968). *The morphology of the folktale.* Austin : University of Texas Press.

Ruse, M. (1996). *Monad to man: The concept of progress in evolutionary biology.* Cambridge, MA: Harvard University Press.

Scollon, R, & Scollon, S. B. K., (1979). *Linguisitic convergence: An ethnography of speaking at Fort Chipewyan.* New York: Academic Press.

Sheehan, K. J. (1999). Playing with the sacrificial child: Brian Sutton-Smith's boys' story *Our Street.* In S. Reifel (Ed.), *Play and culture studies: Vol. 2. Play contexts revisited* (pp. 25–36). Stamford, CT: Ablex.

Spariosu, M. (1989). *Dionysus reborn.* Ithaca, NY: Cornell University Press.

Stewart, S. (1978). *Nonsense.* Baltimore: John Hopkins University Press.

Sutton-Smith, B. (1950).*Our street.* Wellington, New Zealand: A. H. Reed.

Sutton-Smith, B. (1959). *The games of New Zealand children.* Berkeley: University of California Press.

Sutton-Smith, B. (1961). *Smitty does a bunk.* Wellington, New Zealand: Price-Milburn.

Sutton-Smith, B. (1968). Novel responses to toys. *Merrill–Palmer Quarterly, 14,* 151–158.

Sutton-Smith, B. (1975). The importance of the storytaker: An investigation of the imaginative life. *Urban Review, 8*(2), 82–85.

Sutton-Smith, B. (1976). *The Cobbers.* Wellington, New Zealand: Price-Milburn.

Sutton-Smith, B. (1978a). *Die dialektic des spiels.* Schorndorf, Germany: Verlag Karl Hoffman.

Sutton-Smith, B. (1978b). The dialectics of play. In F. Landry & W. A. R. Orbam (Eds.), *Physical activity and human well being* (pp. 759–768). Miami, FL: Symposium Specialists.

Sutton-Smith, B. (1981). *The folkstories of children.* Philadelphia: University of Pennsylvania Press.

Sutton-Smith, B. (1983). The origins of fiction and the fiction of origins. In E. Bruner (Ed.), *Text, play and story* (pp. 117–132). Washington, DC: American Ethnological Society.

Sutton-Smith, B. (1986). The development of fictional narrative performances. *Topics in Language Disorders, 7*(1), 1–10.

Sutton-Smith, B. (1994). A memory of games and some games of memory. In J. Lee (Ed.), *Life and story: Autobiographies for a narrative psychology* (pp. 125–142). Wesport, CT: Praeger.

Sutton-Smith, B. (1995). Radicalizing childhood: The multi vocal mind. In H. McEwan & K. Egan (Eds.), *Narrative in teaching, learning and research* (pp. 69–90), New York: Teachers College Press.

Sutton-Smith, B. (1997). *The ambiguity of play.* Cambridge, MA: Harvard University Press

Sutton-Smith, B. (in press). Play as a tertiary emotion. In J. L. Roopnarine (Ed.), *Play and culture studies* (Vol 4). Stamford,CT: Ablex.

Sutton-Smith, B., Botvin, G., & Mahony, D. (1976). Developmental structures in fantasy narratives. *Human Development, 19,* 1–13.

Sutton-Smith, B., & Heath, S. B. (1981). Paradigms of pretense. *Quarterly Newsletter of the Laboratory of Comparative Human Cognition, 3*(3), 41–45.

Sutton-Smith, B., & Kelly-Byrne, D. (1984). The idealization of play. In P. K. Smith (Ed.), *Play in animals and humans* (pp. 305–322). London: Blackwell.

Sutton-Smith, B., Mechling, J., Johnson, T. W., & McMahon, F. R. (1995.) *Children's folklore: A source book.* Logan: Utah State University Press.

8

*

"He Was the Best Daddy"

Postdivorce Preschoolers' Representations of Loss and Family Life

PATRICIA HERMAN
INGE BRETHERTON

The assumption that preschoolers' pretend play with toy families can reveal some of their deepest emotional concerns underlies many play therapy approaches (e.g., Axline, 1969; Erikson, 1963; A. Freud, 1946; Miller, 1984; Waelder, 1933). That children represent and "work through" emotionally charged personal meanings in pretend play was even noted by cognitive theorists such as Piaget (1951) and Fein (1981). Indeed, in her later work, Fein (1989) came to assign priority to the emotional over the cognitive aspect of pretending, noting that it "may help children fine-tune their emotional reactions to a variety of childhood anxieties" (p. 360).

The suggestion that events young children enact and narrate in the course of pretend play reveal their attempts to make sense of emotionally significant experiences inspired a number of developmental researchers to create enactive story-completion procedures designed to probe preschoolers' thoughts and feelings about salient family and moral issues (e.g., the Attachment Story Completion Task—Bretherton & Ridgeway, 1990; the MacArthur Story Stem Battery—Bretherton, Oppenheim, Buchsbaum, Emde, & MacArthur Narrative Group, 1990; moral and family story stems—Buchsbaum & Emde, 1990; incomplete doll stories about the self—Cassidy, 1988; separation stories—Oppenheim, 1997; for reviews, see Oppenheim & Waters, 1995; Solomon & George, 1999). In these tasks, an interviewer presents children with story beginnings or stems that focus on relationship or moral issues they are likely to have encountered in their everyday lives (e.g., fear, pain, separation, and transgression), followed by the invitation: "Show me and tell me what happens next." The story stems are narrated and enacted with the aid of small family figures and props because these tangible objects not only make it easier for the children to grasp the major issues presented but also allow them to create more elaborate and comprehensible story completions in which narration is clarified and supplemented by dramatic action.

Young children's responses to these family and moral story stems turned out to be significantly correlated with observed patterns of child–mother attachment, ratings of self-worth, and teacher evaluations of social competence in the preschool (e.g., Bretherton, Ridgeway, & Cassidy, 1990; Cassidy, 1988; Oppenheim, Emde, & Warren, 1997; Verschueren, Marcoen, & Schoefs, 1996; for a review, see Page, in press). Children who created constructive resolutions of the story issues and enacted their responses with emotional openness and narrative coherence tended to be securely attached to mother and to exhibit low levels of behavioral problems in the preschool. Findings thus lent support to clinical reports as well as Fein's suggestions that pretense reveals important aspects of young children's inner world.

That story responses predict the quality of actual family and peer interactions should not, however, be taken to mean that children's story completions represent literal replays of remembered family events. Rather, the content and organization of the stories appear to reflect, in addition to actual experiences, children's hopes, wishes, and fears about family life. That is, they appear to capture what one might call, in line with Fein's ideas, their "affective reality." This became especially obvious in the story completions of 71 preschoolers participating in our study of postdivorce families. These children incorporated many instances of family reunification and mother–father affection (hopes) as well as dramatic instances of abandonment or parental death (fears), events that we knew not to be literally true (Bretherton, Munholland, & Page, 1999). That their story completions nevertheless represented an underlying "affective truth" could not be directly demonstrated, though—as in the studies cited previously—it was strongly suggested by correlations of story themes with other assessments, such as reports of the mother–child and mother–father relationship as well as preschool teacher ratings of peer competence (see Bretherton, Page, Golby, & Walsh, 1997; Page & Bretherton, in press).

To provide detailed illustrations of the way in which postdivorce preschoolers portrayed their affective reality through story completions, we undertook an in-depth analysis of their responses to one particular story stem that elicited especially poignant evidence of divorce-related concerns or fears about loss of or separation from the father, parental discord, abandonment, and neglect but also hopes or wishes for parental affection, parental cooperation, and caregiving. This story stem, the "Uncle Fred" story, had been designed by Zahn-Waxler et al.. (1994), not with the aim of eliciting themes concerning fear of loss but to discover the extent to which preschoolers might enact empathy themes when faced with a scenario in which a mother figure was crying over the death of a relative.

Our decision to conduct a systematic qualitative analysis of postdivorce preschoolers' responses to the "Uncle Fred" story seemed especially warranted given the scarcity of information in the divorce literature about how preschoolers from divorced families think and feel about their restructured families (Grych & Fincham, 1999). The many studies that assess child outcome after parental divorce in early childhood do so via later questionnaires and global indicators such as self-esteem. Findings based on these studies suggest that unless there is considerable parental discord in the postdivorce family, most children appear to adjust quite well to the changes resulting from parents' marital separation (Amato & Keith, 1991; Emery, 1994). On the other hand, clinical reports (e.g., Gardner, 1991; Hodges, 1991; Johnston & Roseby, 1997) as well as a seminal divorce study that used diagnostic play therapy with a nonclinic sample (Wallerstein & Kelly, 1975, 1980) reveal that young children's experiences of postdivorce family life are often accompanied by considerable psychological, pain, distress and confusion, interspersed with hope for renewed family togetherness.

The findings by Wallerstein and Kelly (1975, 1980) are especially noteworthy because family members had not been in clinical treatment prior to being recruited for the study, although all were offered a short-term intervention with a primarily preventive focus in return for their participation. The subsample of 26 3- to 5-year-old preschoolers whom Wallerstein and Kelly observed during play therapy interviews frequently enacted themes about parent loss by death, disaster, and abandonment, leaving the child doll to lead a parentless existence. Play therapy portrayals of harmonious, well-ordered family scenes reflecting hope for family reunification were especially common in little girls' play. A number of these girls, however, proceeded to disrupt their initially peaceful family scenes by enacting tragic disasters that befell the whole family or particular family members. In addition, it was fairly common for preschoolers to create play therapy scenarios that portrayed young children (boys and girls) as taking care of each other without adult intervention. During direct interviews about their actual families, many preschoolers described their mothers' crying as upsetting. Many worried intensely about their mothers' and fathers' health and well-being. They also engaged in more aggressive and angry behavior than previously, stimulated perhaps by witnessing parental quarrels. A high proportion held themselves or their wrongdoing responsible for the parents' divorce. These findings suggest that children's resilience in the face of divorce, demonstrated in later survey studies, should not lead us to minimize the repeated emotional readjustments that accompany postdivorce family life for many young children (Emery, 1994).

Given that our procedure borrowed techniques from play therapy, we should perhaps not have been surprised that a play scenario involving maternal distress over the loss of a relative should call forth divorce-related loss themes. However, the children in our study, unlike those studied by Wallerstein and Kelly, had had 2 years to adjust to the restructured family, and many did not even remember their fathers living with them, factors that would lead us to expect fewer divorce themes. In addition, the story stems were not specifically tailored to the divorce situation but only suggested divorce indirectly by placing mother and father figures in different pretend houses. Finally, the families participating in this study were not recruited from a clinical population and were, on the whole, a well-functioning group. For example, means for maternal depression assessed with the Beck Depression Inventory (Beck, 1976) were well within the normal range, although a few mothers scored above the clinical cutoff (Bretherton et al., 1997). Similarly, children's prosocial and problem behaviors with peers as rated by preschool teachers conformed to national norms (Page & Bretherton, in press).

METHOD

Participants

Seventy-one postdivorce families with preschool children participated in the study. Most were identified by searching public court records. Of the 110 mothers who responded to a letter describing the study and inviting their participation or whom we contacted by telephone, 54% ($n = 59$) agreed to participate. The remaining 12 families were recruited through local preschool directors. Mothers received $75 in appreciation of their participation.

About the Mothers

Mothers were eligible for the study if the divorce or permanent separation had occurred at least 2 years previously and if the mothers were employed or engaged in academic studies (or a combination of these). These criteria were applied in order to avoid the normally highly stressful time immediately surrounding the divorce (Hetherington, 1989) and to control for the added stress of extreme poverty. Mothers who were remarried were not included in the study. However, almost two-thirds of the mothers mentioned a stable partner who was actively involved in the children's lives. Only 17% of these mothers were cohabiting with a partner. Seven percent of the mothers lived with their parents and 10% lived with another adult, such as a sibling.

The mothers' ages ranged from 23 to 47 years (m = 33 years). All had graduated from high school and 29% had obtained bachelor's or higher degrees. The mothers' average yearly income (between 1992 and 1995) was $24,000, including child support.

About the Children

Forty-one boys and 30 girls participated in the study. Their ages ranged from 4 years 5 months to 5 years 0 months (m = 4 years 8 months). All but two of the children were White, one was biracial (White mother, African American father), and one had a mother who identified herself as Hispanic. Thirty-four percent were only children; the remainder had siblings. One child had been adopted at birth.

About the Fathers

Information about the fathers was supplied by the mother. The fathers' education and occupation levels (Hollingshead scale, 1978) resembled that of the mothers. Eighty-three percent of the fathers lived in the same town or close vicinity, 6% lived in the same state but at some distance, and 11% lived out of state. Twenty-eight percent of the fathers were reported by the mothers to have serious alcohol or drug problems; one father was in jail for drug dealing.

Custody Arrangements

Seventy-six percent of the mothers had joint legal custody. The remainder had sole custody of the target child. However, the child's primary physical placement was with the mother in 92% of the families and shared equally with the father in the other 8%.

Seventy percent of the children saw their fathers every 2 weeks or more (half of these every week); 6% saw their father every 4 to 6 weeks; 11%, three to four times a year; 3% twice a year; and 10% had not seen their fathers for a year or more. Many of the fathers who saw their children three to four times a year or less lived out of state, but some belonged to the group with alcohol or drug problems.

Assessments

In the course of the larger study, mothers completed a variety of questionnaires and participated in several interviews. In addition, the family was observed at home from dinnertime to bedtime, and preschool teachers or child-care providers filled out questionnaires about the children's social competence, but in this chapter we focus only on the story completion assessment of the child participants.

To establish friendly rapport in the presence of the mother, the interviewer first engaged the child in 10–20 minutes of free play. When the child appeared to feel comfortable with the interviewer, the mother was led to a separate room where she was interviewed about her relationship with the child while the child interviewer administered the story completion task and some other assessments. The story completion sessions were videotaped.

The Expanded Attachment Story Completion Task

The Expanded Attachment Story Completion Task consists of five stories from the original Attachment Story Completion Task described in Bretherton, Ridgeway, and Cassidy (1990). It was supplemented by four stories from the MacArthur Story Stem Battery and a fifth story, the "Uncle Fred" story, created by Zahn-Waxler et al. (1994). The 10 stories focused on attachment, authority, empathy, sibling loyalty, and separation and loss issues but did not explicitly address divorce topics.

The story stems were enacted with a bear family dressed in human clothes. They included a mother, father, grandmother, two children of the same sex as the participating child, and a family dog. Similar animal figures were used to represent two of the children's friends. Not all figures were used in every story. Given that the participating children themselves most often referred to the figures without mentioning that they were bears, we refer to them as mother, father, and children for remainder of this chapter. When this terminology might lead to ambiguities, we distinguish between family figures and actual family members in a variety of ways.

The story completion task was adapted for use with children of divorce as follows. At the beginning of each story stem, the mother and father figures were placed on separate "houses" (felt squares) placed at opposite corners of the child-size table at which the task was administered. In eight of the story stems, the mother was portrayed as the acting parent. In one story stem the children were placed with the father. In the final story, the main protagonists were the two siblings and a friend, with the two parental figures remaining on their respective houses. The participant child was, however, free at all times to include the father figure into their story enactments. Many of the children did so frequently (Page & Bretherton, in press).

After enacting and narrating each story stem according to the standard protocol, the interviewer invited the child to "show me and tell me what happens next," using a prescribed set of prompts if necessary. A warm-up story about a birthday scene, designed to acquaint the children with the story completion technique, preceded 10 story stems that comprised the task proper. A wrap-up story "about the family doing something fun" was used to create a positive ending for the task.

The "Uncle Fred" Story. The "Uncle Fred" story focused on the mother figure's distress about loss of a relative (Uncle Fred). As already noted, this story was designed by Zahn-Waxler et al. (1994) to elicit themes of child empathy with a distressed mother and was the last but one story stem (of a total 10) presented to the child. The story began with the mother figure sitting on a couch and the child figure standing nearby. The father figure remained standing on his "house" some distance away. The interviewer introduced the story as follows: "The mother is sitting on the couch. She is so sad because Uncle Fred has died. Show me and tell me what happens next."

Story Completion Analysis

To analyze the children's responses, we created detailed transcripts of the videotaped sessions. These transcripts captured both the enacted and narrated events created by the child and also included interviewer prompts. A second researcher (the first author) checked the transcripts against the videotapes. Where errors of omission were noticed, the transcripts were corrected. The few errors of commission (disagreements of interpretation) were conferenced with the original transcriber. Although we subsequently coded the transcripts in terms of various parent–child interaction themes (Page & Bretherton, 1993), for purposes of this chapter we relied entirely on the transcripts, making extensive use of the participating children's verbatim narratives.

RESULTS

Our findings are organized around three aspects of the children's responses to the "Uncle Fred" story stem. First, we explore expressions of children's concern about divorce and loss issues. Second, we analyze how children portrayed positive and negative aspects of the father–child and father–mother relationships. Third, we examine enactments of positive and negative aspects of the mother–child relationship.

Themes Related to Divorce and Father Loss

Completions of the "Uncle Fred" story that suggested concern, even preoccupation, with divorce issues took various forms, ranging from family reunification to sadness about loss, anger, and rejection.

Reunifications of the Parental Houses and of the Family

The presence of two houses, one for each parent, provided an opportunity for 7 of the 71 children to suggest family reunifications. Some of the children moved the two houses close together so that they were touching or overlaid on each other. In some cases they accompanied this action with an explanation, such as "we don't need the houses to be two houses," or "the father's house is way too far away"; in other cases they completed the action without comment. When a child made no verbal comment, we cannot be sure that the actions symbolize the family's return to a predivorce state, but this possibility is strongly suggested when all family members are placed together in one house and the participant child hands the other house to the interviewer, saying, "We don't need this anymore." In a strikingly explicit image, a child figure crept under the father's house in order to change it "like it was supposed to be, like before," verbalizing the idea of transformation to a prior state, possibly prior to the divorce. In another story, the mother, father, and child figures took shelter under father's house, "because it's raining and there is a leak." The maternal house was then added to form "a little house." This particular image appeared to be metaphorical, with the leaky house suggesting protection but also disrepair, possibly symbolizing relationships within the family.

Sometimes, reunifications of the parental houses were followed by negative episodes. For example, in pushing the two parental houses together, one study child smiled, saying, "Hook houses like that." Immediately after this move, however, he drew an imaginary line between the houses with his index finger. Similar ambivalence was evident in a reunification sequel that included aggression by the story father toward the story child. The child creating this story seemed to be struggling with wanting things to be as they were before the divorce, at the same time acknowledging family separation and discord.

In addition to uniting the houses, 23 of the participant children united the family by making the father figure join mother and child. In 10 cases, the three figures then interacted amicably, but in 13 other instances the introduction of the father figure into the scenario led to aggression and disasters, either immediately or after a short positive interlude. In 4 of these 13 cases, the whole family died together. More detailed accounts of positive and negative story interactions are provided later.

Sadness at Father Loss and Denial of Loss

Two children's story completions were characterized by sadness at the death of the uncle that seemed to be directly linked to sadness at the loss of the father through divorce. In the first example, the child figure whipped the mother figure and kicked her across the room "because Uncle Fred was dying and he was the best daddy." This suggests anger at the actual mother about the father's absence from the family.

As this story progressed, the participant child wrapped the child figure in the mother's house and laid the "package" on the couch, suggesting an image of simultaneous caring and avoidance (covering up). When asked by the interviewer what the family members did about the mother being sad, the participant child replied, "they were just happy," illustrating further reluctance to address the loss issue.

In one instance in which the father figure was used to portray Uncle Fred, the child figure then said sadly that she was "just going to wait for dad to come, but he'll never come back." Earlier in the story, the child figure had denied that the father (transformed into Uncle Fred) was dead, stating that "he's only hiding," then she said "Daddy's back," and the father figure sat on the couch with mother and child. Subsequently, all three family members died, but mother and child came to life again while the father remained dead, leading to the waiting behavior described previously. This was another instance in which a participant child acknowledged the loss, possibly the loss of the family as it was before the divorce, while also denying the loss.

The example just given illustrates what Fein (1989) refers to as ambiguity in pretense. According to Fein, ambiguity in children's pretense (symbolic play) may be advantageous in that it allows a child to pursue or try out a variety of options. In the case just presented, the child figure was made to display happiness at the father's not being dead as well as sadness at the fact that he will never come back.

Anger toward the Father Figure

Not all depictions of the father figure were amiable. Anger toward the father was enacted by three participant children, including one who used the father figure to represent Uncle Fred. In this story the child protagonist asked the mother why she missed Uncle Fred because "he was a real pain in the butt" and continued "I never want to see him again." The mother figure scolded her daughter for these words, telling her she was "the baddest [sic] girl" and then choked her in severe punishment. However, following this the mother figure tucked the now sick child into bed and wrapped her in the mother's house as a blanket, indicating a return to warmth and nurturance. It is interesting to speculate what mixed messages the child who told this story might have received about her actual father. Perhaps she had overheard her mother speak negatively about him without being allowed to do so herself. This could be confusing to a young child, faced with figuring out an acceptable stance toward the nonresidential father.

Maternal and Child Vulnerability

One image that we repeatedly observed during the "Uncle Fred" story was that of injury, either to the story child (six instances) or to the child participant him- or herself (four instances). For example, in direct response to the story stem, the child figure's finger began to bleed and "they put a big wrapper [the mother's house] on it." The house was also wrapped around the child figure's head "to make sure he never could see." This "made him better, the end." In another story, and once again as the first response to the story stem, the child figure told the mother, "I'm so sick," and then went to the father's house, where the father gave him "medicine for his headache." In yet another example, a participant child feigned injury by sliding under the table during presentation of the story stem and deliberately bumping his hand against the underside of the table.

Several possible explanations of the injury phenomenon occur to us. It could be that the emotionally charged theme of death elicited a sense of vulnerability. Another possibility is that the child was trying to deflect attention away from the anxiety-provoking death scenario by bringing attention to the injury of the child figure or to him- or herself. Alternatively, these examples of injury may metaphorically represent the psychic injury of divorce.

Another version of vulnerability occurred in a story in which the child figure asked the mother why she was crying. The mother responded that she "loved him [Uncle Fred] so much and was going to marry him." The child figure then told the mother "not to marry Uncle Fred" because he will throw the child "in the garbage can when they have a party, and he'll do it to the mom too." This is a striking metaphorical image of disposal or casting away of child and mother.

Another child told a story that appeared to acknowledge the death/divorce situation on one level but enacted a story sequel that revealed a more complex picture. In this story the participant child laid the father figure down in response to the story stem and then said, "Okay, this Uncle Fred is dead, and this mommy lives by herself and with her kids." Chaos then ensued with the couch blowing up and child and mother falling to the floor. This may be symbolic of the participant child's perception of the postdivorce situation as dangerous and volatile. It reminds us of Wallerstein and Kelly's (1975) finding that some preschoolers from postdivorce families fear that one or both of their parents will encounter a disaster, leaving the child without a parent.

Portrayals of the Father–Child and Father–Mother Relationship

To understand the context of the father–child and father–mother relationship as depicted in the "Uncle Fred" story, we remind the reader of the custody arrangements for the children in this study. Their primary physical placement was with the mother in 92% of families. The actual father–child relationships of the study children varied across a range of frequent to infrequent visits and from nurturing relationships to those that were not so nurturing as described by the mothers (Bretherton et al., 1997).

The story task began with the father figure set in his house, apart from the mother and child. Thus, the inclusion of the father figure was not explicitly suggested by the story stem, and the first point to consider was whether he was introduced into the story at all. Fifty of the 71 child participants made use of the father figure in their responses to the "Uncle Fred" story, and 28 associated Uncle Fred with the father figure. In a few instances this association was minimal, such as looking at the father figure or touching the father figure while the interviewer narrated that the mother was crying at Uncle Fred's death, but in most cases it was more explicit (e.g., picking up the father figure and asking, "This guy died?" or saying, "Then dad got shot, and he went in the grave.").

It is, of course, possible that some participant children used the father figure simply because they needed a tangible male character to represent Uncle Fred. However, other children invented imaginary figures for this purpose instead of transforming the father figure. In addition,

21 of the 71 children did not use the father figure. Thus, neither inclusion of the father in the story nor his identification with Uncle Fred was automatic.

When the father figure did appear in a story, his behavior toward child and mother and/or conversely the behavior by mother and child figures directed toward him could be categorized in three ways: benevolent, malevolent, or ambivalent. Examples of each category are discussed next.

The Father–Child and Father–Mother Relationship as Benevolent

Twenty-three of the 50 children who used the father figure did so in ways that primarily suggested benevolence or kind feelings by the father figure toward the child or mother figures and/or by the mother or child figures toward the father.

Benevolence by the Father toward the Mother and/or Child. In 16 instances we observed empathic behavior by the father figure toward mother and/or child. In one story, the father figure moved over to the couch along with the mother and child figures and said, "I'm sad too," but without giving a reason. In other instances the participant child made somewhat more explicit statements, such as: "He [father] got there [couch] because they were sad." Sometimes, the father merely came over and sat with mother and child, which may imply empathy though these instances are less certain. In still other cases, the father expressed empathy through a question he addressed to the mother, such as "Why are you sad?" or "What's wrong?" Overall, these examples portrayed a father figure who expressed concern for the emotional distress of the mother and child.

In some instances of benevolent interaction, the father figure offered companionship rather than empathy in response to the mother figure's crying, such as coming over to sit on the couch with mother and child to watch television (a small television set had been used as a prop in a previous story, which may have prompted inclusion of it in some of these completions). In this case, there was no overt mention of the mother's sadness when the father joined her on the couch, and it is possible that these offers of companionship express avoidance of a difficult issue as well as concern.

In a few instances, the father figure showed affectionate behavior toward mother or child. In one story, after having told the mother figure he was not dead, the father stood close to her and they kissed (touched faces). The mother figure then told the father that she was sad because Uncle Fred died, to which the father replied, "That's okay, honey, I'm sad too." The fact that the father figure used a term of endearment toward the mother and that mother and father figures kissed may symbolize the participant child's hope or wish for an affectionate relationship between his actual divorced parents.

In one particularly striking story portrayal of the father as a benevolent figure, the child cast him as a priest ("we'll pretend the father is a priest"). The father-as-priest went to the funeral and grave site with the mother and put Uncle Fred into the grave while the child figure sat on the sofa (bench at the cemetery). This metaphorical image portrayed the father in the role of protector of the mother and child. It is interesting that in the midst of telling this story, the participant child interjected a related personal narrative about a pet at school dying and being put into a grave. This was one of several examples in which a child associated a story with his or her own real life experiences. In a last example in this category, the father figure, cast as Uncle Fred, came back to life and played a game with the child and mother. It is interesting to note that the game played was peek-a-boo, implying the context of "now you see me, now you don't," which could be related to Uncle Fred coming back to life or, by extension, the father moving in and out of the child's life.

Benevolent Behavior Directed toward the Father. In addition to portraying the father figure's benevolence toward child and/or mother figures, we noted seven instances of benevolent behavior directed by the child or mother figures toward the father. In some of these instances, the mother and/or child figure expressed happiness when the father, who had been previously portrayed as dead, came back to life. In other versions of this theme, mother or child were happy to discover that the father figure was not the dead Uncle Fred after all. These responses may indicate that a participant child initially experienced the divorce as father loss but that this feeling was reversed when the father continued to be part of the child's and mother's life.

Stories in which the child or the mother figures expressed sadness about the father figure's death also imply benevolent feelings toward him. Perhaps understandably, there were more stories in which a child figure was sad about the father's death than stories in which the mother figure was sad. In one such story the child figure cried after being told by the mother figure that "your dad died."

The Father–Child and Father–Mother Relationship as Malevolent

The stories of 17 participant children were categorized as predominantly malevolent with respect to behavior by or toward the father figure.

Malevolence by the Father. Negative behaviors by the father figure toward the child and/or mother figures (five instances) spanned the gamut from neglectful to violent. At the neglectful end of the scale, we categorized the father figure's behavior as malevolent when he "didn't even come, he stayed at his house." Although it might be argued that this is not malevolent behavior in the strictest sense of the word, the use of the word "even" suggests that it was perceived as noncaring behavior by the child who created the story. More active father malevolence also occurred. In one malevolent story, the father figure knocked the mother off the couch; in another, "the dad comes over and scares him [child]," followed by the child figure falling over with a loud cry. When the mother figure then told the father she was "so sad that the cousin [i.e., uncle] died," the father became "so mad the cousin died, he could blast up in the air." The father figure then flew wildly around in the air, not being able "to see where he was" and "so mad he couldn't stand it." In the process he knocked mother figure over. The story ended with mother and child sitting on the couch while the father "got so mad he died." In a further example the father figure "knocked the baby down," then tipped over the couch on which the mother figure was sitting. While tipping the couch back up, the child figure was trapped under it and turned into a ghost. The father figure then commented: "Who's under there? Ah, ghost under there" and prevented the trapped child/ ghost from escaping. In another story, a tornado occurred (represented by rolling the couch over and over) as the father figure entered the scene, and everyone was knocked helter-skelter. We do not know whether these aggressive physical actions related to the father's arrival on the scene were inspired by violence actually experienced or witnessed by the participant child or whether they symbolized more general feelings of hostility or other violent emotions among the actual family members.

In one particularly striking story, the father figure piled the couch on the mother's house, designating it as "garbage." He then put the child and mother on the pile because "because he's really mad at them, he doesn't like them any more." The "garbage" metaphor suggests the idea of the actual mother and child being discarded by the father, presumably by way of the divorce.

Malevolence toward the Father Figure. Malevolent behavior toward the father figure occurred in 12 of the 17 stories in which we noted father-related malevolence. These enactments may represent the participant child's anger toward the actual father. For example, in one story the child protagonist knocked the father over as Uncle Fred's death was narrated by the interviewer, and in several additional instances the participant child laid the father figure down as if he were dead, sometimes with an explicit statement, such as "This Uncle Fred is dead." It is, of course, not clear whether these images (when not followed by empathy) symbolized a participant child's wish to have the actual father out of the way or fear of losing the father.

An outside character was the purveyor of malevolent behavior toward the father in two of the stories. In one instance, a stranger "cut the father right here [father's head]" and the father then died. In another, the mother figure told the child that "someone stuck a knife in him [father], a bow and arrow too." This may represent the participant child's attempt to attribute to someone else the angry thoughts he may have had toward the father. Alternatively, it may reflect the fear held by some preschool children in postdivorce families that something dreadful will happen to their parent or parents and they will be left parentless (Wallerstein & Kelly, 1975).

Ambivalent Father–Child and Father–Mother Interactions

Eight of the 50 stories that included the father portrayed him or interactions with him in a generally ambivalent way. A story was assigned to this category when there was a mixture of benevolent and malevolent behaviors toward or by the father, with neither being predominant. In one example already cited earlier, the father (alias Uncle Fred) was "just hiding" at the cemetery and then came back to life, and joined mother and child on the couch (benevolent). However, he then died again and the child cried, waiting "for the father, but he never came back." This story ended with the child participant displaying anger toward the father figure, facing him away from the mother and child and then hitting him against the table, saying, "Stop it, you daddy!" (malevolent). The expression of anger may represent the participant child's feelings about the actual father not coming back or being less accessible after the divorce.

In another ambivalent story, the father figure defended the mother against the child who had hit the mother and was "biting her on the bottom." After the mother figure put the child in time out, the father arrived and spanked the child. Although this is an example of protective behavior by the father figure vis-à-vis the mother, the spanking was interpreted as malevolent because the father "spanked the baby real hard," indicating severe punishment. The theme of a child figure attacking the mother figure may symbolize anger toward the actual mother for her part in the divorce. At the same time, the participant child may have perceived his own anger as deserving of punishment by the still powerful (though not present in the home) father figure. In another ambivalent story involving both parents and the child, the father came over, kissed the child, and taught him a somersault. However, the somersault went out of control, and the story ended with the mother rescuing the child who had been endangered by the father's actions.

A particularly long and complex ambivalent story started out with the father as Uncle Fred dying "for real" but then becoming "all much better [sic]," possibly symbolizing a reversal of the loss associated with divorce. The father figure then confessed that he had been upstairs playing with the child's "stuff" and that he had "knocked her things down" (malevolent behavior). We wonder whether the "things" that the father "knocked down" represented the disarray in the participant child's world after the divorce. The story continued with the mother figure berating the father for his malevolent actions: "What the hell did you do to her bedroom?" A quarrel between the mother and father figures ensued during which the mother, held up in the air above the father, proclaimed: "I'm bigger than you." Interestingly, the father then defended himself to the mother, claiming that "I'm just a little boy and don't tell me not to do that," which may represent an attempt to absolve himself from being seen as malevolent. The parental argument continued with the mother telling the father emphatically: "Yes, I can. These are my daughters." Whereas this implies a protective stance by the mother toward the children, it also diminishes the father–child relationship. After a few more salvos in the argument, the child figure stood between the parents and asked, "What are you fighting about?" She then addressed the father figure, saying, "Why don't you get out of here in your house . . . ," and placed the father back in his house, continuing, ". . . and don't bother my mommy" (malevolent). In a positive turn of events, the father figure then cleaned up the imaginary bedroom, making a big point of this to the child: "I cleaned it." In response, the mother praised the father: "You are so nice, that's nice of you," and the father apologized: "I'm sorry for break [sic] the shelves. I put shelves back up too, see?" (benevolent). As the story continued, the father slept on the couch with the child which might be seen as nurturing (benevolent), but then the mother entered the room to wake them up and the child told her, "All I want you to do is get dad out of my room" (malevolent). At this request the mother figure asked the father to leave and sleep in his own room. The repeated oscillations between benevolence and malevolence portrayed in this story may reflect the process through which the parents came to the point of divorce, a process that often includes several separations and reunions of the couple prior to the final divorce (Emery, 1994). Alternatively, this many-faceted story may represent emotional swings that accompanied the actual father repeatedly entering and leaving the child's and the mother's lives since the divorce.

The Mother–Child Relationship

To enact the "Uncle Fred" story, the mother figure was placed on the couch (in the center of the table) and expressed her sadness about Uncle Fred's death to the child who stood at some distance. There would hence appear to be no question of the mother figure's involvement in the story as she is depicted as the major protagonist. However, 21 of 71 children enacted no interaction between the mother and child figures at all whether in terms of dialogue or in terms of the child moving toward the mother.

In 3 of these 21 cases, the participant child simply refused to respond to the story; but in the other instances one of three things generally happened: (1) the child figure directed behavior entirely toward the father figure, (2) the mother and father interacted only with each other, or (3) the child figure talked about Uncle Fred's death, without involving the mother figure. Sometimes there was a combination of two or more of these interaction types.

In the 50 story completions that included interactions between mother and child figures, the nature of these interactions was categorized as benevolent, malevolent, or ambivalent. Examples of each category are provided next.

Benevolent Mother–Child Interactions

Thirty of the 71 children portrayed mother–child interactions as benevolent. In 22 of these stories, the child figure expressed empathy for the crying mother. In some cases, expressions of empathy were explicit, as when the child figure said, "I'm sad, too." In other instances, the child figure expressed empathy by reassuring or comforting the mother figure. For example, in one story a child figure first acknowledged the mother's sadness and then told the mother that Uncle Fred was not dead. In some instances, empathy was conveyed by affectionate behavior, as when the story child hugged the mother figure and sat on the couch with her. In a few instances it was difficult to determine whether the expression was one of empathy as story child was merely moved close to the mother on the couch.

In some renderings, expressions of empathy by the child figure were followed by companionable mother–child activities as the mother felt better. For example, in one particularly poignant example, the child figure said to the mother, "I'll make you feel better. Would a story help?" Mother and child then agreed that Peter Pan would be a good choice, and the child figure "read" the mother a story about Peter Pan, who went out to play and "never got home, but he knowed [sic] the way to grandmother's, so he went to grandmother's. The end." The choice of story book is noteworthy: Peter Pan, the boy who never grew up. We wondered whether the participant child's mother characterized the father in this way. Moreover, the fact that the character "never got home" may represent the father not returning to the child and mother after the divorce, with the possibility that he went to live with the grandmother (the father's mother).

In one story, the child figure acknowledged the loss of Uncle Fred without expressing empathy, telling the mother matter-of-factly, "Well, mom, that's the way it goes," to which the mother replied, "I know, but it's hard." In another story the child and mother figures went to the funeral and the child told the mother, "Mommy, don't worry, some people die like that." Yet another example of the child figure seeking to acknowledge and reassure the mother occurred when the child told the mother, "He [Uncle Fred] just got too old, he had to [die], he couldn't help it." In both of these examples we see the child taking the role of advice giver for the parent. The latter story continued with mother and child figures dancing together happily. This dancing might possibly be seen as a celebration of the departure of the male figure, perhaps symbolizing the actual father, and may thus not have been as benevolent as it seemed at first glance.

Benevolent Care by the Mother toward the Child. Benevolence by the mother figure toward the child was also observed. In a story mentioned earlier, the mother's house was placed around the child as a "big wrapper" so that he "never could see" and to "make him [child] feel better." This metaphorical image suggests the mother's house as a nurturing place for the child, a haven in the face of injuries or losses that are part of the divorce. However, preventing the child from seeing the dead uncle suggests an undercurrent of denial. In another rendering of the maternal care theme, the child sucked on a bottle while the mother held her, though this scenario also alludes to feelings of neediness that may have been experienced by the participant child. In another example of benevolent interaction, the mother figure engaged the child in a companionable activity: Both laid down on the rug (a transformation of the mother's house) and "they have a nice thing." However, although the interaction between mother and child figures was benevolent, the mother's distress was not addressed.

Malevolent Mother–Child Interactions

Five participant children presented interactions between mother and child figures that were primarily malevolent, in contrast to 17 stories in which father–child and/or father–mother interactions were so characterized.

Sometimes malevolent behavior took the form of aggression. In one story, the child figure stated that Uncle Fred "turns back into live [*sic*]," followed by the mother figure knocking the child figure down and the child figure reciprocating. When asked "how come?" the participant child merely responded "because." In another story the mother figure "pounded" the child and then the child "stomped" the mother. Again, no explanation for these actions was given. Yet another example of malevolent interaction occurred in a story cited earlier in which the mother choked the child for speaking ill of the father figure.

These examples of aggression between story mother and child may symbolize the participant child's angry feelings toward the actual mother or vice versa. Two stories hint at the participant child's anger for driving the other parent away. In one of these stories, cited earlier, the child figure whipped and kicked the mother, claiming that the dead Uncle Fred was "the best daddy." In the second story, the child figure bit the mother in response to Uncle Fred's death. Interestingly, explicit self-blame for the divorce by child figure was not enacted in the "Uncle Fred" story.

A few of the mother–child interactions were classified as malevolent because the mother figure neglected the needs of the child figure. In one instance, the child figure went to the mother's house "all by herself. She's very sad because no one's over there, and she can't play. She wants to play with Barney [family dog, used in a previous story] . . . because Barney died." The parent figures, in the meantime, had been placed together in the father's house. When the child figure walked over to the father's house to tell her parents that the family dog died, they merely replied "go to bed." After returning alone to the mother's house the child figure was said to be "dreaming about who she used to play with at home." The wording suggests that the death of the dog may have represented the father's absence and unavailability as playmate. In a somewhat similar story, the child figure also went to the mother's house alone, leaving the mother figure sitting on the couch. No further interaction of mother and child figures occurred in this story. The mother figure was then placed with the father figure in the father's house where the father, initially believed to be dead, revealed to the mother that he was "only sleeping, silly." The lack of consideration for the child figure's needs portrayed in these story completions may represent the actual child's feelings of being neglected as a consequence of the divorce.

Ambivalent Mother–Child Interactions

In 13 of the stories, the mother–child interaction was characterized as ambivalent, that is, as portraying a mixture of benevolent and malevolent behaviors with neither being predominant. The ambivalence in these stories may reflect inconsistency in the participant child's interactions with the actual parents during the renegotiation of family relationships that follows the divorce process.

One ambivalent story started out with mother, child, and father figures sitting together on the couch "cause they were sad" (benevolent empathy). After the participant child explained, "We don't need these houses like two houses," the couch was placed on top of the two united parental houses. The child figure then fell off the couch, hurt his hand, and told the mother he got a cut. The mother did not respond and the child figure "didn't know where the band-aids were." The story ended with mother and father figures remaining together on the couch while the child figure went to a friend's house and was pushed off the table. In a few other stories that were classified as ambivalent, maternal caregiving was accompanied by ineffectual behaviors which, it might be argued, could be also seen as a type of neglect. For example, in one story the child figure approached the mother and told her "I can make him [Uncle Fred] come alive, I have powers." The mother answered, "Do you? Well, let's go get him." The child figure then asked, "Aren't you coming, mama?" to which the mother, who had changed her mind, replied: "No, you do it." In another story the child figure approached the crying mother figure, saying: "Oh, yeah? Here let me give you a hug" (indicating benevolent feelings). However, the child figure then began to doubt the mother, saying: "There, let's go to Uncle Bob [sic], and see if you're telling the truth." After going to Uncle Bob's imaginary house, the child figure repeatedly said: "Wake up," to which the imaginary Uncle Bob replied: "Yes?" This was followed by the child figure reproaching the mother: "See? He didn't die. So dry your tears off. You were just making a lie, see? He woke up." This story may indicate a sense of distrust by the participant child vis-à-vis what he is being told by his actual mother.

CONCLUDING REMARKS

Fein (1989) suggests that pretending, with its associated symbolic meaning system, is "a means for regulating emotional life" (p. 360). We argue that the children whose responses to the "Uncle Fred" stories we have described here are revealing this regulatory process by using the story completion task as a vehicle for working on issues and concerns related to their parents' divorce. Many of their themes recall those observed in a small sample of preschoolers during much longer diagnostic play interviews conducted primarily for research purposes (Wallerstein

& Kelly, 1975). They also recall themes observed by clinicians writing about play therapy with children of divorce. For example, Hodges (1991) lists anger, abandonment, and loss themes as particularly common. Gardner (1991) adds grief and depression, denial, blame and guilt, immaturity, hypermaturity, reconciliation preoccupation, self-esteem, sexual identity, quest for the lost parent, deprivation, annihilation, guilt, fear of retribution, and devaluation. Note, however, that the majority of the examples supplied by Hodges and by Gardner refer to stories created by children over 7 years of age rather than preschoolers.

That the preschoolers in our sample created so many divorce-related themes resembling those noted by play therapists working with children of divorce surprised us for several reasons. First, aside from placing the parents in separate houses, the task was not explicitly set up for probing divorce-related themes. Second, the children were younger than many of those described in the play therapy literature. Third, unlike the children in the Wallerstein and Kelly group who were also recruited from a nonclinical population and resembled ours in age, children in our study did not participate in a lengthy diagnostic play interview lasting several hours. They produced the themes described in this chapter in the course of just a few minutes to only 1 of 10 story stems that composed the entire task. Finally, their parents had been divorced or permanently separated for at least 2 years, unlike those participating in the Wallerstein and Kelly study who were observed while their parents were divorcing.

Loss Themes Associated with the Father Figure

Most striking in the "Uncle Fred" story completions was the theme of father loss that was either directly enacted or indirectly suggested. That the identification or association of the father figure with the dead Uncle Fred was so immediate and frequent suggests that many of the postdivorce preschoolers in our study felt anxious about potential loss of the father.

Reunifications

Emery (1994), drawing on his clinical work with postdivorce families, claims that years after a divorce becomes final, children and adults often hold out the possibility of reversing the divorce. Many responses to the "Uncle Fred" story revealed such hopes. In some cases, these were expressed by bringing Uncle Fred, portrayed by the father figure or even identified as the father figure, back to life. Given that children often feel powerless in divorce situations, it was interesting to note that a few children used "powers" to revive Uncle Fred, alias dad.

Hope for family reunification was also expressed symbolically by combining the two pieces of felt that represented the parental houses, or by handing one of the houses to the interviewer as no longer needed. In one particularly poignant instance, the participant child placed the family figures under a tent-like structure formed from the parental houses as protection against the rain.

Yet another quite frequent variation on the reunification theme consisted of the father coming over to join mother and child to express empathy, in one case by becoming the priest who officiated at the grave. In a number of these cases, however, chaos, aggression, and even death to all family members occurred when the father figure was moved close to mother and child. In these cases, contact between the parents led to anger and loss of control (in one case depicted as a tornado). As in Wallerstein and Kelly's accounts, these disruptions sometimes occurred after initially idyllic scenes as if the children telling these stories could not sustain the hopeful image they had initially created.

Blame and Rejection

Wallerstein and Kelly had noted that preschoolers often blame themselves for causing their parents' divorce through naughty behavior. We did not observe explicit depictions of this theme in any of the responses to the "Uncle Fred" story, though they would have been easy to enact. The story in which the mother chokes the child for speaking badly of the father may possibly represent an indirect portrayal of this theme. Interestingly, other recent literature reviews have also reported very low levels of self-blame in school-age children (Grych & Fincham, 1999). In contrast, blame of the *mother* for causing the divorce was explicitly portrayed in the story in which the child figure kicks the mother off the table for causing the death of "the best daddy." In addition, there were two stark instances in which the father was portrayed as putting the mother and child on the garbage. These may symbolic instances of the father blaming mother and child for the divorce.

Deprivation and Injury

Many clinicians writing about marital breakup and marital distress have noted that children sometimes try to distract their parents from spousal conflicts by drawing attention to themselves (e.g., Vuchinich, Emery, & Cassidy, 1988). This might explain the fairly numerous stories in which the participant child enacted injury to the story child or even to him- or herself in response to the mother figure's crying about Uncle Fred's death. We regard it as more likely, however, that the children were depicting deprivation or "neediness" themes in response to the anxiety-provoking scene of a distressed, vulnerable mother figure. In a small number of these stories, the hurt child figure did not receive care from one of the parents and was depicted as lonely and abandoned, with the parental figures placed together elsewhere.

Vulnerability of the whole family was suggested in the stories in which all three family members died or the family was devastated by explosions and storms. However, in one case of mild family vulnerability (the family's house leaks in the rain), the participant child was able to protect the family by covering it with a tent formed from the parental houses.

Alliances, Loyalty Conflicts, Responsibility

Neither Hodges (1991) nor Gardner (1991) listed alliances between a child and one parent against the other parent as a common divorce theme in play therapy, though Emery (1994) reported this to be a pervasive issue for children of divorce. A number of participant children did enact such alliances in response to the "Uncle Fred" story. An example was the mother figure who, after arguing with the father, possessively insisted "these are my daughters," and the child figure (in the same story) who took the mother's side when mediating between the quarreling parents. A child–father alliance was suggested by the previously mentioned story in which the child figure kicked the mother figure off the table, apparently blaming her for the death of "the best daddy."

Being "caught in the middle" and serving as go-between is another common problem that many children of divorce experience (Emery, 1994). Several instances in which the story child went to check on the death of Uncle Fred/dad while the mother remained on the couch suggest that the participant child may have experienced such situations. In a variant of this scenario, a letter announced that Uncle Fred/dad—initially believed to be dead—was alive. The child figure, after checking on the father, then managed to persuade the initially disbelieving mother to come and look for herself that the father figure was still alive. The story of the child figure putting the house back "like it was supposed to be, like it was before," was another example portraying a child as assuming an adult-like, even parent-like, role of responsibility for repairing the family.

Empathy for a Parent and Role Reversal

Empathic behavior by the child toward the mother was enacted in 40% of the stories. Johnston and Roseby (1997) suggested that postdivorce children from high-conflict families are acutely aware of the emotional neediness of their parents and can become intensely concerned about the parents' emotional and physical well-being. Emery (1994) also points out that some postdivorce children reverse roles by taking care of the parents' emotional needs. We would like to caution, however, that it is necessary to distinguish between a child's healthy empathy toward a sad parent and a child taking charge of the situation as if the parent was the child in need of care or discipline (behavior variously termed "role reversal," "parentification," or "inverting the parent–child role"; see Emery, 1994). Although this is not always an easy distinction to draw, we did observe several clear examples of role reversal in responses to the "Uncle Fred" story, such as the already mentioned story in which the mother figure sent the child alone to check on whether the father was dead, even after the child figure asked, "Aren't you coming, mama?"

In summary, through their responses to the "Uncle Fred" story stem, the 71 children participating in this study offered surprisingly many glimpses into continuing concerns associated with postdivorce family life. The richness and depth of many of their stories suggest that this story completion technique can be helpful in probing children's thoughts, hopes, and fears regarding postdivorce family interactions, concerns that only rarely emerged from our direct 2-hour home observations from dinnertime to bedtime (Bretherton, Corey, & Tiwari, 2001) and that may, hence, often be overlooked.

Our analysis underscores the point, eloquently made by Emery (1994), that postdivorce children's general adjustment and resilience does not preclude concurrent feelings of pain, fear of parental loss, sadness or anger, and continued hope for reconciliation. In our studies, these themes were readily evoked well after the parental divorce decree became final and in a standard story completion task that only alluded to the divorce situation through the placement of the parental figures in separate houses. This suggests that these children continued to be preoccupied with making sense of relationship issues facing their reorganized families. The fact that their preschool teachers generally rated them as quite well adjusted indicates that similar preoccupations are likely to be common in other nonclinical groups. Preschoolers' everyday adjustment in the family and with peers should therefore not lead either professionals or parents to trivialize the emotional work with which young children are faced after their parents divorce. Our findings lead us to submit that all children of divorce might benefit from continuing age-appropriate help with clarifying their understanding and feelings about parental divorce. For preschoolers, the enactment and narration of stories may serve as a useful springboard for eliciting their thoughts, hopes, and fears.

ACKNOWLEDGMENTS

The research reported in this chapter was funded by Grant No. R01 HD267766 awarded to Inge Bretherton by the National Institutes of Health (National Institute of Child Health and Human Development). Supplementary support was provided by the University of Wisconsin Graduate School Research Committee, the Waisman Center, and the Vilas Trust. We wish to express our gratitude for this support. We would also like to thank Tim Page for administering and transcribing the stories, and Barbara Golby, Chris Halvorsen, Rhegan Walsh, and Laura Winn for assisting with data collection. Last, but not least, we wish to express our appreciation to the mothers and children who participated in this study.

REFERENCES

Amato, P. R., & Keith, B. (1991). Parental divorce and adult well-being: A meta-analysis. *Journal of Marriage and the Family, 53*, 43–58.

Axline, V. M. (1969). *Play therapy.* New York: Ballantine Books.

Beck, A. T. (1976). *Cognitive therapy and the emotional disorders.* New York: International Universities Press.

Bretherton, I., Corey, J., & Tiwari, G. (2001). *Home observations of postdivorce families as related to maternal and child representations of family life.* Manuscript in preparation, University of Wisconsin-Madison.

Bretherton, I., Munholland, K. A., & Page, T. (1999). *"He lives with them now": Divorce-related themes in preschoolers family story completions.* Paper presented at the Biennial Meetings of the Society for Research in Child Development, Albuquerque, NM.

Bretherton, I., Oppenheim, D., Buchsbaum, H., Emde, R. N., & MacArthur Narrative Group. (1990). *The MacArthur Story Stem Battery.* Unpublished manual, University of Wisconsin–Madison.

Bretherton, I., Page, T., Golby, B., & Walsh, R. (1997). *Fathers in postdivorce families seen through the eyes of mothers and children.* Unpublished report to the Aid Association for Lutherans Scholars Committee, School of Human Ecology, University of Wisconsin–Madison.

Bretherton, I., & Ridgeway, D. (1990). Assessing internal working models of the attachment relationship: Appendix. Attachment Story Completion Task. In M. T. Greenberg, D. Cicchetti, & E. M. Cummings (Eds.), *Attachment in the preschool years: Theory, research, and intervention.* Chicago: University of Chicago Press.

Bretherton, I., Ridgeway, D., & Cassidy, J. (1990). Assessing internal working models of the attachment relationship. In M. T. Greenberg, D. Cicchetti, &

E. M. Cummings (Eds.), *Attachment in the preschool years: Theory, research, and intervention* (pp. 273–308). Chicago: University of Chicago Press.

Buchsbaum, H., & Emde, R. N. (1990). Play narratives in 36-month-old children: Early moral development and family relationships. *Psychoanalytic Study of the Child, 40,* 129–625.

Cassidy, J. (1988). Child–mother attachment and the self in six-year-olds. *Child Development, 59,* 121–134.

Emery, R. E. (1994). *Renegotiating family relationships: Divorce, child custody, and mediation.* New York: Guilford Press.

Erikson, E. H. (1963). *Childhood and society.* New York: Norton.

Fein, G. G. (1981). Pretend play in childhood: An integrative review. *Child Development, 52,* 1095–1118.

Fein, G. G. (1989). Mind, meaning, and affect: Proposals for a theory of pretense. *Developmental Review, 9,* 345–363.

Freud, A. (1946). *The psycho-analytical treatment of children.* London: Imago.

Gardner, R. A. (1991). *Psychotherapy with children of divorce.* Northvale, NJ: Jason Aronson.

Grych, J. H., & Fincham, F. D. (1999). Children of single parents and divorce. In W. K. Silverman & T. H. Ollendick (Eds.), *Developmental issues in the clinical treatment of children* (pp. 321–341). Boston: Allyn & Bacon.

Hetherington, M. E. (1979). Coping with family transitions: Winners, losers and survivors. *Child Development, 60,* 1–14.

Hodges, W. F. (1991). *Interventions for children of divorce.* New York: Wiley.

Hollingshead, A. B. (1978). *The four-factor index of social status.* Unpublished manuscript, Yale University, New Haven, CT.

Johnston, J. R., & Roseby, V. (1997). *In the name of the child: A developmental approach to understanding and helping children of conflicted and violent divorce.* New York: Free Press.

Miller, T. J. (1984). Therapist–child relations in play therapy. In T. D. Yawkey & A. D. Pellegrini (Eds.), *Child's play and play therapy* (pp. 85–103). Lancaster, PA: Technomic.

Oppenheim, D. (1997). The attachment doll play interview for preschoolers. *International Journal of Behavioral Development, 20,* 681–697.

Oppenheim, D., Emde, R. N., & Warren, S. (1997). Children's narrative representation of mothers: Their developments and associations with child and mother adaptation. *Child Development, 68,* 127–138.

Oppenheim, D., & Waters, H. S. (1995). Narrative processes and attachment representations: Issues of development and assessment. In E. Waters, B. E. Vaughn, G. Posada, & K. Kondo-Ikemura (Eds.), Caregiving, cultural and cognitive perspectives on secure base behavior and working models. *Monographs of the Society for Research in Child Development, 60*(2–3, Serial No. 244), 197–233.

Page, T. (in press). The social meaning of children's narratives: A review of the attachment-based narrative story stem technique. *Child and Adolescent Social Work Journal.*

Page, T., & Bretherton, I. (1993). *Manual for coding the Expanded Story Completion*

Task adapted for children of divorce. Unpublished manuscript, University of Wisconsin–Madison.

Page, T., & Bretherton, I. (in press). Mother– and father–child attachment themes as represented in the story completions of preschoolers in post-divorce families: Linkages with teacher ratings of social competence. *Attachment and Human Development*.

Piaget, J. (1951). *Play, dreams and imitation in childhood*. New York: Norton.

Solomon, J., & George, C. (1999). The measurement of attachment security in infancy and childhood. In J. Cassidy & P. R. Shaver (Eds.), *Handbook of attachment: Theory, research, and clinical applications* (pp. 287–316). New York: Guilford Press.

Verschueren, K., Marcoen, A., & Schoefs, V. (1996). The internal working model of the self, attachment and competence in five-year-olds. *Child Development, 67*, 2493–2511.

Vuchinich, S., Emery, R. E., & Cassidy, J. (1988). Family members as third parties in dyadic family conflict: Strategies, alliances, and outcomes. *Child Development, 59*, 1293–1302.

Waelder, R. (1933). The psychoanalytic theory of play. *Psychoanalytic Quarterly, 2*, 208–224.

Wallerstein, J. S., & Kelly, J. B. (1975). The effects of parental divorce: The experiences of the preschool child. *Journal of the American Academy of Child Psychiatry and Child Development, 14*, 600–615.

Wallerstein, J. S., & Kelly, J. B. (1980). *Surviving the breakup: How children and parents cope with divorce*. New York: Basic Books.

Zahn-Waxler, C., Cole, P. M., Richardson, D. T., Friedman, R. J., Michel, M. K., & Belouad, F. (1994). Social problem solving in disruptive preschool children: Reactions to hypothetical situations of conflict and distress. *Merrill–Palmer Quarterly, 40*, 98–119.

9

❧

"I'm So Glad I'm Glad"

*The Role of Emotions and Close Relationships
in Children's Play and Narrative Language*

A. D. PELLEGRINI
LEE GALDA

It is a great personal pleasure and honor to be asked to write a chapter celebrating the career of our friend and colleague Greta G. Fein. Greta is a wonderful person as well as one of the most important persons in our field and we thank her for her many and diverse contributions. Greta, for us, represents a wonderful combination of high positive affect and intellectual acuity.

In many ways Greta's work in children's narrative and play incorporates these affective and intellectual properties. Most influential for us has been Greta's work on the emotional dimensions of pretending (Fein, 1989) and narrative language (Fein, 1995). In the spirit of narrative, we begin with a brief story.

Our work on narrative, play, and children's language began a number of years ago as we were both reading a typed draft of the Rubin, Fein, and Vandenberg (1983) chapter on play. I (L. G.) was struck by the similarity between the design features of pretending and those of narrative. About this time we also got to know Greta personally. Greta was enthusiastic about this line of research and encouraged us to work in what was considered then a rather marginal area of scientific inquiry within the child development community. Guided by the features of pretending, which were more clearly explicated in Greta's *Child Devel-*

opment (Fein, 1981), a review paper on pretend play, we began our work on the relations between play and narrative and play and early literacy (Galda, 1984; Pellegrini, 1985). This work was followed by an edited book on the topic (Galda & Pellegrini, 1985) and a series of empirical studies of preschoolers' pretend play, narrative language (Pellegrini & Galda, 1988), and early literacy (summarized in Pellegrini & Galda, 1991).

After a number of years, our interest and funding in this area waned, despite Greta's ever present encouragement. Upon meeting Greta at a professional meeting, I (ADP) told her about my latest work in another area of play (rough-and-tumble play). Greta listened politely, but then she insisted, with a smile, that we really should return to the area of narrative and play, noting there were many more interesting and important questions to be answered there than in rough and tumble. Greta, we have returned to the study of play, narrative, and language and thank you for your guidance, support, and friendship.

In this chapter we present results from our work with the National Reading Research Center (NRRC) which was housed in Athens, Georgia from 1992 to 1997. Our research at NRRC was concerned primarily with social contextual arrangements as they related to children's first encounters with literacy in a school setting. In this chapter, we examine some ways in which emotional dimensions of peer groups, such as friendships and acquaintances, and instructional settings, such as pretend play and literacy settings, relate to children's use of narrative language.

We, like Fein, propose that emotions serve an important role in children's social pretend play, narrative language, and early literacy. High positive emotions probably motivate children to initiate and sustain activity in these areas. The emotional investment that characterizes children's play and narrative language is evidenced by their talk about emotions—for example, "I'm so glad." Talk about emotions, in turn, enables children to both "cool" those emotions and reflect upon the emotions—"I'm so glad I'm glad" (Bruner, 1987). By cooling we mean that children pause and think about the processes or problems under consideration. This, in turn, enables children to consider the emotional, cognitive, and linguistic processes constitutive of peer interaction (e.g., "I'm so glad I'm glad"). When this sort of interaction occurs in the context of literacy events (e.g., being read to, writing a story), or talking about a story, children typically reflect on the nature of language and literacy per se. This ability to reflect on language and literacy is a powerful predictor of school-based literacy (Pellegrini, Galda, Bartini, & Charak, 1997).

In this chapter, we discuss what we mean by literate language, paying specific attention to the social–contextual configurations, such as friendships, which seem to support its use. We also discuss the instructional dimensions of social context as they relate to literate language. Specifically, we examine how variation in the playful and didactic orientations of context affect the use of literate language. Finally, we present experimental evidence documenting the effects of these contextual variables on children's literate language.

EMOTIONS, NARRATIVES, AND EARLY LITERACY

Narratives have long been the object of scholarly inquiry in numerous fields, such as literary criticism (Burke, 1945), folklore (Sutton-Smith, 1981), linguistics (Chafe, 1980), psychoanalysis, education (Britton, 1970; Hymes & Cazden, 1980), and,most recently cognitive developmental psychology (Bruner, 1986; Fein, 1995). Child developmentalists and educationalists have been especially attracted to the production of narratives and narrative language because of the ubiquity of narrative forms during the preschool period and their possible roles in subsequent development and education. Narrative language resembles the language of stories,in its temporal organization and fictitious characters. Narrative language is typically used by young children as they interact with peers, especially during pretend play (Fein, 1987, 1995). Pretend play and oral narratives, especially of the sort produced by young children, have similar structure (Galda, 1984). For example, each involves pretending, temporal and causal motivations, and characters solving problems. These features, in turn, reflect the narrative structure of many of the stories young children hear.

Narrative language, however, can be described in two ways: It is emotionally laden and literate. Emotionally laden language (Britton, 1970; Bruner, 1986; Hymes & Cazden, 1980) conveys meaning through personal forms, in contrast to language that is more impersonal and often also expository. The stress on the personal over the impersonal implies that emotionality is an important component in children's narrative productions. Thus, narrative language may be one way in which children come to terms with cognitive and emotional ambiguity, inconsistency, and difficulties (Pellegrini & Galda, 1988). As Greta Fein (1995) notes, narratives may help children address "deeply held human concerns" (p. 152). Greta's (1995) elegant experimental investigations into these matters have shown that preschoolers' narratives are often elicited by fear and breach of conventionality.

Literate language is the second dimension of narrative language, and it too has been examined by Fein (Fein, Ardilia-Rey, & Groth, 2000).

Literate language typifies narratives used in school-based literacy events, in the service of early literacy instruction (Galda, Cullinan, & Strickland, 1997). Literate language is represented in the early texts children read, write, and talk about in school and it is used by teachers in literacy events (Cook-Gumperz, 1977). It is this aspect of narrative language, literate language, that we discuss in this chapter.

Early literacy events often involve talk between children and peers and between children and teachers about narratives. Like other forms of story-related language, this talk contains conjunctions marking temporality (e.g., "He ran up to the car *and then* said Boo"), causality (e.g., " *'Cause* he was scary"), and adversity (e.g., "He should, *but* won't"). In addition, literate language involves talk about talk, thought processes, and the literacy events in which the talk is embedded. For example, when children say a text is *hard* or ask *what sound a letter makes*, they are talking about the cognitive and linguistic processes which typically constitute school-based literacy events.

Children's production of this linguistic register is affected by different social–emotional arrangements. In the experiment presented in this chapter, we examine the ways in which pairs of friends, compared to pairs of acquaintances, produce literate language.

USE OF LITERATE LANGUAGE
WITH FRIENDS AND ACQUAINTANCES

We present a comparison of the effects of friendship and acquaintance configuration on children's use of literate language because these two social groupings represent one way in which emotional commitment between peers can be operationalized. Friendships are reciprocal, dyadic relationships (i.e., friends nominate each other as friends) and are characterized by mutuality and emotional ties and commitment (Hartup, 1996). Acquaintances, on the other hand, are familiar with each other but do not share the reciprocity and emotional commitment of friendships.

The reciprocity, and corresponding emotional commitment, which characterizes friendships may be an important reason why friendship groupings, compared to acquaintances, are supportive of cognitive performance. It may be that friends engage in the sorts of conceptual conflicts, which, according to Piaget's equilibration theory, foster cognitive growth. Friends, compared to nonfriends, do indeed engage in more conflicts and they more frequently resolve these conflicts (Hartup, 1996; Pellegrini, Galda, Bartini, & Charak, 1997). The conflict/resolution cycles between friends, compared to acquaintances, are also more likely to result in "mature cognitions" (Nelson & Aboud, 1985; Newcombe & Brady, 1982). For this reason, we hypothesized that friendship, compared to acquaintance, groupings should evidence more literate language.

The process by which conflicts and resolutions lead to "mature cognitions" is mediated by emotionality. We posit a process model whereby conflicts and resolutions arouse high levels of emotionality, especially between friends (Dunn, 1988). For higher-level cognitive interactions to occur subsequently, these intense emotions must be "cooled," to use Bruner's (1987) term. Children's talk about emotions serves to cool the emotions surrounding conflicts/resolutions (Bruner, 1987; Dunn, 1988; Pellegrini, Galda, Flor, Bartini, & Charak, 1998). The mechanism at work to "cool" may be something like Pavlov's second signal system where language mediates thought (Bruner, 1987). More simply, talking about emotions may merely provide the time necessary to lower emotions. Thus, we expect conflicts/resolutions to relate to children's use of emotional terms, both of which should be observed more frequently between friends than acquaintances. Emotional terms should, in turn, relate to higher cognitive processes and talk about language and cognitive processes.

FRIENDS IN DIDACTIC AND PLAYFUL INSTRUCTIONAL SITUATIONS

Friends also provide support for each other in demanding situations. The mutuality of friendship typically means that children have reasonable expectations of support from their friends. Friends know that when they support each other, their efforts will usually be reciprocated. Consequently, we also expect the children in the friendship condition, because of reciprocity and mutuality, to support exhibition of high levels of literate language in a demanding situation (Azimitia & Montgomery, 1993). For this reason we observed friend and acquaintance dyads as they interacted in both a relatively demanding, didactic setting (writing narratives about a story they had just been read) and a relatively undemanding play setting (peer play with narrative-eliciting props).

A demanding, didactic setting was defined as one in which children were presented with a writing task by an adult. Writing lessons are usually associated with formal schooling and, consequently, are governed by a priori rules to which children must accommodate. Also, writing in most classrooms is usually serious business, partially because of these rules.

An undemanding play setting, on the other hand, was defined by the children themselves, not by an adult; pretend play is an example of an informal task. Play with peers, unlike the writing task, is not usually subject to the same level of teacher-imposed rules. Peer play is rule governed, but the rules are presented and negotiated between peers (Garvey, 1990; Garvey & Kramer, 1989; Garvey & Shantz, 1992; Göncü, 1993). In the course of negotiating play roles and defining play transformations, children often talk about linguistic and mental states (Garvey, 1990). That children enjoy peer play motivates them to sustain this difficult social cognitive work (Garvey, 1990).

The idea that young children should exhibit higher levels of literate language in play contexts than in more demanding school lessons is also consistent with Vygotsky's (1967) theory of play. The theory posits that children's play scaffolds their exhibition of competence because in pretending they are motivated to reach fantastic goals (i.e., goals obtainable only through pretense, while simultaneously confronting the rules governing these sorts of behaviors in real life) (see Fein, 1979, for an excellent discussion of these issues).

In contrast, during adult-directed writing, because it may be less motivating than peer play, children may choose not to expend much social cognitive effort to complete these tasks. Thus, formal literacy events, relative to peer play, may actually dampen children's exhibition of competence (i.e., literate language) whereas play may facilitate it (Vygotsky, 1967). Accordingly, we predict a main effect for didactic/play condition such that children should generate more literate language in the play context than in the writing context. We also predict a social context (i.e., friends/acquaintance) by task (i.e., didactic/play context) interaction on measures of literate language such that in the writing condition friends, compared to acquaintances, should exhibit more literate language.

GENDER AND FRIENDSHIP

Gender is also relevant to the study of children's friendships. We know that children's friends are usually of the same gender (Hartup, 1983). We also know (Maccoby, 1990) that boys are more assertive and conflictual than girls; thus, we expect boys to engage in more conflicts and resolutions than girls. Girls, on the other hand, tend to be more emotional and enabling (Maccoby, 1990) than boys; thus we expect girls to generate more emotional terms than boys. These differences are consistent with Maccoby's (1990, 1998) characterizations of interaction styles in gender-segregated groups.

Although the literature on gender and different social relationships is limited (Newcombe & Bagwell, 1995), there are some findings from related literature which allow us to generate hypotheses. Specifically, girls, more than boys, are concerned with close relationships (Waldrop & Halverson, 1975) and girls are more cooperative with friends than with other acquaintances (Feshbach, 1969). Consequently, we expect girls to exhibit higher levels of competence (i.e., generate more literate language) in the friendship, compared to the acquaintance, condition.

THE EXPERIMENT

Participants, Procedure, and Measures

The children who participated in the study were sampled from public school kindergarten classes in Athens, Georgia. After approximately 2 weeks of familiarization, research assistants took individual students out of their classrooms and conducted a friendship nomination procedure where each child was shown pictures of all his or her classmates and asked to nominate friends. Friends were defined, following Hartup (1996), as children with reciprocated friendship nominations; that is, children were friends when they nominated each other as friends. Acquaintances were nonfriends from the same classroom. Based on these nominations, friend/nonfriend dyads were constructed. All dyads were comprised of same-gender, same-race children.

Children were observed in friend or acquaintance dyads 12 times across the school year, in play settings and peer writing settings. The separate play observations involved replica toys from currently popular narrative films: *Aladdin, The Jungle Book,* and *The Lion King.* In the play contexts, children were presented with the replica props and encouraged to play. In this setting children generally engaged in social fantasy play with themes consistent with the toys present.

The demanding setting involved children being read a book by an experimenter, then being asked to write about the book and then to talk about their work. Books were all narratives related to the theme of birthdays: Clarke's (1992), *How Many Days to My Birthday?,* Rylant's (1987) *Birthday Presents,* and Brown's (1989), *Arthur's Birthday.* Order of presentation of play/peer writing and friend/acquaintance contexts were counterbalanced, with one exception, across classrooms and three academic quarters. The exception related to the initial presentation of the books in the writing setting. Because of some new kindergartners' limited literacy skills, the simplest book was presented first (*How Many Days to My Birthday?*).

Children were observed at tables in a hall outside their classrooms. Audiorecordings were made of their interactions and from these recordings, measures of children's oral language were derived.

In the writing setting, researchers first read the assigned book to the group. After each book, researchers followed standardized instructions to encourage children to write and talk about the stories they had just heard. Most of the talk occurred after the writing process per se: Children read their texts to each other, told stories about the texts and pictures, and talked about reading and writing generally.

Oral language tapes were coded by one of the research assistants according to mutually exclusive categories. All measures of oral language derived from audiotapes were expressed in terms of relative frequency. Measures of each category for each dyad were averaged across the three academic quarters.

Conjunctions were coded as *additive* (e.g., *and*), *temporal* (e.g., *and then*), *causal* (e.g., *because*), or *adversative* (e.g., *but*). Linguistic, cognitive, and emotional terms were coded as *regular* and *contrastive*. Use of *regular* linguistic (e.g., *"Talk* louder"), cognitive (e.g., "Let me *think"*), and emotional (e.g., "I'm *happy* now") terms indicates children's knowledge of those processes (Pellegrini et al., 1995). *Contrastive* linguistic (e.g., "You *can't say* that"), cognitive (e.g., "It *doesn't make sense"*), and emotion terms (e.g., "He's *not really sad"*) are most indicative of reflection on the processes they encode (Shatz, Wellman, & Silber, 1983) and predictive of early literacy (Pellegrini & Galda, 1991).

Finally, oral language tapes were coded for *conflicts and resolutions.* Conflicts included any mention of disbelief, disagreement, efforts to substitute one thing for an other, postponements, and evasions. Resolutions were represented by compromise, expression of sorrow/apology, and accepting explanation/alternative.

Results/Discussion

Variation in Language: Effects for Relationships and Writing/Play Settings

In these analyses we address the ways in which social contextual variables affect literate language as well as the conflicts/resolutions and emotional language that accompany it. First, we addressed the hypothesis that children would generate more literate language, conflicts and resolutions, and emotional terms in the friend and play conditions, respectively, compared to the acquaintance and writing conditions. Gender was also expected to interact with social context to the extent that girls should generate more literate language as well as conflict/resolutions and emotional terms with friends than with acquaintances. We also predicted that the social (friend/acquaintance) and setting (play/writing) conditions would have an interactive effect on these forms of language. In the writing condition, we hypothesized, more literate language should be observed between friends, compared to acquaintances.

These hypotheses were tested with gender (2), social context (2: friend/acquaintance), and setting (2: play/writing) analyses of variance (ANOVAs) on separate dimensions of children's oral language production. We begin with literate language.

Literate Language. Dimensions of literate language analyzed included conjunctions (additive, temporal, and causal) and regular and contrastive cognitive and linguistic terms.

First regarding additive conjunctions, a significant social context × gender interaction, $F(1, 15) = 4.90, p < .02$, was observed such that girls generated more in the friend condition ($M = .025$) than in the acquaintance condition ($M = .02$), and boys ($M = .03$) generated more than girls in that latter condition. For temporal conjunctions no significant effects were observed. For causal conjunctions a main significant effect for social context was observed, $F(1, 15) = 7.45, p < .005$, as was a significant social context X gender interaction, $F(1, 15) = 5.87, p < .01$. Like the additive conjunction results, girls generated more causal conjunctions with friends ($M = .015$) than with acquaintances ($M = .01$). Further, in the friend condition, they generated more causals than boys ($M = .01$). These results are consistent with our hypothesis that girls would exhibit their highest levels of competence with friends.

For cognitive terms, no social contextual effects were observed but a significant effect for gender, $F(1, 15) = 8.20, p < .005$, was observed, with girls ($M = .03$) using more cognitive terms than boys ($M = .015$). For the cognitive contrast terms a significant effect for social context was observed, $F(1, 15) = 4.08, p < .03$, where more were observed between friends ($M = .01$) than acquaintances ($M = .001$). This finding is consistent with our predicted relationship effects but not with our writing/play prediction.

For regular linguistic terms significant main effects were observed for the undemanding/play condition, $F(1, 15) = 56.53, p < .0001$, and the social context, $F(1, 15) = 14.76, p < .0001$. More regular linguistic terms were observed in the writing setting ($M = .04$) than in play ($M = .015$), whereas more regular linguistic terms were observed in the friend dyads ($M = .035$) than in the acquaintance dyads ($M = .02$).

Regarding linguistic contrast terms, a main effect was observed for writing/play settings, $F(1,15) = 11.35, p002$, with more being observed in the writing condition ($M = .01$) than in the play condition ($M = .005$). These results are partially supportive of the relationship hypothesis but counter to our writing/play hypothesis.

Emotional Terms and Conflicts/Resolutions. We also predicted main effects for the friendship condition and for gender on regular and contrastive emotional terms and conflicts and resolutions. We expected more conflicts/resolutions from boys than girls and more emotional terms from girls than from boys. Regarding regular emotional terms,no significant effects were observed, though the effect for social context approached significance, $F(1, 15) = 2.32$, $p < .07$, with more emotional terms being observed between friends ($M = .007$) than between acquaintances ($M = .001$). For emotion contrast terms,a significant effect for gender, $F(1, 15) = 6.81$, $p < .005$, was observed where girls ($M = .013$) used more than boys ($M = .01$). Thus, our gender hypothesis was supported but not the relationship hypothesis.

Next we consider conflicts/resolutions (conflict/resolution cycles). A significant gender effect, $F(1, 15) = 5.91$, $p < .01$ (boys: $M = .032$; girls: $M = .02$), was observed, as was a significant effect for the writing ($M = .017$)/play ($M = .035$) setting, $F(1, 15) = 12.94$, $p < .001$. The gender effect was consistent with our hypothesis but the relationship effect was not.

The data from this experiment only partially support our claim for the effects of social relationships. First, we did not observe a significant main effect, as predicted, for the friends/acquaintances context on conflicts/resolutions. However, the data that showed that friends, especially female friends, exhibited more emotional language than acquaintances, did support our hypotheses.

These equivocal results were probably due to our definition of friends as reciprocally nominated friends and acquaintances as familiar children. Meta-analyses of friendship relations suggest that comparisons between friends and acquaintances as defined here often detect few differences, especially for children in this age group (Newcombe & Bagwell, 1995). It may have been the case in this study that children's repeated interactions with acquaintances, who were also in the same classrooms, across the school year resulted in their becoming friends (Hartup, 1996). Although our definitions of friends and acquaintances were based on theories presented in the literature and the ecology of peer relations in classrooms, more extreme, but ecologically valid, contrasts are justified in future research. For example, reciprocal friends should be compared with acquaintances in the same classroom who do not like each other.

That friends, compared to acquaintances, would generate more literate language was generally supported. Specifically, friends exhibited more talk about language and talk about cognitive processes than did acquaintances. For two of the three measures of conjunctions, friendship effects were mediated by gender. Girls exhibited more of this form of talk with friends than with acquaintances. Thus, close relationships facilitate children's aspects of literate language, and these effects seem particularly important for girls. This finding reinforces Waldrop and Halverson's (1975) suggestion, 25 years ago,that close, intensive relationships are important to girls.

However, more research in the area of gender and friendships is needed, particularly as children interact in different task settings. It would be particularly interesting to examine the role of emotionality in male and female friendship groups. For example, under what circumstances, other than following conflict/resolution cycles, do girls use emotional terms? Is this similar for boys?

Our hypotheses for the effects of play/writing settings on children's language were not supported. Indeed, some of the most important results were in the opposite direction: The didactic/writing setting afforded more talk about talk than the play setting.

This finding may have been to due to the age of the children under study. In our earlier work on play and literate language we found that preschool children (3- and 4-year-olds) generated talk about talk in the context of pretend play (Pellegrini & Galda, 1991). Pretend play with peers may have afforded opportunities for youngsters to master a form of language they had learned earlier while interacting with their mothers. When these children reached 5 years of age, however, talk about talk was not significantly correlated with pretend; it co-occurred with realistic peer interaction. Thus, using these terms in pretend settings enables opportunities to master them and use them subsequently in more realistic speech events.

Another, probably complementary, explanation for the writing, not play, setting eliciting more "meta" talk, especially talk about language, was simply that the props in the former setting were more closely related to language than props in the latter setting. In the writing setting, children talked about what they were doing: using language.

These results may have implications for preschool and primary school classrooms. It may be the case that encouragement of pretend play with peers is important to facilitate preschoolers' literate language. For primary school children, on the other hand, the provision of literacy props, such as paper, pens, shared narrative experiences, and, most important, opportunities for children talking with peers,should be encouraged.

Relations of Conflicts/Resolutions with Emotional Terms and Emotional Language with Literate Language

Data analyzed in this section relate to the hypotheses that conflicts and resolutions should relate to encoding of emotional terms and that talk about emotions should, in turn, relate to talk about cognitive and linguistic processes. First, the measures of emotional language and conflicts and resolutions were positively and significantly intercorrelated.

Next, we determined the extent to which the aggregated mean of regular emotional terms, emotion contrast terms, and conflicts/resolutions predicted the use of cognitive language (i.e., the aggregate mean of regular cognitive terms, and cognitive contrast terms) and literate language (the aggregate mean of regular linguistic terms and linguistic contrastive terms). Using regression analyses, the aggregate of emotion terms and conflicts/resolutions predicted a significant portion of the variance in both cognitive ($R^2 = .23$, $p < .0001$) and linguistic language ($R^2 = .46$, $p < .0001$).

We hypothesized that children's "meta" talk, or talk about cognitive and linguistic processes, would correspond to conceptual conflict/resolutions and subsequent emotional "cooling." Our analyses support this contention. Conflicts/resolutions and emotional terms were intercorrelated. These measures, in turn, related to talk about language and cognitive processes. Of course, these data are correlations and directionality is elusive. It could be that conflicts/resolutions and emotional encoding predict "meta" talk or vice versa. Longitudinal data are needed to address this question properly. Our microgenetic analyses, however, support this model (Pellegrini et al., 1998).

CONCLUSION

Guided by Greta Fein's work in this and related areas of study (e.g., symbolic play and Vygotskian theory) we have demonstrated that emotionality is an important component in children's expression of narrative language. In this chapter, we concentrated on one dimension of narrative language: literate language: the story language typifying children's books, early literacy events, and pretend play. Future research should examine the ontogenetic and microgenetic pathways of both forms of narrative language. For example, the emotionally laden language of narrative used to solve social problems (the sort discussed by Bruner) ontogenetically precedes the more school-like forms of literate language. Although longitudinal research is needed to address this issue directly, evidence from a number of sources suggest that children do indeed use the former variety of language well before they use the latter (e.g., Pellegrini & Galda, 1993, 1998). Further, children having a variety of experiences with the specific narrative forms used in school seem to have an easier time learning literate language (Heath, 1983; Michaels, 1981).

At the level of microgenetic development, it would be interesting to examine the extent to which children differentially use each component or dimension of narrative language as they progress through a school-based literacy specific task. Theory (Britton, 1970; Bruner, 1986) and empirical study (Pellegrini & Galda, 1993) suggest that children often use the emotionally laden variant of narrative language when they are confronted with problems. Thus, it may be that when children encounter difficulty or a problem in a literacy event, they use emotionally laden narrative language to address the problem.

In this chapter we also extended our current understanding of the contexts which provide emotional support for the expression of literate language. We have shown that distinctions such as "peer context" are much too global. Different sorts of peer relations and different sorts of instructional settings affect children's interactions and early literacy. Future research should look toward making clearer distinctions among peers. For example, is there a difference between the way friends and best friends interact? If the latter relationship is typified by more trust and investment, we would expect them to also exhibit more literate language.

More provocatively, the theory of Basil Bernstein (1960) is also informative as to the ways in which social configurations affect language. Specifically, 40 years ago Bernstein proposed a theory to account for the ways in which socialization patterns affected language and children's success in school. His seminal discussions of the ways in which socialization experiences affected children's learning of elaborated and restricted codes and the impact on school was well-known, and fortunately is being rediscovered. Basically, his theory predicts that being exposed to a variety, rather than a limited number, of interlocutors should result in cognitive decentering and use of literate language (which he termed "elaborated code").

Bernstein's (1960, 1971, 1972, 1982) elegant discussions of the ways in which social structure and social processes affect language structure and then school performance are a rich source of hypotheses. As part of this discussion, Bernstein suggested that an elaborated code is learned in social contexts that affords speakers opportunities to interact with a variety of different interlocutors. By having to speak with and be understood by a variety of others, he argued, children could not rely on shared background knowledge to convey information. Instead, they would have to lexicalize meaning. To do this,children need to define pronouns; talk about language, thought,and meaning; and use conjunctions to organize their arguments. In short, by interacting with a variety of interlocutors, children have to decenter cognitively and linguistically. These same thought and language processes also typify student–teacher interaction patterns in school.

This "variety" of peers hypothesis is clearly at odds with the "closeness" of peers (in the form of friends) hypothesis put forth in this chapter. It would be interesting to compare the relative impact on literate language of children interacting with a variety of interlocutors with those interacting with friends.

In this chapter we have also shown that the role of play settings in eliciting literate language may be limited for school-age children. Like Greta Fein's most recent work in this area (Fein et al., 2000), future research should address the differential effects of different models of literacy teaching through well-designed field experiments. Certainly much more work is needed in these areas. Greta's theoretical and empirical guidance, as well as her emotional support, will make the work easier.

ACKNOWLEDGMENTS

Work on this chapter was partially supported by grants from the National Reading Research Center and the School of Education at the University of Cardiff. We acknowledge the comments of Artin Göncü on earlier drafts.

REFERENCES

Azimitia, M., & Montgomery, R. (1993). Friendship, transactive dialogues, and the development of scientific reasoning. *Social Development, 2,* 202–221.

Bernstein, B. (1960). Language and social class. *British Journal of Sociology, 1,* 217–227.

Bernstein, B. (1971). *Class, codes, and control* (Vol. 1). London: Routledge & Kegan Paul.

Bernstein, B. (1972). Social class, language, and socialization. In P. Giglioli (Ed.), *Language and social context* (pp. 157–178). Hammondsworth, UK: Penguin.

Bernstein, B. (1982). Codes, modalities and the process of cultural reproduction: A model. In M. Apple (Ed.), *Cultural and economic reproduction in education* (pp. 304–355). Boston: Routledge.

Britton, J. (1970). *Language and learning.* London: Penguin.

Brown, M. (1969). *Arthur's birthday.* New York: Houghton-Mifflin.

Bruner, J. S. (1986). *Actual minds, possible worlds.* Cambridge, MA: Harvard University Press.

Bruner, J. S. (1987, February). *Narrative thought and narrative language.* Paper presented at the Institute for Behavioral Research Cognitive Group Colloquium, Athens, GA.

Burke, K. (1945). *The grammar of motives.* New York: Prentice-Hall.

Chafe, W. L. (Ed.). (1980). *The pear stories.* Norwood, NJ: Ablex.

Clarke, G. (1992). *How many days to my birthday?* London: Andersen Press.

Cook-Gumperz, J. (1977). Situated instructions: Language socialization in school. In S. Ervin-Tripp & K. Mitchell-Kernan (Eds.), *Child discourse* (pp. 103–124). New York: Academy.

Fein, G. G. (1979). Echoes from the nursery: Piaget and Vygotsky, and the relationship between language and play. In E. Winner & H. Gardner (Eds.), *Fact, fiction, and fantasy* (pp. 1–14). San Francisco: Jossey-Bass.

Fein, G. (1981). Pretend play in childhood: An integrative review. *Child Development, 52,* 1095–1118.

Fein, G. G. (1987). Pretend play: Creativity and consciousness. In D. Gorlitz & J. Wohlwill (Eds.), *Curiosity, imagination, and play* (pp. 281–304). Hillsdale, NJ: Erlbaum.

Fein, G. G. (1989). Mind, meaning, and affect: Proposals for a theory of pretense. *Developmental Review, 9,* 345–363.

Fein, G. G. (1995). Toys and stories. In A. D. Pellegrini (Ed.), *The future of play theory* (pp. 151–164). Albany: State University of New York Press.

Fein, G. G., Ardilia-Rey, A., & Groth, L. A. (2000). The narrative connection: Stories and literacy. In K. Roskos & J. Christie (Eds.), *Literacy and play in the early years: Cognitive, ecological, and sociocultural perspectives* (pp. 27–44). Mahwah, NJ: Erlbaum.

Feshbach, N. (1969). Sex differences in children's modes of aggressive responses to outsiders. *Merrill-Palmer Quarterly, 15,* 249–258.

Galda, L. (1984). Narrative competence: Play, storytelling and comprehension. In A.D. Pellegrini & T. D. Yawkey (Eds.). *The development of oral and written language in social contexts* (pp 105–119). Norwood, NJ: Ablex.

Galda, L., Cullinan, B., & Strickland, D. (1997). *Language, literacy, and the child.* Ft Worth, TX: Harcourt Brace Jovanovich.

Galda, L., & Pellegrini, A.D. (1985). *Play, language, and stories.* Norwood, NJ: Ablex.

Garvey, C. (1990). *Play.* Cambridge: Harvard University Press.

Garvey, C., & Kramer, T. L. (1989). The language of social pretend. *Developmental Review, 9,* 364–382.

Garvey, C., & Shantz, C. U. (1992). Conflict talk: Approaches adversative discourse. In C. U. Shantz & W. Hartup (Eds.), *Conflict in childhood and adolescence* (pp. 93–121). New York: Cambridge University Press.

Göncü, A. (1993). Development of intersubjectivity in the dyadic play of preschoolers. *Early Childhood Research Quarterly, 8,* 99–116.

Hartup, W. W. (1983). Peer relations. In E. M. Hetherington (Ed.), *Handbook of child psychology* (Vol 4, pp. 103–196). New York: Wiley.

Hartup, W. (1996) The company they keep: Friendships and their developmental significance. *Child Development, 67,* 1–13.

Heath, S. B. (1983). *Ways with words.* New York: Cambridge University Press.

Hinde, R. (1980). *Ethology, its nature and relation with other sciences.* London: Fontana.

Hymes, D., & Cazden, C.B. (1980). Narrative thinking ans story telling: A folklorist's clue to a critique of education. In D. Hymes (Ed). *Language in education: Ethnolinguistic essays* (pp. 136–138).Washington, DC: Center for Applied Linguistics.

Maccoby, E. E. (1990). Gender and relationships: A developmental account. *American Psychologist, 45,* 513–520.

Maccoby, E. E. (1998). *The two sexes: Growing up apart, coming together.* Cambridge, MA: Harvard University Press.

Michaels, S. (1981). "Sharing time": Children's narrative styles and access to literacy. *Language in Society, 10,* 423–442.

Nelson, J., & Aboud, F. E. (1985). The resolution of social conflict between friends. *Child Development, 56,* 1009–1017.

Newcombe, A. F., & Bagwell, C. L. (1995). Children's friendship relations: A meta-analytic review. *Psychological Bulletin, 117,* 306–347.

Newcombe, A. F., & Brady, J. E. (1982). Mutuality in boys' friendship relations. *Child Development, 53,* 392–395.

Pellegrini, A. D. (1985). The narrative organisation of children's fantasy play: The effects of age and play context. *Educational Psychology, 5*(1), 17–25.

Pellegrini, A. D., & Galda, L. (1988). The effects of age and context on children's use of narrative language. *Research in the Teaching of English, 22,* 183–195.

Pellegrini, A. D., & Galda, L. (1991). Longitudinal relations among preschoolers' symbolic play, metalinguistic verbs, and emergent literacy. In J. Christie (Ed.). *Play and early literacy development* (pp. 47–68). Albany: State University of New York Press.

Pellegrini, A. D., & Galda, L. (1993). Ten years after: A reexamination of symbolic play and literacy research. *Reading Research Quarterly, 28,* 163–175.

Pellegrini, A. D., & Galda, L. (1998). *The development of school based literacy: A social ecological study.* London: Routledge International Library of Psychology.

Pellegrini, A. D., Galda, L., Bartini, M., & Charak, D. (1997). Oral language and literacy learning in context: The role of social relationships. *Merrill-Palmer Quarterly, 44,* 38–54.

Pellegrini, A. D., Galda, L., Flor, D., Bartini, M., & Charak, D. (1998). Close relationships, individual differences, and early literacy learning. *Journal of Experimental Child Psychology, 67,* 409–422.

Rubin, K. H., Fein, G., & Vandenberg, B. (1983). Play. In E. M. Hetherington (Ed.), *Handbook of child psychology: Vol. 4. Socialization, personality, and social development.* New York: Wiley.

Rylant, C. (1987). *Birthday presents.* New York: Orchard.

Shatz, M., Wellman, H., & Silber, S. (1983). The acquisition of mental verbs: A systematic investigation of the reference to mental states. *Cognition, 14,* 301–321.

Sutton-Smith, B. (1981). *The folk stories of children.* Philadelphia: University of Pennsylvania Press.

Sutton-Smith, B. (1998). *The rhetorics of play.* Cambridge, MA: Harvard University Press.

Vygotsky, L. S. (1967). Play and its role in the mental development of the child. *Soviet Psychology, 5*(3), 6–18.

Waldrop, M. F., & Halverson, C. F. (1975). Intensive and extensive peer behavior: Longitudinal and cross-sectional analyses. *Child Development, 46,* 19–26.

10

❧

Playing "Inside" Stories

LOIS A. GROTH
LYNN DIETRICH DARLING

We first embarked on the investigation of narrative in the early 1990s in Greta G. Fein's graduate seminar, "Models of Mind in Young Children's Play." We examined how models of mind are translated into research paradigms and from there into curriculum. Through *Acts of Meaning* (1990), Greta introduced us to Bruner's view of narrative thought as a basic, primary way of thinking; mind likened to a story. Greta shared her fascination with the narratives of dramatic fantasy play. Although Bruner never applied narrative theory to pretend play, Greta did when she described pretend play as "collaborative narrative making." The seminar gave rise to several practical and theoretical questions. High on the practical list was whether children's intuitive understanding of narrative forms could become the basis of a curricular activity. Toward this end, we introduced story dictation and story enactment into a classroom of 4-year-old children. High on the theoretical list was an account of how young children used this activity when it became a regular part of the schoolday. The purpose of this chapter is to describe our efforts to address these issues.

Bruner (1990) claims that children have a natural bent for narrative organization that emerges at an early age. Young children have "an abundant and early armament of narrative tools" (Bruner, 1990, p. 79). In fact, a child's understanding of the world is organized as a story that encodes information about specific events. When children listen to stories or tell stories they call on this understanding. Bruner also claims that a readiness for narrative organization sets the agenda for language acquisition. Taken one step farther, this narrative organization facility also may set the agenda for literacy acquisition. Researchers postulate that narrative thought provides the connective tissue for a variety of literacy activities, including sociodramatic play, storybook enactment, and dialogic reading. These activities encourage the progression from knowledge of print and pretend reading and writing to the real thing (Fein, 1995; Pellegrini, 1985a). Evidence suggests that it is narrative thought that makes it possible for the child to understand how words and text convey meaning (Pellegrini & Galda, 1988, 1991, this volume; Williamson & Silvern, 1991). Thus narrative thought frames the child's understanding of the mysteries of written language, and is enhanced by the emergence of narrative competence as cognitive development progresses.

Narrative competence is an aspect of literate behavior as defined by Heath (1982), Olson (1977), and Scribner and Cole (1978). These researchers defined narrative competence as the ability to comprehend and produce characters' actions, motives, goals and language consistent with a particular story line. As narrative competence develops, children acquire an integrative and interpretive framework to use in their encounters with literacy. Such competence involves an understanding of story events and actions as temporally sequenced and causally motivated (Pellegrini, 1985b; Pellegrini & Galda, 1988). Use of these characteristics results in the creation of a coherent story.

Curricular research in emergent literacy suggests that children's narrative competence emerges through and is enhanced by repeated experiences with narratives, including storybook reading, engaging in dramatic play, and participating in dramatic reenactments. Although early childhood educators have long promoted storybook reading, and more recently storybook enactment, it is only recently and largely through the work of Paley (1981, 1988) that a broader integration of active story making and story sharing has found a place in the preschool classroom. Paley extends the use of enactment beyond fairy tales and published literature to include stories authored by the children in her class. Passive encounters with print may not be enough to connect oral and written literacy. In Paley's classroom, children use print and make print in the service of a social process called literacy. Her reports suggest that early childhood classrooms might benefit from a systematic approach to children's construction of original, oral texts that can be and are recorded and because they are recorded are available for communal sharing.

Our fascination with Paley's work, combined with Greta's prodding, generated many questions, some of which were addressed in the study reported in this chapter. First, we asked whether anyone can create a "Paley" classroom environment? In this exploratory study, we introduced story dictation–story enactment procedures into an intact classroom of 4-year-olds using procedures similar to those described by Paley (1981). Are the children eager or reluctant participants? Does the activity interest many or few? However, we were not sure whether 4-year-olds would take advantage of two unfamiliar scribes in their classroom when the opportunity to dictate stories was provided.

Second, what are the implications for literacy development when opportunities for story dictation are provided? How do young children seem to understand the relation between their own spoken words and the scribe's words written as rendered by pen on paper? Do they pace their telling to the scribe's writing or do they ignore the connection between their words and the scribe's activity? How do they deal with the amount of space written words use on a piece of paper and the need for another piece?

Third, if the children produced narratives, how would they react to the enactment of their own stories and the stories of their peers? How do children respond to the social opportunities provided by story enactment? We were especially interested in the children's reaction to the opportunity to participate in other children's stories and to choose peers to participate in one's own stories. Answers to questions such as these were based on field notes of observations as well as analysis of videotapes of the activities during this exploratory study. The authors were present in the classroom twice a week for 4 weeks to accomplish this task.

METHOD

Participants

Seventeen middle-class Caucasian children attending one preschool classroom in a private preschool participated in this study. Eleven of the participants were boys. Their ages ranged from 4 years, 3 months to 5 years, 1 month at the beginning of the 4-week observation period (mean = 4 years, 5 months).

Design and Procedure

Field Notes

Both researchers conducted observations in the classroom during the 4-week intervention. Observations focused on the periods during which storybook reading, storybook enactment, dictation, and original story enactment occurred. Detailed field notes were made subsequent to observations of these activities. These included analytic notes (Glesne & Peshkin, 1992) in the form of observer comments. The researchers' interpretations of these activities were logged in field books in narrative form.

Videotapes

To aid in the description of the context, the dictation and original story enactment were videotaped once a week, resulting in a total of four taped segments. A camcorder was set on a tripod approximately 25 feet from the group with a remote pressure zone microphone in the group environment.

Original Story Dictation

Prior to this study the participants' only in-school experience with dictation was writing one- or two-sentence captions to describe drawings they had done. The teacher explained to the children on the first day of the study that the researchers were story collectors and would be available during choice time to anyone who wanted to tell a story. On each successive occasion, the story dictation was discussed as an activity on those days the researchers were present. Participation in story dictation was voluntary.

The classroom routine began with a morning circle time. Immediately following this was a block of free choice time. Free choice time allowed the children to select from a number of activities such as block play, art activities, and dramatic play. Twice a week the researchers were seated at an established writing center to take story dictations. The writing center consisted of a table and four chairs, separated from other centers by a divider and a couch. This configuration allowed the researcher and the child author to sit side by side.

The researchers wrote the stories on brightly colored paper (the author's copy) and used carbon paper to make copies for themselves. During the dictation the researcher/scribe read the words as she wrote them. The story was also audiotaped for future reference. At the conclusion of the dictation the researcher read the story back to the child to be sure it said just what the child intended. If the author made changes, the story was amended. When the story was finished, the child author was given the chance to illustrate it. Markers were available at the art table for this purpose.

Enactment

Story enactment was a novel experience in this classroom. The children's original fictional narratives were dramatized during a second circle time immediately following choice time. The group sat on the edges of a rug area that delineated "the stage." Seated in a chair, with the children gathered around in a semicircle, one of the researchers read a story aloud. The stories were read in no particular order, although efforts were made to begin with those who had not had a story enacted previously.

After the initial reading, the researcher invited the author to stand on the stage. She asked the author what characters were needed for the dramatization. As the author listed the characters the researcher asked who the author would like to portray the character. At that point the child author invited a peer to accompany him or her on stage. The child author controlled the casting. When all the characters were chosen, the researcher reread the text as narration for the enactment. The actors improvised their own dialogue and action, sometimes getting prompts from the author.

RESULTS

Analysis

Constant comparative methods (e.g., Glaser & Strauss, 1967), whereby instances of a phenomenon are compared across a range of situations, over time, and through a variety of methods, were used to guide coding, thematic analysis, and interpretation during the analysis of these data. The field notes were used in conjunction with the videotapes. At the end of data collection, all sessions of the activity were used for in-depth analysis. An event sampling procedure was employed (Bakeman & Gottman, 1986) as the researchers created a descriptive log of each taped session, noting time, who was involved, and what students and researchers were doing. Then, themes were generated from the descriptive logs. Finally, specific episodes in each session that illustrated these themes were identified and transcribed. These themes are discussed under separate headings for the dictation process and the enactment process in the results section.

The Dictation Process

One purpose of this study was to examine the implications for literacy development during story dictation. The following section describes what happened during story dictation. These observations reveal insights about the children's understanding of the idea-to-print relationship. Field notes and videotapes provided clues to the children's understanding of the dictation process—specifically, the relationship between one's ideas, spoken and written words, writing materials, and the events that yielded written text.

Participation

The decision to author a story was made by the child. At no time did any of the adults in the room send, direct, cajole, or invite the children to tell a story. During the monthlong intervention all but one child told at least one story and 15 of the 17 told two or more. The children chose when they would author a story. However, their enthusiastic response to the dictation created situations in which the researchers might be busy with other children when a child was ready to compose. At first those children were sent to make other choices until they noticed a vacancy. Eventually the children solved the problem by creating a "waiting room" (their term) on a couch behind the writing table. The book read in the morning circle was left on the couch, and the children enjoyed "reading" it while waiting for a turn to tell their own story.

Transformation and Copies

Transformation of oral text into written text was facilitated by a scribe. These children were intrigued by their words written conventionally on paper. An example of the awe this created in our young authors was their fascination with our use of carbon paper. One girl fingered the pages often, looking from the original to the carbon after each sentence was written. Another youngster tried pushing on her story and tapping it. After each of these motions she checked to see if these "marks" had gone through the carbon paper. It was amazing for the children to see their spoken words transformed into words on paper and to end up with two copies of one story.

Words into Print

The children differed in their grasp of the process whereby the adult transformed their oral words into print. At one end were children who seemed not to recognize the role of the scribe as a manual story recorder. At this end were the children whom we continuously asked to "wait" so that we could write down all that they had said. For the most part this group kept talking, oblivious of what their scribe's hand was doing. This excerpt illustrates the researcher's concern:

> Jay comes to me and begins rattling off a story about his cats. First I
> try to explain to him that I will have to ask him to wait so I can write
> down what he tells me. I continually have to ask him to wait. He
> seems to have more trouble with the notion of dictation than any of
> my previous storytellers. He finishes the story somewhat abruptly. I
> wonder if he was put off by my having to wait for me to catch up.
> (Field notes, Darling, 3/17)

At the other extreme were the handful of youngsters who spoke in
phrases, stopping to wait while we wrote, and continuing just as we finished. These children seemed better tuned to the socially mediated process of story dictation.

> Sue came over to tell me a story. I explained to her that I would be
> writing it as she told it to me, so I might have to ask her to stop. She
> was very patient and would stop when I asked her to, then watch me
> write until I stopped. Then she would resume her story. A few times I
> read the line as I was writing it then she picked it right up and contin-
> ued her thought. (Field notes, Darling, 3/15)

A couple of these authors could be heard repeating their words in whis-
pers as the scribes wrote them down. One student even "shared the
pen" as she composed. Each time that the word "to" or "too" occurred
in her story, she insisted on writing it herself. Although she inserted
"too" regardless of the correct usage, this small bit of ownership was
very potent for this young author. Other children achieved ownership
of the text by writing their name on the page.

Concepts about Print

Children construct hypotheses about print during naturally occurring
events. These hypotheses become progressively more complex, enabling the children to use their texts functionally in the social context of
the classroom. Analysis of the children's comments and actions during
storytelling make it clear that in this project, the children were acquiring
an understanding of various aspects of writing. The dictation process
provided insights into children's thoughts about stories as well as their
concepts about print. For example, children were concerned with how
their stories were represented on paper. Story length is determined by
the end point of a tale. Orientation on the page is important to authors
and readers alike. And a title has a specific narrative function. The following section outlines the episodes we observed concerning these particular concepts about print.

Story Length

Story length concerned some of the young authors. How does an author decide where the end of a tale is? For one child the determining factor was physical; when we reached the bottom of the page while dictating, her story was over. For another child similar constraints had different implications. After the daily dramatization, he complained that we had only acted out one of his stories. As we looked back at the day's texts we realized his confusion stemmed from the fact that his story was written on two pieces of paper. He reasoned that two pieces of paper meant two stories.

Consider the power in realizing that as an author, one controls just how much story there will be. This was evident in a young girl's comment as she entered the room one morning. Before doing anything else, she approached the researchers and informed them that she was going to need two pieces of paper for her story that day.

The Meaning of a Page

These young authors contemplated complex concepts concerning text orientation on a page. What is a page and what are the constraints of a page? Through our own questioning, we learned about the children's understanding of these issues. As one girl began her story, the researcher asked if it was okay to write the child's name at the top of the page. The child asked where the top was. The researcher pointed; the child nodded and began spinning her tale. This child certainly has experience with stories even if that does not include where to begin "writing" them on the page. It seems that this information is not a prerequisite to being a competent storymaker.

The Function of a Title

One day a child asked why the researcher had drawn a line under her title. The researcher explained that the line signified that the title was a special part of the story. The youngster added, "Sometimes to show that it's not part of the story. To keep it away from the start of the story. Right?" In setting off a title with a title page are authors attempting to differentiate between the name of the story and the story itself? A title carries a metacommunicative or metanarrative function. It announces to the reader or listener that a story is forthcoming. This child's insightful observation indicates a deepening understanding of the framework of the written story and reveals volumes about this child's experiences with books and print. Our recording of children's dictation behaviors opened the door to questions about the many intricacies of young children's emerging understanding of print and the writing process. To become a literate person requires knowledge of such seemingly obvious things as written forms, the spaces occupied by these forms, and the physical medium on which words are inscribed.

The Story Enactment Process

The following section describes what happened during story enactment. Our observations reveal how these children reacted to the enactment experiences. Field notes and videotapes provided clues to the children's understanding of the enactment process—specifically, the relationship between written text and its dramatic recreation and the social dynamics between the author and the other characters, as well as the audience. In the following paragraphs we describe two sets of findings, one set refers to our observations of mutual respect observed among children during story enactment and the second refers to actual procedural considerations during casting.

Mutual Respect

We derived attention, interest, and participation validation as indices of mutual respect. It was quite striking that the children were absolutely riveted to the words of their peers and listened carefully to each story as it was read. Even the most convoluted and disjointed stories were attended to with great respect. This attention was achieved by the words alone as the majority of the stories were not illustrated, and if they were, the illustrations were often not shown.

The children were enchanted as their classmates' stories were read aloud. The children sat still, some of them with their chins cupped in their hands, elbows resting on their knees as we read their work. One or two could be caught smiling at the author at the culmination of the initial reading. They clamored to be in their peer's productions, so much that at least two children warned that they would not choose children who were saying "Me, me." Just as it did in other studies of enactment (e.g., Fein, Ardila-Rey, & Groth, 2000), authorship conveyed prominence and respect from peers.

There was an extremely high level of interest in this project on the part of the young children. This interest carried over to all facets of the project in this classroom. As they passed the writing table, children would stop and listen to a story being told. The following illustrates this.

> Sue was telling a story entitled "Cinderella." It was another retelling of "Aladdin." Cindi stopped by the table and listened to Sue's story. Then Jenna came over too and squeezed herself onto the chair next to Sue. After listening for a bit Jenna helped Sue remember the name "Jafar." As Sue continued dictating Jenna interrupted to ask if she could be next. Sue replied affirmatively. (Field notes, Darling, 4/7)

At the art table children would share their stories as they worked on illustrations. On the first day of the intervention, Matt explained his pictures to Nick. His story was about a Tyrannosaurus but the picture was a coffee grinder, "which was a scary machine" with a monster peeking over it. Nick agreed that a monster was behind the machine.

Perhaps the greatest validation of these children as authors was that they chose ideas from each others' stories and included them in their own tales. As the children borrowed themes from literature, they also borrowed themes from classmates. This could be viewed as the ultimate validation: "You have become a 'real' author when someone uses something out of your story to make his own!" This is depicted by the following excerpt:

> Katherine comes over to the table as the rest of the children have begun cleaning up. This is the first time she has volunteered a story. She begins telling a story about some mischievous mice. This may have been influenced by *Mousepaint*. She adds a part about a spinning wheel up in a tower. This seems to be directly related to the work that Emily and Cindi have been doing with a modified *Sleeping Beauty* theme. They have each included spinning wheels in their latest stories that were dramatized. (Field notes, Groth, 4/5)

Casting Procedure

In addition to listening carefully to the plot of the story during the initial reading, the children seemed to be listening to decide which characters they wanted to play in the enactment. When casting a story, most authors had several willing volunteers crying, "I want to be the fox," or "I want to be the machine." Rarely did an author have trouble finding a volunteer to act out a part. On occasion a child was forced to compromise. When casting a very complicated story replete with characters, Kyle could not find anyone who wanted to portray the sun. He eventually gave up. And the story was performed without a sun.

On another day Adam's story included 18 bees and he was determined to cast them all. He walked around the circle, from child to child, asking, "Do you want to be a bumblebee?" Only a few replied affirmatively. He ended up with three bees who all had a delightful time buzzing about throughout the production. It appeared as if some authors had specific actors in mind when dictating their stories (i.e., Adam and the 18 bees and Emily and her friends). This effort on their part to craft stories that include particular people supports Sutton-Smith's idea that storytelling is a dialogical process, with context-specific stories that are dependent on an audience, the occasion, and the social context in which the stories are told (Sutton-Smith, 1979).

Actor selection was an exciting and powerful job. Interpreting the dramatization experience through the lens of the storyteller affords us a view of the unique way these child authors were able to relate to their peers. The storyteller directed the activity. Paley (1984) recognized this opportunity to be "the boss" as one significant advantage of authorship. This control was most evident in the activities surrounding the casting of characters. One child told his classmates, "I am not going to pick you if you don't raise your hand." Teachers of young children hear their own voices echoed in these words.

These child authors were autonomous directors. As they cast their productions they were able to remember exactly what characters were in their stories even though up to an hour may have passed between the telling and the doing. In addition, once the parts were cast, the author/director had no trouble remembering who was who. The actors and the researchers occasionally needed reminders, and, when necessary, the authors clarified the confusion. The audience members were also able to remember available roles and who was cast in each part. If an individual was eager to play a specific part and was not chosen for that part, he or she was usually ready with a second choice.

Casting Styles

There were many different methods of actor selection. A number of children picked their friends to be in their productions. This was most evident in second and subsequent stories. We could predict which names these children would call as their characters were listed. Callie, Emily, and Cindi would always cast each other in their productions. Jay and Matt often cast each other and proved to be rather rambunctious together. During other classroom activities the two were encouraged by their teachers to seek out other children as companions. We did not discourage them from performing together, which may explain part of their joy in performing.

In most of these cases parts were cast quickly, with the call of a name. Within this group it was perfectly acceptable to request a different part than the one originally assigned. The author would usually agree to the modification then call the next friend's name to portray the leftover character. A number of these children also omitted the same children from their productions. As their friends were automatically cast, their "nonfriends" were ignored, even when it was clear that these ignored children were extremely interested in participating as a character. The following excerpt illustrates one such episode:

> Emily took a long time choosing actors today. At one point Joe was asking to be something. She ignored him even after the teacher drew her attention to the fact that he would like to be in her story. She picked Sue to be the red bird and Cindi to be the blue jay. Cindi wanted to be the butterfly so Emily let her switch. Ultimately no child is selected to portray the queen. This may have been to avoid including Joe. (Field notes, Darling, 3/22)

Some children were more deliberate in their casting selections. They took more time, relishing every moment spent "center stage." These children seemed to labor over decisions. Some of them called children's names as they were cast, literally inviting their peers to accept roles. Adam deliberately approached a child and bent down and quietly asked that child if he would like a certain part. Katherine wordlessly walked around the circle and ever so gently tapped seven children on top of the head as though bestowing a special honor on them. The children seemed to easily adapt to different casting styles and waited quietly as Katherine proceeded with her task. With these directors, if a child turned down a part, that child was omitted entirely from the production. When the cast was set, it was time to begin the production.

Production

The action and dialogue for the dramatizations of the children's stories were the province of the actors. They added dialogue of their own when a story was devoid of it and took their cues for what type of movement to include from the story and their knowledge of the character they were portraying. The following excerpt includes the text on the left and the actors' motions and dialogue on the right to illustrate a typical enactment.

A statue doesn't move.

There's a castle with armor.

And a dungeon where a person gets lost.

He gets handcuffed.

Someone carries an American flag, to hang on top of the castle.

A silly guy with a mustache comes on a horse to the castle.

And the tyrannosaurus rex bited the bad guy and he had blood.

A robot was in the castle too.

And they were hanging some fire on the castle.

And G. I. Joe came. He got in the bad armor.

Then Superman came. He did something bad to the bad guys. He fighted them with a sharp sword.

Then a dragon blew fire.

Then a spaceship came to the castle.

A boat was there.

And a vacuum vacuumed the bad guys up.

That's the end.

Boy 1 stands straight and tall, hands at his sides.

Boy 2 walks around.

Boy 2 puts his hands behind his back.

Boy 3: "That's me!" He marches, hands together, waist high. He reaches overhead.

Boy 4 gallops in and says, "Whoa. This horse is moving."

Boy 5: "Who's the bad guy?"

The researcher asks the author, "Is Boy 3 the bad guy?"

Author responds, "No. He's the American."

The researcher asks, "Who's the bad guy? Is he the one who handcuffed boy 2?"

Boy 5 makes a biting motion.

Boy 6 walks stiff armed and stiff legged.

The robot puts his hands up and down as if hanging something.

Boy 7 walks with his hands in his pockets.

Girl 1: "Where is he?"

The researcher says, "They're all bad guys."

Girl 1 makes stabbing motions.

Boy 8 says, "I'll get you bad guys." He blows.

Boy 9 makes a whooshing sound.

At times, the author took control of the production by choreographing it or telling the other actors what to do. One morning, before the storybook reading, Emily told us that she would have to show people how to walk before we acted out her story. She obviously had a story she was ready to tell and had planned the dramatization as well. After her story was cast, she began by demonstrating choreography for several of her characters, demonstrating and asking them to practice walking like she did. Then she stretched her arms out to her sides raising them slightly above shoulder level and picked her leg up with the knee locked and the toes pointed. As she demonstrated she told her characters they had to "walk like this." They obliged her and practiced a bit before the production began. During the enactment, they all walked the way they had been instructed.

The intense interest that this group of children had in the dramatizations is illustrated by the fact that every author opted to dramatize his or her story. And during the eight sessions the researchers were present, every child told at least one story, with most telling more than one. In fact, after the researchers ended their activities in this classroom, the teacher continued to implement dictation and dramatization as a result of the children's insistence that she do so. The implementation of activities modeled after Paley's was certainly successful in this classroom.

DISCUSSION

We set out to explore three issues during this exploratory study. First, we wondered whether we could create a "Paley" classroom in which 4-year-olds would be willing participants. Second, if the children did dictate and act out the stories, what opportunities for literacy development might story dictation provide? And, finally, how would children react to the social opportunities provided by story enactment? A discussion of these three issues follows.

One purpose of this study was to ascertain the efficacy of creating a "Paley" classroom. This project provided rich, if incomplete, answers to our questions about Paley's work. Exploratory research provides insights for future endeavors. We discovered that it is indeed possible to recreate a Paley classroom environment. Certainly our experience was atypical in that we were two extra adults in this classroom, which alleviated some of the management issues. However, it remains clear that a teacher could incorporate storytelling by means of dictation and dramatization of child-authored stories into the preschool curriculum. The children involved in this project had stories to tell, even to relative strangers. Involvement of the classroom teacher as opposed to outside researchers could enhance opportunities for mediation within the social context of these literacy activities.

During this study, the opportunity to enact the stories seemed to motivate even the most hesitant children to write. Joe's participation in story dictation is particularly noteworthy. He refused to dictate for the first few weeks, pointedly telling us, "I am *not* going to tell a story, no way." However, he was often ignored in casting and when cast was liable to improvise to such an extent that he altered the story. When he would complain about being left out, we would remind him that if he dictated a story, he would then be able to play any part he chose. The last week of the intervention, he dictated, and enacted, two of his own stories.

A second purpose of this study was to explore what happened during dictation and story enactment in terms of participants' literacy development. Through the children's willing and enthusiastic participation in story dictation and enactment and their subsequent insistence that both activities continue after the researchers left, it is clear that this outlet for narrative expression had a significant impact in the classroom. Story dictation created a context rife with literacy implications. The context created by story dictation in this preschool classroom provided an outlet for tapping children's literacy knowledge, including their concepts about print and understanding of sense of story.

During dictation, it was evident that children in this project were actively thinking about text on paper, their own and of others'. The children acquired an understanding of the links that occur between thoughts, spoken words, marks on paper, and the space occupied by these marks. The children also came up against the idea that human beings mediate among thoughts, sounds, and print as they compose text.

The third purpose of this study was to examine the social opportunities provided by story dictation and story enactment. Paley's use of enactment in the classroom is based on the belief that literacy is a social process (Paley, 1981, 1988, 1990). In this project, story dictation and story enactment were social endeavors. Literate behavior is enhanced through social interaction in varied contexts. Holdaway (1979) identified four processes related to social interaction that facilitate literate behavior. They include *observation* of others involved in their own literacy activities, *collaboration* with others in a socially interactive manner, individual or collaborative *practice* of literacy behaviors, and sharing literacy through *performance* . Instituting enactment of children's original stories in the classroom provided ample opportunities for all four of these processes with emphasis on performance.

The enactment of the children's stories was a communal celebration of their creative literary achievements. The children respected one another as authors. Simply reading the stories aloud might achieve this, but dramatization extends it. By inviting others to "play inside their stories" actors as well as audience members were relating in unique ways. As a prospective actor, each child listened attentively as a story was read. Then when the story was dramatized, each participant's performance had to make sense in relation to the other actors as well as the author's intentions.

CONCLUSION

For years teachers have been including storybook reading in their literacy curricula. Storybook enactment has been viewed as a natural supplement to these readings. However, recent research indicates that storybooks are not the panacea we once believed (Scarborough & Dobrich, 1994). Our challenge is to discover how best to enrich children's experiences with stories in order to create more literate classrooms. Story dictation and story enactment of child-authored texts have the potential to become powerful tools in providing young children with increased opportunities to enhance literate behavior.

Story dictation followed by enactment completes the cycle: Imagine a story, tell the story, write the story, read the story, and dramatize the story. In this way narrative thought is transformed into language, then one step further, into narrative action, and last, into narrative community. It then becomes a part of the "corporate memory" solidified in the oral tradition of the classroom community. Children's participation in these social interactive narrative processes may scaffold their literacy learning.

According to Bruner (1990), "while we have an innate and primitive predisposition to narrative organization that allows us quickly and easily to comprehend and use it, the culture soon equips us with *new powers of narration* through its tool kit and through the traditions of telling and interpreting in which we soon come to participate" (p. 80).

Perhaps by providing young children with opportunities to participate in story enactment, whereby they take the role of a character and actively explore the possibilities of theme, setting, and action which make a story interesting and exciting, we foster narrative competence. Because 4-year-old children's narrative abilities are sensitive to context (Fein, Darling, & Groth, in press), further research of the role that story dictation and story enactment play in the child's development as an able storyteller is needed. Thanks to Greta, those of us interested in children's narrative competence are encouraged to pursue it.

REFERENCES

Bakeman, R., & Gottman, J. M. (1986). *Observing interaction: An introduction to sequential analysis*. New York: Cambridge University Press.

Bruner, J. (1990). *Acts of meaning*. Cambridge, MA: Harvard University Press.

Fein, G. G. (1995). Toys and stories. In A. D. Pellegrini (Ed.), *The future of play theory: Essays in honor of Brian Sutton-Smith* (pp. 151–164). Albany, NY: State University of New York Press.

Fein, G. G., Ardila-Rey, A. E., & Groth, L. A. (2000). The narrative connection: stories and literacy. In K. Roskos & J. Christie (Eds.), *Play and literacy in early childhood: Research from multiple perspectives* (pp. 27–44). Hillsdale, NJ: Erlbaum.

Fein, G. G., Darling, L. D., & Groth, L. A. (in press). Replica toys, stories, and a functional theory of mind. In R. Mitchell (Ed.) *Pretense in animals, children, and adult humans*. Boston, MA: Oxford University Press.

Glaser, B. C., & Strauss, A. L. (1967). *The discovery of grounded theory: Strategies for qualitative research*. New York: Aldine de Gruyter.

Glesne, C., & Peshkin, A. (1992). *Becoming qualitative researchers*. New York: Longman.

Heath, S. B. (1982). What no bedtime story means: Narrative skills at home and school. *Language in Society, 11*, 49–76.

Holdaway, D. (1979). *The foundations of literacy*. Sydney: Ashton Scholastic.

Olson, D. (1977). From text to utterance. *Harvard Educational Review, 47*, 257–281.

Paley, V. G. (1981). *Wally's stories*. Cambridge, MA: Harvard University Press.

Paley, V. G. (1984). *Boys and girls: Superheroes in the doll corner*. Chicago: University of Chicago Press.

Paley, V. G. (1988). *Bad guys don't have birthdays*. Chicago: University of Chicago Press.

Paley, V. G. (1990). *The boy who would be a helicopter*. Cambridge, MA: Harvard University Press.

Pellegrini, A. D. (1985a). The relations between symbolic play and literate behavior. A review and critique of the empirical literature. *Review of Educational Research, 55*, 1051–1070.

Pellegrini, A. D. (1985b). Relations between preschool children's symbolic play and literate behavior. In L. Galda & A. Pellegrini (Eds.), *Play, language and stories: The development of children's literate behavior* (pp. 79–97). Norwood, NJ: Ablex.

Pellegrini, A. D., & Galda, L. (1988). The effects of age and context on children's use of narrative language. *Research in the teaching of English, 22*, 183–195.

Pellegrini, A. D., & Galda, L. (1991). Longitudinal relations among preschooler's symbolic play, metalinguistic verbs, and emergent literacy. In J. F. Christie (Ed.), *Play and early literacy development* (pp. 47–67). Albany, NY: State University of New York Press.

Scarborough, H. S., & Dobrich, W. (1994). On the efficacy of reading to preschoolers. *Developmental Review, 14*, 245–302.

Scribner, S., & Cole, M. (1978). Literacy without schooling: Testing for intellectual effects. *Harvard Educational Review, 48,* 448–461.

Sutton-Smith, B. (1979). Presentation and representation in children's fictional narrative. In E. Winner & H. Gardener (Eds.), *New directions for child development: No. 6. Fact, fiction and fantasy in childhood* (pp. 53–65). San Francisco: Jossey-Bass.

Williamson, P. A., & Silvern, S. B. (1991). Thematic fantasy play and story comprehension. In J. F. Christie (Ed.), *Play and early literacy development* (pp. 69–90). Albany, NY: State University of New York Press.

PART IV

❧

Children in School

11

✖

Day Care and the Strange Situation

ALISON CLARKE-STEWART
VIRGINIA ALLHUSEN
FRITS GOOSSENS

A PERSONAL NOTE
FROM ALISON CLARKE-STEWART

All the contributors to this book have been touched by Greta G. Fein's influence, but none, I suspect, more than I. Greta and I were graduate students at Yale, barely acquainted with each other or with research on day care, when we were tapped by our adviser and mentor, William Kessen, to take on a critical task. It seemed that Bill had been asked by the Foundation for Child Development to compile and collate the reports then flooding into Washington, DC, describing the effects of various early childhood programs on children and their test scores. Bill was busy and he quickly passed the job on to Greta and me. We were a logical choice: we were interested in child development research with policy implications, we had time on our hands (we were only graduate students), and we could use the money. That was the beginning of my day-care career. It was 1970.

In the next month or so, Greta combed the research literature for relevant background materials (one didn't just do a PsycINFO search in

1970), and we packed up 16 cartons of reports and reprints and headed to Cape Cod to assemble and assimilate them. We rented a house for a month, with the explicit plan of working in the mornings and playing in the afternoons—and the plan worked. Of course, as the month wore on, Greta was getting up earlier and earlier to begin work and I was working later and later into the afternoon, but still there was always clamming or tanning at some point. By the end of the month we had a skeletal report, which over the course of the next few months back in New Haven developed chapters and acquired an advisory panel convened by the Foundation. Eventually the report evolved into a book, *Day Care in Context*, published in 1973.

Little did I know to what extent my professional life would grow out of that publication. Because of that book, people associated me with research on "day care" and kept asking me about its effects. I felt I had to undertake some original research to answer their questions. The publication of that research then led to another chapter and another book. . . . And then, just when I thought I was going to change directions and study something new, Greta renewed my attachment to day care with an innocent little request. Would I write a critical review of an article Jay Belsky had submitted to the *Early Childhood Research Quarterly* (1988), in which he claimed that day care was harmful for children's emotional development? Naively, I entered the fray of the "infant day-care wars" (Belsky, 1992; Karen, 1994). That special issue of the *Quarterly*, which Greta and Nathan Fox put together showcasing Jay's article in a bed of critiques, led down the road to the "Infant Day Care Summit Conference," sponsored by Zero to Three, which led to the National Institute of Child Health and Human Development (NICHD) Study of Early Child Care, of which I became a part. Today, I remain involved in the study of day care (now called "child care"), and I spend 3 days every 3 months in a closed room with Jay Belsky and the other 20 principal investigators and co-investigators of the NICHD Study hammering out the details of how to do that best. We have followed a cohort of more than 1,000 infants from birth through fourth grade and are continuing to follow the children through to the threshold of adolescence. I will probably be studying this sample and looking for lingering effects of infant day care on their behavior until the end (of my life, theirs, or federally sponsored research). And I owe it all to Greta!

I also owe this chapter to Greta. It is a direct outgrowth of the ideas I developed when at her behest I wrote my critical review of Jay Belsky's conclusions about the negative effects of day care. I wouldn't have reached this point without her invitation. So this one's for you, Gretum—I hope you like it!

AN EXPERIMENTAL INVESTIGATION OF DAY CARE AND INFANT–MOTHER ATTACHMENT

The crux of the "infant day-care wars" that began in the late 1980s was whether infants in nonmaternal care during the first year of life suffer from their experience so that their emotional development is impaired. Specifically, the issue was whether the quality of these children's attachment to their mothers was as emotionally secure as that of infants who were reared exclusively by their parents.

The security of children's attachments to their mothers had been a central concern in the field of child development since Bowlby first published his theory of early emotional development (Bowlby, 1969). He suggested, and subsequent studies confirmed, that the relationships infants develop with their mothers in the first year of life are critical for their subsequent development and psychological well-being (see Fox & Bar-Haim, this volume, for a discussion of lifespan theories of attachment). Without developing an attachment to a primary caregiver, children flounder. Bowlby's theory was extended and empirically verified by Mary Ainsworth (Ainsworth, Blehar, Waters, & Wall, 1978), who made two important discoveries: (1) that it is not simply the development of any kind of attachment that is important for the child's well-being but the development of an emotionally *secure* attachment, and (2) that evidence for the emotional security of a child's attachment could be gleaned from a relatively brief laboratory-based assessment—the Strange Situation.

The Strange Situation assessment Ainsworth devised consisted of the following seven 3-minute episodes (Ainsworth & Wittig, 1969):

1. Mother and child enter an unfamiliar room and play with toys alone.
2. A stranger enters and interacts with child.
3. The mother leaves the room and the stranger responds to the child and tries to get the child to play with the toys.
4. The mother returns to the room and tries to get the child involved in play; the stranger leaves.
5. The mother leaves the child alone in the room.
6. The stranger returns to the room, comforts the child if necessary, and once again attempts to engage the child in play with toys.
7. The mother returns to the room and the stranger leaves.

Children's behavior in the Strange Situation, particularly during the two reunion-with-mother episodes, could then be observed and coded into the following categories: (A) insecure-avoidant attachment—the baby ignores or avoids the mother; (B) secure attachment—the baby actively seeks proximity and contact or interaction with mother; (C) insecure–ambivalent or resistant attachment—the baby displays both proximity seeking *and* conspicuous contact- and interaction-resisting behavior. Children's behavior in the Strange Situation, Ainsworth and her colleagues discovered, offered a window into the young child's emotional life. The instrument was used in a great many studies (e.g., Waters, Vaughn, Posada, & Kondo-Ikemura, 1995) to demonstrate that attachment in the Strange Situation was related to children's competence in a variety of settings and contexts.

At the same time, in the 1980s, as more and more mothers entered the work force sooner and sooner after their babies were born, researchers started to question whether the quality of infants' attachments to their mothers was as strong and secure if those infants were spending significant amounts of time away from the mother in a day-care setting. It seemed reasonable to expect that when an infant was separated from mother for 8 or 10 or more hours a day, their attachment relationship would be at risk. These researchers explored the question of whether the quality of the relationships day-care children had with their mothers was as secure as the relationships of infants who were being raised exclusively at home by comparing the behavior of day-care and non-day-care children in the Strange Situation. Unfortunately, the results of their efforts provided ammunition rather than resolution for the day-care wars.

By the end of the 1980s, almost 20 studies had accumulated in which researchers compared the Strange Situation behavior of day-care and mother-care infants. Their results were quite consistent. Children in day care were more likely than children at home to exhibit insecure attachments to their mother in the Strange Situation. But the debate did not end there. The question was raised as to whether the Strange Situation provided a fair assessment of day-care children's attachment relationships (Clarke-Stewart, 1988, 1989). Could it be that infants who routinely experience separations from their mothers do not behave the same in the Strange Situation as children who do not have this experience because the components of the Strange Situation are more familiar to them? It was this question that motivated our study, in which an alternative method of assessing the infant–mother attachment, which does not involve experiences that "favor" children in day care, was used to compare the attachment relationships of day-care and home-care children.

THE DATA LINKING DAY CARE
WITH ATTACHMENT INSECURITY

Studies in the 1970s and 1980s

The suggestion that infant day care is a "risk factor" for the development of emotional insecurity was made first and most forcefully by Belsky in 1986. He had discovered on the basis of his own and four other carefully selected studies ($n = 491$) that the rate of insecure infant–mother attachments for children with 20 or more hours of nonparental care per week in first year of life was 43%, whereas for children with less nonmaternal care it was only 26%. Other reviewers, spreading their research net more widely, found differences that paralleled these, although not quite as large. Lamb, Sternberg, and Prodromidis (1992), combining data from 13 studies ($n = 897$), reported a rate of 37% insecure attachments for children in regular nonmaternal care compared to 29% for infants in exclusive maternal care, and, in the most inclusive tabulation of available studies (17 studies, 1,247 children), Clarke-Stewart (1989) found that of the infants of full-time working mothers, 36% were classified as insecure, whereas only 29% of the infants of non-employed or part-time working mothers were so classified. These were the data that provided the fuel for the "day-care wars."

Studies in the 1990s

More recent studies, conducted after these results were compiled and the battle joined, have not confirmed the significant differences obtained in these earlier investigations. Roggman, Langlois, Hubbs-Tait, and Rieser-Danner (1994), Stifter, Coulehan, and Fish (1993), and Burchinal, Bryant, Lee, and Ramey (1992) did not find significant relations between attachment security and mothers' employment or infants' day-care attendance in the first year, in their day-care studies, nor did the most comprehensive investigation—the one inspired by the Infant Day Care Summit Conference as a way of settling the day-care issue—the NICHD Study of Early Child Care. In this longitudinal study of more than 1,000 infants and their mothers at 10 sites around the United States, the security of infants' attachments to their mothers was not related to the quality, amount, stability, or type of day care or to the age at which care began, when family and child factors were taken into account statistically (NICHD Early Child Care Research Network, 1997).

There are a number of possible explanations for the virtual disappearance of the difference in attachment security that was previously reported. For one thing, relatively more mothers of infants were employed in the 1990s than were earlier, and, therefore, the group of mothers who work may be more similar to the group of mothers who do not than in the earlier studies. For another, mothers may have become more aware of the potential risks involved in leaving their infants in child care and therefore improved their own behavior at home. The quality of available child care may have improved or the number of child-care options increased. Perhaps, though, the most likely explanation is that what has improved is our research methods. Studies in the 1970s and 1980s were small and exploratory. In the 1990s, investigations were larger, better controlled, and less biased in their recruitment of subjects. Coding of children's attachment security is now always done "blind" to the child's daycare status, and researchers routinely control for "selection variables" such as parents' education, family income, mothers' attitudes, and child gender, in multivariate statistical analyses. In the NICHD Study, children were recruited from hospital births rather than from child-care settings, thus allowing researchers to follow them prospectively into whatever types of care their parents chose.

So is there any difference left to fight over? In the NICHD Study, an unpublished analysis was done comparing the attachment of children who had experienced more than 30 hours of care each week from the time they were 4 months old until they were 15 months with the attachment of children who had experienced less than 10 hours of care during this time period (NICHD Strange Situation Differential Validity Task Force Report—1C, 1994). In this analysis, child and family factors were not statistically controlled. Although there was no significant difference in the percentage of secure versus insecure attachments in this subsample, there was a near-significant difference when attachment insecurity was divided into anxious–avoidant and anxious–ambivalent types (chi square [$df = 2, 520$] = 5.24, $p = < .07$). In the group with extensive day-care experience, 20% had avoidant attachments, whereas in the group without day-care experience, only 13% did. This analysis of extreme groups suggests that there still may be some small difference in attachment between day-care and mother-care children (as assessed in the Strange Situation), when family factors are not controlled, and that difference is most apparent in the proportion of *avoidant* attachments specifically, as it was in the earlier studies (Clarke-Stewart, 1989). Moreover, when child and family selection factors were controlled, and the interactive effects of child care and maternal variables were calculated, in multiple regression analyses for the *entire* NICHD sample, an elevated rate of insecurity was found for those day-care children whose mothers were less positively involved with them at home (NICHD Early Child Care Research Network, 1997).

INTERPRETATIONS

The question that has led to disagreement, though, is not whether there is a measurable difference in the rate of insecurity between day-care and mother-care children but what that difference means. It has been suggested that infants of working mothers are at risk for emotional insecurity because they interpret their mothers' absence as rejection (Barglow, Vaughn, & Molitor, 1987), because repeated separations disturb their emerging attachment relationship and lead them to develop a coping style that masks their anger (Belsky, 1988), and because daily separations cause the infant to lose confidence in the availability and responsiveness of the parent and reduce opportunities for ongoing tuning of the emerging infant–caregiver interactive system (Sroufe, 1988). These interpretations are extrapolated from knowledge of the correlates of insecure attachment in children with nonemployed mothers and reflect the kinds of processes that characterize development in children who are in their parents' care exclusively. Psychologists from the attachment school believe that, regardless of etiology, infants who have insecure attachments to their mothers are predisposed to psychopathology (Main & Weston, 1982).

LIMITATIONS IN THE ASSESSMENT OF ATTACHMENT (OR, IS THE STRANGE SITUATION THE SAME FOR EVERYONE?)

But there may be a problem with these interpretations—because the observed difference in attachment between children in day care and mother care is based on behavior observed in a single assessment procedure, Ainsworth's Strange Situation. The Strange Situation is indeed a reliable and useful measure of the mother–infant relationship and a powerful predictor of later behavioral problems in mother-care children (Ainsworth et al., 1978). But the question is, is the Strange Situation equally valid for infants in day care? The validity of the Strange Situation procedure depends on creating a situation in which infants feel moderately stressed and therefore display proximity-seeking behavior to their attachment figure. It involves two brief separations from the mother and interactions with a stranger, in an unfamiliar room. The quality of attachment is assessed primarily by observing the child's behavior when the mother returns to the room. If the child goes to or greets the mother, this is a sign of a secure relationship. If the child avoids or ignores her or is ambivalent toward her, these are signs of an insecure relationship. Children with insecure avoidant attachments readily separate to explore during preseparation. They ignore the mother on her return, greeting her casually if at all, show little tendency to seek proximity to the mother, and treat the stranger much as they treat the mother (Ainsworth et al., 1978).

But the Strange Situation may not be psychologically equivalent for infants with daycare experience; for them it may not be as stressful as it is for children without this experience. In the SS, infants play with someone else's toys in a room that is not their own, are left by their mother with another woman, with whom they play and by whom they are comforted in the mother's absence, and then the mother returns to pick them up. Experiences such as these are more common for children in day care. Perhaps the Strange Situation does not create enough stress in infants who are accustomed to these experiences for them to exhibit attachment behavior. If children are not as stressed by the unfamiliar room, the mother's departure, or the presence and comfort of another woman, they may be less likely to seek comfort, proximity, and contact when the mother returns. If they are used to their mother's comings and goings, they may be less likely to stop their play to greet her. Behavior that might be considered avoidance from the standpoint of Strange Situation coding may simply reflect the fact that the mother's departure and absence did not activate the child's attachment behavior system.

Reason to Believe That Behavior in the Strange Situation Is Related to Familiarity

Is there any reason to believe that greater familiarity with the elements of the Strange Situation procedure would change the way infants react? There are some indications in the research literature that this may be the case. First, there is evidence that the familiarity of the room affects the infants' behavior. Infants seek less proximity with mother (move farther away, stay away longer, and are more likely to avoid the mother) when Strange Situation-like brief separations occur in a more familiar setting, at home rather than in the laboratory (Brookhart & Hock, 1976; Rinkoff & Corter, 1980).

Second, there is evidence that experience with strangers affects the child's behavior in the Strange Situation. In a meta-analysis of Strange Situation data from laboratory playrooms around the world, Sagi, van IJzendoorn, and Koren-Karie (1991) found that infants' behavior in the reunion episodes was related to their behavior in the preseparation episodes, and that the only differences between groups in different countries occurred in Israel, where infants in kibbutzim were more "impressed" by the Strange Situation than infants in day care. Specifically, these children, who seldom encounter strangers in the normal course of events, were anxious about the presence of a stranger in the Strange Situation. Kroonenberg, van Dam, van IJzendoorn, and Mooijaart (1997) further demonstrated that stranger wariness is an important component of Strange Situation behavior, so that infants who are wary of the stranger in earlier episodes of the Strange Situation more intensely display their attachment concerns in the subsequent episodes. This concurs with the finding of Sagi, Lamb, and Gardner (1986), who measured stranger sociability in a separate procedure prior to the Strange Situation.

Third, there is evidence that familiarity with being separated from their mother affects children's Strange Situation behavior. Japanese infants, who in the course of their daily lives are rarely separated from their mothers (and, in fact, sleep on the same futon with them at night), have been observed in several studies of the Strange Situation to exhibit only proximity seeking to their mothers, never avoidance (Nakagawa, Lamb, & Miyaki, 1992; Takahashi 1986). It is generally assumed that this is because they find the Strange Situation particularly strange (unusual) and stressful. It has been suggested more recently that the lack of avoidant behavior observed in the Strange Situation in Japan may have been exacerbated by a procedural problem: The Japanese infants were allowed to cry longer when the mother left the room than is conventionally done (more than 30 seconds), and this may have led to more than mild or moderate stress. If so, this just confirms the premise that Strange Situation classification depends on the level of stress created by the Strange Situation procedure.

Other evidence supporting the possibility that infants' behavior in the Strange Situation may be affected by their familiarity with separation from the mother comes from studies showing that infants adapt to repeated separations from mother under other circumstance, such as when the mother is away at conferences (Field, 1991) or the child is in day care (Fein, Gariboldi, & Boni, 1993; Howes & Oldham, this volume; Kagan, Kearsley, & Zelazo, 1978).

Evidence That Day Care Infants Are Less Stressed by Events Like Those in the Strange Situation

So is there any evidence that infants with experience in day care, because of their greater familiarity with the components of the Strange Situation, are less stressed by the procedure? In a systematic meta-analysis of 14 studies relevant to this question, McCartney and Phillips (1988) found that there was no overall statistically significant difference in children's distress or exploration in laboratory assessments involving brief separations from mother and the presence of a stranger. But half the studies included in their analysis involved children who were older than those for whom the Strange Situation is appropriate (ranging in age from 2½ to 5 years old). Therefore, we cannot rely on their analysis alone. Lurking in those studies, and others conducted subsequently, there is some suggestion that day-care children (under age 2) may find the kinds of events included in the Strange Situation less stressful than children without experience in nonmaternal care.

Mother-care children have been observed to stare longer at a stranger when she entered the lab, suggesting that this is a more novel event for them (Doyle, 1975). Day-care infants have been observed to act less wary toward a stranger (Ramey, MacPhee, & Yeates, 1982) and to be less likely to resist contact with the stranger (Hock, 1980). They have been observed to be less disturbed by the mother's absence, playing more and crying less when they are left alone (Doyle & Somers, 1978). Children with a moderate amount of day-care experience (in terms of hours of care per week) have been found to show less distress at separation than children with no day-care experience or very high amounts of care (Jacobson & Wille, 1984). Day-care children also have been observed to be more comfortable in a new situation—such as a visit to an unfamiliar day-care center (Kagan et al., 1978). Finally, Goossens's (1987) finding that in the standard laboratory Strange Situation even securely attached infants were more likely to be low in proximity seeking and contact maintaining if their mothers worked (more B1 and B2s and fewer B4s), suggests that infants with day-care experience find the standard Strange Situation less stressful.

Furthermore, not only are the infants of working mothers more likely to be familiar with features of the Strange Situation, so are their mothers. This too might affect infants' behavior. Researchers have found that mothers' behavior in the Strange Situation reunion is related to their anxiety about separation from their infants (McBride & Hock, 1984), and we know from other studies that infants are sensitive to their mothers' emotional signals in ambiguous situations (Saarni, Mumme, & Campos, 1998). All these are merely hints, not proof, of the possibility that day-care infants find the Strange Situation less stressful—but they do offer a justification for our attempt to explore the issue experimentally.

ATTEMPTS TO VALIDATE THE STRANGE SITUATION FOR DAY CARE CHILDREN

In three studies conducted since the "day-care wars" began, researchers have attempted to disprove the hypothesis that the elevated likelihood of attachment insecurity in infants with extensive day-care histories is a result of the fact that these children with routine experience of separation are less stressed by the Strange Situation. Belsky and Braungart (1991) compared 11 infants who had experienced more than 20 hours of nonparental care per week with 9 infants who had experienced less than 20 hours per week. The infants with more child care whimpered, fussed, and cried more and played with toys less in the reunions than the children with no care. A more substantial sample in the NICHD Study of Early Child Care (NICHD Early Child Care Research Network, 1997) allowed a more convincing test of the hypothesis. The subsample of infants who were in more than 30 hours of nonmaternal care from 4–15 months ($n = 257$) was compared with the subsample of infants who experienced less than 10 hours ($n = 263$) for distress in the Strange Situation during mother-absent episodes. No significant difference in distress was observed, either overall or within attachment types. These analyses do not offer support for the differential-stress hypothesis, it is true. But they do not disprove it either. There may still be differences in infants' anxiety and lack of comfort in the Strange Situation that do not show up in overt *dis*tress. Distress in the Strange Situation has not proven to be a useful behavior for making attachment classifications (Moore, Cohn, Belsky, & Campbell, 1996; Richters, Waters, & Vaughn, 1988), presumably because it is related to infants' temperament (Thompson, Connell, & Bridges, 1988; Vaughn, Lefever, Seifer, & Barglow, 1989; Weber, Levitt, & Clark, 1986).

A second test of the differential stressfulness hypothesis was carried out in the NICHD Study by comparing the confidence with which coders (all at a central site) assigned attachment classifications to children in day care and mother care. Presumably if any day-care children's behavior was not "true" avoidance, coders might be less confident about their classification of these children. Instead, these analyses revealed that children in day care were coded with greater confidence than children who were not in day care—in two attachment categories. In the NICHD (1997) report, this was interpreted as evidence *against* the hypothesis of differential stressfulness. But the two categories about which coders were more confident were the "D" (disorganized) and "U" (unclassifiable) categories. Because Main originally developed the D classification to cover cases that did not neatly fit into Ainsworth's A, B, and C prototypes (Main & Solomon, 1986), and because it is not clear what it means to be more confident that a child is *unclassifiable*, perhaps these results do not offer evidence disconfirming the hypothesis after all.

A third attempt to validate the Strange Situation with day-care children was made by Berger, Levy, and Compaan (1995). Infants were videotaped while they were given routine pediatric checkups, and the tapes were coded for attachment security by an investigator who had been trained in Strange Situation coding conventions by Sroufe and Main. Attachment classifications were highly concordant with classifications based on the Strange Situation—regardless of the children's day-care status, and of the 10 infants who were classified as insecure in the Strange Situation and secure in the pediatric visit, 8 were maternal care. This is the strongest evidence gathered so far against the differential stressfulness hypothesis. But it should be cautioned that this sample, especially the children in day care, exhibited an unusually high level of insecurity. Of the day-care children, 59% were insecure in the Strange Situation and 63% in the pediatric visit; of the children in maternal care, 48% were insecure in the Strange Situation and 29% in the pediatric visit. Only the results of this last assessment are in line with rates of insecurity observed in most U.S. studies. Thus, this study does not settle the question whether day-care children behave differently in the Strange Situation because they experience it as less stressful.

NEED FOR A NEW ASSESSMENT OF ATTACHMENT FOR DAY CARE CHILDREN

To explore more thoroughly the hypothesis that children with regular day-care experience react differently from those with no such experience in the Strange Situation because they find it less stressful, we devised a procedure for assessing attachment that does not depend on separations from mother or confrontations with unfamiliar women— events that differentiate the experiences of home-reared and day-care infants. Like the Strange Situation, the California Attachment Procedure (CAP) is a method for assessing attachment security in a laboratory setting. It is designed to provide events that universally activate the infant's attachment behavior control system. It capitalizes on Bowlby's (1969) suggestion that attachment behavior and withdrawal behavior are distinct behavioral systems that, although frequently compatible with each other, can easily be in conflict. Bowlby (1969) argued that "an individual's susceptibility to respond with fear whenever he meets a potentially alarming situation is determined in very large part by the type of forecast he makes of the probable availability of attachment figures, and that these forecasts derive from the structure of the working models of attachment figures and of self with which he is operating" (p. 297) . Like the Strange Situation, the CAP is based on the assumption that all human beings withdraw from stimuli that act as natural clues to impending danger and that it is in the patterning of these behaviors with reference to the mother that the security or insecurity of the infant's relationship with mother can be discovered. However, the CAP differs from the Strange Situation in the ways in which withdrawal from the strange is elicited. Although the infant is confronted with an unfamiliar person in the CAP, that person is "strange" in ways that are likely to be equally unfamiliar for both home-reared and day-care infants; the stranger does not act or look like a day-care provider. A wider array of stimuli is used to evoke fear in the CAP than in the Strange Situation and this increases the probability that at least one of the varied stimuli will successfully activate attachment behaviors. Finally, the mother does not leave the room in the CAP, and thus she is not the source of the child's distress and she is available for the child to use as a source of comfort and security should the child choose to do so.

VALIDATING ATTACHMENT ASSESSMENTS: LINKS WITH MATERNAL SENSITIVITY

Most authors (Main, 1990; Hinde & Stevenson-Hinde, 1990; van IJzendoorn, 1990) agree that the validity of a new instrument to assess the quality of infants' attachment also needs to be assessed in terms of its association with known antecedents of attachment security. The most obvious antecedent of attachment security is maternal sensitivity. Research consistently has documented a significant link between mothers' sensitivity and the security of infants' attachments. In fact, it was the link between sensitivity and attachment that led Ainsworth and her followers to believe that the Strange Situation reflected something important in the first place. Ainsworth obtained a high correlation of .78 between maternal sensitivity and infant attachment in her Baltimore study. Subsequent studies reviewed by Clarke-Stewart (1988) and meta-analyzed by Goldsmith and Alansky (1987) showed consistent and significant, though considerably smaller, associations between sensitivity and attachment (average correlation = .16), and a more recent meta-analysis carried out by De Wolff and van IJzendoorn (1997), which combined the results of 21 studies, including the NICHD Study of Early Child Care, showed that preceding or concurrent observational measures of sensitivity had a combined effect size on attachment security of $r = .24$. It was therefore also our purpose to investigate the prediction of children's behavior in the CAP from a measure of their mothers' sensitivity.

A STUDY OF THE
CALIFORNIA ATTACHMENT PROCEDURE

To explore the hypothesis that children in routine child care would appear more secure in the CAP—because it does not involve separations from mother or care by an unfamiliar woman—we examined a sample of 60 toddlers (32 of them girls), from white, middle- to upper-middle-income two-parent families, in both the Strange Situation and the CAP (Clarke-Stewart, Goossens, & Allhusen, in press). About half of the children experienced regular, routine separations from their mothers; the others did not. Because we expected that the experience of frequent separations from the mother rather than the length of time away from the mother during any given separation would be the critical factor in predisposing some children to be less stressed by Strange Situation separations, we used the number of regular weekly separations from mother as well as the number of hours spent apart from mother to define our day-care and mother-care groups. The day-care group consisted of 34 children who were in the care of someone other than their mothers on a regular basis at least 3 days a week. On average, children in this group spent 33 hours a week in nonmaternal care (time in care ranged from 10 to 50 hours). All but two of these children had begun nonmaternal care some time during their first year of life (on average, at 4 months of age). The type of day care varied, from nannies in the children's homes to formal day-care centers; for one child, the only nonmaternal caregiver was the father. The 26 children in the mother-care group experienced little or no regular nonmaternal day care (on average, only 1 hour per week); no child in this group spent more than 5 hours or 2 days a week in day care.

Data were collected on two separate occasions, when children and their mothers visited a laboratory playroom at the university. All procedures were videotaped for later scoring. On the first visit, when the children ranged in age from 14 to 19 months, the Strange Situation was conducted following Ainsworth's standard laboratory procedure (Ainsworth & Wittig, 1969; Ainsworth et al. 1978). Strange Situation tapes were then coded by certified raters according to the guidelines described by Ainsworth et al. (1978) for A, B, and C types of attachment (and their subcategories).

At the second visit to the laboratory, 1 month later, when the children ranged in age from 16 to 20 months, the CAP was conducted. In the CAP, the child is presented with three different stimuli designed to elicit moderate distress. Before introducing each new stimulus, the research assistant waited until the child was at least a short physical distance from the mother so that approach behavior could be observed at the onset of the stressful event. The mother was instructed to remain quiet for a moment at the beginning of each stressful episode so that the child's initial reaction could be observed without her interaction, then to respond however she saw fit. Each of the stressful episodes was followed by a brief period of recovery in which the mother and child returned to playing with a set of toys available in the room. The three stressful stimuli were the following:

1. *A loud noise.* A loud noise was made by a remote-controlled hovercraft toy hidden in a box in the corner of the room. The research assistant activated the toy from the observation booth, creating a loud engine noise. The mother was then instructed via a bug-in-the-ear device to encourage the child to go to the box to investigate the source of the noise.

2. *A strange person.* The strange person was an adult, dressed in a wizard costume, who entered the room and invited the child to play. The wizard sat alone for a minute, played alone with balls and scarves for a minute, then invited the child to play. After another minute the mother was instructed to encourage the child to join in the play if he or she had not already done so. Finally, after another minute, the mother was instructed to join in the play herself.

3. *A mechanical robot.* The robot was a small black mechanical toy with flashing red lights. The research assistant entered the room swiftly and quietly, put the robot on the floor facing the child, turned it on, and quickly left the room. The robot advanced toward the child for 15–30 seconds; then the mother was instructed to turn it off.

The CAP was coded following the Ainsworth guidelines for Strange Situation coding, with appropriate modifications. Children coded as secure (Type B) in the CAP approached or looked to their mother at the onset of the stressful event and were successful in deriving comfort and security from her so that they were able to return to constructive play and exploration, either during the stressful episode or shortly after it. Children coded as avoidant (Type A) ignored their mother (Type A1) or seemed ambivalent about approaching her (Type A2). The stressful stimuli clearly elicited distress in these children, as evidenced by their inability to explore the new object or activity, and they were unable to use their mothers to overcome this discomfort. Children coded as resistant (Type C) went to their mothers in search of comfort when the stressful events began, but they were unable to settle, even while in their mother's arms. Their distress continued throughout the stressful episodes, and they often showed anger toward the mother, as if blaming her for this unfortunate turn of events. An attachment classification was given for each stressful episode, then an overall classification (at the subcategory level) was assigned, based on the pattern of behavior observed across all three episodes. An A-B-C classification (and subclassification) system was used, as in the Strange Situation.

At the beginning of the visit at which the CAP was administered, before the stressful events began, we also assessed the mother's sensitivity to the child's behavior. According to Pederson et al. (1990), sensitivity is best measured when the mother is not entirely focused on the child. In their research, it was when mothers were induced to selectively attend to the child and to respond to bids by the child in the context of other tasks that important aspects of sensitivity became apparent. In our study, we used a measure of sensitivity based on both free mother–child interaction and a structured distraction. The mother and child were escorted into the playroom and left alone to play with an array of toys. There was a telephone on a table in the corner of the room next to an armchair where the mother could sit. After several minutes, a research assistant called the mother on the telephone and engaged her in a 12-minute interview. This scenario provided an opportunity to observe the mother's behavior toward the child while she was otherwise occupied. The mother's sensitivity toward the child (including her responsiveness, warmth, quality of interaction, and lack of rejection) was rated at the end of each of the two periods (free play and telephone call) by two different raters who were not aware of how the children had behaved in the Strange Situation or the CAP.

DIFFERENT DISTRIBUTIONS OF ATTACHMENT TYPES IN THE STRANGE SITUATION AND THE CALIFORNIA ATTACHMENT PROCEDURE

In the Strange Situation, 67% of the children were classified as securely attached (Type B), 21% were avoidant (Type A), and 12% were resistant (Type C). This distribution is practically identical to that obtained by van IJzendoorn and Kroonenberg (1988) in their international meta-analysis (65% Bs, 21% As, and 14% Cs). However, in the CAP, a higher rate of secure attachments was obtained. The CAP distribution was 83% Bs, 12% As, and 5% Cs. This raises the question whether 83% is a unreasonably high rate of security, because it is higher than the two-thirds rate usually obtained in the Strange Situation. It seems unlikely that there is anything sacrosanct about the two-thirds/one-third split of secure/insecure attachments typically seen in the Strange Situation. Perhaps this division reflects the unique characteristics of the Strange Situation procedure rather than a universal rate of attachment security. In the attachment Q-sort, a comparable two-thirds rate of security was created in order to make the distribution similar to that of the Strange Situation. But it is noteworthy that mothers using Q-set items to describe their own children place almost *all* of them in the secure range (Posada et al., 1995), which these authors take to support the conjecture by Bowlby and Ainsworth that secure-base behavior is characteristic of our species. Thus perhaps it is not unreasonable that in our new assessment of attachment, 83% of the children exhibited secure attachment behavior.

DIFFERENCES BETWEEN DAY-CARE
AND MOTHER-CARE CHILDREN

When we looked at the distributions of the three different types of attachment exhibited by children in day care and children in maternal care, we discovered that the percentage of Type A avoidant children in the Strange Situation was higher for day-care children than for mother-care children (27% vs. 15%). This difference parallels the results of previous research in showing that in the Strange Situation, the rate of avoidant attachments is higher for day-care children than for mother-care children. The magnitude of the difference is somewhat larger than that found in Clarke-Stewart's (1989) compilation of 17 studies (22% vs. 16%) and the NICHD substudy of children in full-time nonmaternal child care versus no nonmaternal child care (NICHD Strange Situation Differential Validity Task Force Report—1C, 1994) (20% vs. 13%). Nevertheless, the difference in this study was not statistically significant, presumably because of its much smaller sample size. In the CAP, however, unlike the Strange Situation, the percentage of avoidant children for maternal-care and day-care children was identical (12% in each). Thus we have the first evidence to support the hypothesis that the Strange Situation may be eliciting disproportionately high levels of avoidance in day-care children.

AGREEMENT BETWEEN STRANGE SITUATION
AND CALIFORNIA ATTACHMENT PROCEDURE
SECURITY CLASSIFICATIONS

The next question we asked was whether there was any agreement between Strange Situation and CAP classifications. Were children who were coded as secure in the Strange Situation also secure in the CAP? Among the children in mother care, we found, 85% received the same attachment classification in the two assessments. This concordance rate is quite similar to the rates that have been observed in other studies comparing Strange Situation attachment classifications with attachment measured by other assessment instruments. Berger et al. (1995) obtained a concordance rate of 76% between the Strange Situation and a pediatric checkup visit for mother-care children; Pederson and Moran (1996) found a concordance rate of 86% between the Strange Situation and an assessment of attachment made at home during Bayley testing and an interview with the mother, and Finkel, Wille, and Matheny (1998) observed a concordance rate of 78% between the Strange Situation and a more lengthy Strange Situation-like assessment of attachment for twins. The concordance rate for the day-care children in our study, however, as predicted, was substantially lower—only 59%. Here, then, is evidence supporting the suggestion that day-care children are not as likely as home-care children to perceive the Strange Situation and the CAP as equally stressful.

THE "SHIFT TO SECURITY" IN ATTACHMENT SUBTYPES

The difference in these concordance rates for day-care and mother-care children was not random. The reason that there was less agreement between the two assessments for the children in day care was that those children were disproportionately likely to be *insecure* in the Strange Situation and *secure* in the CAP. Of the 9 mother-care children who were insecure in the Strange Situation, fewer than half (44%) were secure in the CAP, but of the 11 day-care children who were insecure in the Strange Situation, almost all (91%) were secure in the CAP.

To explore this difference further, we conducted finer-grained analyses of the discrepancies between attachment classifications in the Strange Situation and the CAP for children in day care and those in mother care. For each child, a number was calculated, which was the difference between the attachment classification subtype assigned in the Strange Situation and the attachment classification subtype assigned in the CAP, with positive signs indicating a "shift" toward being assigned a more secure subtype in the CAP than in the Strange Situation and negative signs indicating a "shift" toward being assigned a less secure subtype in the CAP than in the Strange Situation. We then looked at the percentages of children who made "shifts" of each magnitude ranging from −3 to + 4.

In the first examination, we looked at the shifts from both directions (from both Type A and Type C) to B3, which is often considered to be the most secure attachment category. Among the mother-care children, 27% shifted in a positive direction, that is toward greater security in the CAP, and 27% shifted in a negative direction. Among day-care children, 54% shifted in the direction of increased security in the CAP and only 18% shifted in the direction of decreased security. We then looked at shifts toward B3 *or* B2, because both of these subtypes can be considered very secure. The results were similar: for children in mother care, 58% did not shift, 20% shifted in a positive direction, and 23% shifted in a negative direction, whereas, for children in day care, 38% did not shift, 48% shifted in a positive direction, and 15% shifted in a negative direction. We also calculated the shift from a more avoidant attachment subtype (A, B1, or B2) to a more secure one (B3), dropping the children who received B4 or C1 classifications in the Strange Situation, because in previous research it was avoidant attachment that was overrepresented among day-care children. The difference between mother-care and day-care children remained apparent in this analysis as well. Thus, in all three analyses, among day-care children, approximately three times as many increased in security from the Strange Situation to the CAP as decreased in security, whereas, among mother-care children, the probability of increasing or decreasing in security from Strange Situation to CAP was about equal (i.e., the same as would be expected by chance).

RELATIONS WITH MATERNAL SENSITIVITY: STRANGE SITUATION VERSUS CALIFORNIA ATTACHMENT PROCEDURE

Finally, we examined whether the CAP classifications were comparable to Strange Situation classifications in terms of their associations with maternal sensitivity. As it turned out, they were not. Mothers' sensitivity was unrelated to children's attachment security assessed in the Strange Situation—for the whole sample, the mother-care sample, and the day-care sample. However, maternal sensitivity was related to attachment security assessed in the CAP (significantly so for the whole sample and the day-care sample and approaching significance for the mother-care sample). As Figure 11.1 shows, the most sensitive mothers had the most securely attached infants (B3s) in the CAP. Levels of sensitivity increased the closer the child's CAP attachment classification was to B3. (The quadratic trend for others' sensitivity with attachment subtypes in the CAP, ordered from A1 to C1, was significant, $F[1, 53/59]$ quadratic $= 14.3$, $p < .001$.) On the other hand, maternal sensitivity was not related to specific attachment subtypes in the Strange Situation, and there was no significant curvilinear association between maternal sensitivity and attachment classifications in the Strange Situation ($F[1, 59]$ quadratic $= < 1$). When the same analyses were performed for the two groups, those in mother care and those in day care, the findings paralleled those for the whole sample: Mothers' sensitivity was curvilinearly related to attachment subtype in the CAP but not in the Strange Situation for both mother-care and day-care children.

The finding that maternal sensitivity was higher for B infants than for infants classified as either A or C in the CAP replicates findings by Pederson and Moran (1996) and Kochanska (1998) and is consistent with the results of the meta-analysis by De Wolff and van IJzendoorn (1997). The fact that sensitivity was more strongly related to the CAP attachment classification than to the Strange Situation classification parallels the difference between attachment Q-sort classifications and Strange Situation classifications. In their meta-analysis of studies in which the Strange Situation was used, De Wolff and van IJzendoorn (1997) found that the association between maternal sensitivity and attachment security was .24, whereas in a meta-analysis of studies using the Q-sort, the association was .50 (van IJzendoorn, Vereijken, & Riksen-Walraven, in press). In the present study, too, the correlation between sensitivity and security measured in the CAP was .50. It is not too sur-

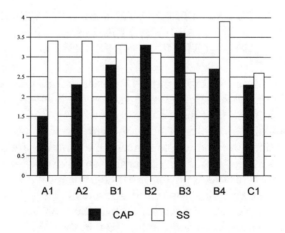

FIGURE 11.1. Maternal sensitivity related to children's attachment classifications in the CAP (California Attachment Procedure) and the SS (Strange Situation).

prising that a significant association between maternal sensitivity and security in the Strange Situation was not found; not every study has revealed a significant relation. Because of this, previous reviewers claimed that the association between mothers' sensitivity and security of infants' attachment was weak (Goldsmith & Alansky, 1987; Lamb, Thompson, Gardner, & Charnov, 1985).

WHAT WE HAVE LEARNED
AND WHAT LIES AHEAD

In brief, then, the results lend support to the possibility that differences in attachment insecurity, which, in earlier studies, were linked to day-care participation, may have been affected by the use of the Strange Situation as the sole method of assessing attachment. Using a method that was designed to be psychologically equivalent for children with and without experience in day care indicated that a substantial number of children who were classified as insecure in the Strange Situation were secure in the new procedure. Although this issue may be practically moot, now that contemporary, multivariate research controlling for family factors suggests that the difference in attachment associated with day care has shrunk, it is valuable to have more than a single attachment assessment instrument available. Moreover, this one was found to have the advantage of providing attachment classifications that were more closely related to maternal sensitivity than classifications based on the Strange Situation.

The results of this study suggest that the CAP is an instrument worth further empirical investigation. It supplements the Strange Situation procedure and provides a valuable addition to the slim library of available attachment assessments. This study represents a first attempt to validate this new measure of attachment. In future studies we hope to replicate these findings with a larger sample (approximately 100 children participating in the longitudinal NICHD Study of Early Child Care). In addition we plan to validate the CAP against a series of later child outcomes including social competence at age 3 and behavioral problems at ages 2 and 3. We will also examine the stability of attachment classifications through age 5, using measures of attachment that resemble the CAP as well as those that resemble the Strange Situation. Together, these data will provide the foundation necessary to support the CAP as a valid new measure of attachment security.

Having a new and valid instrument for assessing infants' attachments is particularly important as we enter the changed and changing world of experiences for mothers and children in the next century (cf.

Klein & Tarullo, this volume). The concerns parents have about when and whether the mother should return to work after the baby's birth have not diminished over the past decade and are unlikely to do so in the next. To allay parents' fears about the negative consequences of day care without leading them to abdicate their parental responsibility will require cold hard facts and continued mental effort. As a source of such facts and a stimulus for that effort, we need research that extends beyond the Strange Situation and probes the parameters of children's experiences. We hope that the CAP can play a role in such research.

ACKNOWLEDGMENTS

The following people were particularly helpful in carrying out this study, and we wish to express our appreciation to them: Ellen Greenberger, for consultation in the development of the CAP and the maternal sensitivity measure; Andrea Karsh, Cornelia Biermeier, and Maureen Fitzpatrick for data collection—excellent wizards, all; Andrea Karsh for coding the CAP; Luke Thelen, for analyzing the data; and Tracy Spinrad for her pink scarves and red and blue balls. This study was funded by the National Institute of Child Health and Human Development as part of the cooperative agreement for the NICHD Study of Early Child Care. The sample, however, was not part of the NICHD Study of Early Child Care. Portions of the chapter are taken from Clarke-Stewart, Goossens, and Allhusen (in press). Copyright 2001 by Blackwell Publisher. Reprinted by permission.

REFERENCES

Ainsworth, M. D. S., & Wittig, B. A. (1969). Attachment and exploratory behavior of one-year-olds in a strange situation. In B. M. Foss (Ed.), *Determinants of infant behaviour* IV (pp. 111–136). London: Methuen.

Ainsworth, M. D. S., Blehar, M. C., Waters, E., & Wall, S. (1978). *Patterns of attachment: A psychological study of the Strange Situation.* Hillsdale, NJ: Erlbaum.

Barglow, P. Vaughn, B. E., & Molitor, N. (1987). Effects of maternal absence due to employment on the quality of infant-mother attachment in a low-risk sample. *Child Development, 58,* 945–954.

Belsky, J. (1986). Infant day care: A cause for concern? *Zero to Three, 6,* 1–7.

Belsky, J. (1988). The "effects" of infant day care reconsidered. *Early Childhood Research Quarterly, 3,* 235–272.

Belsky, J. (1992). Consequences of child care for children's development: A deconstructionist view. In A. Booth (Ed.), *Child care in the 1990s: Trends and consequences* (pp. 83–94). Hillsdale, NJ: Erlbaum.

Belsky, J., & Braungart, J. M. (1991). Are insecure–avoidant infants with extensive day-care experience less stressed by and more independent in the Strange Situation? *Child Development, 62,* 567–571.

Berger, S. P., Levy, A. K., & Compaan, K. M. (1995, March). *Infant attachment outside the laboratory: New evidence in support of the Strange Situation.* Paper presented at the biennial meetings of the Society for Research in Child Development, Indianapolis.

Bowlby, J. (1969). *Attachment and loss: Vol. 1. Attachment.* Harmondsworth: Penguin.

Brookhart, J., & Hock, E. (1976). The effects of experimental context and experiential background on infants' behavior toward their mothers and a stranger. *Child Development, 47,* 333–340.

Burchinal, M. R., Bryant, D. M., Lee, M. W., & Ramey, C. T. (1992). Early day care, infant-mother attachment, and maternal responsiveness in the infant's first year. *Early Childhood Research Quarterly, 7,* 383–396.

Clarke-Stewart, K. A. (1988). Parents' effects on children's development: A decade of progress? *Journal of Applied Developmental Psychology, 9,* 41–84.

Clarke-Stewart, K. A. (1989). Infant day care: Maligned or malignant? *American Psychologist, 44,* 266–273.

Clarke-Stewart, K. A., Goossens, F. A., & Allhusen, V. D. (in press). Measuring infant-mother attachment: Is the Strange Situation enough? *Social Development.*

De Wolff, M., & van IJzendoorn, M. H. (1997). Sensitivity and attachment: A meta-analysis on parental antecedents of infant attachment. *Child Development, 68,* 571–591.

Doyle, A.-B. (1975). Infant development in day care. *Developmental Psychology, 11,* 655–656.

Doyle, A.-B., & Somers, K. (1978). The effects of group and family day care on infant attachment behaviours. *Canadian Journal of Behavioural Science, 10,* 38–45.

Fein, G. G., & Clarke-Stewart, A. (1973). *Day care in context.* New York: Wiley.

Fein, G. G., Gariboldi, A., & Boni, R. (1993). The adjustment of infants and toddlers to group care: The first 6 months. *Early Childhood Research Quarterly, 8,* 1–14.

Field, T. M. (1991). Young children's adaptations to repeated separations from their mother. *Child Development, 62,* 539–547.

Finkel, D., Wille, D. E., & Matheny, A. P., Jr. (1998). Preliminary results from a twin study of infant-caregiver attachment. *Behavior Genetics, 28,* 1–8.

Goldsmith, H. H., & Alansky, J. A. (1987). Maternal and infant temperamental predictors of attachment: A meta-analytic review. *Journal of Consulting and Clinical Psychology, 55,* 805–816.

Goossens, F. A. (1987). Kwaliteit van de hechtingsrelatie van jonge kinderen aan hun moeder, vader en crecheleidster. [Quality of the attachment of young children to their mother, father, and professional caregiver] *Nederlands Tijdschrift voor de Psychologie en haar Grensgebieden, 42* 308–320.

Hinde, R. A., & Stevenson-Hinde, J. (1990). Attachment: Biological, cultural and individual desiderata. *Human Development, 33,* 62–72.

Hock, E. (1980). Working and nonworking mothers and their infants: A comparative study of maternal caregiving characteristics and infant social behavior. *Merrill–Palmer Quarterly, 26,* 79–102.

Jacobson, J. L., & Wille, D. E. (1984). Influence of attachment and separation experience on separation distress at 18 months. *Developmental Psychology, 20,* 477–484.

Kagan, J., Kearsley, R. B., & Zelazo, P. R. (1978). *Infancy: Its place in human development.* Cambridge, MA: Harvard University Press.

Karen, R. (1994). *Becoming attached: Unfolding the mystery of the infant–mother bond and its impact on later life.* New York: Warner Books.

Kochanska, G. (1998). Mother–child relationship, child fearfulness, and emerging attachment: A short-term longitudinal study. *Developmental Psychology, 34,* 480–490.

Kroonenberg, P. M., van Dam, M., van IJzendoorn, M. H., & Mooijaart, A. (1997). Dynamics of behaviour in the Strange Situation: A structural equation approach. *British Journal of Psychology, 88,* 311–332.

Lamb, M. E., Sternberg, K. J., & Prodromidis, M. (1992). Nonmaternal care and the security of infant–mother attachment: A reanalysis of the data. *Infant Behavior and Development, 15,* 71–83.

Lamb, M. E., Thompson, R. A., Gardner, W., & Charnov, E. L. (1985). *Infant–mother attachment: The origins and development significance of individual differences in Strange Situation behavior.* Hillsdale, NJ: Erlbaum.

Main, M. (1990). Cross-cultural studies of attachment organization: Recent studies, changing methodologies, and the concept of conditional strategies. *Human Development, 33,* 48–61.

Main, M., & Solomon, J. (1986). Discovery of an insecure–disorganized/disoriented attachment pattern. In T. B. Brazelton & M. W. Yogman (Eds.), *Affective development in infancy* (pp. 95–124). Norwood, NJ: Ablex.

Main, M., & Weston, D. (1982). Avoidance of the attachment figure in infancy: Description and interpretation. In C. M. Parkes & J. Stevenson-Hinde (Eds.), *The place of attachment in human behavior* (pp. 31–59). New York: Basic Books.

McBride, S., & Hock, E. (1984, April). *Relationship of maternal behavior and anxiety associated with mother–infant separation.* Paper presented at International Conference on Infant Studies, New York.

McCartney, K., & Phillips, D. (1988). Motherhood and child care. In B. Birns & D. Hay (Eds.), *The different faces of motherhood* (pp. 157–183). New York: Plenum.

Moore, G. A., Cohn, J. F., Belsky, J., & Campbell, S. B. (1996). A comparison of traditional and quantitative classification of attachment status. *Infant Behavior and Development, 19,* 265–268.

Nakagawa, M., Lamb, M. E., & Miyaki, K. (1992). Antecedents and correlates of the Strange Situation behavior of Japanese infants. *Journal of Cross-Cultural Psychology, 23,* 300–310.

NICHD Early Child Care Research Network. (1997). The effects of infant child care on infant-mother attachment security: Results of the NICHD Study of Early Child Care. *Child Development, 68,* 860–879.

NICHD Strange Situation Differential Validity Task Force Report—1C. (1994). Unpublished report. National Institute of Child Health and Human Development, Washington, DC.

Pederson, D. R., & Moran, G. (1996). Expressions of the attachment relationship outside of the Strange Situation. *Child Development, 67*, 915–927.

Pederson, D. R., Moran, G., Sitko, C., Campbell, K., Ghesquire, K., & Acton, H. (1990). Maternal sensitivity and the security of infant–mother attachment: A Q-sort study. *Child Development, 61*, 1974–1983.

Posada, G., Gao, Y., Wu, F., Posada, R., Tascon, M., Schoelmerich, A., Sagi, A., Kondo-Ikemura, K., Haaland, W., & Synnevaag, B. (1995). The secure-base phenomenon across cultures: Children's behavior, mothers' preferences, and experts' concepts. In E. Waters, B. E. Vaughn, G. Posada, & K. Kondo-Ikemura (Eds.), Caregiving, cultural, and cognitive perspectives on secure-base behavior and working models: New growing points of attachment theory and research. *Monographs of the Society for Research in Child Development, 60*(2–3, Serial No. 244), 27–48.

Ramey, C. T., MacPhee, D., & Yeates, K. O. (1982). Preventing developmental retardation: A general systems model. In L. Bond & J. Joffe (Eds.), *Facilitating infant and early childhood development* (pp. 343–401). Hanover, NH: University Press of New England.

Richters, J. E., Waters, E., & Vaughn, B. E. (1988). Empirical classification of infant-mother relationships from interactive behavior and crying during reunion. *Child Development, 59*, 512–522.

Rinkoff, R. F., & Corter, C. M. (1980). Effects of setting and maternal accessibility on the infant's response to brief separation. *Child Development, 51*, 603–606.

Roggman, L. A., Langlois, J. H., Hubbs-Tait, L., & Rieser-Danner, L. A. (1994). Infant day care, attachment, and the "file drawer problem" *Child Development, 65*, 1429–1443.

Saarni, C., Mumme, D. L., & Campos, J. J. (1998). Emotional development: Action, communication, and understanding. In W. Damon (Ed.) & N. Eisenberg (Vol. Ed.), *Handbook of child psychology* (5th ed.: *Vol. 3. Social, emotional, and personality development* (pp. 237–310). New York: Wiley.

Sagi, A., Lamb, M. E., & Gardner, W. (1986). Relations between Strange Situation behavior and stranger sociability among infants in Israeli kibbutzim. *Infant Behavior and Development, 9*, 271–282.

Sagi, A., van IJzendoorn, M. H., & Koren-Karie, N. (1991). Primary appraisal of the Strange Situation: A cross-cultural analysis of preseparation episodes. *Developmental Psychology, 27*, 587–596.

Seifer, R., Schiller, M., Sameroff, A. J., Resnick, S., & Riordan, K. (1996). Attachment, maternal sensitivity, and infant temperament during the first year of life. *Developmental Psychology, 32*, 12–25.

Sroufe, L. A. (1988). A developmental perspective on day care. Special Issue: Infant day care. *Early Childhood Research Quarterly, 3*, 283–291.

Stifter, C. A., Coulehan, C. M., & Fish, M. (1993). Linking employment to attachment: The mediating effects of maternal separation anxiety and interactive behavior. *Child Development, 64*, 1451–1460.

Takahashi, K. (1986). Examining the Strange-Situation procedure with Japanese mothers and 12–month-old infants. *Developmental Psychology, 22*, 265–270.

Thompson, R. A., Connell, J. P., & Bridges, L. J. (1988). Temperament, emotion, and social interactive behavior in the Strange Situation: A component process analysis of attachment system functioning. *Child Development, 59,* 1102–1110.

van IJzendoorn, M. H. (1990). Special topic: Cross-cultural validity of attachment theory. *Human Development, 33,* 2.

van IJzendoorn, M. H., & Kroonenberg, P. M. (1988). Cross-cultural patterns of attachment: A meta-analysis of the Strange Situation. *Child Development, 59,* 147–156.

van IJzendoorn, M. H., Vereijken, C. M. J. L., & Riksen-Walraven, M. J. M. A. (in press). Is the Attachment Q-Sort a valid measure of attachment security in young children? In B. E. Vaughn & E. Waters (Eds.), *Patterns of secure base behavior: Q-sort perspectives on attachment and caregiving.* Hillsdale, NJ: Erlbaum.

Vaughn, B. E., Lefever, G. B., Seifer, R., & Barglow, P. (1989). Attachment behavior, attachment security, and temperament during infancy. *Child Development, 60,* 728–737.

Waters, E. Vaughn, B. E., Posada, G. & Kondo-Ikemura, K. (Eds.). (1995). Caregiving, cultural, and cognitive perspectives on secure-base behavior and working models: New growing points of attachment theory and research. *Monographs of the Society for Research in Child Development, 60*(2–3, Serial No. 244).

Weber, R. A., Levitt, M. J., & Clark, M. C. (1986). Individual variation in attachment security and Strange Situation behavior: The role of maternal and infant temperament. *Child Development, 57,* 56–65.

12

❧

Processes in the Formation of Attachment Relationships with Alternative Caregivers

CAROLLEE HOWES
ERIN OLDHAM

It is well documented that children construct attachment relationships with caregivers in the child-care setting (Howes, 1999). However, little research attention has been paid the processes involved in relationship formation in this particular developmental context. That children form and maintain multiple attachment relationships is theoretically consistent with Bowlby's attachment theory (Bowlby, 1969/1982). However, Bowlby's account of the formation of attachment relationships assumes that an adult and an infant begin to construct their relationship from the moment of birth. In this scenario, children's repertoire of social signals and their capacities for memory, internal representation, and affective cognitions develop at the same time as the child–adult attachment. The formation of infant–mother attachment relationships can be observed as children track or follow the mother, cry to alert her to their distress, or maintain social contact through smiles and vocalizations. A different scenario occurs when toddlers begin child care. These children already have a repertoire of social signals and a beginning set of internal representations of relationships with the important caregivers in their lives. The nature of their relationship history predisposes the toddlers to act as if this new child-care caregiver will be a delightful new person to be enjoyed and trusted, or a person to distrust. Of course, the new caregiver may fit these expectations or behave in ways that disconfirm the toddler's internalized model of relationships. The purpose of the research reported in this chapter is to examine the formation of attachment relationships when children have prior experience in attachment relationship formation, have a repertoire of social signals, and the capacity to develop internal representations. We were interested in examining what behavior repertoires children brought to child care, how they approached the task of trusting someone taking care of them, and how long it appeared to take to build a new relationship.

Fein's research describes entry into child care as a stressful experience (Fein, 1995; Fein, Gariboldi, & Boni, 1993; Fox & Field, 1989). Regular child-care caregivers serve as attachment figures because they are, over time, responsible for mundane, everyday caregiving tasks and for keeping the child safe in the absence of the parent. If entry into child care is stressful, and if parents by leaving the child with the caregiver explicitly or implicitly tell the child that the caregiver is responsible for the child's welfare, then we expect that the children's attachment system will be activated upon child-care entry. That is, we expect children to direct attachment behaviors to the caregiver even if initially he or she is a stranger.

In Bowlby's (Bowlby, 1969/1982; Bretherton, 1985) formulation of attachment theory, attachment behaviors are those social bids that permit the child to maintain proximity to the caregiving adult. Thus the child tracks or follows the caregiver, cries to alert the caregiver, or maintains social contact with the caregiver through smiles and vocalizations. A child's attachment organization is the particular way the child uses or represents the caregiver, resulting in felt security (or insecurity). Through numerous experiences of social interaction with the caregiver using attachment behaviors, the child internalizes an attachment organization. When attachments are formulated within the family, with parents present from birth, there is a synchrony between developmental advances in using attachment behaviors, in the capacity to form internal representations, and in the development of particular attachment organizations around the parent caregiver.

In contrast to this theoretical formulation, when toddler-age children enter child care they have in place a repertoire of attachment behaviors and the experience of forming an attachment with at least one parent. By examining the process of formation of attachment in these children we are able to consider the role of attachment behaviors in the formation of attachment organization separately from the social and cognitive underlying developmental processes inherent in the formation of attachment during infancy.

The literature on entry into child care suggests that children beginning child care initially are demanding of and oriented to adults rather than to peers. As the experience becomes more familiar over the next 2 to 3 weeks, children become more sociable with peers and active with materials. After a few weeks in child care children are indistinguishable from children longer in the setting (Feldbaum, Christenson, & O'Neal, 1980; Fox & Field, 1989; McGrew, 1972). Although none of these previous studies directly examined attachment behaviors, these observations suggest an activation of the attachment system at child-care entry and the establishment of relationships at some time thereafter.

Studies of children who have been in child care for 2 or more months find that there is great variation in their attachment security with primary caregivers. Some children form trusting secure relationships with caregivers while others are anxious and distrustful. Typical children, as opposed to children from extremely difficult life circumstances, form relationships with caregivers that are independent in quality of their maternal attachment relationships (Howes, 1999). The variation in child–caregiver attachment quality is linked to the sensitivity and responsiveness of the caregiver (Howes & Smith, 1995). Caregivers, of course, vary greatly in their sensitivity and responsiveness to children. We know that some children more readily elicit kind behavior while others frustrate and annoy caregivers. It often requires a great deal of professionalism and commitment for caregivers to be sensitive and responsive to the more difficult children. A complete study of the formation of attachment relationships in child care would require studying variability in children and in caregivers' capacities to build relationships. To narrow the issue we chose to focus on variability in children. We limited our study to children entering high-quality center-based child-care programs. The teachers in these programs were above average in their knowledge of and commitment to providing a positive child-care experience for all children who entered the center. No child no matter how difficult would be asked to leave, and the teachers saw it as their job to form a positive relationship with each child. Children were not assigned to a primary caregiver as they entered the program, but teachers (as well as the researchers) monitored the establishment of relationships and expected that children (and caregivers) would form preferential pairings.

We were particularly interested in examining whether the kind or intensity of attachment behaviors the children used at entry influenced their attachment security in child care 6 months later. Fein (1995; Fein et al., 1993) suggests that the initial encounters of children and child-care caregivers continue to influence children's adjustment following 6 months in care. To explore this finding, we also examined whether caregiver responsiveness at child-care entry influenced children's attachment security 6 months following entry.

Attachment relationships are constructed between a particular adult and a particular child (Bowlby, 1969/1982; Bretherton, 1985). In the child-care settings we studied, entering children always had more than one caregiver available. Furthermore, in no setting were children assigned to caregivers. When caregivers are assigned to children they are expected to be differentially responsive to their assigned children. Therefore, with multiple caregivers available and no assignment of caregivers, children in our study had the task of differentiating among caregivers. Prior research suggests that in such child-care settings children and caregivers differentially prefer each other. With differential preferences or primary caregivers, children direct disproportionate amounts of their attachment behaviors to one caregiver rather than to the others (Rubenstein & Howes, 1979). In most cases the primary caregiver of the child can be identified by adults in the setting (Howes & Smith, 1995). In the current research, we examined how and when these matches between caregivers and children emerged. Specifically, we asked when in the process of entering child care do children organize their attachment system around a particular or primary caregiver? That is, when do children begin to differentiate their attachment behaviors between caregivers?

Prior research in which children's attachment relationships have been observed assumed that after 2 months in care children would have attachment relationships (Goossens & van IJzendoorn, 1990; Howes & Smith, 1995). There is little empirical basis for this assumption. Several studies of child-care entry suggest that social and emotional adjustment to child care is complete in two months (Blanchard & Main, 1979; Fox & Field, 1989). In contrast, a study of infants adopted from an orphanage suggested that emotional bonds to new parents may form more rapidly (Dontas, Maratos, Fafoutis, & Karangelis, 1985). In our study, all the children had readily identified primary caregiver after 6 months in child care. We explored the assumption that attachment relationships form within 2 months of child-care entry by examining whether the interaction patterns across time between children and the caregivers who would become primary caregivers.

METHOD

Sample

Ten children, five girls and five boys, participated in this research. At the beginning of the study the children ranged in age from 15 to 28 months (mean age = 21.3 months, SD = 3.65 months). The children were ethnically diverse (33% Asian, 40% white, 20% African American, 10% Latino). All of the children lived with their two biological parents. In each family, one or both of the parents were faculty or were graduate students, at a major urban university.

As the study began, all of the children were beginning their first out-of-home child-care experience. They began full-day, full-week care in one of three child-care centers serving the university campus. The average group size of the child-care classroom for the children was 6.3 (SD = 1.2) and the average child-to-adult ratio was 4:1 (SD = 0.3). The Infant–Toddler Environmental Rating Scale (ITERS) ratings (Harms, Clifford, & Cryer, 1990) on the classrooms entered by the children ranged from 5.02 to 6.16 (average rating = 5.34, SD = 0.2). The ratio and ITERS scores indicate that the care in the classrooms was generally good in quality. The caregivers assigned to the children's classrooms over the 6 months of observation remained constant. Therefore, no child experienced caregiver turnover.

Procedures and Measures

Observations

Eighteen observations were conducted on each child over a 6-month period. The observations were divided into four periods. Observations were more densely spaced during the child's initial time in child care and then were more broadly spaced to cover the child's first 6 months in child care. The first period consisted of four observations, conducted on the first, third, seventh, and ninth day of child-care attendance without the parent. The second period consisted of eight observations conducted weekly for 2 months (16th, 23rd, 30th, 37th, 44th, 51st, 58th, and 65th day in child care). The third period consisted of four observations conducted biweekly for 2 months (79th, 93rd, 107th, and 121st day in child care). The final period consisted of two once-a-month observations (151st and 181st day in child care). If a child was absent on the target observation or if the target observation day was on a weekend, the next first available day was used for observation.

Observations were conducted by a team of trained graduate students. An observer was assigned to a child for the duration of a period. In the next period another observer was assigned to the child. This shifting of the observers prevented any observer from becoming overly familiar with the child.

Each observation lasted 2 hours. Only behaviors occurring within three social contexts were observed. The three contexts were separation from parent; routine caregiving, including feeding, clothing, diaper changing, and naptime; and child distress. The parent departure context was selected because the separation from parent was expected to be sufficiently stressful to activate the attachment system. Routine caregiving and distress contexts were selected because theoretically they are optimal periods for observing security seeking and secure base phenomenon behaviors.

Each day's observation began when the parent who had brought the child to child care left the room. Parent departure, routine caregiving, and distress served as triggers or start points for coding interactive episodes. Once coding began it continued until the child or caregiver ended the interaction by walking away and not making a social bid for at least 20 seconds.

Within an interactive episode, child and caregiver behaviors were coded from a predetermined list every 20 seconds. Interactive behavior categories were derived from the Strange Situation (Ainsworth, Blehar, Waters, & Wall, 1978; Clarke-Stewart, Allhusen, & Goossens, this volume) and from the Attachment Q-Set (Waters, 1990). Child behaviors were *tracks* the caregiver (physically approaches the caregiver, physically follows the caregiver or gazes at the caregiver, and/or visually checks in with caregiver), *positively initiates* to the caregiver (vocalizes to the caregiver, signals to be picked up by the caregiver, or initiates hugs or cuddles with the caregiver); *positively responds* to the caregiver (relaxes in the lap or arms of the caregiver, follows the caregiver's suggestions or instructions, vocally responds to the caregiver, or smiles or laughs in response to the caregiver's behavior), *cries or fusses* while looking at the caregiver, and *avoids* the caregiver (holds body stiff or apart when held by caregiver, looks away when caregiver attempts to engage or pulls or moves away when caregiver attempts to engage). Caregiver behaviors were *positive initiation* (approaches child, places self within 3 feet of child and looks at child, picks up the child without a child signal, verbally attempts to engage child, or initiates hugs or cuddles), *positive response* (picks up child upon child's signal, laughs or smiles in response to child behavior, or talks to child in response to child behavior), *ignoring child* (does not appear to notice child initiations or distress), and *reprimanding* a fussing or distressed child and *comforting* a distressed child. Frequencies of reprimand were too low to analyze so this variable was dropped.

Interobserver reliability prior to coding was established with 15 observational visits to children not in the study. Coders were trained to an 85% exact agreement criteria (kappa ranges on composite variables .82 to .96). Interobserver reliability was reestablished at 3-month intervals during the 18 months of data collection.

Ratings

At the conclusion of each observation, the observers assigned global ratings to children on four scales. These ratings provided an index to the emotional tone and climate of the child–caregiver interactions during the 2-hour observation visit. A *sensitivity* rating for each caregiver with whom the child engaged during the visit was made using the Ainsworth maternal sensitivity scale (Ainsworth, Blehar, Waters, & Wall, 1978). The three additional 4-point scales were based on composite behavioral measures used by Fein (Fein et al., 1993) in her study of infants' adjustment to child care. A high score on the *Affect* scale means that the predominate emotional tone of the child during the observation period was positive—smiling, laughing, and vocalizing—rather than crying, fusing, frowning, or looking sad. A high score on the *Activity Involvement* scale means that the child was involved in complex object and motor play and interested in classroom activities as opposed to being immobile or inattentive. A high score on the *Interaction* scale means that the child was involved with the other people in the classroom—adults and peers—as opposed to social withdrawal.

Interobserver reliability prior to coding was established with 15 observational visits to children not in the study. Coders were trained to a 85% exact agreement criteria (kappa ranges on composite variables .93 to .97). Interobserver reliability was reestablished at 3-month intervals during the 18 months of data collection.

Q-Set

After the final observation session, the last observer assigned to the child in consultation with the author (C. H.) determined the child's primary caregiver in the child-care center. A primary caregiver was defined as the caregiver to whom the child directed the largest proportion of his or her attachment behaviors and appeared to prefer. A different observer then spent 2 to 4 hours in the classroom watching while the child and primary caregiver pursued normal activities in the child-care setting. Following the observation, the observer completed the 90-item Attachment Q-Set (AQS; Waters, 1990).

Observers were trained to an 85% exact agreement criterion on each item prior to data collection. Interobserver reliability checks were conducted throughout data collection. Median interobserver reliability was kappa = .91 (range kappa = .85 to .97). To obtain security scores the raw scores from the AQS were correlated with the criterion scores provided for security by Waters (1990). The correlation coefficients are the children's security scores. Security scores can vary from –1.0 to 1.0. A higher score indicates greater security.

RESULTS

Interactive Episodes

Nine hundred and eighty interaction episodes were observed. The episodes lasted an average of 8.2 ($SD = 4.9$) intervals or approximately 2.7 minutes. Each child contributed an average of 90.8 ($SD = 6.4$, range = 52 to 124) episodes. Children did not significantly vary in their number or in the length of their episodes.

Every child contributed 18 departure of parent episodes (total number of episodes = 180). The other 728 episodes were distributed between routine caregiving (53%) and distress (47%) contexts. There was a significant association between child and context for the nondeparture episodes ($\chi^2(9) = 105.97$, $p = .000$). At one extreme one child had 95% routine caregiving and 5% distress episodes; at the other extreme a child had 30% routine caregiving and 70% distress episodes.

Because the children were in group child care, at all times there was more than one adult present in the classroom. Overall, 28% of the episodes were between the caregiver identified as the child's primary caregiver at 6 months after entry and the child. The children were significantly more likely to be with the primary caregiver during parent departure episodes than the nondeparture contexts ($\chi^2(2) = 11.99$, $p = .003$). There were no differences in the number of units of episodes with the primary and other caregivers ($t(906) = 1.16$, n.s.).

Attachment Q-Set

Children's attachment security scores with their primary caregiver ranged from .15 to .72 ($M = .47$, $SD = .17$). A convention with the Attachment Q-Set is to use .33 as a threshold score to indicate security (Raikes, 1993). Using this convention 70% of the children were classified as secure and 30% as insecure.

Differentiating the Primary Caregiver

The first step in the analysis was to examine whether the children differed in the frequency of attachment behaviors directed to the person who would become the primary caregiver versus other caregivers over time. To complete this analysis, we calculated, for each child, the frequency of units of each category of attachment behavior directed to primary versus other caregivers during each of the four time periods (entry, second, third, and fourth) corrected for differences in number of observations per time period. Table 12.1 presents descriptive statistics.

Because of the small sample size we made comparisons between behaviors to primary and other caregivers at each period using Wilcoxen Matched-Pairs Signed-Rank Tests. During the entry period children were more likely to track the caregiver who would become the primary caregiver than were the other caregivers ($z = 2.07, p = .04$). During the third ($z = 3.47, p = .02$) and fourth periods ($z = 2.73, p = .02$) children were more likely to respond to the person who would become the primary caregiver than to other caregivers.

We then compared behaviors received from the person who would become the primary caregiver and other caregivers. Table 12.2 presents descriptive statistics. Again, the frequencies were corrected for differences in number of observations per period. As before, Wilcoxen Matched-Pairs Signed-Rank Tests were used to make comparisons. During the third ($z = 1.99, p = .05$) and fourth periods ($z = 2.80, p = .005$) the persons who would become the primary caregivers were more likely to be responsive than were other caregivers.

TABLE 12.1. Children's Attachment Behaviors Directed to Primary and Other Caregivers over Time

| | Observation period | | | | | | | |
| | Entry | | 2 | | 3 | | 4 | |
Behavior	M	SD	M	SD	M	SD	M	SD
Track								
Primary	3.23	(1.59)	2.14	(1.41)	2.16	(1.41)	2.11	(1.98)
Other	2.25	(1.16)	2.35	(1.51)	1.76	(0.66)	1.51	(0.98)
Positive initiation								
Primary	0.90	0.76	1.16	1.24	0.91	0.78	0.56	1.24
Other	1.08	1.16	1.27	0.81	0.81	0.61	0.84	0.90
Positive response								
Primary	5.46	3.54	2.49	2.68	6.56	5.72	5.73	6.01
Other	4.19	2.34	4.02	2.34	4.10	2.72	2.78	1.83
Cry/fuss								
Primary	2.49	2.60	0.93	0.71	0.94	0.78	0.40	0.66
Other	3.15	2.99	1.02	0.83	0.55	0.56	0.54	0.59
Avoid								
Primary	1.67	1.72	0.35	0.55	0.40	0.49	0.10	0.32
Other	2.07	2.09	0.57	0.67	0.41	0.47	0.25	0.30

TABLE 12.2. Comparisons of Behaviors Received from Primary and Other Caregivers over Time

	Observation period							
	Entry		2		3		4	
Behavior	M	SD	M	SD	M	SD	M	SD
Positive initiation								
Primary	2.57	0.87	1.63	1.04	2.95	0.91	2.40	2.73
Other	2.78	1.07	2.28	1.04	2.17	0.43	2.71	1.11
Positive responses								
Primary	5.19	1.73	3.33	1.84	6.24	4.20	6.93	4.23
Other	5.09	1.55	3.39	1.23	3.94	2.31	3.36	2.28
Ignore								
Primary	0.45	0.60	0.14	0.06	0.16	0.33	0.15	0.34
Other	0.78	1.38	0.32	0.39	0.24	0.14	0.15	0.32
Comfort								
Primary	1.41	1.95	0.77	0.90	0.31	0.39	0.13	0.19
Other	1.40	1.82	0.34	0.44	0.13	0.13	0.12	0.24

Changes in Children's Attachment Behaviors over Time

Figure 12.1 presents changes in frequencies of children's attachment behaviors to all caregivers by observation day. We used two strategies to assess changes in children's attachment behaviors over time—growth curve modeling and nonparametric, Wilcoxen Matched-Pairs Signed-Rank Tests for change.

Growth Curve Modeling

Growth curve modeling permits examining the structure and predictors of individual growth (Bryk & Rasdenbush, 1992). We used a two-level hierarchical model to examine individual variations at entry and in change over time in the five child attachment behaviors. We also tested whether variations in entry behaviors or in change over time could be explained by the child's age, gender, or final attachment security score. There were no effects for age or gender. Table 12.3 presents the results of the analyses, including security scores. There was considerable individual variation in children's entry-level attachment behaviors; the t-ratios for entry for all five attachment behaviors were significant. There was less individual variation in growth rates, only tracking and avoiding showed significant individual variation. The coefficients for growth rate

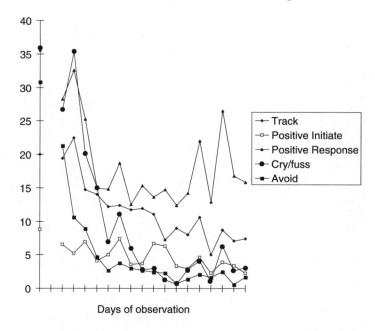

FIGURE 12.1. Changes in behaviors over time.

tend to be relatively small relative to the coefficients for entry indicating that the growth rates of these behavior were fairly flat. The negative coefficients for growth indicate that the behaviors tended to decrease over time.

The tau statistic provides a correlation between individual change and initial status. For all attachment behaviors it was high in magnitude and negative in direction, indicating that children who engaged in fewer attachment behaviors at entry tended to gain them at a faster rate. The low and insignificant t-ratios for both entry and growth for security indicate that final security scores did not explain significant variation in either entry behaviors or in growth rates for any attachment behavior.

Wilcoxen Matched-Pairs Signed-Rank Tests

Inspection of the graphs in Figure 12.1 suggests that attachment behaviors decrease sharply and then level off. We used Wilcoxen Matched-Pairs Signed-Rank Tests to examine the period in which attachment behaviors decreased. Given the small sample size and the large number (18) of data points we tested differences between a limited number of

TABLE 12.3. Linear Model of Growth in Attachment Behaviors

Fixed effect	Coefficient	SE	t-ratio	Tau
Track				
Model for initial status				
Entry	16.08	3.10	5.18**	−0.62
Security	2.31	17.55	0.13	
Model for growth rate				
Time	−0.07	0.02	2.98**	
Security	−0.16	0.12	0.13	
Positive initiation				
Model for initial status				
Entry	9.56	3.45	2.76*	−0.51
Security	−6.94	6.97	1.00	
Model for growth rate				
Time	−0.04	0.03	1.48	
Security	0.03	0.05	0.61	
Positive response				
Model for initial status				
Entry	13.11	13.27	0.99	−0.91
Security	20.55	26.68	0.77	
Model for growth rate				
Time	0.07	0.11	0.60	
Security	0.03	0.23	0.11	
Avoid				
Model for initial status				
Entry	10.99	3.90	2.82*	−0.76
Security	18.96	19.56	0.97	
Model for growth rate				
Time	−0.09	0.03	2.29*	
Security	−0.17	0.17	0.97	
Cry or fuss				
Model for initial status				
Entry	16.98	5.48	3.10**	−0.73
Security	6.90	10.09	0.68	
Model for growth rate				
Time	−0.12	0.06	2.24*	
Security	0.08	0.11	0.68	

$*p < .05$; $**p < .01$.

time points. The selection of which time points to test was guided by previous research which found the entry period and subsequent weeks most stressful for children (Blanchard & Main, 1979; Fein, 1993; Feldbaum et al., 1980; Fox & Field, 1989; McGrew, 1972) and by inspection of the graphs.

Tracking behaviors significantly decrease between the end of the entry period (day 9) and the beginning of period 2 (day 16) ($z = 1.97$, $p = .05$). Positive responses significantly decreased between the first day (day 0) and the beginning of period 2 (day 16) ($z = 2.55$ $p = .01$) and then significantly increased between the end of the second period (day 65) and the end of the third period (day 121) ($z = 2.15$, $p = .05$). Avoiding behaviors ($z = 2.55$, $p = .01$) and crying and fussing ($z = 2.07$, $p = .04$) significantly decreased between the first day (Day 0) and the beginning of period 2 (day 16). There were no significant changes in positive initiations.

Changes in Ratings of Children's Behavior over Time

We used the same strategies, growth curve modeling and nonparametric tests for change, to examine changes in ratings of children's behaviors over time. Figure 12.2 presents changes in children's ratings over the 6 months of the study.

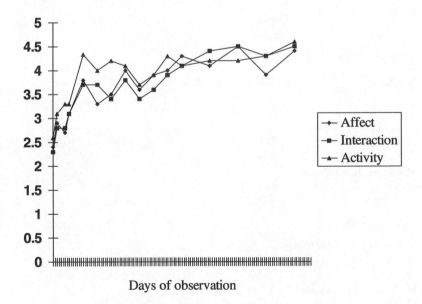

Days of observation

FIGURE 12.2. Changes in ratings over days of observation.

Growth Curve Modeling

Again, we used a two-level hierarchical model to examine individual variations in ratings at entry and in change over time and tested whether variations in entry ratings or in change in ratings over time could be explained by the child's age, gender, or final attachment security score. There were no effects for age or gender. Table 12.4 presents the results of the analyses, including security scores. There was considerable individual variation in children's scores for both entry and growth; t-ratios for entry and for time for all three (affect, activity involvement and interaction) ratings were significant. The coefficients for growth rate tend to be relatively small relative to the coefficients for entry, indicating that the growth rates of the ratings were fairly flat. The positive coefficients for growth indicate that the behaviors tended to increase over time.

The tau statistic provides a correlation between individual change and initial status. For all ratings behaviors it was high in magnitude and

TABLE 12.4. Linear Model of Growth in Rating of Children's Behavior

Fixed effect	Coefficient	SE	t-ratio	Tau
Affect				
Model for initial status				
Entry	3.15	0.34	9.39**	−0.93
Security	−0.07	1.82	0.04	
Model for growth rate				
Time	0.01	0.00	2.39*	
Security	0.01	0.02	0.44	
Activity				
Model for initial status				
Entry	3.51	0.32	10.99**	−0.61
Security	0.84	1.72	0.49	
Model for growth rate				
Time	0.01	0.00	2.93*	
Security	0.01	0.01	0.47	
Interaction				
Model for initial status				
Entry	3.09	0.31	9.83**	−0.72
Security	0.24	1.69	0.14	
Model for growth rate				
Time	0.01	0.00	3.65**	
Security	0.00	0.01	0.13	

$*p < .05; **p < .01.$

negative in direction, indicating that children who received lower ratings at entry at entry tended to gain at a faster rate. The low and insignificant t-ratios for both entry and growth for security indicate that final security scores did not explain significant variation in either entry ratings or in growth rates for any rating.

Wilcoxen Matched-Pairs Signed-Rank Tests

Inspection of the graphs in Figure 12.2 suggests that ratings of affect, activity involvement, and interaction increased over time. We used Wilcoxen Matched-Pairs Signed-Rank Tests to examine whether ratings increased after the entry period. Ratings of affect ($z = 2.37, p = .02$), activity involvement ($z = 2.52, p = .01$), and interaction ($z = 2.29, p = .02$) increased significantly from the entry to the second period.

Relations between Attachment Behaviors and Child Ratings and Attachment Security with Caregiver at 6 Months after Entry

We examined relations between children's attachment behaviors and ratings by computing Spearman correlation coefficients. Attachment behavior scores were the frequency of units of each category of attachment behavior directed to primary caregiver during each of the four periods (entry, second, third, and fourth) corrected for differences in number of observations per time period (see Table 12.1). Table 12.5. presents the correlations. Significant correlations between behaviors and security scores were found only in the fourth period. Children with higher security scores also had high frequencies of tracking and more positive initiations and responses during the fourth period. As well, children with higher security scores had higher ratings of activity involvement and interaction during the fourth period.

The pattern of correlation coefficients displayed in Table 12.5 suggests that with a larger sample individual differences in child behavior, correlates of attachment security could emerge in the third period—2 months after child-care entry. Correlations between behaviors and security were low in magnitude during entry and the second period but approached significance by the third period.

Relations between Caregiver Behaviors and Sensitivity Ratings and Attachment Security with Caregiver at 6 Months after Entry

We examined relations between caregiver behaviors and sensitivity ratings by computing Spearman correlation coefficients. Caregiver behav-

TABLE 12.5. Relations between Attachment Behaviors and Child Ratings and Attachment Security with Caregiver at 6 Months after Entry

	Attachment security
Attachment behaviors	
Track	
Entry	.04
Second period	.01
Third period	$.43^t$
Fourth period	.55*
Positive initiation	
Entry	−.36
Second period	−.22
Third period	.35
Fourth period	.49*
Positive response	
Entry	.02
Second period	.39
Third period	$.44^t$
Fourth period	.65*
Avoid	
Entry	−.04
Second period	−.35
Third period	−.17
Fourth period	−.25
Cry or fuss	
Entry	−.26
Second period	−.13
Third period	−.21
Fourth period	−.26
Ratings	
Affect	
Entry	.21
Second period	.14
Third period	.32
Fourth period	.35
Activity involvement	
Entry	.38
Second period	.22
Third period	.33
Fourth period	.67*
Interaction	
Entry	.18
Second period	.15
Third period	.26
Fourth period	.56*

$^t p < .10$; *$p < .05$.

ior scores were the frequency of units of each category of primary caregiver behavior during each of the four periods (entry, second, third, and
fourth) corrected for differences in number of observations per period
(see Table 12.2). Table 12.6 presents the correlations. Significant correlations were found between security scores and positive initiation, positive responses and sensitivity ratings in the third and fourth periods.
Caregiver comforting behavior was significantly associated with security in the fourth period and approached significance in the third
period.

DISCUSSION

In her 1995 study of Italian infants entering center-based child care,
Greta G. Fein documented individual differences in adjustment to child
care entry. She concluded that "the quality of interaction provided by
caregivers is crucial" (p. 274) for modulating the distress most infants
experience as they enter the world of child care. In this study, we have
expanded on the work of Fein and others to examine individual differences in children who eventually construct secure and insecure child–
caregiver attachment relationships.

As did the Italian children studied by Fein, the toddlers in our
study showed large individual differences in their distress upon entry
into child care. Some children entered the child-care center howling,
while others smiled their way through the initial period. And as in previous work (Feldbaum et al., 1980; Fox & Field, 1989; McGrew, 1972),
this initial distress was relatively short term. Children's crying and
avoidance of the new caregivers decreased rapidly, so that by the end of
2 months, frequencies of these indications of distress were fairly low.
This ratification of previous findings gives some support to the belief
system common to many child-care teachers (and teenage baby-sitters)
that if only the parents would just leave all will be well. The children
will calm down.

The assurance that all will be well is, of course, too simplistic and
not supported by this or Fein's earlier work, which underlines the importance of caregiver support for children who are distressed at child-
care entry. The children in this study were not left to cry, but, instead,
whether they cried or smiled, they were individually supported
through their transition into child care. It would be a mistake to interpret these findings as if no extra caregiver effort is needed during the
entry period.

The unique contributions of our study are both in finding that initial variations in attachment behaviors at child-care entry could not pre-

TABLE 12.6. Relations between Caregiver Behaviors and Sensitivity Ratings and Attachment Security with Caregiver at 6 Months after Entry

	Attachment security
Caregiver behaviors	
Positive initiation	
Entry	−.02
Second period	.47[t]
Third period	.59*
Fourth period	.59*
Positive response	
Entry	−.09
Second period	.20
Third period	.55*
Fourth period	.59*
Ignore	
Entry	−.13
Second period	−.18
Third period	−.38
Fourth period	−.18
Comfort	
Entry	−.09
Second period	−.13
Third period	.47[t]
Fourth period	.52*
Sensitivity Rating	
Entry	−.09
Second period	.20
Third period	.55*
Fourth period	.59*

[t]$p < .10$; *$p < .05$.

dict attachment security 6 months later and that from the first few days in child care children begin to differentiate between caregivers. The lack of relation between individual variations in attachment behaviors at entry and attachment security after 6 months in care supports the findings from other work (Howes, 1999) that child–caregiver attachments are independent of child–mother attachments. As well, these findings refute the idea that the smiling, happy infants at entry become securely attached to caregivers while more troublesome infants do not.

Our definition of primary caregiver meant that we were looking for the "best match," the caregiver–child combination that best met the child's needs for emotional security. In the current work, children began to track their best-match caregiver immediately and by the third month in child care they were more likely to engage in reciprocal interaction with that caregiver. Because we did not rate or record the behaviors of the primary caregiver to all the other toddlers in the classroom, we cannot tell whether the primary caregiver was more or less sensitive and skilled in social interactions with the children than were other potential primary caregivers. Therefore, we cannot determine if the toddlers really made the best choices among caregivers in directing their attachment behaviors. However, as in prior work (Howes, 1999) children who were more emotionally secure with caregivers after 6 months in care were associated with caregivers who received higher sensitivity ratings.

Taken together, our findings underscore Fein's (1995) conclusion that "the quality of interaction provided by caregivers is crucial" (p. 274). Our findings suggest that most children enter child care "ready" to construct positive attachment relationships. They act as if they hope or expect caregivers to take care of them. To the extent that caregivers play their part and sensitively engage the children in positive social interaction, these hopes or expectations will be fulfilled.

But our work cannot answer several critical questions. What if there was only one caregiver? This is the case in most family child-care homes and many child-care centers. In this scenario children do not have the opportunity to be savvy and to direct their behavior to the "best" caregiver. Moreover, the match goes both ways, caregivers adequate in many ways may be inappropriate with children who "rub" them the wrong way, reminds them of a personal tragedy, and so on.

Although we suspect that there were individual variations in the responsivity of the teachers we observed, we chose not to study these variations. The literature on teacher behavior suggests large variability in teacher skill (see Patt & Göncü, this volume). A future study needs to examine both child and teacher variability during the period of establishment of attachment relationships.

Increasing numbers of young children are entering our child-care system regardless of the capacity of our system to ensure that they will be able to move past a period of transitional distress to form a positive and trusting attachment relationship with a caregiver. This study points to the need to focus the attention of child-care caregivers on forming positive relationships with all children in child care.

ACKNOWLEDGMENTS

An Academic Senate Research Grant supported portions of this research. Special thanks to Vivian Cho for her work in designing the study and to Vivian Cho and Shira Rosenblatt, who served with Erin Oldham as observers for the study.

286 CHILDREN IN SCHOOL

REFERENCES

Ainsworth, M. S., Blehar, M., Waters, E., & Wall, S. (1978). *Patterns of attachment.* Hillsdale, NJ: Erlbaum.

Blanchard, M., & Main, M. (1979). Avoidance of the attachment figure and social and emotional adjustment in day care infants. *Developmental Psychology, 15,* 445–447.

Bowlby, J. (1982). *Attachment and loss: Loss, sadness and depression.* New York: Basic Books. (Original work published 1969)

Bretherton, I. (1985). Attachment theory: Retrospect and prospect. In I. Bretherton & E. Waters (Eds.), Growing points of attachment: Theory and research. *Monographs of the Society for Research in Child Development, 50*(1–2, Serial No. 209), 3–38.

Bryk, A., & Rasdenbush, S. W. (1987). Application of hierarchical linear models to assessing change. *Psychological Bulletin, 101,* 147–158.

Dontas, C., Maratos, O., Fafoutis, M., & Karangelis, A. (1985). Early social development in institutionally reared Greek infants: Attachment and peer interaction. In I. Bretherton & E. Waters (Eds.), Growing points of attachment: Theory and research. *Monographs of the Society for Research in Child Development, 50*(1–2, Serial No. 209), 135–175. Chicago: University of Chicago Press.

Fein, G. (1995). Infants in group care: Patterns of despair and detachment. *Early Childhood Research Quarterly, 10,* 261–275.

Fein, G. G., Gariboldi, A., & Boni, R. (1993). The adjustment of infants and toddlers to group care: The first six months. *Early Childhood Research Quarterly, 8,* 1–14.

Feldbaum, C. Christenson, T. E., & O'Neal, E. C. (1980) An observational study of the assimilation of the newcomer to the preschool. *Child Development, 51,* 497–507.

Fox, N., & Field, T. M. (1989). Individual differences in children's adjustment to preschool. *Journal of Applied Developmental Psychology, 10,* 527–540.

Goossens, F. A., & van IJzendoorn, M. H. (1990). Quality of infant's attachment to professional caregivers: Relation to infant–parent attachment and daycare characteristics. *Child Development, 51,* 832–837.

Harms, T., Clifford, R., & Cryer, D. (1988). *Infant–Toddler Environmental Rating Scale.* New York: Teachers College Press.

Howes, C. (1999). Attachment relationships in the context of multiple caregivers. In J. Cassidy & P. R. Shaver (Eds.), *Handbook of attachment: Theory, research, and clinical applications* (pp. 671–687). New York: Guilford Press.

Howes, C., & Smith, E. (1995). Children and their child care teachers: Profiles of relationships. *Social Development, 4,* 44–61.

McGrew, W. C. (1972). Aspects of social development in nursery school children with emphasis on introduction to the group. In N. Blurton-Jones (Ed.), *Ethological studies of child behavior* (pp. 129–156). London: Cambridge University Press.

Raikes, H. (1993). Relationship duration in infant care: Time with a high ability teacher and infant–teacher attachment. *Early Childhood Research Quarterly, 8*, 309–325.

Rubenstein, J., & Howes. C. (1979). Caregiving and infant behavior in daycare and homes. *Developmental Psychology, 15*, 1–24.

Waters, E. (1990). *The Attachment Q-Set*. Stony Brook: State University of New York Press.

13

❧

Conceptual Gaps in the Lifespan Theory of Attachment

NATHAN A. FOX
YAIR BAR-HAIM

The development of social relationships has long been of interest to psychologists who wish to understand how we learn to relate to other people. We are by nature a social species, interested from birth in faces, and producing in the early months of life smiles that attract adult attention. At least at an early age, we are playful, imaginative, and seemingly full of creative potential. Greta G. Fein recognized the potential within each child and the manner in which children use play creatively to express their individuality. She also understood that through play and positive social interaction children develop important social skills and form social relationships. Greta's approach to the development of the relationship between infant and parent was through the lens of positive affect and play. She often spoke about the opportunities parents have to play with their children, providing them with an environment in which their creativity can be expressed and a context in which they can have fun. In our discussions with each other about her approach to the development of social relationships we often brought up attachment theory, which has been one of the dominant theories in developmental psychology. The origin of attachment theory is the notion that infants need to feel secure in order to express exploratory behavior. Insecurity may arise from the fear or anxiety of being left alone or having one's distress or discomfort unattended to. Although never denying the importance of attachment, Greta emphasized the importance of play and positive interaction in the development of social relationships. This emphasis has remained an important cornerstone of our work and we are indebted to her for her insights.

First described and elaborated by John Bowlby (Bowlby, 1969, 1973, 1980) and later adapted and expanded by Mary Ainsworth, Alan Sroufe, Everett Waters, and their students (Ainsworth, Blehar, Waters, & Wall 1978; Sroufe & Waters, 1977), attachment theory has found a central place in the field of psychology as a basis for understanding the origins of social and personality development. The method used to assess the quality of the attachment relationships between caregivers and their infants, the Strange Situation (Ainsworth & Witting, 1969), is a procedure consisting of eight episodes designed to exert a gradual increase in stress through the introduction of a stranger and through two sets of separations from the parent (see Clarke-Stewart, Allhusen, & Goossens, this volume, for a description of the measure). It is assumed, that infants' behavioral reactions to this procedure reflect their internalized pattern of relationships with their parent (i.e., secure, avoidant, ambivalent, or disorganized). The antecedents and consequences of different patterns of attachment in infancy have been well studied now for at least 30 years. And the Strange Situation has been used across different cultures and with parent–infant pairs who vary in almost every conceivable manner (e.g., van IJzendoorn & Kroonenberg, 1988).

In recent years, attachment theorists have expanded their thinking on the importance of the initial attachment relationship. A good deal of research has examined life span changes that occur in the child's concept of attachment and the role that such concepts have in social development. This work has led to conceptualizations on the part of some attachment researchers as to the lifespan changes in working models of attachment (Main, Kaplan, & Cassidy, 1985). And it has led to great interest toward examining states of mind with regard to attachment experiences in older children (e.g., Cassidy, 1990; Cassidy & Marvin, 1992; Shouldice & Stevenson-Hinde, 1992) and adults (Main & Goldwyn, 1998; van IJzendoorn, 1995).

Attachment theorists have attempted to incorporate these new ideas regarding lifespan changes in working models and perceptions of attachment into their research and thinking about the importance of attachment in infancy. However, these growing points within attachment theory and research alongside the attempt to conceptualize attachment as a lifespan process challenge to a significant degree some of the basic tenets of the original theory. In particular, these reconceptualizations may stand in contrast to the critical nature attachment research assigns to the formation of internal working models of attachment in the first year of life.

In this chapter we discuss some of the inherent limitations of this new lifespan direction taken by attachment theory and research. We specifically focus on issues of continuity and discontinuity in attachment organization and representation. The possible contribution of family life events and nonparental caregivers to stability and change of attachment behavior and internal representation is also discussed. Finally, we discuss the implications that the existing research evidence has for the criticality assigned by attachment theoreticians to infant–mother attachment in the first year of life.

STABILITY OF INTERNAL WORKING MODELS:
SOME BASIC ASSUMPTIONS
OF ATTACHMENT THEORY

The relatively long period of time during which the human infant has extreme dependence on its parents for survival was part of the foundation of Bowlby's theory (1969). This extreme dependence, particularly during the first year of life, was presumed by Bowlby to be at the core of the attachment behavioral system, the ultimate goal of which was to promote caregiving and protection for the young.

According to attachment theory, repeated interactions with the caregiver and the overwhelming need to form an efficient attachment bond to him or her result in a behavioral and emotional adaptation on the part of the infant to the specific characteristics and demands of its caretaking environment. These emerging emotional, cognitive, and behavioral adaptations are sometimes referred to as internal working models of attachment. Such internal working models of attachment are postulated to be the underlying psychological structures that guide behaviors and social interactions first with the parents and later with other people as well.

The internal working model formed during the first year of life through repeated interactions with primary caregivers is thought to produce expectations and biases in the child with respect to the nature of relationships in general, the self, and the trustworthiness of others. When the child enters new relationships or social interactions later in life, that is, with nonparent others, it is hypothesized that the expectations and biases formed in the parent–infant relationship will be extrapolated and thus will play a major role in thinking and behavior in new relationships. Furthermore, the specific behaviors and feelings related to the internal working models formed with the parents may be reinforced by the dynamics of the actual interaction with others. For example, an insecure–ambivalent child may enter a social encounter with peers displaying high levels of anxiety and social ambivalence and may become highly demanding for attention and inappropriately impinge on his or her partner's activities. A common reaction of an interaction partner could be distancing and avoidance. This reaction could then serve as reassurance for the anxious/ambivalent child of his or her currently held internal working model of self as unworthy of love and attention and others as inconsistent and insensitive. In that respect, internal working models of attachment are expected to be self-perpetuating and remain relatively stable over time (Bar-Haim & Kaitz, 2000).

A lifespan theory of attachment in which events occurring in infancy are thought to affect later outcomes implies continuity or stability in attachment classification or at the very least an influence of infant security or insecurity with his or her primary caregivers on later working models. Furthermore, a lifespan model should offer theoretical and empirical frameworks for the study of developmental shifts in attachment representation throughout the life cycle.

STABILITY AND CHANGE
OF ATTACHMENT IN INFANCY

The data on stability of attachment classification in infancy have shown mixed results and often received conflicting interpretations. Goossens, van IJzendoorn, Tavecchio, and Kroonenberg (1986) measured the stability of attachment in infants at 18 and 19 months of age. They reported perfect stability of attachment classifications when the Strange Situation was conducted in the laboratory and 90% stability when the assessment was conducted at the home. Other research on the stability of attachment classifications in the Strange Situation between 12 and 18 months has shown that in stable middle-class samples, percentages of children obtaining the same attachment classification at both ages has been fairly high, 73 to 96% (Connell, 1976; Main & Weston, 1981; Waters, 1978). Others reported a more moderate yet statistically significant stability of attachment classifications in infancy. Bar-Haim, Sutton, Fox, and Marvin (2000) found stability of 64% in attachment classification between 14 and 24 months of age and Frodi, Grolnick, and Bridges (1985) reported stability of 66% between 12 and 20 months of age.

Stability of attachment has been found to be considerably lower and nonsignificant, with bidirectional changes in attachment classifications, in families undergoing changing life circumstances such as stressful life events, onset of maternal employment, onset of regular nonmaternal care, birth of a sibling, and onset of maternal depression (Owen, Easterbrooks, Chase-Lansdale, & Goldberg, 1984; Thompson, Lamb, & Estes, 1982, 1983; Touris, Kromelow, & Harding, 1995; Vaughn, Egeland, Sroufe, & Waters, 1979). Percentages of infants classified to the same attachment group at two age points in these studies ranged from 53 to 62%.

In a recent study of two large middle-class samples, Belsky, Campbell, Cohn, and Moore (1996) reported attachment stability rates of 53 and 46% between 12 and 18 months. Based on their findings and a review of the relevant literature, they concluded that it might not be appropriate to assume that stability rather than instability is the norm when it comes to the measurement of attachment security using the Strange Situation.

Apart from the possibility that attachment relationships with a particular caregiver may change over time, instability of attachment over time might also reflect other changes in the infant's environment. One possible factor might be that the actual social environments of infants are more complex than attachment relationships with just one parent. Interactions with a wide range of adults (other than the infant's parents) and peers may serve as important moderators of infants' behavior in the Strange Situation.

Many infants nowadays are exposed to care by professional caregivers. Predictions from attachment theory were that routine nonmaternal care in the first year of life would adversely affect the security of the infant's attachment to the mother. Several psychosocial mechanisms were offered to explain this prediction. For example, Barglow, Vaughn, and Molitor (1987) suggested that infants might experience repeated daily separations as maternal rejection. Sroufe (1988) argued that daily separations could result in the infant losing confidence in the availability and responsiveness of the mother. And other researchers drew attention to the possibility that nonmaternal care might adversely affect proximal processes of infant–mother interaction (Owen & Cox, 1988). Such theories typically predicted an elevated level of insecure attachment classifications in day-care-attending infants.

Initial analyses of aggregated data from several independent samples indicated that infants who experienced 20 or more hours per week of routine day care in the first year of life were more likely to be classified as insecurely attached to their mothers between 12 and 18 months of age as compared with infants who experienced less child care (Belsky & Rovine, 1988; Clarke-Stewart, 1989; Lamb & Sternberg, 1990). However, an extensive research program sponsored by the National Institute of Child Health and Human Development (NICHD Early Child Care Research Network, 1997), which included 10 independent data collection sites and 1,153 infants, failed to reveal the same pattern of elevated insecure attachment classifications. Instead, infants with extensive child-care experience did not differ in their Strange Situation classifications from infants without child care. These later findings suggest that mother–infant attachment is not affected by extensive exposure to other caregivers, and that reasons for instability of attachment classifications should be looked for elsewhere (also see Clarke-Stewart, Allhusen, and Goossens, this volume; Howes and Oldham, this volume).

STABILITY OF ATTACHMENT CLASSIFICATION BEYOND INFANCY AND INTO THE PRESCHOOL YEARS

Over the past 15 years procedures have become available to assess the quality of child–parent attachment beyond the infancy period (e.g., Cassidy & Marvin, 1992; Main & Cassidy, 1987; Main et al., 1985). It is widely recognized by researchers and theoreticians that the assessment of attachment quality of preschoolers must necessarily take into account a broader range of behaviors than those considered during the assessment of attachment in the infancy period. For infants, crying and physical movement for gaining or avoiding proximity and contact with the mother are of primary interest. By 3 or 4 years of age attention must also be given to body position, visual attention, content and manner of speech directed at parents, and verbal expressions of affect. Although the specific behaviors associated with attachment may differ at each age, attachment researchers assume that the underlying organization of attachment behaviors or the internal working models tend to remain stable. Specific strategies at each age were theoretically and empirically associated with secure, avoidant, resistant, and disorganized types of relationships (Cassidy & Marvin, 1992; Cicchetti, Cummings, Greenberg, & Marvin, 1990; Main, 1981; Main et al., 1985).

The research literature on the stability of attachment classification from infancy to the preschool years is rather limited and once more reveals inconsistencies in findings. Two studies, one of U.S. samples and one of a German sample, both composed of mother–child dyads from middle-class families, examined stability of attachment between infancy and 6 years of age. Both studies revealed relatively high levels of stability in attachment classifications, 84, 85, and 88%, respectively (Main & Cassidy, 1988; Wartner, Grossman, Fremmer-Bombik, & Suess, 1994). A correlation of .76 between infant and 6-year attachment status was also reported (Main et al., 1985). Stevenson-Hinde and Shouldice (1993) provided further evidence for the stability of attachment classification between 2.5 years in the Strange Situation and 4.5 years using the attachment classification system of Cassidy and Marvin (1992). When using forced classification into the conventional three attachment classes—avoidant, secure, or ambivalent—stability was at 72%. However, at least two studies failed to replicate the foregoing findings and reported nonsignificant stability rates of only 38 to 41% between Strange Situation classification at 1 year of age and the Cassidy and Marvin attachment classification at 4.5 years (Bar-Haim et al., 2000; Goldberg et al., 1998). In addition, Bar-Haim et al. failed to find significant stability in attachment classification between 24 months and 4 years of age.

STABILITY OF ATTACHMENT IN INFANCY AND EARLY CHILDHOOD: SUMMARY AND IMPLICATIONS

Although there is some evidence for short-term stability of attachment classifications over the first 2 years of life, the evidence for stability into the preschool and school years is decidedly mixed. Findings from the NICHD Study of Early Child Care point to the unique nature of the infant–mother attachment relationships in that that it does not seem to be affected by the infant's exposure to extensive interactions with nonmaternal figures. Overall, however, the existing data fail to support a "strong stability" of attachment position, which holds that in the face of normative developmental change, the pattern of attachment strategies established around the end of the first year of life remains a stable and consistent template for subsequent interactions with others. Findings from several studies seem to indicate that current life events and changes in family's lifestyle are associated with instability of attachment classification (e.g., Bar-Haim et al., 2000; Owen et al., 1984; Thompson et al., 1982).

Taken together, the total corpus of evidence suggests that change in attachment classification between infancy and early childhood is just as probable as the case of attachment classification stability. This conclusion poses a major obstacle for the formulation of a simple epigenetic model for attachment as a lifespan process. It seems that in the absence of highly stable environments and nonchanging representations of parents, it would be rather unusual to find stability of mental representations about attachment. Rather, any new lifespan theory of attachment should define the life events around which normative variation in attachment relationships takes place (e.g., Eiden, Teti, & Corns, 1995).

A MOVE TOWARD THE LEVEL OF REPRESENTATION: INTERNAL REPRESENTATION OF ATTACHMENT RELATIONSHIPS

The assessments of attachment relationships used with infants, toddlers, and preschoolers discussed previously, have all been based on laboratory procedures that allow for the observation of child behaviors during separation and reunion situations with the parent. Main et al. (1985) pointed out that one could not infer the nature of internal working models solely by observing the parent–child interaction. Moreover, even if underlying working models of attachment guide social interactions, it is not clear whether these models represent the history of parent–child relationships since infancy as assumed by most attachment students or merely the short-term current state of mind with respect to attachment and current parent–child relationships.

There are several methods for assessing individual differences in inferred mental representations of attachment relationships that are administered in the absence of the parent. It is assumed that children's responses to representational tests will be analogous in some ways to their responses to real separations measured through behavior classification protocols (e.g. Bretherton, 1985; Cassidy, 1990; Main et al., 1985; Shouldice & Stevenson-Hinde, 1992; Sroufe & Fleeson, 1986). The underlying supposition is that the existence of internal working models of attachment is reflected in both behavior and representational material. One method, the Separation Anxiety Test (SAT) (Hansburg, 1972; Klagsburn, & Bowlby, 1976), involves presenting children with photographs of various separation situations and asking the participant what the child in the picture feels and what she or he would do in the situation. Main et al. (1985) have used similar procedures with a sample of 6-year-old children and found a significant correlation between attachment classifications in infancy and children's emotional openness at 6 years of age. Main et al. (1985) also found that mental representations of attachment at 6 years of age, based on ratings of children's responses to the picture of 2-week separation from parents in the SAT, were significantly correlated with security of attachment to the mother in infancy.

Shouldice and Stevenson-Hinde (1992) reported a significant association between children's reactions to the SAT and attachment classification at 4.5 years coded by the Cassidy and Marvin (1992) system.

Taking Main et al.'s (1985) work further they employed contemporaneous comparisons between attachment classifications of reunion behavior and discrete responses to the SAT pictures rather than single rating scales. Children classified as secure in reunion, compared with those classified as insecure, were more emotionally open to appropriate negative feeling, were not overly expressive, and showed a greater ability to tolerate security distress aroused by the separation pictures without raising defenses against it. Slough and Greenberg (1990) found significant correlations between avoidance behavior in a separation–reunion procedure and avoidant reactions to the SAT of 5-year-olds. In this particular study, behaviors associated with secure attachment were reflected to a lesser and nonsignificant degree in the representational realm. Finally, Bar-Haim et al. (2000) found a significant correlation between concurrent attachment classification and children's mental representations of attachment derived from the SAT at 4.5 years of age. However, this study failed to replicate the associations previously reported between attachment classification in infancy or early childhood and later mental representations of attachment.

The increasing emphasis within attachment theory and research on representational knowledge and working models in childhood and adult life, combined with the lack of solid evidence for stability in attachment classifications and representations from infancy to the preschool and school years, argues for some rethinking of previous theoretical positions. In particular, those positions having to do with the criticality assigned to attachment at the end of the first year of life for later relationships may have to be reconsidered.

ATTACHMENT ORGANIZATION MODELS IN INFANCY AND EARLY CHILDHOOD

van IJzendoorn, Sagi, and Lambermon (1992) have acknowledged that attachment classifications derived from the Strange Situation may not be stable over time and have limited success in outcome prediction. They therefore suggested that attachment research might benefit from the study of a larger network of significant adults beyond that of the infant–mother relationship. van IJzendoorn and his colleagues describe four possible attachment organization models for infants who grow up in extended childrearing environments, and who had experienced intensive interaction with multiple caretakers. The first and most traditional model (Bowlby, 1951) implied that only one adult, mostly the mother, is a significant attachment figure. According to this model, the influence of other caregivers in terms of attachment relationship would be only marginal, and a child's internal working models of self, other, and relationship will evolve based on the characteristics of the infant–mother interactions. The second model (Bowlby, 1969) proposes a hierarchy among attachment figures. In this theoretical model, several caregivers may serve as a secure base in the absence of the primary caregiver; however, only one caregiver, typically the mother, is perceived as the most important attachment figure. The third model of internal attachment organization suggested by van IJzendoorn et al. (1992) implies that the infant may be attached with similar intensity to several different caregivers. However, the working model derived from each particular attachment relationship may be functional only in those domains in which the infant and the specific caregiver have been interacting over an extended period. Finally, an attachment integration model postulates a process of internal organization that integrates all the infant's important attachment relationships into one functional working model. From this point of view, secure attachments may compensate for insecure attachments or one insecure relationship might overshadow a set of otherwise secure attachments. According to this model, a child would optimally function in a network of secure attachments and would be most compromised if the attachment network were totally composed of insecure attachments.

The predictive value of some of these theoretical models was tested in childrearing environments that expose children to intensive care from caregivers other than their parents. The childrearing practices of Israeli kibbutzim provided one such setting. Kibbutz infants are exposed to multiple caregiving early in life. The mother and the *metapelet* (professional caregiver) jointly care for the infant during the first months of life. Later, during the second half of the first year of life, the *metapelet* gradually assumes responsibility for the infants' needs as the mothers increase their workload. By the infants' second year, they come under the full care of the *metapelet* and interaction with the parents is typically confined to the afternoon hours (Aviezer, van IJzendoorn, Sagi, & Schuengel, 1994). Oppenheim, Sagi, and Lamb (1988) assessed 5-year-old kibbutz children who were seen in the Strange Situation in infancy with their mothers, fathers, and professional caregivers. They found no significant associations between attachment to the parents and a set of socioemotional measures (e.g., being empathic, dominant, independent, and achievement oriented). However, they did find associations between these measures and attachment classifications with the professional caregivers. In accord with the third model of attachment organization described previously, it has been suggested that these findings are the result of domain-specific attachment and that attachment relationships with the parents may not influence behaviors and competencies that were acquired in contexts outside of the home. van IJzendoorn et al. (1992) reanalyzed the original kibbutz data of Oppenheim et al. (1988) along with additional data from Dutch infants who were also exposed to intensive nonparental caregiving. They have shown that an attachment model based on a network of multiple relationships (mother, father, and professional caregiver) was the most powerful predictor of socioemotional development 5 years later, when compared with predictions based on attachment to mother, father, or professional caregiver alone. These findings were particularly strong for children living in Israeli kibbutzim, presumably because they grew up in an environment in which it was ideologically believed that multiple caregiving is beneficial for children (Aviezer et al., 1994).

Taken together, these findings suggest that more complex models, which include infants' interactions with several important adult figures in addition to social structure and cultural context, are required for better prediction of children's social and emotional adaptation. It appears that internal representations of relationships and self are molded via more complex and continuous processes than those originally proposed by attachment theory.

ADULTS' STATES OF MIND REGARDING ATTACHMENT THEMES: THE ADULT ATTACHMENT INTERVIEW

According to some attachment theory students, discontinuities in attachment classification are not necessarily discordant with current life-span attachment theory. Indeed, it is the very fact that "states of mind," as Main sometimes calls internal working models, change across development that led her and others to call for reformulation of attachment theory (Main, 1991; Main et al., 1985). Main argued that it was necessary to develop the methods to probe children, adolescents, and adults about their states of mind regarding attachment in order to understand continuities and discontinuities in these working models. Main's work on the development and use of the Adult Attachment Interview (AAI) brought sharply into focus the role that adult perceptions of their own personal histories with their parents have in their parenting of their own children (Fonagy, Steele, & Steele, 1991; Pederson, Gleason, Moran, & Bento, 1998). But it may have exposed a logical inconsistency in attachment theory that reflects fundamentally on the critical nature of attachment in the first year of life.

Just how critical is the association between infant classification derived from the Strange Situation and adult classification derived from the AAI for attachment theory? It would seem to be critical for any lifespan theory that argues for the centrality of the infant's initial relationship with the parents as a determining factor for most subsequent relationships. On the other hand, our knowledge about short-term stability of infant attachment classifications speaks to the importance of supporting environments and the destabilizing influence of life's stresses on the stability of the working model (cf. Bar-Haim et al., 2000; Thompson et al., 1982). Thus, it seems unlikely that one would find this long-term association between attachment in infancy and current states of mind about attachment in adulthood.

In a chapter dedicated to a description of the AAI in the recently published *Handbook of Attachment*, Hesse (1999) reports the existence of five studies in which continuity between infant attachment security and security as categorized in the AAI was examined. The idea behind these studies was that the quality of the relationship established with the mother in the first year of life would predict the state of mind that someone has as an adult concerning attachment themes. Infants who were secure would present as autonomous individuals in the AAI whereas infants who were insecure would present as insecure under the AAI classification. Two of these studies (Hamilton, 2000; Waters, Merrick, Treboux, Crowell, & Albersheim, 2000) reported moderate but significant continuity of attachment classification between 12-month Strange Situation and AAI classifications (64 and 63%, respectively). Both studies, however, also reported major effects of life events on the predictability of AAI classification from the 12-month Strange Situation data. The remaining three studies (Lewis, 1997; Weinfield, Sroufe, & Egland, 2000; Zimmermann, Grossmann, & Fremmer-Bombic, 1998) failed to find continuity in attachment classification from infancy to early adulthood.

Based on the studies described by Hesse (1999), we conclude that the predictability of adults' states of mind regarding attachment themes from behavioral attachment classification during infancy is inconsistent and low. We contend that attempts to show continuity in attachment style from infancy to adolescence or adulthood are bound to fail considering the inability of previous research to show clear consistency in attachment classification or representations over much shorter periods of time. Moreover, assessment of attachment security in adults relies on description and interpretation of subjects' mental representations and memories of their childhood relationships with their parents and other significant adults. Such recollections are inherently unstable (e.g., Loftus, 1994) and subject to multiple life-event factors. Thus, in the absence of highly stable environments and nonchanging representations of parents, it would be unusual to find stability of mental representations of attachment.

Attachment theorists recognize this "missing link" in their research. Some of these writers have even stated that adult state of mind regarding attachment as derived from the AAI may have little to do with the actual events or caregiving experiences that the person had as an infant (e.g., Hesse, 1999; van IJzendoorn, 1995). This logic is included in the AAI classification manual. For example, even when an individual had a rejecting parent (and presumably insecure attachment in the first year of life) he or she may still be classified in the "earned security" category as an adult if their current view about themselves and their discourse in relation to this experience are coherent and emotionally resolved. Alternatively, adults whose parents divorced when they were young adolescents may harbor great anger toward them, and although they may have been classified as secure in infancy, their current views on parental care might reflect the unresolved anger due to the divorce that occupied their later childhood. Among the empirical data which support this view are those of Pearson, Cohn, Cowan, and Cowan (1994), who report that parents who received an earned security classification (classified as autonomous despite reporting difficult and unloving early relationships with their parents) were comparable to other autonomous parents in their parenting warmth. This finding may illustrate how the representations derived from early experiences of care can evolve and change. Thus, adults' contemporary "states of mind" with regard to attachment do not seem to depend on the actual support received from a parent in early childhood but, rather, appear to depend on the adults' capacity to subsequently come to terms with their perceived early childhood attachment experiences. It seems likely that normative life experiences in later childhood, adolescence, and adulthood provide valuable catalysts to such reflection and reassessment. Here again are data which make the point that it is the context and family structure and changes in this structure that are most likely to influence how we feel about ourselves and our perceptions of our caregiving histories. Lewis (1997) boldly proposed the following questions: First, do adult representations of attachment derived from the AAI correspond to the actual caregiving experience in infancy? Second, if not, how did the representations change over time? And, finally, if the representations are not a photograph of the original event, why should we study the earlier event at all? Lewis's longitudinal data do not confirm that AAI representations correspond to the actual caregiving experiences during infancy. Thus, Lewis concludes that the study of infant–parent attachment removed from the study of ongoing contextual changes is futile for later prediction of developmental pathways.

INTERGENERATIONAL TRANSMISSION OF ATTACHMENT

A good deal of work on the AAI has taken the opposite tack and examined longitudinal prediction in a forward manner. Numerous studies have demonstrated that parent perception of their own caregiving experiences influences their own behavior with their infants. The impressive findings from these studies are that parent state of mind in respect to attachment is significantly associated with infant attachment classification in the next generation (e.g., Benoit & Parker, 1994; Fonagy et al., 1991; van IJzendoorn, 1995). This has given rise to that part of attachment theory known as intergenerational transmission of attachment. Simply put, the state of mind of adults regarding their own caregiving history will influence the manner in which they parent their children. Most impressive is the fact that the different styles of remembering or states of mind are related to infant attachment classifications.

There are, clearly, a number of interesting links to be explored here. The first is with regard to the processes by which adult perceptions about their own caregiving histories get translated into behaviors that in turn influence the behavior of the infant in the Strange Situation and hence infant attachment classification. One obvious candidate would be sensitivity and responsivity of the caregiver that would be expected to vary as a function of AAI status. This, in turn, should predict infant attachment classification. However, both van IJzendoorn (1995) and Pederson et al. (1998) note that there is a marked "transmission gap" in researchers' understanding of the nature of relations between the AAI, parental sensitivity, and the Strange Situation. In a meta-analysis of all the studies examining sensitivity and responsivity in relation to attachment classification since the Goldsmith and Alansky (1987) article, DeWolff and van IJzendoorn (1997) found the same low magnitude of association between parental sensitivity and attachment classification. This finding indicates that a large part of the influence adults' representation of attachment has on their infant's attachment security could not be accounted for by parental sensitivity and responsiveness.

Thus, researchers will have to examine closely exactly what forges the link between parent perceptions and infant attachment classification. On the other hand, it is not surprising to most developmental or clinical psychologists that parent personality and mental health predict style of caregiving. In fact, given the lack of substantial proof of correspondence between actual early caregiving experiences or early attachment classifications and adult's states of mind regarding these experiences, the AAI should most adequately be considered a semistructured psychodynamic interview technique that assesses adult personality based on interviewee's discourse style. This powerful interview may very well predict the interviewee's parenting style considering the intense focus it has on parent–child relations and its pre-planned attempts to probe the interviewee's unconscious regarding these issues.

GENERAL CONCLUSION AND POSSIBLE DIRECTIONS FOR FUTURE RESEARCH

When attachment theorists write about the intergenerational transmission of attachment it is perhaps best to think about this process as being multidetermined. No one factor or parameter (e.g., insecurity in infancy) should be given prominence in determining the trajectories of children in the development of their social relationships. Indeed, the evidence for prediction from infancy in the absence of supporting environments is quite weak and would argue for discontinuity and change rather than determinism as a function of that early social relationship. As children mature, changing family experiences, interaction with adults other than their parents, and peer relationships are likely to contribute to the reconstruction of the affective and representational legacy of early childhood relationships. This may be especially true when parental separation or divorce, or the serious illness or death of a family member, significantly alters family functioning. In addition, representations of early family relationships are likely to be influenced by later experiences in close relationships as well as by changes in personality, self-reflection abilities, and implicit theories of personal growth and continuity.

If, as is likely, there is little continuity from infancy with regard to attachment classification, and if, as is currently claimed by attachment theorists, AAI report of current state of mind about caregiving experiences need not reflect with any veridicality that individual's history, and if, indeed, continuity and prediction from infancy and early childhood are dependent more on the family ecology and the events which occur to children as they grow, learn, and interact with their environments and their cultures, then how is one to use the knowledge of the quality of the attachment relationship between mother and infant at the end of the first year of life?

All this points to the fact that prediction of the child's state of mind with respect to attachment themes will depend greatly on the particular family environment, the particular life circumstances, and the consistency with which adults care for children within specific developmental periods. Social development is marked by important transitions but also by periods of stability between these transitions. It is likely that during these periods of stability there will be continuity in the child's state of mind with respect to attachment assuming that other factors having to do with family ecology are themselves stable. One should, on the other hand, expect change and discontinuity across transition points, particularly transition points that call into question the child's relationship to his or her parents. One obvious example of such a transition point would be the period of adolescence. This is a time of reorganization of the self-system in relation to personal identity, peers, and to one's own parents. This transition should be marked by great discontinuity in working models of attachment. A similar transition point would have occurred much earlier in social development, during the toddler period. This period that Mahler (Mahler, Pine, & Bergman, 1975) and others noted as marked by separation and individuation would likely involve a reorganization of states of mind about self and representations of the caregiver. Again, one should expect discontinuities to occur across this transition point, with relations to previous "states of mind" as a function of how parents handle this transition point. The onset of more extensive nonparental caregiving and children's first ventures into the world beyond the family may serve as important catalysts for internal reorganization of attachment models.

The major conceptual advances in attachment theory have highlighted the degree to which working models change over the lifespan, so much so that adult states of mind may have little to do with actual degrees of security during earlier periods of time. If one were to suggest a research program for a lifespan version of attachment theory it would be to first identify periods of transition across which one would expect normative changes in working models. One should use existing measures or devise methods for the assessment of these working models in order to test the existence of these changes. And one should make the extraordinary effort to assess parental and environmental factors that will undoubtedly contribute to these changes in perception about oneself and one's parents as well. One should probably spend less time and effort focusing on the Strange Situation with regard to both its antecedents and its consequences of different attachment classifications. If anything, one should focus more on the toddler period during which the first true attachment themes of separation and individuation are clearly present.

Thinking about attachment themes across the lifespan necessitates a broader view of the infancy period and a less sharply defined notion of the criticality of the first year of life. The process by which individuals develop the capacity to form intimate and healthy relationships with significant others is a complex one involving a long and detailed history complete with many changes, twists and turns of fate, and instabilities and inconsistencies in parental response. That instability seems to be the human condition, and it is our ability to adapt to those changes and to change ourselves that remains the hallmark of the human condition.

REFERENCES

Ainsworth, M. D., Blehar, M. C., Waters, E., & Wall, S. (1978). *Patterns of attachment: Assessed in the Strange Situation and at home.* Hillsdale, NJ: Erlbaum.

Ainsworth, M. D., & Witting, B. A. (1969). Attachment and exploratory behavior of one-year olds in a strange situation. In B. M. Foss (Ed.), *Determinants of infant behavior* (Vol. 4, pp. 111–136). London: Methuen.

Aviezer, O., van IJzendoorn, M. H., Sagi, A., & Schuengel, C. (1994). "Children of the Dream" revisited: 70 years of collective childrearing in Israeli kibbutzim. *Psychological Bulletin, 116,* 99–116.

Barglow, P., Vaughn, B., & Molitor, N. (1987). Effects of maternal absence due to employment on the quality of infant–mother attachment in a low-risk sample. *Child Development, 58,* 945–954.

Bar-Haim, Y., & Kaitz, M. (2000). *Adult attachment style and interpersonal distance.* Manuscript submitted for publication.

Bar-Haim, Y., Sutton, D. B., Fox, N. A., & Marvin, R. S. (2000). stability and change of attachment at 14, 24, and 58 months of age: Behavior, representation and life events. *Journal of Child Psychology and Psychiatry, 41,* 381–388.

Belsky, J., Campbell, S. B., Cohn, J. F., & Moore, G. (1996). Instability of infant–parent attachment security. *Developmental Psychology, 32,* 921–924.

Belsky, J., & Rovine, M. (1988). Nonmaternal care in the first year of life and the security of infant–parent attachment. *Child Development, 59,* 157–167.

Benoit, D., & Parker, K. (1994). Stability and transmission of attachment across three generations. *Child Development, 65,* 1444–1456.

Bowlby, J. (1951). *Maternal care and maternal health.* Geneva, Switzerland: World Health Organization.

Bowlby, J. (1969). *Attachment and loss: Vol. 1. Attachment.* New York: Basic Books.

Bowlby, J. (1973). *Attachment and loss: Vol. 2. Separation.* New York: Basic Books.

Bowlby, J. (1980). *Attachment and loss. Vol. 3. Loss.* New York: Basic Books.

Bretherton, I. (1985). Attachment theory: Retrospect and prospect. In I. Bretherton & E. Waters (Eds.), Growing points in attachment: Theory and research. *Monographs of the Society for Research in Child Development, 50*(1–2, Serial No. 209), 3–38.

Cassidy, J. (1990). Theoretical and methodological considerations in the study of attachment and the self in young children. In M. T. Greenberg, D. Cicchetti, & E. M. Cummings (Eds.), *Attachment in the preschool years* (pp. 87–119). Chicago: University of Chicago Press.

Cassidy, J., & Marvin, R. S. (1992). *Attachment organization in three- and four-year olds: Coding guidelines.* Unpublished manuscript, Department of Psychology, University of Maryland, College Park, MD.

Cicchetti, D., Cummings, E. M., Greenberg, M. T., & Marvin, R. S. (1990). An organizational perspective on attachment beyond infancy: Implications for theory, measurement, and research. In M. T. Greenberg, D. Cicchetti, & E. M. Cummings (Eds.), *Attachment in the preschool years* (pp. 3–49). Chicago: University of Chicago Press.

Clarke-Stewart, K. A. (1989). Infant day-care: Maligned or malignant. *American Psychologist, 44,* 266–273.

Connell, D. B. (1976). *Individual differences in attachment: An investigation into stability, implications, and relationships to structure of early language development.* Unpublished doctoral dissertation, Syracuse University.

DeWolff, M. S., & van IJzendoorn, M. H. (1997). Sensitivity and attachment: A meta-analysis on parental antecedents of infant attachment. *Child Development, 68,* 571–591.

Eiden, R. D., Teti, D. M., & Corns, K. M. (1995). Maternal working models of attachment, marital adjustment, and the parent–child relationship. *Child Development, 66,* 1504–1518.

Fonagy, P., Steele, H., & Steele, M. (1991). Maternal representations of attachment during pregnancy predict the organization of infant–mother attachment at one year of age. *Child Development, 62,* 891–905.

Frodi, A, Grolnick, W., & Bridges, L. (1985). Maternal correlates of stability and change in infant-mother attachment. *Infant Mental Health Journal, 6,* 60–67.

Goldberg, S., Washington, J., Myhal, N., Janus, M., Simmons, R. J., MacLusky, I., & Fowler, R. S. (1998). *Stability and change in attachment from infancy to preschool.* Unpublished manuscript, Hospital for Sick Children, Toronto, and University of Toronto.

Goldsmith, H. H., & Alansky, J. A. (1987). Maternal and infant predictors of attachment: A meta-analytic review. *Journal of Consulting and Clinical Psychology, 55,* 805–816.

Goossens, F. A., van IJzendoorn, M. H., Tavecchio, L. W., & Kroonenberg, P. M. (1986). Stability of attachment across time and context in a Dutch sample. *Psychological Reports, 58,* 23–32.

Hamilton, C. E. (2000). Continuity and discontinuity of attachment from infancy through adolescence. *Child Development, 71,* 690–694 .

Hansburg, H. G. (1972). *Adolescent separation anxiety: A method for the study of adolescent separation problems.* Springfield IL: Charles C. Thomas.

Hesse, E. (1999). The Adult Attachment Interview: Historical and current perspectives. In J. Cassidy & P. R. Shaver, *Handbook of attachment: Theory, research, and clinical applications* (pp. 395–433). New York: Guilford Press.

Klagsburn, M., & Bowlby, J. (1976). Responses to separation from parents: A clinical test for young children. *British journal of Projective Psychology, 21,* 7–27.

Lamb, M., & Sternberg, K. (1990). Do we really know how day-care affects children? *Journal of Applied Developmental Psychology, 11*, 351–379.

Lewis, M. (1997). *Altering fate: Why the past does not predict the future.* New York: Guilford Press.

Loftus, E. F. (1994). The repressed memory controversy. *American Psychologist, 49*, 443–445.

Mahler, M., Pine, F., & Bergman, A. (1975). *The psychological birth of the human infant.* New York: Basic Books.

Main, M. (1981). Avoidance in the service of attachment: A working paper. In K. Immelmann, G. Barlow, L. Petrinovich, & M. Main (Eds.), *Behavioral development: The Bielefeld interdisciplinary project.* New York: Cambridge University Press.

Main, M. (1991). Metacognitive knowledge, metacognitive monitoring, and singular (coherent) vs. multiple (incoherent) models of attachment: Findings and directions for future research. In C. M. Parks, J. Stevenson-Hinde, & P. Marris (Eds.), *Attachment across the life cycle* (pp. 127–159). London: Routledge.

Main, M., & Cassidy, J. (1987). *Reunion-based classifications of child–parent attachment organization at six years of age.* Unpublished scoring manual, University of California at Berkeley.

Main, M., & Cassidy, J. (1988). Categories of response to reunion with parent at age six: Predictable from infant attachment classifications and stable over a one month period. *Developmental Psychology, 24*, 415–426.

Main, M., & Goldwyn, R. (1998). *Adult attachment scoring and classification system.* Unpublished manuscript, University of California at Berkley.

Main, M., Kaplan, N., & Cassidy, J. (1985). Security in infancy, childhood, and adulthood: A move to the level of representation. In I. Bretherton & E. Waters (Eds)., Growing points of attachment theory and research. *Monographs of the Society for Research in Child Development, 50* (Serial No. 209), 66–106.

Main, M., & Weston, D. R. (1981). The quality of the toddler's relationship to mother and to father: Related to conflict behavior and the readiness to establish new relationships. *Child Development, 52*, 932–940.

NICHD Early Child Care Research Network. (1997). The effects of infant child care on infant-mother attachment security: Results from the NICHD study of early child care. *Child Development, 68*, 860–879.

Oppenheim, D., Sagi, A., & Lamb, M. E. (1988). Infant–adult attachments in the Kibbutz and their relation to socioemotional development 4 years later. *Developmental Psychology, 24*, 427–433.

Owen, M. T., & Cox, M. J. (1988). Maternal employment and the transition to parenthood: Family functioning and child development. In A. E. Gottfried & A. W. Gottfried (Eds.), *Maternal employment and children's development: Longitudinal research* (pp. 85–119). New York: Plenum Press.

Owen, M. T., Easterbrooks, M. A., Chase-Lansdale, L., & Goldberg, W. A. (1984). The relation between maternal employment status and the stability of attachments to mother and father. *Child Development, 55*, 1894–1901.

Pearson, J, L., Cohn, D. A., Cowan, P. A., & Cowan, C. P. (1994). Earned- and continuous-security in adult attachment: Relation to depressive symptomatology and parenting style. *Development and Psychopathology, 6,* 359–373.

Pederson, D. R., Gleason, K. E., Moran, G. & Bento, S. (1998). Maternal attachment representation, maternal sensitivity, and the infant–mother attachment relationship. *Developmental Psychology, 34,* 925–933.

Shouldice, A., & Stevenson-Hinde, J. (1992). Coping with security distress: The Separation Anxiety Test and attachment classification at 4. 5 years. *Journal of Child Psychology and Psychiatry, 33,* 331–348.

Slough, N. M., & Greenberg, M. T. (1990). Five-year-olds' representations of separation from parents: Responses from the perspective of self and other. *New Directions for Child Development, 48,* 67–84.

Sroufe, L. A. (1988). A developmental perspective on daycare. *Childhood Research Quarterly, 3,* 283–291.

Sroufe, L. A., & Fleeson, J. (1986). Attachment and the construction of relationship. In W. Hartup & Z. Rubin (Eds.), *Relationships and development* (pp. 51–72). Hillsdale, NJ: Erlbaum.

Sroufe, L. A., & Waters, E. (1977). Attachment as an organizational concept. *Child Development, 48,* 1184–1199.

Stevenson-Hinde, J., & Shouldice, A. (1993). Wariness to strangers: A behavior systems perspective revisited. In K. H. Rubin & J. B. Asendorpf (Eds.), *Social withdrawal, inhibition and shyness in childhood* (pp. 101–117). Hillsdale, NJ: Erlbaum.

Thompson, R. A., Lamb, M. E., & Estes, D. (1982). Stability of infant–mother attachment and its relationship to changing life circumstances in an unselected middle class sample. *Child Development, 53,* 144–148.

Thompson, R. A., Lamb, M. E., & Estes, D. (1983). Harmonizing discordant notes: A reply to Waters. *Child Development, 54,* 521–524.

Touris, M., Kromelow, S., & Harding, H. C. (1995). Mother–firstborn attachment and the birth of a sibling. *American Journal of Orthopsychiatry, 65,* 293–297.

van IJzendoorn, M. H. (1995). Adult attachment representations, parental responsiveness, and infant attachment: A meta-analysis on the predictive validity of the Adult Attachment Interview. *Psychological Bulletin, 117,* 387–404.

van IJzendoorn, M. H., & Kroonenberg, P. M. (1988). Cross-cultural patterns of attachment: A meta-analysis of the strange situation. *Child Development, 59,* 147–156.

van IJzendoorn, M. H., Sagi, A., & Lambermon, M. W. E. (1992). The multiple caretaker paradox: Some data from Holland and Israel [Special issue on relationships between children and nonparental adults]. *New Directions in Child Development, 57,* 5–24.

Vaughn, B., Egeland, B., Sroufe, L. A., & Waters, E. (1979). Individual differences in infant–mother attachment at twelve and eighteen months: Stability and change in families under stress. *Child Development, 50,* 971–975.

Wartner, U. G., Grossmann, K., Fremmer-Bombik, E., & Suess, G. (1994). Attachment patterns at age six in south Germany: Predictability from infancy and implications for preschool behavior. *Child Development, 65,* 1014–1027.

Waters, E. (1978). The reliability and stability of individual differences in infant attachment. *Child Development, 49,* 483–494.

Waters, E., Merrick, S. K., Treboux, D., Crowell, J., & Albersheim, L. (2000). Attachment security from infancy to early adulthood: A 20–year longitudinal study. *Child Development, 71,* 703–706.

Weinfield, N., Sroufe, L. A., & Egland, B. (2000). Attachment from infancy to early adulthood in a high risk sample: Continuity, discontinuity, and their correlates. *Child Development, 71* 695–702.

Zimmermann, P., Grossmann, K. E., & Fremmer-Bombic, E. (1998). *Attachment in infancy and adolescence: Continuity of attachment or continuity of transmission of attachment?* Manuscript submitted for publication.

14

§

Talking the Talk

Constructivist Teachers Guiding Children's Problem Solving

MICHELLE B. PATT
ARTİN GÖNCÜ

Four-year-old Ana slowly turned each small rectangular block on its end, building a 3-foot wall across the block area. She then placed a square block on the first rectangular block. "Oh, I see you're balancing the square on top of the block," the teacher said. Without a response, Ana continued placing one square block on the top of each rectangle. After placing squares on the entire row of rectangles, Ana began to place another row of square blocks on top.

"I see you're making another layer," the teacher said. Ana smiled and continued. Several of the rectangles fell over under the weight of the squares. "Hmm, some of the blocks are falling," the teacher observed. "What do you think made that happen?" Ana carefully removed the top layer of squares from the remaining blocks. "Oh, you're taking the top squares off," said the teacher.

Ana turned to the teacher and said, "Teacher, you talk way too much."

This story, and others like it, represent some of the difficulties the constructivist teacher faces. What should I say to children at play? What if I talk too much? What does it mean to be a "facilitator" without interfering in children's activities? Constructivist teachers working with young children constantly ask these and similar other questions because as we strive to be collaborators, guides, and companions, we try to avoid being didactic in children's explorations. At the same time, however, we struggle with the question of when we *should* intervene in children's activities, and whether imposing some of our adult concepts on children might actually be the best solution in some circumstances.

As an example of the latter, consider the case of 3-year-old Brandon, who pours an extra cup of water into the batter while making pancakes. The teacher knows that that will make the batter too thin and the pancakes will not cook properly. When the pancakes turn out looking and tasting strange, perhaps she can help Brandon reconstruct what happened and help him to develop an understanding of mixing substances in proportion. On the other hand, there are the real concerns of how the other children will react, what they will eat for a snack, and the waste of food and money from the tight cooking budget. Is this a teachable moment worth allowing Brandon's mistake to become public discussion for 14 of his peers?

As former preschool teachers committed to constructivist philosophies, we struggled with these questions on a daily basis in our interactions with children. However, what once was a part of daily practice has gained a dimension of formal inquiry for both of us, with our changing roles from teachers to academic researchers. Examples of such efforts can be found in the work Göncü (e.g., Göncü & Becker, 2000; Göncü & Cannella, 1996; Göncü & Weber, 2000). This chapter is based on the work of Patt conducted at the University of Illinois as a research requirement toward a doctoral thesis. Our goal is to piece together a portrait of what constructivist teachers do while interacting with children in their classrooms. We explore the conditions under which constructivist teachers use different types of guidance with their students. Our goal is to illustrate that constructivist teachers' guidance of children varies as a function of activity demands.

We felt that this would be an appropriate question to explore in a chapter written to honor the contributions of Greta G. Fein to the study of child development and early education. Over the years, Greta served as a constructivist teacher to many us, bringing important scholarly questions to our attention by guiding us to seek the experiential roots of those questions in our lives as well as guiding us through her explicit statements abundantly sprinkled throughout the literature. In keeping with Greta's constructivist teaching, we explored our question on both personal and more formal theoretical and research grounds. Toward that end, we first present Patt's experiences in the beginning of her teaching career as personal background to our inquiry. This is followed by a discussion of the constructivist theories and the relevant research literature that has examined teacher–child collaboration and influenced Patt's practice, as well as how such theory and research guided us to conduct the study reported in the subsequent section. As an illustration of the varying nature of teacher guidance, we present and discuss the patterns of interaction that emerged between children and their teachers during classroom cooking activities. Finally, we discuss the implications of this study for future research and for constructivist teaching practices in preschool classrooms.

CONSTRUCTING THE TEACHER ROLE

A Teacher Seeks Understanding

I had become a teacher not because I had any urge to provide formal instruction, but instead, because I was simply fascinated by how children explore their environment and make discoveries. I envisioned myself as a participant observer, or, at most, a facilitator who would help create the perfect milieu for children to become a part of an exciting world, full of discoveries. Thus, I approached my first week of teaching in a constructivist preschool with great excitement, as I looked forward to creating an ideal setting in which children could explore and create.

My coteacher and I enthusiastically shared ideas about room arrangement and materials. As we chose books and puzzles, water table scoops, and unit blocks, my coteacher and I talked about how this would enable the children to explore independently or that would encourage the children to construct understandings of mass and of number. But when we began to discuss the dramatic play area, we reached our first disagreement.

In my previous classroom, I made extensive use of prop boxes, transforming the dramatic play area into themed centers, such as a restaurant, a fire station, or a jungle. I excitedly shared these experiences with my new coteacher, as I pointed out a box that might make a perfect fire truck, or a space where we could fit several tables to make a restaurant dining room. She did not share my enthusiasm. She maintained that children should decide what they wanted to pretend, and that creating a dramatic play theme imposed our ideas on the children and, in fact, limited their ability to create for themselves. Pointing to the box that I had envisioned as a fire truck, she explained that if children decided it was a fire truck, we could follow their lead and suggest ways to expand their play. If they thought it was a fire truck, maybe *then* they would want to paint it or add ladders and hats. We could help them think their ideas through, plan, and find the materials they needed, but any greater adult involvement would be interference with their own creative processes.

From a theoretical standpoint, this position made sense: Of course we should be encouraging children's autonomy and independent discovery. Wasn't that one of the reasons I became a teacher? But, on the other hand, there was the reality of a preschool classroom environment. In certain circumstances, teachers make decisions for children. From the arrangement of the schedule to the materials provided in traditional areas of a classroom (e.g., blocks, dramatic play, and art), teachers set up tacit expectations for how children should spend their time. Also, teachers do intervene, if not with directions, then with suggestions and comments that are intended to push children toward the teacher's way of thinking. My coteacher and I reached an agreement that if children were using the box as a fire truck, then we could help them figure out ways to make it look more like a fire truck, or to think of things we could add to the area to "play fire station." Perhaps children would truly gain ownership of the ideas if they were involved in the implementation. Or, is this simply a way teachers justify their intrusion into children's pretend worlds, by gaining children's assent for the adults' ideas?

To my dismay, during my first teaching year, and in subsequent years of teaching, these doubts were not resolved but instead expanded into every corner of our classroom curriculum. At times, decisions about which materials to choose and which activity plans to follow seemed to impose our adult wills on children. Other times, following children's leads simply seemed wrong. As much as I did not want to consider myself a "teacher," I conceded that the 3-year-old children who shared my classroom were not always capable of making the organizational and educational decisions that had to be made.

I also became concerned about how our classroom environment might influence their interactions in the world outside our classroom. The constructivist classroom seemed to be a vacuum separate from the outside world. However, children exist in other social contexts as well, and I wondered how well we were preparing them for later school experiences in more structured settings, or whether our practices might conflict with social norms in their families and homes (see Klein & Tarullo, this volume; Powell, this volume, for a discussion of these contexts). The central question that emerged was what constructivist teachers do, and what constructivist teachers *should* do, to help children develop understandings and make sense of the world around them. Guided by these questions, I continued to examine constructivist views on early education, which we present here.

Constructivist Theories and Research on Teacher–Child Collaboration

One main theoretical influence on constructivist early childhood practice is the work of Jean Piaget. Preschool curricula based on the theories of Piaget emphasize that children should have the primary responsibility for constructing their own questions and discovering the answers independently (DeVries, this volume; DeVries & Kohlberg, 1987). According to Piaget (1932/1965), the teacher should not impose or reveal rules to child, in fact, " 'a priest' is the last thing a schoolmaster should be: he should be an elder collaborator, and, if he has it in him, a simple comrade to the children" (p. 364). In Piagetian-based curricula, the teacher's role is thus limited to one of support, such as figuring out what the child is thinking and responding in a way that stimulates the child to construct understandings of relationships between objects and events (Kamii & DeVries, 1978/1993). It is the children's responsibility to have "wonderful ideas" which are meaningful to them and which they can explore with their own intellectual tools, to construct knowledge through their own discoveries (Duckworth, 1987). This emphasis on children's roles in constructing their own knowledge suggests that children would have greater responsibility for, and greater participation in, classroom activities than would teachers. In this model, teachers would play a supporting role by following children's leads and initiatives rather than direct the activity themselves.

However, based on our own previous teaching of preschool children and examination of the relevant literature, it occurred to us that the Piagetian approaches do not address the question of how to balance the unstructured explorations of the child with the real demands of the social world. The Piagetian approaches provide an opening for future work to explore how teacher guidance varies both from one activity to another and within the context of the same activity as the activity demands change. For example, during pretend play, teachers might follow children's initiations more than during a cooking activity, and while cooking, some parts of the activity may require structure and planning from adults that other parts do not.

To examine these issues at the theoretical level we turned to the work of Vygotksy (1978), who considered teachers' and children's joint participation in the learning process. Vygotsky (1978) described "learning in the zone of proximal development," which occurs when adults assist children by providing guidance to allow children to perform a task that they would be unable to perform independently (Rogoff & Wertsch, 1984). Other researchers have expanded Vygotsky's theory by providing detailed descriptions of how the teaching and learning are accomplished. For example, Wood, Bruner, and Ross (1976) and Rogoff (1990) described a process in which the adult provides support for a problem-solving activity by assisting or providing structure for the child and then gradually decreases the level of assistance as the child takes on more responsibility for the task.

Research in the area of adult guidance of children's problem solving has demonstrated that this type of guidance is beneficial; however, much of this research involved experimental tasks (e.g. Göncü & Rogoff, 1998; Radziszewska & Rogoff, 1988). Naturalistic studies on the types of guidance provided by teachers have often focused on children of elementary rather than preschool children (e.g., Mercer, 1995). The existing research on teacher–child interaction in early childhood classrooms has concentrated on teacher-led, large-group activities, such as "sharing time" (Cazden, 1988) and reading aloud (French & MacLure, 1983; Martinez & Teale, 1993), or on small-group instruction (Fowell & Lawton, 1992), but has not extensively addressed activities in which the teacher and child collaborate jointly. Other research has examined aspects of teacher–child interaction during child selected problem-solving or play activities, such as the extent to which teachers collaborated with children (Göncü & Weber, 2000) and the negotiation strategies and level of interpersonal understanding demonstrated by the teacher (DeVries, Haney, & Zan, 1991), but did not directly address the ways in which teacher guidance occurs.

We sought to extend the previous research by examining how teachers facilitate and guide children's problem solving in actual cooking activities in preschool classrooms and what teachers do to help children accomplish a complex task such as cooking. Cooking provides opportunities for children to develop skills such as temporal reasoning, quantification, reading, and cooperation with peers (Kamii & DeVries, 1978/1993). In addition, these teachers aimed to encourage children's autonomous problem solving by using recipes and other tools which decreased reliance on the teacher as the source of information (DeVries & Kohlberg, 1987; Kamii & DeVries, 1978/1993). Therefore, the cooking activities were viewed as an ideal setting to observe how teacher guidance facilitates children's problem solving.

Our specific goal was to examine whether or how teachers' interaction styles vary with evolving demands of cooking. We addressed two questions in this study. First, how were responsibility for planning and implementing cooking activities shared between the teachers and children? Following the Vygotskian model of scaffolding, we anticipated that the initial structure of the activities would require a high level of adult participation and guidance. Previous research using experimental tasks has demonstrated that adult guidance and shared responsibility in planning (Gauvain & Rogoff, 1989; Radziszewska & Rogoff, 1988, 1991) or in structuring a task (Göncü & Rogoff, 1998) helped children complete them in more efficient and sophisticated ways than children who were not involved in that type of planning or organization. In addition, research on adult guidance of children's everyday activities in a variety of cultures has demonstrated that adults provide structure for children during the initial stages of their joint activity (for a review, see Rogoff, 1990). Thus, we expected that planning and negotiation of plans would comprise a large portion of the activity, would continue throughout the activity, and that the adult would have much of the responsibility in this area.

Once the planning stages were accomplished, we expected that the actual task of cooking would be turned over to the children with minimal adult intervention, especially if the experience involved physical, observable events. Piagetian-based curricula emphasize that children construct understanding of physical phenomena and logical consequences by performing actions on objects and by establishing relations between their actions and transformations in the objects (Kamii & DeVries, 1978/1993). Thus, we expected that much of the problem-solving activities in which children engaged would involve physical manipulation of materials, and that children would have the primary responsibility for such tasks. In addition, because the educational aspects of these "physical knowledge" activities are not only to perform actions on objects but to develop understandings from these events, we expected to see frequent evaluation, with the children having primary responsibility.

The second question addressed the interactional strategies used by teachers while guiding children's problem solving. There has not been extensive naturalistic research on interactional strategies used by preschool teachers, although several studies identified forms used in particular situations. For example, work focusing on teacher-directed lessons reported that teachers initiate the topic and regulate the lesson as it progresses, mostly by asking closed-ended questions to which the children respond (Cazden, 1988). Other research focusing on constructivist teaching reported that teachers also ask open-ended questions intended to stimulate children's thinking and use indirect methods, such as giving suggestions, providing prompts or hints, and making comments (DeVries & Kohlberg, 1987; Fowell & Lawton, 1992; Kamii & DeVries, 1978/1993). However, such work did not address whether the interactional style of teachers' guidance varies with different demands of the activity.

The connection between adult guidance and interaction style is addressed in some experimental work. For example, adults provided explicit instruction or strategies to the child (e.g., "After going to a store, we will see what is the next closest store") during complex tasks such as grocery shopping (Radziszewska & Rogoff, 1988, p. 843). Further, this type of adult support is related to greater child competency in performance of the task (Göncü & Rogoff, 1998; Radziszewska & Rogoff,

1988). Based on this evidence, we expected that during planning teachers would engage in directing and questioning, which are strategies that involve greater teacher responsibility or control. In some contrast, during cooking when responsibility is transferred to the child (Rogoff, 1990), and when activity involves observable physical phenomena, the interactional style would involve less directing and more questioning or narrating, strategies which encourage children's autonomy (DeVries & Kohlberg, 1987; Kamii & DeVries, 1978/1993).

METHOD

Setting

The setting we chose for the present study was a mixed-age classroom of 3- and 4-year-olds at a university-based day-care center. The center subscribed to constructivist theories of development, particularly that young children develop understanding about their world through participating in hands-on activities, exchanging opinions with peers, and having opportunities to solve problems independently. This philosophy was implemented throughout the daily routine. For approximately 2 hours at the start of the day, the children were free to choose and move between a variety of activities, positioned in various areas of the room. These included Play-Doh, blocks, water table, writing, dramatic play, and other activities common to early childhood classrooms. During this morning period, teachers occasionally worked with small groups of children on specific activities, such as cooking, art, and writing activities. After this morning free-play time came group time, then outdoor play, lunch, and naptime. After naptime, free play in the classroom and outdoors continued until the end of the day.

I (Patt) and the two classroom teachers jointly discussed which classroom activity should be the focus of the study. We searched for an activity or routine that involved a high amount of problem-solving opportunities and in which most of the children in the classroom participated. We narrowed our choices to cooking, group time, and preparation to go outside. Ultimately, cooking was chosen, as the teachers felt that the cooking curriculum embodied most of the principles of their constructivist philosophy (as discussed earlier in this chapter).

Eleven children (five boys, six girls) and two teachers (both female) participated in the study. There were a total of 14 children in the classroom, but three of the children did not participate in any of the observed activities. The children represented a variety of cultural backgrounds, and their ages at the beginning of the study ranged from 36 months to 57 months. The two teachers were the children's regular classroom teachers. Both teachers had bachelor's degrees in education and had taught for 9 and 14 years, respectively.

Cooking took place in either the cooking area or the house corner. The cooking area measured approximately 4' × 6', and was furnished with a child-size table and chairs. The classroom sink was nearby, as was a shelf containing eating utensils and recipes. Two charts on the wall indicated which children's turn it was to cook. The house corner measured approximately 5' × 8', and was furnished with toy kitchen appliances and utensils, and a child-size table and chairs. This area was used when access to an electrical outlet was needed. Cooking utensils and food items were stored in areas outside the classroom.

Opportunity to cook was determined by a system established by the teachers. Each child's name was written on a wall chart, and the teachers followed the list to determine who would have the next turn to cook. The teachers used a clothespin to mark the name of the child who would have the next turn. The day before the designated cooking day, a teacher would inform the child that it was his or her turn, then ask that child to choose a partner, and to choose what to cook. The teacher or child would then place photographs of the two participating children and an illustration of the food to be cooked on a poster labeled "Look Who's Cooking." The foods that were prepared during observed sessions were macaroni and cheese, English muffin pizzas, pancakes, and waffles. The two teachers alternated responsibility for supervising cooking, including making sure all necessary materials, such as ingredients and utensils, were available.

Observations were recorded by Patt, who was a former teacher at the day-care center and was known to the teachers. The teachers introduced her to the children before data collection and explained that she used to be a teacher at their school and that she was interested in seeing how children cook. She sat at the edge of the area where cooking took place and accompanied the children and teacher when leaving the classroom to go to the kitchen. Eight weekly cooking sessions were observed during a 10-week period. Observed sessions were audiotaped, and field notes were taken. Patt also had informal conversations with the teachers both during and after the observation period. During these conversations, they discussed the teachers' educational philosophies and how classroom activities were planned and implemented.

Coding

Patt (who had recorded the observations) coded the data with the assistance of two graduate students. The audiotapes were transcribed, using the field notes for clarification (such as determining the identity of the speaker or identifying an unclear word). Transcripts consisted of verbatim accounts of verbal interaction that took place during the cooking sessions as well as actions involved in manipulating materials (e.g., taking spoons out of a drawer or stirring a pot). The transcripts were edited to include only data relevant to cooking. Data were considered relevant if they involved speech or actions that contributed to the ongoing cooking activity, and if the teacher and at least one of the participating children were present.

Variables

The transcripts were examined according to the number of turns that were involved in a given task. A turn was considered to start when a topic was introduced, and lasted until the *topic, speaker,* or *addressee* changed. Each turn was coded as enacted by teacher, by child, or jointly (saying or doing the same thing simultaneously). Turns by each child participating in the activity were recorded separately, and the participants enacting a joint turn were noted.

The turns were then categorized according to the process of cooking it involved. Three processes involved in cooking activities were identified. *Planning* included all aspects of preparation for implementing the cooking project, such as determining what to cook, who would participate, what materials were needed, and how many servings to make, such as, "We have to grate the cheese," or "How many pizzas do we need?" *Doing* included utterances and actions directly related to the actual preparation of food, such as cutting, stirring, or measuring food, such as, "Put some sauce on each one." *Evaluating* included decisions or discussions about how previous tasks had been implemented, such as whether enough servings had been made, or whether the food was prepared correctly, such as, "How much more water do we need?" or, "Do we need to put them back in the oven?"

Teacher turns were additionally coded according to whether they involved directing, questioning, or narrating. *Directing* turns involved the teacher explicitly telling the child what to do or what will be done, or telling the child the correct or appropriate answer to a question or problem such as, "You need to get some water," or "Actually, we need sixteen." *Questioning* involved the teacher asking the child a question phrased to elicit a response, such as, "Did you bring me the two bowls?" or "How many more muffins do you think we need to cut?" Directions that were phrased in question form but did not allow the child to reply (e.g., "We have to go to the kitchen now, okay?") were not included in this category. *Narrating* turns were those in which the teacher made comments that provided information about ongoing activity but that were not directly addressed to the child, or were not phrased in a way that suggests the child must respond, such as, "It looks like Michael got a little more water in his cup this time," and "That's a good idea the way you're doing that, you're pushing the plate closer to the waffle iron."

RESULTS AND DISCUSSION

Data Analysis

The data were analyzed using Friedman tests to determine group differences between (1) the number of turns enacted by teachers and children, (2) the number of turns enacted during the various processes of cooking, and (3) the number of turns involving the different teacher interactional styles during the various processes of cooking.

Turns by Teachers and Children

Teachers enacted a significantly greater overall number of interactional turns than did children ($p < .01$). Teachers also enacted a significantly greater number of planning turns than did children ($p < .01$). However, no significant differences were found between the number of doing turns or of evaluating turns enacted by teachers and children (see Table 14.1). Consistent with our expectation, these findings suggest that more teacher participation occurred during the planning process of cooking, but as the activity progressed, children's participation increased, with teachers and children sharing the responsibility for the actual doing and the evaluation of cooking.

TABLE 14.1. Mean Numbers of Turns per Observed Cooking Session

Process	Teachers	Children	Combined
		Group	
Planning	116	77	193
Doing	43	37	80
Evaluating	33	26	59
All Processes	192	140	332

Planning

Planning involved a significantly greater number of turns than did doing or evaluating. These results were found when looking at the overall number of turns ($p < .01$), only teacher turns ($p < .01$), or only children turns ($p < .05$) (see Table 14.1). This further emphasizes the importance of planning to the cooking, as planning occurred more than twice as frequently as doing and three times as frequently as evaluating. Although planning occurred at all points in the activity, and varied in length, a typical sequence of planning turns occurred at the beginning of each cooking activity, as the teacher went over the recipe, helped the children to decide what tools or ingredients were needed, and discussed the procedure for how the food would be made. An example follows (all are planning turns):

> Paula is the teacher who is working with Michael (4 years, 9 months) and Wendy (4 years, 8 months) as they make macaroni and cheese. Paula takes out the recipe, and shows the first page, which is an illustrated list of ingredients, to the children. She points to each picture as she labels it or asks about it.

> PAULA: Let's see if we have all the things that it says we need. These pictures aren't so great so we'll have to kind of look at them. This is macaroni. You know what this is?

> MICHAEL: Butter.

> PAULA: Well, it's really cheese.

> MICHAEL: It looks the same.

> PAULA: It looks the same. And what is this?

> MICHAEL: Spoons.

> PAULA: We got our spoons. And what is this?

> MICHAEL AND WENDY: Bowls.

> PAULA: OK, over there we got our bowls. And what is this?

> MICHAEL: Kitchen.

> PAULA: Well, it's something that goes in the kitchen but it has a handle on it.

> MICHAEL: Pan.

> PAULA: A pan, or a pot. Yes, and this is our pot that we're gonna use today, OK? And what is this?

> MICHAEL: A pitcher.

> PAULA: OK, a pitcher, or measuring cup. OK, and it says we need to grate the cheese. And these are the graters. And it says we

need a colander. We don't have a colander so we can just use one of our other bowls today. And this is a stove. Now it says fill the pot with water. So you all need to go get some water, so you can pour it into our pot, okay?

In this excerpt, the teacher clearly guided the planning process, and participated in the activity more than the children did. Her style was a combination of directing and questioning, as she presented information and asked questions to elicit a specific response. However, the questions were not open-ended, meaning that the teacher knew what the answer should be, and was merely trying to elicit the correct response. When the child's answer was incorrect, such as Michael misidentifying cheese as butter, or calling a pan a "kitchen," the teacher either directly corrected him or provided a prompt to lead him to the right answer.

During planning, teachers engaged in directing significantly more often than questioning or narrating ($p < .005$) (see Table 14.2). This is illustrated in the following example, during which another teacher, Gail, helped Sharon (3 years, 6 months) and Daisy (4 years, 3 months) make English muffin pizzas (all are planning turns, and all teacher turns are directing).

GAIL: [The recipe says] Open up the tomato sauce. (*Opens the jar.*) Daisy, can you get two bowls?

DAISY: Sure.

GAIL: Little bowls? OK, and it says to put the muffin halves—

DAISY: (*interrupts.*) Two or one? Two or one?

GAIL: Get two bowls. That way we can put some sauce in each one.

DAISY: (*Brings two bowls to Gail.*): Here you go.

GAIL: Oh, you know what, We're gonna, I think we're gonna need some small spoons—

TABLE 14.2. Mean Numbers of Turns per Session Involving Teacher Interactional Styles

	Interactional style		
Process	Directing	Questioning	Narrating
Planning	71	34	7
Doing	29	2	2
Evaluating	9	15	9
All processes	109	51	18

DAISY: Why?

GAIL: Do you think—it's one thing that it didn't say on the list, but we might need another spoon. Do you think the tablespoon is to scoop the sauce on? But we might need another spoon. We only have one tablespoon. Unless Daisy you want to use a little plastic spoon. I don't really want to go back to the kitchen.

This teacher made the decisions for how the cooking activity would proceed and directed Sharon and Daisy to follow her instructions. Although some of the directions were phrased in a question form ("So you think the tablespoon is to scoop the sauce on?"), it is clear that the teacher did not expect a response, but was giving instructions to be followed.

It is not surprising that the teachers used directing so extensively during the planning process. Although previous research has not extensively addressed how teachers and children interact during small-group activities such as those described here, adults' use of direction as a guidance tool in classroom settings (see Cazden, 1988) and in experimental situations (e.g., Radziszewska & Rogoff, 1988) has been well documented. Providing structure for the activity is a part of the scaffolding process, allowing the children to gradually receive responsibility from the adult, and increase their participation in the activity.

Doing

As expected, children's participation increased during the doing process of cooking. No significant differences were revealed between the number of doing turns enacted by teachers and children (see Table 14.1). This suggests that as the activity progressed, the teachers and children shared the responsibility for the actual doing of cooking. However, doing turns also involved significantly more directing than questioning or narrating ($p < .005$), as in the following example (all are doing turns, and all teacher turns are directing):

The recipe says to put two spoons of sauce on each muffin half. Sharon has 12 muffin halves on a baking sheet in front of her but is putting all her sauce on one muffin.

GAIL: I'm gonna take a little bit off of that one and put it on this. (*Takes a spoon and lifts sauce off of Sharon's muffin and distributes it between the other muffins.*)

GAIL: Now, Sharon, here's some cheese that you can put on your pizza. Did you want to put oregano? Did you want to put this on, Sharon? You wanna put some of that on. You know what I'm gonna ask you to do, this is what—I'm gonna pour some of this into your bowl, and what I want you to do is pick some up with your fingers like this. (*Demonstrates sprinkling a pinch of oregano on each muffin.*)

SHARON: (*Begins to sprinkle oregano, putting on more than Gail suggested.*)

GAIL: Just a little bit—no that's enough. Just a little bit. Just a little bit 'cause it's very strong. (*Guides Sharon's hand to sprinkle the rest of the pizzas, then gives her a spoon.*) You might wanna spread it around a little bit. Spread it around, Sharon, all over it.

The use of directing as a primary strategy during the doing process of cooking is not consistent with the existing literature. According to theory and research concerning guided participation (Rogoff, 1990), after providing an initial structure as scaffolding, the teacher would be expected to gradually transfer responsibility for the task to the child. During the doing process, the proportion of child responsibility in relation to teacher responsibility did increase. However, at the same time, teachers used directing with a much greater frequency ($p < .005$) than they used questioning or evaluating, which are less controlling styles of interaction. These findings are also surprising considering the philosophical orientation of the classroom, particularly that the cooking curriculum emphasized children's autonomous problem solving and active manipulation of objects (Kamii & DeVries, 1978/1993). However, in this particular situation, and in similar situations throughout the cooking activities, perhaps the child was not yet ready to assume primary responsibility for the task. Another possibility is that other considerations, such as the time, the monetary cost of wasting oregano, or the possibility that too much oregano would make the pizzas unpalatable, made it less practical for that particular task to be turned over to the child.

Evaluating

Although directing was used more frequently than other styles during planning and doing, no significant differences were revealed between teacher styles during evaluating (see Table 14.2). Evaluating comprised the smallest number of turns; however, it appears that during evaluating, teachers and children shared responsibility, and teachers did not rely on only one interactional style. This is consistent with the constructivist philosophy of the classroom, which values making observations and judgments about events and physical phenomena as a key component of children's learning. For example, in the macaroni-and-cheese activity introduced earlier, once Paula, the teacher, introduced the task of filling the pot with water, Michael and Wendy began to fill pitchers with water and pour the water into the pot. After two pitchers were poured in, Paula clarified the task. All the turns in the following sequence are evaluating, and interactional style of teacher turns is indicated by the letter following the turn (Directing, Questioning, Narrating).

> PAULA: OK, we need to fill the water up to about to this line (*points to line on inside of pot*), so how much more do you think we need to put in that pitcher? Huh? [Q]
>
> MICHAEL: (*points to about two-thirds line on pitcher.*)
>
> PAULA: Well, you can go see. [D]
>
> MICHAEL AND WENDY: (*Each pours another pitcher into the pot.*)
>
> PAULA: OK, is it up here yet? [Q]
>
> MICHAEL AND WENDY: Nooooo.
>
> JON: You have to use more water first.
>
> MICHAEL AND WENDY: (*Each pours another pitcher into the pot.*)
>
> PAULA: Is it up there yet? [Q]
>
> MICHAEL AND WENDY: Nooooo.

This process of filling the pitchers and Paula asking if they have filled the pot up is repeated three more times. After Michael pours his sixth pitcher into the pot, Paula uses narration and questioning to encourage the children to evaluate whether they have gotten the necessary amount of water.

> PAULA: OK, let's see what happens when Wendy brings hers. Ooh, Wendy, you've got *a lot* more this time. (*Laughs.*) You have to walk slower, cause it's very close to the top. [N]
>
> WENDY: (*Pours her pitcher into the pot.*)
>
> PAULA: OK, it's very close. [N] How many more you think we need? [Q]
>
> MICHAEL: One.
>
> PAULA: One? OK, so go get one more, then. And then we'll be done. [D]
>
> WENDY: Not me?
>
> PAULA: Not you? That's up to you. Do you think you need to get one more? [Q]
>
> WENDY: (*Shakes her head.*)

Paula transferred responsibility for the task to Michael and Wendy. She did not tell them how much water was needed but structured the task in a way that they could perform and evaluate it independently. Even when Wendy asked if she should get more water, Paula simply commented, "That's up to you," turning the question back to Wendy: Does *she* think more water is needed? In this part of the macaroni-and-cheese activity, the children had the responsibility for solving the problem and accomplishing the task. However, in the overall analyses, the lack of significant differences between number of teacher turns and number of child turns during evaluating implies that although children increased their participation and shared responsibility with adults, they did not have primary responsibility. As a whole, cooking in this classroom remained an endeavor that was overshadowed by adults.

Thematic Elements

The inconsistencies between the findings and our original expectations led us to question whether there were subtle aspects of the cooking activities, classroom environment, or specific tasks that led to the high level of teacher participation and direction. Preliminary qualitative analyses identified three thematic elements occurring throughout the cooking sessions: procedural, academic, and physical knowledge.

As already discussed, tasks related to procedure, such as planning, performing steps in a specific order, and performing steps a particular way, generally involved the teacher providing explicit direction to the children, such as telling them what to do or how something would be done. When tasks involved traditional academic topics, such as reading the recipe and counting how many servings to make, the teachers shifted emphasis from directing to questioning. For example, in the earlier example of reading the macaroni-and-cheese recipe, the teacher asked what each item was and continued to ask questions until all the necessary ingredients had been correctly identified. This emphasis on questioning occurred each time a recipe was read.

Another academic task that commonly involved teacher questioning was counting the people in the room to determine how many servings to make. While the children counted, the teachers' contributions consisted primarily of guidance strategies rather than evaluative comments or corrections. For example, before Daisy and Sharon began preparing their English muffin pizzas, they counted how many servings they needed to prepare.

> GAIL: Well, what do we have to do before we really start? How will we know how many we need?
>
> DAISY: Count! Let's count. (*Walks around the room counting people, then after several minutes, returns to the table.*)
>
> GAIL: How many did you count?

DAISY: I didn't count all.

GAIL: You didn't count all of them? You know what, Paula thought of a different way that we can count. Instead of counting all the people who are walking around, we could count our cooking chart people. Why don't you get the basket, Sharon and Daisy. I've never done it that way but I think it's a good idea.

Daisy and Sharon get basket of photographs of children in the class and bring it to the table. Daisy lifts out the photos, saying the name of each child.

DAISY: Robbie—

GAIL: Is Robbie here today? Yeah.

DAISY: Freddie.

GAIL: Is Freddie here today?

DAISY: Yes.

This question-and-answer sequence continues until all the photos are counted.

In this example, Gail first presented the problem, "How will we know how many we need?" then allowed Daisy to figure out the problem independently. However, when it became apparent that Daisy needed extra support to count everyone in the classroom, Gail introduced a strategy the children could use to determine who was at school that day. She used guiding questions to help them get started and then left Daisy and Sharon to complete the task independently. When they were finished, she asked them for their solution:

GAIL: OK. How many children did you find? And how many teachers and everything?

DAISY: Paula, Gail.

GAIL: But how many? Did you count how many?

DAISY: We count all of them.

GAIL: Everybody's here today? Oh, my goodness. We're gonna have to make a lot of pizza. And remember we make a couple extra, in case one of them falls or something? We make a couple extra, OK?

GAIL: (*Takes photos from basket, counts people who are here.*) Paula, 1, 2, 3—

SHARON, DAISY, AND GAIL: 4, 5, 6, 7, 8, 9, 10, 11, 12, 13, 14, 15.

GAIL: 16, 17.

SHARON: Seventeen!

DAISY: Seventeen.

GAIL: Seventeen. You're right. 16, 17—17. So we need to make a lot
of pizzas. We wanna make a few extra in case one falls down or
something, OK? In case somebody drops theirs.

Sharon and Daisy were unable to complete the entire task independently, so Gail provided additional, and more direct guidance. Once
she realized that the children were not applying the strategy she had
given them to solving the problem, "How many do we need?" she demonstrated how to figure it out. Although this style could be considered
directive, Gail used it in the overall context of providing guidance and
did not directly provide the children with the correct answer until she
had exhausted several other methods of encouraging them to figure out
the problem themselves.

The third thematic element identified involved performing actions
on objects and observing physical phenomena (referred to by Kamii &
DeVries, 1978/1993, as physical knowledge). When the cooking activities involved making decisions about physically observable phenomena, the children tended to have primary responsibility, and teacher
strategies emphasized guidance in the form of narrating. Although the
teachers had used directing and questioning to set up the structure of
the cooking activities, the children accomplished much of the actual
food preparation independently, without as much teacher participation.
Decisions about *how* to perform a task (such as grating cheese or mixing
batter), how much of an ingredient was needed, or whether a step was
completed were generally left to the child to determine independently,
or, if the child needed assistance, with teacher guidance. Exceptions to
this pattern occurred when an incorrect decision could adversely affect
the final outcome, such as adding too much water to the pancake batter
or letting something cook too long. However, the majority of food preparation tasks involved physical knowledge experiences of manipulating
materials and observing changes in physical state (Kamii & DeVries,
1978/1993). In the following example, Michael and Wendy were determining how to get butter out of the individual tablespoon-size pack-
ages:

PAULA: We need to put the butter in the pan. I don't know what
you need to get the butter out with. What do you think you
need to get the butter out?

MICHAEL: My hands.

PAULA: Do you think your hands will do?

Michael and Wendy pull the tops off the butter, and try to squeeze it out of the package into the pan. They try for several minutes but are unsuccessful.

PAULA: Yeah, how you gonna get the butter out of there?

MICHAEL: I know. With a knife.

PAULA: OK, why don't you go get a knife.

WENDY: Squeeze it out.

MICHAEL: Let's get a knife, Wendy. (*Goes to shelf.*)

WENDY: I can push it.

PAULA: Push it? Well, you can try that.

Wendy tries unsuccessfully to push the butter into the pan.

PAULA: Do you need a knife? You can go ahead and get what you need.

Michael returns with two knives, and gives one to Wendy. They spread the butter around the pan with their knives.

Paula presented the task as a problem to be solved and initially provided no assistance to the children. When Michael or Wendy proposed an idea, Paula simply suggested they try it out. The children were allowed to experiment with the materials and collaborate with each other to figure out how to perform the task. It was only when Wendy continued to have difficulty that Paula made a suggestion, and even this suggestion was a repetition of Michael's idea, presented as an option rather than a direction.

In addition to these thematic elements, another pattern emerged that occurred across cooking processes and across thematic elements. Teacher direction seemed to be greatest during tasks that involved "high stakes"—when an incorrect decision could ruin or seriously hamper the cooking project. In the earlier pizza example, the teacher intervened when Sharon put all the tomato sauce on one muffin and again when she put too much oregano on each pizza. In other instances, such as measuring exact proportions for pancake batter or deciding when something has finished cooking, the teachers also exerted more control. In an activity such as cooking, it makes sense that teachers are more directive in planning, and as well as other high-stakes aspects of the activity, because cooking involves preparation of a product which is created in part to fulfill a specific goal in social context: making food to share with the group at mealtime. In this context, there is not much room for error, and, especially when the participants are such young children, a higher level of teacher guidance is necessary.

CONCLUSIONS AND FUTURE DIRECTIONS

When we first examined the transcripts described here we were puzzled: Here were constructivist teachers, implementing a curriculum designed to increase children's autonomy, yet most of their interactions with the children involved direction. However, as the patterns in the data emerged, it became clear that cooking with young children is distinctly different from other child-directed or play-based activities in early childhood classrooms. In fact, in many ways cooking does not seem to be a truly child-selected activity. Although children participated in choosing a partner and a food to cook, the cooking routine was already established by the teachers, and the recipes, utensils, and ingredients were not a matter of choice but tools that exist in a cultural context beyond the range of children's control. This suggests that the teachers' strategies were not always a function of their teaching philosophies or of the curriculum but of characteristics of activities and day-to-day classroom living.

Cooking with young children is distinctly different from other child-directed or play-based activities in early childhood classrooms. Although the process of preparing food involves hands-on manipulation of objects, the primary goal is to create a finished product correctly. In addition, there may be concerns about safety (e.g., boiling water or sharp knives), wasting food, and social issues (whether the other children will like the food). These constraints leave little room for error, requiring the teacher to provide direction to ensure that the project proceeds successfully.

However, not every task involved in cooking involves the same risk of error: Choosing a less effective method of removing butter from the package would not have the same detrimental effect as putting an entire bowl of sauce on one muffin. The teachers in the present study appeared to adjust their levels of direction and control according to the level of allowable error in the task, as well as in response to the level of difficulty the child had completing the task independently. Through this process of scaffolding (Wood et al., 1976) the teachers adjusted their interactional styles, helping the children to complete tasks as independently as possible. For example, teachers made decisions about what to do next but transferred responsibility for deciding how to perform a task and for actual task completion to the children.

Another explanation for the discrepancy between the teachers' general philosophies and their particular teaching styles during certain aspects of cooking may be related to cultural meanings and goals for cooking. In conversations with the researcher, the teachers discussed cooking in terms of curricular goals, such as literacy, number, and physical knowledge involved in cooking. However, in the context of actually implementing the cooking activities, the main goal emphasized by the teachers was making food that could be eaten that morning for snack.

The difference between the teachers' reports and their practices can be explained by the distinction made by Wertsch, Minick, and Arns (1984) between formal schooling activities and the learning that occurs within the context of home economic activities. In school students are encouraged to participate in goal-directed actions even if they are unable to complete them efficiently and correctly. In contrast, activities in the home (which would include cooking) focus on efficient, error-free performance, in which children are allowed to perform tasks for which they developed some competence while more complex tasks are introduced one step at a time. Rogoff (1990) describes a similar process in which children develop into skilled participants in society through routine, guided participation in ongoing cultural activities. In the present study, the teachers seemed to be "teaching how to cook" as a cultural activity rather than facilitating exploration and experimentation. It could be that the cooking activities, although conceptualized by the teachers as educational and process-oriented, actually emphasized production, and reproduction of cultural activities, thereby requiring changes in the styles used by the teachers. In future research, it would be important to examine how interactional styles during cooking compare to those process-oriented activities, such as problem solving in blocks, Play-Doh, or pretend play. A comparative examination of various classroom activities would reveal more comprehensive picture of teacher guidance in constructivist classrooms.

In conclusion, the results of our study demonstrate that teacher–child interaction is complex and flexible, changing to meet the many, sometimes conflicting, demands of various tasks. The constructivist teachers we observed did not simply implement the instructional techniques endorsed by their philosophical orientation but, instead, used different interactional styles in various circumstances. Our findings suggest that more attention be paid to the situations in which teachers use particular strategies and thus call for expansion of previously theorized teacher–child interactional styles as exemplifying constructivist orientation (DeVries et al., 1991; DeVries & Zan, 1994).

Based on our observations and previous experiences, we cast the role of a constructivist teacher as one of a guide who understands how much and what type of collaboration the child needs to solve a problem or complete a task as independently as possible. A constructivist teacher recognizes the social and cultural expectations which may at times lead adults to give directions as he or she is aware of the many opportunities for exploration and invention that are not bound by these constraints. Perhaps this conceptualization can help constructivist teachers develop a new understanding of the "teachable moment," that constructivist teaching, like constructivist learning, is a process that is discovered and explored, manipulated, and evaluated.

REFERENCES

Cazden, C. B. (1988). *Classroom discourse: The language of teaching and learning.* Portsmouth, NH: Heinemann.

DeVries, R., Haney, J. P., & Zan, B. (1991). Sociomoral atmosphere in direct-instruction, eclectic, and constructivist kindergartens: A study of teachers' enacted interpersonal understanding. *Early Childhood Research Quarterly, 6,* 449–471.

DeVries, R., & Kohlberg, L. (1987). *Programs of early education: The constructivist view.* New York: Longman.

DeVries, R., & Zan, B. (1994). *Moral classrooms, moral children: Creating a constructivist atmosphere in early education.* New York: Teachers College Press.

Duckworth, E. (1987). *The having of wonderful ideas and other essays on teaching and learning.* New York: Teachers College Press.

Fowell, N., & Lawton, J. T. (1992). Dependencies between questions and responses during small-group instruction in two preschool programs. *Early Childhood Research Quarterly, 7,* 415–439.

French, T., & MacLure, M. (1983). Teachers? questions, pupils? answers: An investigation of questions and answers in the infant classroom. In M. Stubbs & H. Hillier (Eds.), *Readings on language, schools, and classrooms* (pp. 193–211). London: Methuen.

Gauvain, M., & Rogoff, B. (1989). Collaborative problem solving and children's planning skills. *Developmental Psychology, 25,* 139–151.

Göncü, A., & Becker, J. (2000). The problematic relation between developmental research and educational practice. *Human Development, 43,* 266–272.

Göncü, A., & Cannella, V. (1996). The role of teacher assistance in children's construction of intersubjectivity during conflict resolution. In M. Killen (Ed.), *Children's autonomy, social competence, and interactions with adults and other children: Exploring connections and consequences* (pp. 57–69). San Francisco: Jossey-Bass.

Göncü, A., & Rogoff, B. (1998). Children's categorization with varying adult support. *American Educational Research Journal, 35,* 333–349.

Göncü, A., & Weber, E. (2000). Preschoolers' classroom activities and interactions with peers and teachers. *Early Education and Development, 11,* 1, 93–107.

Kamii, C., & DeVries, R. (1993). *Physical knowledge in preschool education: Implications of Piaget's theory.* Washington DC: National Association for the Education of Young Children. (Original work published 1978)

Martinez, M. G., & Teale, W. H. (1993). Teacher storybook reading style: A comparison of six teachers. *Research in the Teaching of English, 27,* 175–199.

Mercer, N. (1995). *The guided construction of knowledge*. Clevedon, UK: Multilingual Matters.

Piaget, J. (1965). *The moral judgement of the child*. London: Free Press. (Original work published 1932)

Radziszewska, B., & Rogoff, B. (1988). Influence of adult and peer collaborators on children's planning skills. *Developmental Psychology, 24*, 840–848.

Radziszewska, B., & Rogoff, B. (1991). Children's guided participation in planning imaginary errands with skilled adult or peer partners. *Developmental Psychology, 27*, 381–389.

Rogoff, B. (1990). *Apprenticeship in thinking: Cognitive development in social context*. New York: Oxford University Press.

Rogoff, B., & Wertsch, J. (Eds.). (1984). *Children's learning in the "Zone of Proximal Development"*. San Francisco: Jossey-Bass.

Vygotsky, L. S. (1978). *Mind in society*. Cambridge, MA: Harvard University Press.

Wertsch, J. V., Minick, N., & Arns, F. (1984). The creation of context in joint problem-solving. In B. Rogoff & J. Lave (Eds.), *Everyday cognition* (pp. 151–171). Cambridge, MA: Harvard University Press.

Wood, D., Bruner, J. C., & Ross, G. (1976). The role of tutoring in problem solving. *Journal of Child Psychology and Psychiatry, 17*, 89–100.

15

❧

Visions and Realities
of Achieving Partnership
Parent–School Relationships
at the Turn of the Century

DOUGLAS R. POWELL

Parents' relationships with early childhood programs and schools received renewed and sharpened attention in the final decade of the 20th century. Recent public- and private-sector recommendations on ways to improve children's learning and development consistently include policies and practices aimed at strengthening continuity in children's experiences across families, early childhood programs, and schools.

The need to maintain positive ties between families and schools, including programs of early education and care, is a familiar theme in the United States, but prominent blueprints and vision statements issued in the last decade have strengthened the language commonly used to describe the desired nature of family–school relationships. Increasingly the emphasis is on family–school *partnerships* that entail shared decision making about children's program and school experiences. This is progress in an arena that generally dodges the delicate matter of power by using fuzzy terminology (e.g., parent involvement and parent participation). It also is a major conceptual shift from the conventional approach to parent–teacher relationships as a task of parents serving as helpmates in implementing school-determined agendas.

Rationales for fostering parent–school partnerships are rooted in the idea that children's experiences and outcomes are strengthened when parents and teachers help children effectively manage the inevitable differences between family and school (Powell, 1989). Interpersonal relationships—between teachers and children, and between teachers and parents—are viewed as central to the task of facilitating continuity and linkages between children's experiences in family and school settings (Elicker, 1997). Increasingly the quality of teacher–child attachment security is considered a key indicator of quality in early childhood programs (e.g., Howes & Oldham, this volume), and children's learning is thought to be most effective when it builds on what children bring to the setting, including their existing understandings and cultural practices and beliefs (Bransford, Brown, & Cocking, 1999) as well as their family and cultural backgrounds (Bredekamp & Copple, 1997). Parent–teacher relationships provide a means by which "complementary and mutually reinforcing environments" for young children can be cultivated at home and at school (Bowman, Donovan, & Burns, 2000, p. 14) and also are an important dimension of children's social environments (Bronfenbrenner, 1979).

In many ways, attention to school–family relationships is a uniquely American interest driven by a democratic spirit of citizen participation in schools and other institutions that contribute to the common good, and by a doctrine of parental rights in decisions about the child's best interest. These principles are evident in legislative provisions for parent participation, such as the "maximum feasible participation" of parents in programs sponsored by the Economic Opportunity Act of 1964 and laws governing parents' decision-making role in educational placement and service plans for children with special needs. Attention to the involvement of parents in schools and early childhood programs is higher in the United States than in many other Western, industrialized countries (e.g., Cochran, 1993).

Despite the traditions of citizen participation and parental rights, the emphasis on shared decision making and program responsiveness to families is a relatively recent development. A "professional knows best" assumption dominated school–family relationships for a good portion of the 20th century, and parental attempts to influence school policies and practices were carefully controlled (Powell & Diamond, 1995). There are notable exceptions to this pattern in the early childhood field, especially the parent cooperative preschool movement and Head Start (Powell, 1991). Generally, however, the task of achieving continuity between home and school has been approached through parent education and other school-initiated strategies aimed at encouraging parents to understand and hopefully subscribe to teachers' views of child development and appropriate ways of teaching children (Powell & Diamond, 1995). As Fein (1980) submits in a thoughtful historical perspective on contrasting approaches to relations between professionals and parents, the boundaries between home and school called for the "informed professional" to govern at school and the "informed parent" to govern at home (p. 155). The "informed professional" idea entered a period of decline and disparagement beginning in the late 1960s, as Fein notes, and the notion of parent as full-fledged participant in children's education has gained at least rhetorical support in the last three decades.

Probably the most prominent vision of parent–school partnerships set forth in the 1990s is the National Education Goal that expects every school to "promote partnerships that will increase parental involvement and participation in promoting the social, emotional, and academic growth of children." This goal was added in 1994 as the eighth and last goal of the National Education Goals, originally established in 1989. Specific objectives include "shared educational decision-making at school" and "parental responsibility for ensuring that schools are ... held to high standards of accountability" (National Education Goals Panel, 1994, p. 11). Within the private sector, notable attempts to influence the shape of home–school relations include a Carnegie Corporation blueprint for improving educational outcomes (Carnegie Task Force on Learning in the Primary Grades, 1996) and a corporate-led report that recommends collaborations among schools, businesses, and parent employees (Casey & Burch, 1997).

The federal Department of Education has been particularly active in promoting the concept of parent–school partnership. The same year home–school partnership was added to the National Education Goals, the U.S. Secretary of Education issued a widely disseminated report on the benefits of family–school connections (U.S. Department of Education, 1994). The current emphasis on partnership is striking in comparison to claims made nearly two decades earlier by the nation's education commissioner about parent education as the key to improved educational outcomes ("every child has a right to a trained parent," Bell, 1975, p. 271). The Secretary of Education's 1994 report also moves beyond simplistic notions of how to improve connections between families and schools by acknowledging, for example, that difficult conditions faced by many families today and "mismatches between the practices of schools, the skills of their staffs, and the needs and circumstances of many students' families" contribute to the formidable nature of fostering family–school partnerships (U.S. Department of Education, 1994).

This chapter examines emerging expectations regarding the nature of parent–school partnerships as represented in theoretical perspectives and professional practice standards. I also review research depicting the state of parent–teacher relationships and offer needed directions in achieving parent–school partnerships. The chapter's focus is early childhood programs and elementary schools. It is organized into three major sections: visions of partnership, realities of partnership, and needed directions.

VISIONS OF PARTNERSHIP

Theoretical Perspectives

The growing use of partnership language in visions of parent–school relations reflects an underlying shift in theoretical perspectives on family–school connections. For a major portion of the 20th century, a specialization model prevailed in approaches to family–school relations at the elementary and secondary school level. In this model, schools and families are seen as having unique missions or spheres of responsibility that are best carried out by maintaining "optimal social distance" between the two (Litwak & Meyer, 1974). Sociological theory has contributed significantly to the idea that schools and families have special functions and therefore separate influences on the child. In an early sociological analysis of teaching, Waller (1932) argued that conflicts between parents and teachers are an inevitable and natural result of differences in the scope and function of families and schools. He submitted it would be a "sad day" if parent–teacher relations succeeded in "getting parents to see children more or less as teachers see them" (Waller, 1932, p. 69). The "separate influences" view calls for schools to maintain "optimal social distance . . . between the extremes of intimacy and isolation" (Litwak & Meyer, 1974, p. 6). A premise is that basic educational processes require experts to handle uniform tasks and nonexperts to handle nonuniform tasks. According to this view, communication between families and schools should not bring them into such close contact that "they impair the social structures that are required to sustain each" (Litwak & Meyer, 1974, p. 13). Early childhood programs never fully fit this model because the scope of responsibility cast by programs (usually the "whole child") typically extends to domains that are also the clear responsibility of families (Powell, 1989). In general, the younger the child, the greater the overlap of tasks assumed by parents and early childhood workers (Katz, 1980).

For several decades now, the focus on schools and families as separate influences has been replaced by attention to shared responsibilities (Connors & Epstein, 1995). Theoretical recognition of shared or joint responsibilities of schools and families received major attention in Bronfenbrenner's (1979) propositions about the conditions that enhance the development of individuals who function in multiple settings (a meso-system). His hypotheses about ways to enhance a setting's developmental potential pertain to the compatability of role demands and goal consensus between settings, supportive linkages between settings, entry into a new setting in the company of a familiar and trusted person, and the mode (personal) and nature (open and two-way) of communications between settings. The intent of interconnections is not to strive toward sameness across settings, however. Bronfenbrenner's theoretical work recognizes the developmental benefit of unique experiences in different settings and the need to maintain respectful boundaries. Sustained participation in diverse environments may enhance cognitive competence and social skills, for instance. Also, he argued that interconnections should not "undermine the motivation and capacity of those persons who deal directly with the child to act on his behalf" (e.g., school personnel who degrade parents or parental demands that undermine the morale or effectiveness of the teacher) (Bronfenbrenner, 1979, p. 218).

More recently, Fitzgerald and Göncü (1993) have applied several Vygotskian ideas to a theoretical framework of parent–teacher relations in which Vygotsky's concept of intersubjectivity is defined as shared understanding constructed by parents and school staff in interaction with each other about what children should learn and how they should learn it. They envision parents and school staff working sensitively within each other's zone of proximal development to negotiate an acceptable plan of education. Further, for young children in low-income, urban neighborhoods in particular, Fitzgerald and Göncü submit that early education is most beneficial if school activities are made meaningful for children through the incorporation of activities that parents value and in which the children engage at home.

Partnership concepts also are prominent in recent theoretical treatments of relations between helping professionals and their "clients," and between researchers and their "subjects." In the conception of partnerships in research, clinical, and educational settings offered by Bibace (1999), professionals and their counterparts strive toward complementarity and reciprocity in their interactions with one another through an appreciation and encouragement of the distinctive contributions that each participant brings to the relationship. Bibace notes that in traditional relationships between professionals and their counterparts, interactions follow a sequence controlled by the professional in which the professional asks questions about areas he or she considers to be relevant and then independently evaluates the counterpart's responses. In the partnership ideal set forth by Bibace, interactions follow a question–answer–feedback sequence characterized by flexible dialogue and symmetry in the flow of questions and information. Each participant asks and receives answers to his or her questions and provides the other with feedback. Interactions are to address issues as well as problems and, moreover, are to recognize that in contrast to problems, issues do not have solutions and thus the professional has no greater authority than his or her counterpart in discerning a course of action. Similarly, a conceptualization of helping professionals as "resource collaborators" by Tyler, Pargament, and Gatz (1983) assumes that both parties are origins or active agents and experts in organizing, conducting, and evaluating their joint work. The words in quotation marks in the lead sentence of this paragraph are deemed inappropriate in the emerging partnership language system. Indeed, the fourth edition of the publication manual of the American Psychological Association (1994) recommends that "participant" be used instead of "subject" in references to human beings engaged in research.

Recent Practice Standards

Images of relations between parents and early childhood programs as collaborative ventures are set forth in practice standards issued recently by the National Association for the Education of Young Children (NAEYC) and the National Parent–Teacher Association (PTA). Both sets of standards—one from a professional group and the other from a parent organization—embrace a two-way flow of influence between families and schools that modifies long-standing assumptions of school–family relations: (1) "parents may go too far" if entitled to a direct role in shaping program policies and practices, and (2) professionals have greater insight than do parents into matters of childrearing. Historically, the first assumption has led to policies and practices that curtail parental influence on curriculum and classroom, and the second assumption has given educators an implicit license to tell parents how to rear their child.

The NAEYC vision of program–family relationships is an integral part of the association's statement on developmentally appropriate practice (Bredekamp & Copple, 1997) and its criteria for accreditation of early childhood programs (NAEYC, 1998). The revised version of the developmentally appropriate practice statement issued in 1997 includes "establishing reciprocal relationships with families" as one of five interrelated dimensions of good early childhood professional practice. There are eight specific guidelines for program practices in this area, including the desired qualities of reciprocal relationships (see the description of the 1997 NAEYC statement two paragraphs below); regular and frequent two-way communication, parent participation in child and program decisions such as child assessment and program planning, and assistance to families in connecting with community resources. In addition, there are 11 policy and practice items pertaining to relationships among teachers and families in the current NAEYC program accreditation criteria (NAEYC, 1998). For instance, the criteria call for procedures for orienting children and families to a program and for communication systems that enable parents and staff to share day-to-day happenings that may affect children.

Two other NAEYC position statements emphasize a family-centered approach to early education and care. The statement on linguistic and cultural diversity recommends that teachers become familiar with the child's community, for example (NAEYC, 1996a). The NAEYC code of ethical conduct emphasizes principles of mutual trust in parent–teacher relations as well as teacher respect for family childrearing values and decision-making rights (NAEYC, 1996b). The themes of collaboration and working within family contexts also are central to practices recommended by the Division for Early Childhood (DEC) of the Council for Exceptional Children, which note that "practices should honor and facilitate the family's caregiving and decision-making roles . . . (and) may be delivered in a manner that conforms to the family's life style, priorities, and concerns" (Sandall, McLean, Santos, & Smith, 2000, p. 9).

The 1997 NAEYC statement provides greater clarity and guidance on the nature of the program–family relationships than the original developmentally appropriate practice statement issued in 1986 (Bredekamp, 1986). Specifically, the 1997 view of program relations with families emphasizes "reciprocal relationships" between teachers and families, and indicates the desired qualities of collaborative partnerships with families entail "mutual respect, cooperation, shared responsibility, and negotiation of conflicts toward achievement of shared goals" (Bredekamp & Copple, 1997, p. 22). The 1986 statement framed parents' contributions to decisions about their child's care and education as a right and a responsibility and did not emphasize the process dimensions of program–family relations highlighted in the 1997 report.

A basis of stronger language about program–family relations in the 1997 NAEYC statement is that there is explicit recognition that social and cultural contexts are major influences on children's development, and need to be respected in decisions about developmentally appropriate practice. Knowledge of social and cultural contexts was not a major factor in the 1986 statement, which emphasized age and individual appropriateness. Consistent with the elevated attention to social and cultural contexts of child development, the 1997 statement uses the term "families" rather than "home" (1986) in the main guideline about program–family relations.

Importantly, the 1997 statement specifies that "teachers *and parents* share their knowledge of the child and understanding of children's development and learning as part of day-to-day communication and planned conferences. Teachers support families in ways that maximally promote family decisionmaking capabilities and competence" (Bredekamp & Copple, 1997, p. 22, italics added). The 1986 statement did not include *and parents* in the main (boldface type) guideline about information sharing or the sentence about teachers supporting families in ways that "maximally promote family decisionmaking."

Language also has changed in the federal performance standards for Head Start. The process of learning about families through needs assessments is now to occur through an individualized Family Partnership Agreement that sets forth family goals, responsibilities, timetables, and strategies for achieving the goals plus monitoring progress. The intent is to establish a collaborative partnership with parents that is built on mutual trust and an understanding of family goals, strengths, necessary services, and other supports (Powell, 2000).

The NAEYC and DEC practice standards are mirrored in the guidelines for the preparation of early childhood professionals developed by NAEYC, DEC, and the National Board for Professional Teaching Standards (NAEYC, 1996c). For example, the NAEYC guidelines indicate that institutions of higher education should prepare early childhood personnel to establish and maintain positive, collaborative relationships with families; demonstrate sensitivity to differences in family structures and social and cultural backgrounds; apply family-systems theory and knowledge; and link families with a range of family-oriented services based on identified resources, priorities, and concern.

In 1997, the National PTA established six national standards for parent/family involvement programs: (1) communication between home and school is regular, two-way, and meaningful; (2) parenting skills are promoted and supported; (3) parents play an integral role in assisting student learning; (4) parents are welcome in the school, and their support and assistance are sought; (5) parents are full partners in the decisions that affect children and families; and (6) community resources are used to strengthen schools, families, and student learning (National PTA, 1997). The standards are consistent with Epstein's widely used typology of family–school collaboration (e.g., Epstein, Coates, Salinas, Sanders, & Simon, 1997).

Indicators of successful programs are provided for each of the six standards in the PTA's position statement. One of the quality indicators for the fifth standard pertaining to decision making, for example, calls for schools to provide "understandable, accessible, and well-publicized processes" for parents to influence decisions, raise issues or concerns, appeal decisions, and resolve problems (National PTA, 1997, p. 18). Indicators of success in meeting this standard also focus on the inclusion of parents in decision-making and advisory committees, the provision of current information regarding school policies and practices, and parent participation in setting goals and evaluating progress in meeting goals.

The PTA's 1997 standards—issued during the organization's 100th year—are in stark contrast with ideas about the parent–teacher relationship promoted by the PTA during the first half of the 20th century. In this earlier period, the PTA had a bylaw stipulating that all local units and branches of the organization should "not seek to direct the administrative activities of the schools or to control their policies" (National Congress of Parents and Teachers, 1944, p. 184). Accordingly, a study of 1924–1925 activities of almost 800 local parent–teacher associations in nine states found that attempts to influence school boards regarding teaching staff decisions represented the smallest amount of local association activity (2.6%). Even feedback from parents on school-driven decisions was generally deemed to be out of bounds. Less than one-third of superintendents and principals surveyed in this study believed that "giving school officials judgment as to where school fails or succeeds" was an appropriate PTA objective; most believed an appropriate PTA role was facilitating acquaintance among parents and teachers. The director of the study, Professor Julian Butterworth of Cornell University, claimed it was doubtful a parent–teacher association should ever evaluate the work of the school because the association "may do much harm by attempting to exert undue influence in such matters" (Butterworth, 1929, p. 62). His concern was that "parents may go too far. They may insist that their point of view be adopted, when the professional officers with their greater insight may realize that it is neither feasible nor sound . . . " (p. 62).

What Is Emphasized, What Is Not

Concern that parents "may go too far" in influencing classroom or school decisions continues to persist in professional thinking about relations with families. The 1997 NAEYC statement on developmentally appropriate practice acknowledges that a family-centered approach to early childhood programs may be "misunderstood to mean that parents dictate all program content and professionals abdicate responsibility, doing whatever parents want regardless of whether professionals agree that it is in children's best interest." This concern "oversimplifies" relationships with families and falls far short of acknowledging the impor-

tance of an "environment in which parents and professionals work together to achieve shared goals for children" (Bredekamp & Copple,
1997, p. 22). Nonetheless, NAEYC's developmentally appropriate practice statement and program accreditation criteria do not offer detailed
provisions for ensuring that parents' contributions to decision making
are more than token exercises. Far stronger provisions are found in
Head Start's performance standards regarding program partnerships
with families, well-known for the requirement of a parent voting majority on the program policy council (Powell, 2000) and the legally mandated authority of parents in contributing to the development and ap-
proval of educational plans for children with identified special needs.
For example, the recommended practices issued by the Division for
Early Childhood of the Council for Exceptional Children specify that
family members and professionals "jointly develop appropriate family-
identified outcomes" (Sandall et al., 2000, p. 45).

The idea that lay persons need to be informed about appropriate
ways of rearing young children is perpetuated in current practice standards, but the 20th century's earlier view of program–family relations as
primarily a parent education activity has been abandoned. A significant
departure from the past is that now professional and parent perspectives
are to be joined in a common set of understandings and goals. Accordingly, both the NAEYC and National PTA standards include support for
the parenting role as an element of parent–school connections within the
framework of a two-way exchange of information about the child.

The absence of a "professional knows best" assumption in current
standards is particularly noticeable in the field of early childhood education, where roots of the parent education tradition run deep. The
nursery school movement of the early 1900s ambitiously approached
parent–teacher relations as a task of educating parents about child development. The title of the first National Society for the Study of Education yearbook devoted to early childhood education is indicative of this
trend: *Preschool and Parental Education* (Whipple, 1929). Nursery schools
typically provided parent education through home visits, individual
conferences and consultations with teachers, opportunities to observe
children and teacher–child interaction in the classroom, and parent
group meetings focused on childrearing topics. An impressive institu-
tional infrastructure was created during this era to support the dissemination of child development information to parents. Key players included the Child Study Association, which provided readings for
parent discussion groups; the federal Children's Bureau, which sponsored a series of publications for parents entitled *Infant Care*; the National Council on Parent Education, devoted to professional education
for parent educators; the U.S. Department of Agriculture's 2,000 county
home demonstration agents who taught parents home management

and childrearing skills, supported through the Smith-Lever Act of 1914; and *Parents* magazine, founded in 1926 as a tool for disseminating expert child development knowledge to parents and lay persons.

The prevailing assumption that teachers hold greater insight than parents into matters of childrearing was challenged on a number of grounds beginning with the civil rights movement in the 1960s and the parent advocacy efforts of families with children with special needs in the early 1970s (Powell & Diamond, 1995). Widespread demographic changes in the United States also contributed to greater sensitivity to issues of class, race, ethnicity, and culture in relations between professionals and laypersons. Scholars argued that the presumed superiority of professionals in defining parents' needs and prescribing solutions may undermine parents' sense of confidence, foster parental dependence on professionals, and diminish the authority of the family (e.g., Hess, 1980). Also, there were criticisms of the imposition of white, middle-class values on low-income and ethnic minority parents (e.g., Laosa, 1983), and questions about the validity and usefulness of expert knowledge about child development (e.g., Cochran & Woolever, 1983). At the same time, there was growth in popularity of the idea that what parents need most are support systems for a range of family functions such as managing work–family tensions (Bronfenbrenner, 1978).

A "parent knows best" assumption also is absent in current practice standards despite the growing policy interest in market-driven school reform initiatives. This comes as no surprise in practice guidelines prepared by a professional membership organization; research has long documented the desire for autonomy in decisions about curriculum and the general affairs of the classroom among early childhood (Joffe, 1977; Powell & Stremmel, 1987) and elementary school (Lortie, 1975) teachers. Because a tenet of professional status is freedom from client or lay control, it is a bold step for a professional group to embrace the idea of shared goals negotiated between parent and teacher. The field of early education and care is clearly cognizant of the "parent knows best" assumption of government funding and regulatory provisions. Policies in the United States emphasize parental choice in a diverse child-care marketplace as an extension of the country's support of religious, ideological, and cultural diversity in childrearing practices and the rights of parents in decisions affecting their child. One of the early childhood program field's responses to this condition is to provide parent consumers with expert information on indicators of high-quality environments for children (see Klein & Tarullo, this volume). An expectation is that this will raise the quality of programs overall, although research suggests that this intervention alone is unlikely to improve program quality on a widespread basis (Holloway & Fuller, 1992).

Do parent and professional have *equally* valuable views on what is best for the child's education? Existing practice standards vary in the explicitness of their guidance on this question. The NAEYC statement on developmentally appropriate practice includes this statement: "Teachers acknowledge parent choices and goals for children and respond with sensitivity and respect to parents' preferences and concerns without abdicating professional responsibility to children" (Bredekamp & Copple, 1997, p. 22). The Division for Early Childhood of the Council for Exceptional Children practice standards note that "family members and professionals work together and share information routinely and collaboratively to achieve family-identified outcomes" (Sandall, McLean, & Smith, 2000, p. 45), and the National PTA (1997) standards call for mechanisms that ensure that parent voices are heard in decision-making processes. Implicit in current practice standards is acknowledgment of the different and essential views of parent and professional (i.e., the professional has detailed knowledge of children in general; the parent has detailed knowledge about a particular child). Yet guidance on how to accommodate what is likely to be inevitable conflict in the parent–school relationship is missing or vague.

In sum, theoretical underpinnings of the growing emphasis on parent–school partnerships pertain primarily to anticipated benefits for the child when home and school complement and support one another. Recent conceptualizations of parent–teacher partnerships focus on a two-way flow of information and influence aimed at developing shared understandings of the child within a family's cultural and social context. This approach is in contrast with the view of parent–school communication as mostly a unidirectional, school-to-home system that maintains school and family as separate rather than connected influences on the child's development. The themes of partnership and collaboration in the theoretical literature are well represented in professional practice standards issued in the 1990s. Current standards offer important refinements in definitions of partnership, particularly an emphasis on shared decision making as a core attribute of parent–teacher collaborations. Yet existing standards vary in their perspective on the balance of power in the parent–teacher relationship and generally offer little or no guidance on how to accommodate conflict.

REALITIES OF PARTNERSHIP

The available evidence indicates that limited rather than full partnerships prevail in parent–teacher relationships in early childhood programs and elementary schools. The nature and extent of parent–teacher information exchange and shared decision making have received little research attention, even in programs or settings with decision-making provisions for parents. Studies show that communication is valued by both parents and child-care providers (Elicker, Noppe, Noppe, & Fortner-Wood, 1997; Kontos, Howes, Shinn, & Galinsky, 1995), but in center-based programs the frequency of communication is highly uneven across settings and parent–teacher dyads, and both parents and teachers are generally dissatisfied with the level of discussion (for a review, see Powell, 1989). Teachers have been found to hold negative judgments about the parenting skills of mothers (Kontos, 1984) and to have less daily communication with mothers held in low versus high esteem (Kontos & Dunn, 1989). In a review of the literature on parent involvement in early childhood education, Fitzgerald and Göncü (1993) conclude that conditions leading to shared parent–teacher understanding about what and how children should learn (intersubjectivity) do not exist or are not fully realized through common approaches to parent participation in programs.

A survey of a nationally representative sample of 900 public elementary schools enrolling kindergarten through eighth-grade students found that a majority provided information to parents on curriculum and student performance plus ways to promote learning at home and provided parent open houses, parent–teacher conferences, and opportunities to volunteer in school functions. Nearly half used compacts or learning contracts or other forms of voluntary written pledge agreements that define expectations and responsibilities of schools and parents as partners in student learning (Carey, Lewis, & Farris, 1998).

A separate national survey of 16,151 parents of first- through eighth-graders suggests that there is considerable room for improvement in school practices to involve families (Vaden-Kiernan & Chandler, 1996). On average, two of seven school practices were done "very well," according to parents. Specifically, more than one-half of parents indicated that their child's school did "very well" at letting them know between report cards how their child was doing in school (59%) and making them aware of chances to volunteer at the school (57%). Less than half of parents reported that their child's school did "very well" in five other practices: providing information about why their child was placed in particular classes (41%); providing information about how to help their child with his or her homework (38%); providing workshops, materials, or advice about how to help their child learn at home (37%); helping the parent understand what children at their child's age are like (35%); and providing information on community services to help the child or family (33%).

The two surveys just described focus on one-way flow of information, from school to family, and do not address the extent to which parents contribute to views of or decisions about their children or to what degree they feel welcome to do so with school personnel.

The growing ethnic, racial, and cultural diversity of the population in the United States has heightened concern about discontinuities between family and school or early childhood programs experienced by children from ethnic minority and/or low-income backgrounds. Today there are increased chances of children being cared for and taught by nonfamilial adults whose behavioral expectations and practices may be different from those of the children's parents or other family members (Cochran, 1993). For example, one study conducted in California found that significant numbers of minority children were in child-care centers where there was not an adult from the same ethnic or racial background. Some 40% of staff reported difficulty communicating with parents because they do not share a common language (Chang, 1993). Another California study found a relatively low percentage of centers enrolling children who spoke a language other than English also employing a teacher who spoke the same language. More than half of directors and one-third of the teaching staff across these centers reported that language barriers contributed to parent–staff communication difficulties (Whitebook, Sakai, & Howes, 1997).

In general, it appears that children from ethnic minority and/or low-income families are more likely than children from Euro-American and/or middle-class families to experience discontinuity between family and early childhood or school experiences (Powell, 1989). Home–school discontinuity has long been viewed as contributing to low academic achievement of ethnic minority children and children of parents with relatively limited levels of education (e.g., Laosa, 1982), although recent research on the academic achievement of children from ethnic minority backgrounds points to a good deal of complexity in how family factors influence children's academic performance (Okagaki & Frensch, 1998).

Parents and teachers have less contact when parents have low income or are ethnic minorities. In the aforementioned national survey of 900 public elementary schools, 28% of schools with a high poverty concentration reported that "most or all" parents attended the school open house compared to 72% of schools with a low concentration of poverty and 48% of schools with a moderate poverty concentration. There was a similar pattern for schools regarding the percentage of minority students. Schools with minority enrollments below 20% reported higher levels of parent attendance at school-sponsored events than did schools with minority enrollments of 20% or more (Carey et al., 1998).

For families receiving welfare, the Personal Responsibility and

Work Opportunity Reconciliation Act of 1996 (Public Law 104-193) appears to be transforming conventional understandings about the parenthood role. The Welfare-to-Work requirements now imposed on mothers suggest that "motherhood is second to work" in the eyes of the government (Holloway, Fuller, Rambaud, & Eggers-Pierola, 1997, p. 215). Welfare reform generally places serious constraints on parents' ability to participate fully in Head Start and other two-generation intervention programs that provide parenting education, early childhood education, adult education or job training, and other family support services. Parents' participation in activities aimed at self-sufficiency has been found to be associated with less involvement in Head Start (Parker et al., 1997). Also, a recent case study of the impact of welfare reform on the federal Even Start Family Literacy Program found that parents were less available for program participation and the intensity of some program components, especially those focused on parenting content, has been reduced to accommodate parents' time constraints (Alamprese & Voight, 1998). Thus, one of the expected outcomes of low-income parents' participation early childhood programs—that parents' feelings of self-worth and job-related skills would be enhanced by participating in classrooms and program decision-making structures—is quickly becoming less important if not irrelevant in the current era of welfare reform.

Contemporary views of family–school relations cast parents as a catalyst for improvements in school or program quality. As noted earlier, the National Education Goal on parent participation expects parents to hold schools to high standards of accountability, and parental choice policies (e.g., vouchers) expect that parents will improve program quality through a free-market selection process. Realities fall far short of these expectations.

The Carey et al. (1998) survey of 900 elementary schools found that parent input was not considered to a great extent in school decision making about allocation of funds, curriculum, design of special programs, library books or materials, discipline policies and procedures, and drug or alcohol abuse or health-related policies. Almost 75% of schools did not consider parent input at all in monitoring or evaluating teachers. School consideration of parent input did not vary by school characteristics (e.g., size, urbanicity, poverty level, and percent of minority enrollment), but schools with parent representation on policy councils or advisory boards were more likely to report considering parent input to a great or moderate extent than schools without these types of groups (Carey et al., 1998).

Advisory or decision-making committees that include parents are not the norm in early childhood programs. As noted earlier, an exception is Head Start, where performance standards have long mandated significant parent decision making on local policy councils. There also are legal provisions for parent decision making in educational plans for children with special needs. For child-care services, parent choice is commonly viewed as a market-driven mechanism for improving and maintaining quality programs. However, research indicates that parents are generally satisfied with their child-care arrangements, typically engage in a cursory examination of various child-care settings in relation to professional criteria, and usually include criteria that are not a part of (and sometimes in conflict with) professional benchmarks of quality (Holloway & Fuller, 1992). For example, in the Cost, Quality and Outcome study of 401 centers in four regions of the United States, parents placed their children in centers that did not fare well on experts' indicators of good quality, and they significantly overestimated the quality of care their children received. The sample was generally well educated with incomes that were higher than the median household income (Cryer & Burchinal, 1997).

High-quality child care is in short supply in the United States (e.g., Helburn, 1995; Kontos et al., 1995) and good care is not equally available to different family income groups (see Klein & Tarullo, this volume). While child-care subsidies for low-income parents appear to have enabled some families to access relatively better quality care, the 1996 welfare reform law gives states greater flexibility in how child-care funds are spent to help Welfare-to-Work populations. For example, states are encouraged but no longer required to conduct market rate surveys or to pay costs of care up to the 75th percentile of child-care rates (Zaslow, Tout, Smith, & Moore, 1998). Low-income parents' options for child care are limited, sometimes exclusively to the less expensive forms of informal family child care (Holloway et al., 1997), and recent data collected on nearly 1000 single mothers moving from welfare to work in California, Connecticut, and Florida indicate that their toddlers and preschool-age children are often in low-quality care characterized by hours in front of television or aimless wandering (Fuller & Kagan, 2000).

Since the 1970s, an image of early childhood programs as modern-day versions of the traditional extended family has been advanced as a vision of the multiple ways programs can connect with and support families (Galinsky & Hooks, 1977; Powell, 1987, 1998). Little is known about the role of programs in formally or informally helping families deal with a range of family support needs, although studies conducted in the 1970s suggest that some staff are resourceful helpers and listeners (Joffe, 1977). One service delivery model aimed at easing family stress is the Parent Services Project: this program comprises local parent committees that set policies, plan, and allocate funds for activities tailored to the interests of parents in an early childhood program (e.g., practical skills workshop such as car repair, family outings with children, adult social events without children, peer support groups) (Link, Beggs, & Seiderman, 1997). Research is needed on how such program provisions contribute to parent–teacher partnership development, especially shared decision making regarding program practices with children.

NEEDED DIRECTIONS
FOR ACHIEVING PARTNERSHIP

To achieve the parent–teacher partnerships envisioned in recent policy directions and practice standards, changes are needed in at least four areas: conceptual framework; resources available to families, schools, and programs; definitions of quality; and professional preparation.

Framework

Parent–teacher partnerships are relationship systems that evolve over time and accommodate unique characteristics and circumstances of all parties involved (e.g., Pianta & Walsh, 1996). A program or school view of relations with parents as a series of discrete events (e.g., parent–teacher conferences and open houses) that follow a teacher-directed protocol is unlikely to yield shared understandings or mutual exchange of information. Even the form of communication between parent and teacher for considering shared goals may need to be negotiated as a clear signal to a parent that his or her knowledge is valued and necessary to good practice (Fitzgerald & Göncü, 1993).

Parents and teachers are likely to approach their connection with one another through different relationship emphases. Elicker et al. (1997) found that confidence was a strong factor in both parents' and infant/toddler caregivers' views of what is important in the parent–staff relationship, but confidence meant somewhat different things to each party. Parents emphasized the caregivers' knowledge and skills and trust that the caregiver would give good care and be a caring person. Caregivers emphasized the importance of open communication and agreement about caregiving issues and the parents' childrearing knowledge and skill. Collaboration was a second major factor important to both parents and caregivers, but again each had a slightly different emphasis. A third factor was unique to each; parents emphasized affiliation or friendship ties with the caregiver, whereas the caregiver emphasized the caring capacities of the parent. Research along these lines is especially useful for guiding strategies to strengthen relationship development.

Clarity also is needed in practice standards on options for responding to conflict. Serious differences in the pedagogical preferences of parent and teacher are likely in some instances (e.g., the classic case is the parent who insists on teacher-directed drill and practice methods and the teacher who insists on child-initiated learning experiences). As noted earlier, limited help is offered in existing practice standards on ways to respond to conflict, although the field has other resources on this issue such as the antibias curriculum's suggested strategies for situations where teachers and parents disagree (Derman-Sparks and the ABC Task Force, 1989). There is variation in levels of conflict, of course, and more generally there is a need for practice standards to fully acknowledge that conflict is inevitable between families and schools and, when addressed through a balance of power and responsibilities between family and school, may yield positive benefits for the child (Lightfoot, 1978).

Resources

Relationship development requires time and other resources increasingly not available to families, early childhood programs, and schools. It is common to identify parent time constraints as a reason for limited involvement in school or early childhood programs, yet school and program resources are often stretched, too. The staff turnover rates in child-care and other early childhood programs jeopardize the quality of children's experiences as well as meaningful ties with parents. Perceived lack of staff time was identified as an impediment to fostering connections with parents by 56% of the some 900 elementary schools in the Carey et al. (1998) survey. Although lack of time can serve as a convenient excuse for avoiding tasks that are unfamiliar or threatening, it is also true that resource allocations such as class size and staff–child ratio have a direct influence on the capacity to individualize work with children and their families. Similarly, parents need calm, plentiful periods of time to tend to childrearing matters. Policies such as welfare reform need to consider the requirements of employment alongside cultural traditions associated with good parenting (Holloway et al., 1997).

Quality

Serious incorporation of parents' perspectives into ideas about quality education and care outside the home are needed if parent–teacher partnerships are to yield genuinely shared goals for children. In the early childhood field especially, existing definitions of quality have been developed by professionals without the contribution of parents (Larner, 1996). Moreover, widely used tools for assessing program quality give scant attention to relations with parents (Raab & Dunst, 1997). Many parents prefer teaching strategies that are more didactic and structured than encompassed by the profession's developmentally appropriate practice guidelines (for reviews, see Dunn & Kontos, 1997; Powell, 1994), and until recently the expectation was that early childhood professionals would promote the superior virtues of developmentally appropriate practice rather than engage in dialogue with parents about ways to accommodate preferences that, at least on the surface, appear to be developmentally inappropriate. The revised statement on developmentally appropriate practice moves beyond a good/bad dichotomy to enhance greater flexibility in approaches to children (Bredekamp & Copple, 1997), and recent recommendations for improving early education and care call for the inclusion of parents' perspectives in definitions of quality (e.g., Kagan & Cohen, 1996).

Preparation

Teachers need knowledge and skills for forming and sustaining partnerships with parents. Current provisions for addressing this need run from meager to nonexistent. A study of professional teacher preparation for family involvement found that most state teacher certification requirements do not mention working with parents or families. Of the 22 state requirements that do mention family involvement, typically the language entails vague phrases and imprecise terms. Nearly all state certification requirements that contain family involvement requirements and training were at the K–6 level, and some states mention it for early childhood certification only. A survey of 60 teacher education programs in the 22 states that mention family involvement in their certification requirements reveals that family involvement training was most often offered as part of a required course and in student teaching; fewer than half the teacher education programs provided a full course on family involvement (Shartrand, Weiss, Kreider, & Lopez, 1997). Findings of a recent study suggest that teachers need planning time and information about family and community issues as part of professional preparation for working with parents. One of the needs here may be to broaden teachers' conceptions of "parent involvement"; in this study, most teachers believed that homework supervision and enrichment experiences at home are the most valuable forms of parent involvement (Shumow & Harris, 2000).

CONCLUSION

A significant shift is under way in the prevailing conceptualization of parent–school relationships. Professionals are being asked to think about children's school and early childhood program experiences as part of the family's experience rather than focus narrowly on parents as part or extensions of the school. Accordingly, some long-standing terms such as "parent involvement" are increasingly useless and a new language to describe the desired family–school relationship is emerging. The concept of partnership as a shared decision-making process is now dominant in professional practice standards. The evolving image of the ideal relationship between parents and schools emphasizes jointly constructed understandings of appropriate educational experiences for the child that come about through flexible dialogue characterized by symmetry in the flow and initiation of questions and information among all participants. As demonstrated in this chapter, there is a huge gap between partnership ideals and realities, although research information is limited, generalizations are especially difficult in the diverse early childhood program field, and most of the extant literature has not been driven by recent conceptualizations of parent–school relationships. Nonetheless, available evidence suggests that major advances are needed in refinements of a conceptual framework, resources, and personnel preparation for supporting parent–teacher partnership development.

Professionals, parents, families, and schools have interests and concerns that, at best, are tangential to the care and education of young children yet can dominate the form and substance of parent–school interactions. Major stressors in a parent's (or teacher's) life, for example, can readily become the continuing focus of parent–teacher discussions or the recipient of program resources (e.g., workshops on stress management). Creating environments that facilitate a child's learning and development within the context of a family system requires respectful yet selective interest in family and program matters. Central to this task is the process of understanding and balancing multiple adult perspectives on what is best for a particular child and what is desired in the parent–teacher relationship. Clearly there is much to process—to sort through, make sense of, figure out how to act on—during the time-limited exchanges between parents and teachers. A challenge, then, is to maintain a clear eye on the fundamental purpose of parent–school relationships: to create a complementary and mutually supportive environments for each young child.

REFERENCES

Alamprese, J. A., & Voigt, J. D. (1998, December). *Delivering family literacy in the context of welfare reform: Lessons learned.* Cambridge, MA: Abt Associates.

American Psychological Association. (1994). *Publication manual of the American Psychological Association* (4th ed.). Washington, DC: Author.

Bell, T. H. (1975). The child's right to have a trained parent. *Elementary School Guidance and Counseling, 9,* 271–276.

Bibace, R. (1999). A partnership ideal. In R. Bibace, J. J. Dillon, & B. N. Dowds (Eds.), *Partnerships in research, clinical, and educational settings* (pp. 275–306). Stamford, CT: Ablex.

Bowman, B., Donovan, M. S., & Burns, M. S. (Eds.). (2000). *Eager to learn: Educating our preschoolers.* Washington, DC: National Academy Press.

Bransford, J. D., Brown, A. L., & Cocking, R. R. (1999). *How people learn: Brain, mind, experience, and school.* Washington, DC: National Academy Press.

Bredekamp, S. (Ed.). (1986). *Developmentally appropriate practice in early childhood programs serving children from birth through age 8.* Washington, DC: National Association for the Education of Young Children.

Bredekamp, S., & Copple, C. (Eds.). (1997). *Developmentally appropriate practice in early childhood programs* (rev. ed.). Washington, DC: National Association for the Education of Young Children.

Bronfenbrenner, U. (1978). Who needs parent education? *Teachers College Record, 79,* 767–787.

Bronfenbrenner, U. (1979). *The ecology of human development: Experiments by nature and design.* Cambridge, MA: Harvard University Press.

Butterworth, J. E. (1929). *The Parent–Teacher Association and its work.* New York: Macmillan.

Carey, N., Lewis, L., & Farris, E. (1998, January). *Parent involvement in children's education: Efforts by public elementary schools, NCES 98–032.* Washington, DC: National Center for Education Statistics, U.S. Department of Education.

Carnegie Task Force on Learning in the Primary Grades. (1996, September). *Years of promise: A comprehensive learning strategy for America's children.* New York: Carnegie Corporation of New York.

Casey, J. C., & Burch, P. E. (1997). *A catalyst for educational change: Promoting the involvement of working parents in their children's education.* Boston: Boston College Center for Work and Family.

Chang, H. (1993). *Affirming children's roots: Cultural and linguistic diversity in early care and education.* San Francisco: California Tomorrow.

Cochran, M. (1993). Public child care, culture, and society: Crosscutting themes. In M. Cochran (Ed.), *International handbook of child care policies and programs* (pp. 627–658). Westport, CT: Greenwood Press.

Cochran, M., & Woolever, F. (1983). Beyond the deficit model: The empowerment of parents with information and informal supports. In I. Sigel & L. Laosa (Eds.), *Changing families* (pp. 225–245). New York: Plenum Press.

Connors, L. J., & Epstein, J. L. (1995). Parents and schools. In M. Bornstein (Ed.), *Handbook of parenting* (pp. 437–458). Hillsdale, NJ: Erlbaum.

Cryer, D., & Burchinal, M. (1997). Parents as child care consumers. *Early Childhood Research Quarterly, 12,* 33–58.

Derman-Sparks, L., & the ABC Task Force (1989). *Anti-bias curriculum: Tools for empowering young children.* Washington, DC: National Association for the Education of Young Children.

Dunn, L., & Kontos, S. (1997). What have we learned about developmentally appropriate practice? *Young Children, 52*(5), 4–13.

Elicker, J. (1997). Developing a relationship perspective in early childhood research. *Early Education and Development, 8,* 5–10.

Elicker, J., Noppe, I. C., Noppe, L. D., & Fortner-Wood, C. (1997). The parent–caregiver relationship scale: Rounding out the relationship system in infant child care. *Early Education and Development, 8,* 83–100.

Epstein, J. L., Coates, L., Salinas, K. C., Sanders, M. G., & Simon, B. S. (1997). *School, family, and community partnerships: Your handbook for action.* Thousand Oaks, CA: Corwin Press.

Fein, G. G. (1980). The informed parent. In S. Kilmer (Ed.), *Advances in early education and day care* (Vol. 1, pp. 155–185). Greenwich, CT: JAI Press.

Fitzgerald, L. M., & Göncü, A. (1993). Parent involvement in urban early childhood education: A Vygotskian approach. In S. Reifel (Ed.), *Advances in early education and day care: Vol. 5. Perspectives on developmentally appropriate practices* (pp. 197–212). Greenwich, CT: JAI Press.

Fuller, B., & Kagan, S. L. (2000). *Growing up in poverty.* Berkeley: University of California, School of Education.

Galinsky, E., & Hooks, W. H. (1977). *The new extended family: Day care that works.* Boston: Houghton Mifflin.

Helburn, S. W. (Ed.). (1995). *Cost, quality, and child outcomes in child care centers. Technical report.* Denver: University of Colorado, Department of Economics, Center for Research in Economic and Social Policy.

Hess, R. D. (1980). Experts and amateurs: Some unintended consequences of parent education. In M. Fantini & R. Cardenas (Eds.), *Parenting in a multicultural society* (pp. 3–16). New York: Longman.

Holloway, S. D., & Fuller, B. (1992). The great child-care experiment: What are the lessons for school improvement? *Educational Research, 21,* 12–19.

Holloway, S. D., Fuller, B., Rambaud, M. F., Eggers-Piérola, C. (1997). *Through my own eyes: Single mothers and the cultures of poverty.* Cambridge, MA: Harvard University Press.

Joffe, C. E. (1977). *Friendly intruders: Childcare professionals and family life.* Berkeley: University of California Press.

Kagan, S. L., & Cohen, N. E. (1996). A vision for a quality early care and education system. In S. Kagan & N. Cohen (Eds.), *Reinventing early care and education: A vision for a quality system* (pp. 309–332). San Francisco: Jossey-Bass.

Katz, L. G. (1980). Mothering and teaching: Some significant distinctions. In L. G. Katz (Ed.), *Current topics in early childhood education* (Vol. 3, pp. 47–63). Norwood, NJ: Ablex.

Kontos, S. (1984). Congruence of parent and early childhood staff perceptions of parenting. *Parenting Studies, 1,* 5–10.

Kontos, S., & Dunn, L. (1989). Attitudes of caregivers, maternal experiences with day care, and children's development. *Journal of Applied Developmental Psychology, 10,* 37–51.

Kontos, S., Howes, C., Shinn, M., & Galinsky, E. (1995). *Quality in family child care and relative care.* New York: Teachers College Press.

Laosa, L. (1982). School, occupation, culture, and family: The impact of parental schooling on the parent–child relationship. *Journal of Educational Psychology, 74,* 791–827.

Laosa, L. (1983). Parent education, cultural pluralism, and public policy: The uncertain connection. In R. Haskins & D. Adams (Eds.), *Parent education and public policy* (pp. 331–345). Norwood, NJ: Ablex.

Larner, M. (1996). Parents' perspectives on quality in early care and education. In S. Kagan & N. Cohen (Eds.), *Reinventing early care and education: A vision for a quality system* (pp. 21–42). San Francisco: Jossey Bass.

Lightfoot, S. L. (1978). *Worlds apart.* New York: Basic Books.

Link, G., Beggs, M., & Seiderman, E. (1997). *Serving families.* Fairfax, CA: Parent Services Project.

Litwak, E., & Meyer, H. (1974). *School, family and neighborhood: The theory and practice of school-community relations.* New York: Columbia University Press.

Lortie, D. (1975). *School teacher.* Chicago: University of Chicago Press.

National Association for the Education of Young Children. (1996a). NAEYC position statement: Responding to linguistic and cultural diversity—Recommendations for effective early childhood education. *Young Children, 51,* 4–12.

National Association for the Education of Young Children. (1996b). NAEYC's code of ethical conduct: Guidelines for responsible behavior in early childhood education. *Young Children, 51,* 51–60.

National Association for the Education of Young Children. (1996c). *Guidelines for preparation of early childhood professionals.* Washington, DC: Author.

National Association for the Education of Young Children. (1998). *Accreditation criteria and procedures of the National Association for the Education of Young Children.* Washington, DC: Author.

National Congress of Parents and Teachers. (1944). *The Parent–Teacher Organization: Its origins and development.* Chicago: Author.

National Education Goals Panel. (1994). *National Education Goals Report: Building a nation of learners.* Washington, DC: Author.

National Parent–Teacher Association. (1997). *National standards for parent/family involvement programs.* Chicago: Author.

Okagaki, L., & Frensch, P. A. (1998). Parenting and children's school achievement: A multiethnic perspective. *American Educational Research Journal, 35,* 123–144.

Parker, F. L., Piotrokowski, C. S., Kessler-Sklar, S., Baker, A. J. L., Peay, L., & Clark, B. (1997). *Parent involvement in Head Start. Final report.* New York: National Council of Jewish Women, Center for the Child.

Pianta, R. C., & Walsh, D. J. (1996). *High-risk children in schools: Constructing sustaining relationships.* New York: Routledge.

Powell, D. R. (1989). *Families and early childhood programs* (Research Monograph Series No. 3). Washington, DC: National Association for the Education of Young Children.

Powell, D. R. (1991). Parents and programs: Early childhood as a pioneer in parent involvement and support. In S. L. Kagan (Ed.), *Ninetieth Yearbook of the National Society for the Study of Education, Part I: The care and education of America's young children: Obstacles and opportunities* (pp. 91–109). Chicago: National Society for the Study of Education.

Powell, D. R. (1994). Parents, pluralism, and the NAEYC statement on developmentally appropriate practices. In B. Mallory & R. New (Eds.), *Diversity and developmentally appropriate practices* (pp. 166–182). New York: Teachers College Press.

Powell, D. R. (1997). Parents' contributions to the quality of child care arrangements. In S. Reifel (Series Ed.) & C. J. Dunst & M. Wolery (Vol. Eds.), *Advances in early education and day care: Vol. 9. Family policy and practice in early child care* (pp. 133–155). Greenwich, CT: JAI Press.

Powell, D. R. (1998). Reweaving parents into the fabric of early childhood programs. *Young Children, 53,* 60–67.

Powell, D. R. (2000). The Head Start program. In J. L. Roopnarine & J. E. Johnson (Eds.), *Approaches to early childhood education* (3rd ed., pp. 55–75). Upper Saddle River, NJ: Prentice-Hall.

Powell, D. R., & Diamond, K. E. (1995). Approaches to parent–teacher relationships in U.S. early childhood programs during the twentieth century. *Journal of Education, 177,* 71–94.

Powell, D. R., & Stremmel, A. J. (1987). Managing relations with parents: Research notes on the teacher's role. In D. L. Peters & S. Kontos (Eds.), *Continuity and discontinuity of experience in child care* (pp. 115–127). Norwood, NJ: Ablex.

Raab, M. M., & Dunst, C. J. (1997). Early childhood program assessment scales and family support practices. In S. Reifel (Series Ed.) & C. J. Dunst & M. Wolery (Vol. Eds.), *Advances in early education and day care: Vol. 9. Family policy and practice in early child care* (pp. 105–131). Greenwich, CT: JAI Press.

Sandall, S., McLean, M. E., Santos, R. M., & Smith, B. J. (2000). DEC's new recommended practices: The context for change. In S. Sandall, M. E. McLean, & B. J. Smith (Eds.), *DEC recommended practices in early intervention/early childhood special education* (pp. 5–13). Denver, CO: Division for Early Childhood of the Council for Exceptional Children.

Sandall, S., McLean, M. E., & Smith, B. J. (Eds.). (2000). *DEC recommended practices in early intervention/early childhood special education.* Denver, CO: Division for Early Childhood of the Council for Exceptional Children.

Shartrand, A. M., Weiss, H. B., Kreider, H. M., & Lopez, M. E. (1997). *New skills for schools: Preparing teachers in family involvement.* Cambridge, MA: Harvard Graduate School of Education, Harvard Family Research Project.

Shumow, L., & Harris, W. (2000). Teachers' thinking about home-school relations in low-income urban communities. *School Community Journal, 10,* 9–24.

Tyler, F. B., Pargament, K. I., & Gatz, M. (1983). The resource collaborator role: A model for interactions involving psychologists. *American Psychologist, 38,* 388–398.

U.S. Department of Education (1994). *Strong families, strong schools.* Washington, DC: Author.

Vaden-Kiernan, N., & Chandler, K. (1996). *Parents' reports of school practices to involve families: Statistics in Brief.* Washington, DC: National Center for Education Statistics, U.S. Department of Education.

Waller, W. (1932). *The sociology of teaching.* New York: Russell and Russell.

Whipple, G. M. (Ed.). (1929). *Twenty-eighth Yearbook of the National Society for the Study of Education, Part I: Preschool and parental education.* Bloomington, IL: Public School Publishing.

Whitebook, M., Sakai, L., & Howes, C. (1997). *NAEYC accreditation as a strategy for improving child care quality: An assessment.* Washington, DC: National Center for the Early Childhood Work Force.

Zaslow, M., Tout, K., Smith, S., & Moore, K. (1998). Implications of the 1996 welfare legislation for children: A research perspective. In N. G. Thomas (Ed.), *Social policy report* (Vol. 12; pp. 1–34). Ann Arbor, MI: Society for Research in Child Development.

16

❧

Contexts of Quality

Implications for U.S. Child-Care Policy

ELISA L. KLEIN
LOUISA B. TARULLO

In the introduction to her chapter in this volume, Alison Clarke-Stewart describes the genesis of *Day Care in Context* (Fein & Clarke-Stewart, 1973). As a fledgling student in developmental psychology, with a nascent but passionate interest in child care and early education, Greta G. Fein's synthesis of the early work on day care provided Elisa L. Klein with a means to connect a growing understanding of concepts and contexts of development with variations found in young children's care and education. More than a quarter century later, *Day Care in Context* stands as one of the first texts to address the complex relationship between child care and issues of quality. Well before the genesis of three successive "waves" of research (Clarke-Stewart, 1987a) that have subsequently been viewed as shaping the direction of our understanding of child care (Howes & Hamilton, 1993; Lamb, 1998; Love, Schochet, & Meckstroth, 1996; Scarr, 1998), Fein and Clarke-Stewart accurately presaged one of the defining issues in child-care research today: the identification of quality and its relationship with child outcomes in early childhood settings.

How we define, identify, and measure essential indicators of quality, and how those indicators interact with characteristics of children and families, has become the primary focus of research in child care. Recent federal initiatives have targeted the quality issue as central to all research efforts. This investigation has a sense of urgency attached to it as the number of infants and young children in some form of nonparental care (13 million, or approximately 60% of all children under the age of 6 according to recent estimates; Hofferth, Shauman, Henke, & West, 1998) continues to increase at a brisk pace. The overall influx of women to part- and full-time employment, including the rapid movement of many mothers into the work force as a direct result of the implementation of welfare reform, has swelled the need for child care at an unprecedented rate. Three out of four children of employed mothers are in some form of child care (Urban Institute, 2000). In addition, there are many children of nonworking mothers who participate in child care and early education programs (National Center for Education Statistics, 1996).

With the increase in children entering care and early education programs such as Head Start and Early Head Start, various state prekindergarten programs, and a wide array of other child-care and preschool settings, it becomes imperative to examine the changing context of child care. There is mounting evidence that much of the quality of this care is often mediocre at best (Newman et al., 2000), and that the cost of even minimally adequate care is beyond the reach of many low- and moderate-income working families, despite federal and state subsidies (Administration on Children, Youth and Families, 1999a; Wertheimer, 1999). Several large-scale, longitudinal studies have persuasively shown that child-care quality does have an important and sustained impact on children's well-being on a number of important indicators (Cost, Quality and Outcomes Study, 1995, 1999; NICHD Early Childhood Care Research Network, 1994, 1998a, 1998b, 1999). This research, combined with what we already know about the long-term outcomes of early intervention (Barnett, 1995; Ramey & Campbell, 1991, 1994; Ramey et al., 2000), puts child-care quality issues at the forefront of concern for educators and psychologists today.

The increase of information and research on child care quality is unprecedented and there is much to learn from this work. A major source of funding for this research is from federal programs that have targeted quality as a critical issue. Concurrently, other policy initiatives have helped to establish an increased presence and focus on child care in various government agencies, as well as many private foundations, policy programs, research institutions, and advocacy groups. As a direct result of these initiatives, there are now meaningful ways in which the connections between research knowledge, policy, and practice are being articulated. It is too early to determine whether these intersections have resulted in a more rapid and/or a sustained impact on the quality of child care for families. Yet there is a growing acknowledgment of the importance of quality care for all young children, and there are now more directly identifiable links between recommendations for action and actual implementation of child-care policy. For instance, under federal law, a minimum of 4% of funds from each state's Child Care and Development Fund (CCDF; a combination of the federal Child Care and Development Block Grant (CCDBG), Social Security Act funds, and state matching funds) is to be set aside to improve the quality of child care and other services to parents (Administration on Children, Youth and Families, 1999a). However, whether these monies are being used appropriately and are resulting in tangible changes remain to be seen. Recent analyses demonstrate that only one in nine children eligible for child-care subsidies through the CCDF program is actually receiving this support, with wide variation across different states (Administration on Children, Youth and Families, 1999a; Newman et al., 2000; Schumacher & Greenberg, 1999).

As we move into this new century, the increase in our understanding about the effects of differential contexts of child care, combined with the concern related to the large number of young children in low-quality settings, prompts us to consider these issues closely. What does quality mean? What do we know about child-care quality and its connection to children's growth and development? How is this information being used to develop policy and inform practice? And, ultimately, is practice meeting the needs of young children and their families?

In this chapter, we address the emerging connections between research on child-care quality and policy and practice initiatives at the federal level in child care in the United States today. A review of the research on child-care quality is not the focus of this chapter as there are several excellent, timely reviews already available (see, e.g., Lamb, 1998; Love et al., 1996; Smith, 1998; Vandell & Wolfe, 2000). Rather, we explore the linkages between our increasing knowledge of child-care quality and how this work is influencing policy directions in the United States, particularly with respect to the changing face of initiatives related to low-income children and their families . We start with a brief overview of the historical antecedents of modern child-care issues in this country and tie current research on child-care quality into this perspective. Connections between this research and the establishment of policy priorities at the federal level are identified. Finally, we speculate on the future directions of research, policy, and practice initiatives aimed at improving the quality of child care in the United States.

FEDERAL INVOLVEMENT IN CHILD-CARE PROGRAMS: HOW DID WE GET HERE?

There has been government involvement in child-care programs throughout the past century, often tied to significant events such as the World War I and World War II or the Great Depression. Modern U.S. policies on child care and early education may be traced to the beginning of two distinct programmatic threads. The first was the early-intervention movement intended to ameliorate the effects of poverty, hallmarked by the authorization of the 1964 Economic Opportunity Act and the inauguration of Head Start in 1965 (Zigler & Styfco, 1996). The second was the initial attempt to meet the growing need for child care in the early 1970s, identified by the 1970 White House Conference on Children as the "most serious problem confronting U.S. families" (Zigler & Gilman, 1996, p. 103). The Comprehensive Child Development Act of 1971 was designed to include high-quality care for all families (with a sliding scale based on income), as well as the development of new child-care centers, and would have incorporated Head Start programs and other family services into these centers (Zigler & Gilman, 1996). Although the bill was passed by Congress, it was vetoed by President Nixon. Public disagreement about the role of government in the care of young children, early results from Head Start that initially did not appear promising, the expense of the appropriation, concern about uniform standards, and differing views on federal versus state control of regulations were all pivotal in the bill's demise (Barnett, 1993; Fein & Clarke-Stewart, 1973; Zigler & Gilman, 1996). Subsequent to this veto, similar proposals (e.g., the Child Care Act of 1979) also failed and reflected public disagreement about social issues such as working mothers and the role of the federal government in family life. Attempts to strengthen and enforce national child care standards, first developed as the Federal Interagency Day Care Requirements (FIDCR) in the late 1960s and reactivated during the Carter Administration, also languished well into the 1980s as child-care legislation continued to be a flashpoint for disagreements related to intersections between public policy, children's development and care, and family function (Barnett, 1993; Zigler & Gilman, 1996).

Although there were ongoing federal programs that supported certain components of child care and early education (with Head Start as the most notable example) in effect during this time, it was not until the late 1980s that some movement toward more comprehensive policies began to occur. Compelling evidence about the importance of early education and care for all children, but especially for children who were the most vulnerable due to poverty and other environmental risks, was mounting. This evidence, combined with the surge of women into the work force, brought about the call for a reexamination of extant policies and the advent of modern child-care reforms (Zigler & Gilman, 1993).

Still, there was hesitancy, or even opposition, on the part of many regarding the establishment of any sweeping changes in child care or other policies to support families in the United States, as well as disagreement about just whom these policies should target. Although most other industrialized nations have already established a long history of support for family and child policies that include child-care and family-leave programs, (for a review of such policies, see Boocock, 1995; Kammerman, 1996), the United States has not. Kammerman (1996) notes:

> The premise undergirding family policy wherever it develops, is that society needs children, and needs them to be healthy, well-educated, and, eventually, productive workers, citizens and parents. . . . Characteristic of family policy in the advanced industrialized world is 1) a concern for *all* children and their families, not just poor families or families with problems, although these and other family types may receive special attention; and 2) an acknowledgment that doing better by children requires help for parents and the family unit as well. (pp. 31–32)

U.S. social policy does not share these characteristics, at least not yet. Despite calls for a shared vision of a future that enhances child and family well-being through a variety of services and systems of support (e.g., Carnegie Task Force on Meeting the Needs of Young Children, 1994; Kagan & Cohen, 1997), it has been difficult to get off the "starting block." Kagan and Cohen (1997) speculate on the reasons for this failure:

> Over the last decade, scholars have argued persuasively that the quality crisis in early care and education may also be rooted in the profound ambivalence within American culture toward mothers and their care-taking roles. On the one hand, we revere the primacy and privacy of motherhood and family, resisting policies and programs that appear to intervene in domestic life. Indeed, many Americans continue to believe that out-of-home care is harmful, despite evidence to the contrary. On the other hand, we dismiss the care of young children as mindless, custodial work, devaluing the contributions of stay-at-home mothers as well as paid caregivers. We pursue national policies that lead to non-parental care for more and more young children,

by favoring "workfare," for example, or by not providing paid parental leave. (p. 4)

This ambivalence about the role of women, the effectiveness of early education programs, and the value of child-care work is further influenced by deeply held beliefs that poor children and families got there by their own design and, with few exceptions, do not deserve governmental supports. Taken together, these attitudes mitigate heavily against any public support for developing a comprehensive approach to child care and early education.

Despite the reluctance and general antipathy, there has been some movement toward developing federal child-care policies in the United States. These efforts have been primarily linked to changes in regulations related to child-care subsidies for low-income families and recipients of welfare, which are discussed later. Proposals to more fully fund other child-care and early education programs either have not been approved or have been underfunded. For example, in 1998, President Clinton proposed major new funding of child-care and early education programs, but these proposals failed when tobacco settlements, intended to be the source for some of the monies, were not approved (Sawhill, 1999). A broader national policy, similar to those of other industrialized countries that encompass *all* children and families, still remains elusive.

A Growing Federal Presence in Child-Care Issues

Within the last decade, a growing federal interest in child-care and early education issues began to take shape. Spurred on by new attention to the importance of early development and mounting evidence that type of child care differentially influences development (e.g., Burchinal, Roberts, Nabors, & Bryant, 1996; Clarke-Stewart, 1987b; Cost, Quality and Outcomes Study, 1995; Howes, Phillips, & Whitebrook, 1992; Phillips & Howes, 1987), increased focus was being paid to understanding the factors that contribute to quality programs for young children.

Definitions of Quality

Although there is no standard definition of quality for child care, both structural features of the setting and the program (e.g., regulative components such as health and safety requirements, group size, child–staff ratio, and teacher education and training), as well as features related to the processes of instruction and adult–child interaction (e.g., curricula, quality of the teacher–child relationship, teacher stability, and daily routines), have been examined in a wide array of studies and have been found to contribute to the overall quality of the program (Howes et al., 1992; Phillips & Howes, 1987; Ruopp, Travers, Glantz, & Coelen, 1979; Wiltz & Klein, in press). Love, Raikes, Paulsell, and Kisker (2000) suggest that an expanded concept of quality in infant programs would incorporate seven key features: (1) structural features, (2) process features, (3) relationships, (4) continuity in relationships and services, (5) cultural relevance, (6) comprehensive services, and (7) contextual elements. These features combine to form a broad framework where quality variables would be considered at four levels: program, teacher/caregiver, child, and community/policy (Love et al., 2000). By considering this broad array of variables, definitions of quality will not be uniform. Indeed, as Lamb (1998) notes, "It is . . . impossible to write a recipe for high-quality care that is universally acceptable. High-quality care needs to be defined with respect to the characteristics and needs of children and families in specific societies and subcultures rather than in terms of universal dimensions" (p. 75).

Influence of Welfare Reform

The burgeoning interest in early care and education coincided with the welfare reform movement, and together, these forces have joined to forge a new direction in child care. There has been a phenomenal growth in the number of federal offices attending to issues related to child care and early education, to research funded by these agencies, to collaborative efforts and the sharing of information, and to the dissemination of this new knowledge to the public. This growth has occurred at about the same time as the "devolution" of public assistance programs to the states. There has been replacement of traditional entitlement programs supporting low-income families (e.g., Aid to Families with Dependent Children; AFDC) with programs that time-limit support and require mothers of young children to seek work, as well as the transfer of delivery mechanisms and certain eligibility decisions to the states through the "New Federalism" (Bridgman & Phillips, 1997; Fuller & Kagan, 2000; Mead, 1996; Urban Institute, 2000; Zaslow, McGroder, & Moore, 2000).

In 1996, President Clinton signed the Personal Responsibility and Work Opportunity Reconciliation Act (PRWORA; Public Law 104-193), which effectively ended the traditional conceptualization of welfare established by President Roosevelt and carried forward through much of this century (see also Powell, this volume). Assistance to families was now designated as temporary. The Temporary Assistance to Needy Families (TANF) regulations stipulated a lifetime limit on support and required mothers to seek work and move off welfare. States were given flexibility in designing how funds would be delivered to families, determining assistance levels, and, to a certain extent, establishing eligibility requirements (Administration for Children and Families, 1999a).

Welfare reform has had many implications for child care. With a limit of 5 years of TANF support and the requirement that even mothers of young children show evidence of seeking jobs within 2 years of initiation of assistance, the role of child-care subsidies and availability of care has become paramount. Subsidies are delivered through the CCDGB/CCDF system mentioned earlier in this chapter: federal monies are supplied through the CCDGB to the states, and the states provide matching funds that are combined to form the CCDF. However, recent analysis of state distribution of subsidies indicates that only a small percentage of children eligible for CCDBG subsidies are actually receiving them: rates range from under 5% in Mississippi to almost 25% in West Virginia, with an overall average of one in nine eligible children served (Administration on Children, Youth and Families, 1999a; Children's Defense Fund, 2000). A study conducted by the Center for Law and Social Policy found that in all states, less than 50% of responding families that had left welfare and were currently working were receiving any sort of child care assistance; in most sites surveyed the average rate of utilization was 30% or less (Schumacher & Greenberg, 1999). Many families were unaware that such assistance was even available. Clearly, all families that would benefit from support monies for child care are not being served (Wertheimer, 1999). The overall cost of child care is a large percentage of the budget for low-income families: estimates are that from 20 to 40% of annual income is paid for child-care expenses. Such a huge proportion stands in stark contrast to moderate and upper-income families, where child-care costs typically make up less than 10% of the family budget (Wertheimer, 1999).

Changes brought about by welfare reform are being closely watched. The support of the Welfare-to-Work movement intended to be provided by child-care subsidies has yet to be successful; it is an open question whether low-income working mothers will be able to move from poverty into the mainstream of the U.S. economy. With almost 90% of the families eligible for child-care subsidies not receiving them, it seems unlikely that movement away from poverty will happen in a timely manner.

Moreover, the underenrollment of children in subsidized care calls into question the quality of the care they do receive. How many are left to fend for themselves while their mothers work? How many are in inadequate care settings? Subsidy requirements allow parents to select any setting they desire (care by relatives, family day care, group care).

To qualify for subsidy payments, these settings must be operating legally, although this does not necessarily ensure licensed care (Administration on Children, Youth and Families, 1999a; Newman et al., 2000). Legal unregulated care, sometimes referred to as license-exempt care, is provided in caregivers' homes, for small numbers of children, with size limits varying by state (Love et al., 2000). Subsidized settings are required to meet minimal health and safety standards. Although by no means a guarantee of quality, these stipulated standards within the subsidy guidelines are at least a starting point for addressing the quality-in-care issue from the federal perspective.

INTEGRATING CHILD CARE AND EARLY EDUCATION

There has been an historical division between child care and early education in this country. Child-care programs developed out of need; as mentioned earlier, this was often in response to times of crisis when women were essential to the work force and their children needed care (Zigler & Gilman, 1996). Early childhood education programs, on the other hand, have their roots in progressive education reform and developmental psychology. Within early education, programs designed for middle-class children and programs designed for children at risk occupied separate trajectories for many years. Programs for middle-class children were seen as enrichment opportunities, but the early intervention movement, epitomized by programs such as Head Start and the Perry Preschool Project (Zigler & Styfco, 1996), was designed to combat the ill effects of poverty and provide young children with a "head start" as they began school. Although the literature on malleability in early development (e.g., the work of Hunt, 1961, Bloom, 1964, and others) did serve as the scientific rationale for early-intervention programs in general, initial expectations for Head Start were unreasonably high:

> It grew ... out of policy makers' efforts to combat the problem of poverty in the United States. In the ensuing three decades, early childhood intervention has been imbued with goals such as reducing welfare dependency, crime, and low educational attainment—goals inspired more by politicians' campaign promises than by scientific findings. ... Head Start was not so much a result but a victim of the optimism of the 1960's. The preschool program was meant to be one small piece in an arsenal of programmatic weapons to combat poverty, but its appeal and popularity turned it into the centerpiece. Social scientists raised the hopes placed in it by proclaiming that in-

telligence could be raised easily during the preschool years. The un-
fettered enthusiasm on both the political and scientific fronts changed
the perception of Head Start as a school readiness program to a panacea that would create a great society and quite possibly a generation
of geniuses. (Zigler & Styfco, 1996, pp. 132, 135)

Although the initial expectations of Head Start were not realized,
in its 35-year history, this program has served almost 18 million children and their families (Administration on Children, Youth and Families, 1999b) and has been an important entry point into early intervention and schooling for a large number of children. Research efforts
under way today are focusing on improving Head Start quality, understanding the lives of families served by the program, and addressing
the mental health needs of Head Start children (Administration on
Children, Youth and Families, 1999c). Unfortunately, even with the increased federal supports for Head Start in the recent reauthorizations,
the more than 800,000 children currently enrolled are still only about
half of those eligible (Children's Defense Fund, 2000). It is estimated
that approximately 27% of eligible 3-year-olds and 48% of eligible 4-
year-olds (defined as being from families at or below the poverty line)
are being served (Administration on Children, Youth and Families,
1999c). However, many programs still are part day and thus cannot
fully meet the needs of working families.

A growing recognition that to be truly effective, early intervention
needs to start even earlier, with infants and toddlers, brought about the
initiation of the Early Head Start program, which today serves approximately 39,000 infants and toddlers and their families (Administration
on Children, Youth & Families, 1999b). Care for infants and toddlers is a
special subset of child care that deserves special attention to provision
of quality and staff development (see Love et al., 2000).

Head Start and other early-intervention programs were not originally intended to provide care for children while their parents worked.
Indeed, most early-intervention programs started off on part-day
schedules and many continue as such. Yet early childhood educators
see the division between "education" and "care" for young children as
essentially being artificial. How could we separate the care needs and
the educational needs of children? Prominent psychologists and educators have called for a way to bring these two strands of early education
together for many years. Indeed, Bettye Caldwell coined the term
"educare" to reflect this joint commitment to all aspects of young children's development and well-being (Caldwell, 1991). Although this
term did not catch on when it was initially introduced, there have been
renewed proposals for such integration:

Historically, there have been two separate and at times conflicting traditions in the United States that can be encapsulated in the terms *child care* and *preschool*. A central premise of this report (National Research Council's report on early childhood pedagogy, *Eager to Learn*), one that grows directly from the research literature, is that *care and education cannot be thought of as separate entities in dealing with young children*. Adequate care involves providing quality cognitive stimulation, rich language environments, and the facilitation of social, emotional and motor development. Likewise, adequate education for young children can only occur in the context of good physical care and of warm affective relationships. (National Research Council, 2001, p. 2)

The integration of early care and education is beginning to be seen in the approaches and initiatives developed through different federal agencies. Whereas public perception still tends to view child care as a custodial enterprise and early education as enrichment, there is clear consensus among early childhood educators and researchers that there should be no divisions between these two. From Head Start, which now incorporates child-care services into a small (approximately one-third) but growing proportion of its programs (Administration on Children, Youth and Families, 1999b), to the larger direction of federally funded research, the separate strands of child care and early education are beginning to merge.

Shared Responsibility for Early Care and Education

The last decade has witnessed an increasingly integrated approach to targeting early care and education within governmental agencies. The primary cabinet-level agencies responsible for early childhood services, the Department of Health and Human Services (DHHS), and the Department of Education (DOE), have moved to establish a more visible presence and have developed mechanisms for interaction and sharing of new research in the field across agencies.

Within the Department of Health and Human Services, the Administration for Children and Families (ACF) is the primary office for programs related to child care and child and family services. It is responsible for some 60 programs which provide services and assistance to needy children and families, regulate the new state–federal welfare program—TANF—oversees the national child support enforcement system, administers the Head Start program, provides funds to assist low-income families in paying for child care, and supports state programs to provide for foster care and adoption assistance (Administration for Children and Families, 2000a). The Head Start Bureau has long been a primary department within the Administration on Children, Youth and

Families (ACYF) in ACF. In 1995 the Child Care Bureau was established to "enhance the quality, affordability, and supply of child care available for all families" (Administration for Children and Families, 2000a, p.1). CCDBG funds are administered through the Child Care Bureau, while TANF oversight and administration resides within the Office of Family Assistance.

The Child Care Bureau also directs the National Child Care Information Center, which acts as a clearinghouse on child-care information for parents and professionals, and has a comprehensive Web site that disseminates information to the public. The Child Care Policy Research Consortium is a research grant program within the Child Care Bureau; it serves as a central point for research and information about child care as a support for low-income families and is composed of a range of national, state, and local child-care agencies, universities, resource and referral agencies, professional organizations, providers and parents, and businesses (Administration for Children and Families, 2000a).

The ACYF Commissioner's Office of Research and Evaluation (CORE) provides research support for a variety of projects related to child care and early education across Head Start, the Child Care Bureau, and the Children's Bureau. The Assistant Secretary for Planning and Evaluation (ASPE) is the "principal adviser to the Secretary of the DHHS on policy development and is responsible for major activities in the areas of policy coordination, legislation development, strategic planning, policy research and evaluation, and economic analysis" (U.S. Department of Health and Human Services, 2000, p. 1). ASPE has commissioned relevant research and policy papers related to child care (see, e.g., Vandell & Wolfe, 2000).

The National Institutes of Health (NIH) is of course the primary research arm for physical and behavioral health for the federal government. Several institutes within NIH conduct research essential to children's well-being, including child care issues. The National Institute of Child Health and Human Development (NICHD) and the National Institute of Mental Health (NIMH) have several ongoing programs which target children's development in child care centers. The NICHD Study of Early Child Care and Youth Development (NICHD Early Child Care Research Network, 1994, 1998a, 1998b, 1999), a comprehensive study of children's development across different child-care settings, is a collaborative research project headquartered at the NICHD (see also Clarke-Stewart, Allhusen, & Goossens, this volume; Howes & Oldham, this volume).

Many cross-collaborative and interagency programs within and beyond DHHS focus on child-care issues. For example, the Federal Interagency Forum on Child and Family Statistics was established in

1994 to coordinate data production and dissemination across federal agencies interested in child and family issues. Ten cabinet-level departments, the Office of Management and Budget, and the National Science Foundation jointly produce the annual report, *America's Children: Key National Indicators of Well-Being*. This report monitors the status of children in the United States, charts trends, and compares changes in status of a wide range of well-being indicators, including numbers of children in poverty and in child-care and early education programs (National Institute of Child Health and Human Development, 2000).

Within the U.S. DOE, the National Institute for Early Childhood Development and Education, a program of the Office of Educational Research and Improvement (OERI), provides research support and direction for the education and care of young children. The Institute funds a variety of projects related to early childhood teacher training and professional development, evaluation of educational programs, child-care issues, educational television, school readiness, and transition from preschool to public school. Funded by the Institute is the National Center for Early Development and Learning, housed at the Frank Porter Graham Center at the University of North Carolina at Chapel Hill, which directs a number of research strands devoted to the mission of the Institute, and engages in a variety of dissemination activities. In 1994, OERI established the Early Childhood Research Working Group, which is an interagency initiative designed to explore ways to share information and link federal resources to develop a collaborative research agenda across federal agencies (National Institute on Early Childhood Development and Education, 1999). The National Center for Education Statistics conducts major national surveys such as the Early Childhood Longitudinal Survey, and serves as a clearinghouse and dissemination point for important statistical information about early care and education programs.

This is by no means an exhaustive list of federal agencies, institutes, and centers focused on issues, programs, and research on early care and education . For example, the Department of Defense has a large program of child-care centers at military installations and has developed its own child-care policies and initiatives. The General Services Administration coordinates child-care programs at federal sites across the country. And the Census Bureau regularly issues reports on the demographics of young children and their families, including child-care concerns. However, the primary setting for research and policy formulation related to child care and early education is with the DHHS and the DOE.

CURRENT RESEARCH DIRECTIONS

Perhaps the most significant and far-reaching way in which the federal government has had an impact on our national perspective on child care and early education is through the funding of research projects designed to examine salient child-care issues. Although funds have come through private foundation sources (separately or combined with federal monies), several federal agencies have provided the direction and the financial support to develop, integrate, and disseminate a substantial research literature that makes a strong contribution to our understanding of the effects of child care on the lives of young children. The following summary is not comprehensive, but it provides an overview of the type of research related to child care and early education that is currently being supported through federal monies.

As noted, the ACF, the NICHD, and the OERI have made child-care quality a research priority, and this has been supported through the targeting of research monies within various funding streams. For instance, fiscal year 2000 funding to the Child Care Bureau included $10 million for child-care research, demonstration, and evaluation activities. The Child Care Bureau's research agenda focuses on five key questions which address concerns related to the current status of child care, the issue of quality with respect to variations in quality and individual child and family outcomes, the quality of the early childhood work force, availability and costs associated with quality, and the translation of these outcomes into specific policies at the national, state, and local levels and for particular subgroups of families (Ad ministration for Children and Families, 2000b). Funding for the NICHD Study of Early Child Care has continued for much of the past decade and supports a team of researchers across the country who have studied approximately 1,200 children as they have moved through infancy into elementary school, and across naturally occurring care contexts (NICHD Study of Early Child Care, 2000). Across the DHHS, more than 40 different research initiatives on child care were in progress or had recently been completed in 1999, according to a recent inventory of funded projects (U.S. Department of Health and Human Services, 1999). Projects focused on a wide array of child-care and early education concerns, including implications of child care for low-income families, the impact of welfare reform for child-care access and choice, effects of home and out-of-home care on child development, Head Start program quality, child outcomes, and experiences of families (the Family and Child Experiences Survey [FACES]), Head Start Quality Research Centers, the demand and supply of quality in child care, improving state capability to evaluate child-care policy options, the impact of child-care regulations on the delivery of services and family choice options, and economic rationales for government intervention in the child care market. Recent initiatives through the National Center for Educational Statistics, the National Early Childhood Institute, and the National Center on Early Development and Learning through the DOE focus on an in-depth study and knowledge synthesis of international early childhood initiatives, relationships between child-care quality and school readiness, effects of comprehensive mental health interventions on young children's school readiness, evaluating the Schools of the 21st Century Project (a year-round preschool care, education, extended day and family support program) (Zigler & Finn-Stevenson, 1996), evaluating universal prekindergarten programs in targeted states, examining the movement of young children in poverty from preschool to formal schooling as part of the Early Childhood Longitudinal Survey (West, Denton, & Germino-Hauskens, 2000), and engagement as a relevant indicator of program quality (National Institute on Early Childhood Development and Education, 1998; Office of Educational Research and Improvement, 1999).

These agencies have also joined forces with nonfederal, often foundation-based partners in reviewing and integrating scientific findings and drawing conclusions for policy and practice. A recent examples of such successful partnership is the Child Mental Health Foundations and Agencies Network (FAN), whose membership includes key agencies and institutes within DHHS and DOE as well as major foundations investing in children's well-being. FAN recently published a monograph and research report focused on the importance of social and emotional factors in children's school readiness (Children's Mental Health Foundations and Agencies Network, 2000). Another major effort has been conducted through the auspices of the National Academy of Sciences/National Research Council (National Research Council and Institute of Medicine, 2000) and funded by both federal and private foundation sponsors. A distinguished panel of researchers and practitioners has conducted a comprehensive review of the multiple domains of early childhood development and offered strong recommendations favoring integrating research and policy in the years to come. The report focuses on the future, asking how society can use knowledge about early childhood development to maximize human capital and ensure democracy. However, the panel also advocates using scientific knowledge to "nurture, protect and ensure the health and wellbeing of all young children as an important objective in its own right, regardless of . . . measurable returns" (p. 3). The committee is clear about the importance of speaking to ethical and moral values as well as to economic, political, and social interests.

CONCLUSIONS

In many ways, there has been astonishing growth in our knowledge and understanding of the contexts of child care in the last 25 years. Research has become increasingly sophisticated in its focus on a complex array of variables that influence development in the many different care settings that make up a large part of the daily environment for most young children in this country. There has been movement beyond the early arguments about whether or not child care is harmful for young children. Successful collaborative research initiatives have been formed that have yielded important information about how differential quality does indeed affect the well-being of young children and their families. Calls for more sophisticated approaches to research methodology which will provide more reliable forms of measurement, address issues of reliability, and more clearly delineate causal implications between quality of care and child development outcomes (Lamb, 2000; Love et al., 1996) indicate that more remains to be done before our understanding of the mediating effects of quality may be fully realized. Still, the implications of these research findings are beginning to be felt at both the policy and the practice levels.

In other ways, we have not moved far. No coherent, comprehensive child-care policy exists in this country. Instead, we have a patchwork of programs that while targeted at ameliorating the effects of poverty, moving mothers off welfare, and helping young children be "ready" for formal schooling, have not yet achieved these goals. Large numbers of young children who would greatly benefit from quality child-care programs have not gained access to even minimally adequate care. The premise of broad-based family and child policies — to enhance the lives of all children, not only those in the greatest need - has yet to be addressed in this country.

The importance of developing and implementing child-care policies designed to improve the quality of care has been a consistent message stemming directly from current research in the field. There is still a long way to go to achieve this end. Changes brought about through the policy and research initiatives described in this chapter will be examined closely as we move into a new century in our efforts to support children and families in child care.

ACKNOWLEDGMENTS

The views expressed are solely our own and do not necessarily represent the views or policy of the U.S. Department of Health and Human Services. We wish to thank Abbey Showalter-Loch and Sunkyoung Yi for their assistance in the initial research for this chapter.

REFERENCES

Administration for Children and Families. (1999). *Welfare fact sheet*. Washington, DC: U.S. Department of Health and Human Services [On-line]. Available: http://www.acf.dhhs.gov/programs/opa/facts/tanf.htm.

Administration for Children and Families. (2000a). *Fact sheet* [On-line]. Available: http://www.acf.dhhs.gov/programs/opa/facts/majorpr.htm.

Administration for Children and Families. (2000b). *Introduction to the Child Care Bureau* [On-line]. Available: http://acf.dhhs.gov/programs/ccb/geninfo/index/htm.

Administration on Children, Youth and Families. (1999a). *Access to child care for low-income working families*. Washington, DC: U. S. Department of Health and Human Services [On-line]. Available: http://www.acf.dhhs.gov/programs/ccb/reports/ccreport.htm.

Administration on Children, Youth and Families. (1999b). *Project Head Start: Statistical fact sheet*. Washington, DC: U.S. Department of Health and Human Services.

Administration on Children, Youth and Families. (1999c). *Evaluating Head Start: A recommended framework for studying the impact of the Head Start program*. Washington, DC: U.S. Department of Health and Human Services.

Barnett, W. S. (1993). New wine in old bottles: Increasing the coherence of early childhood care and education policy. *Early Childhood Research Quarterly, 8*, 519–558.

Barnett, W. S. (1995). Long-term effects of early childhood programs on cognitive and school outcomes. In *The future of children: Vol. 5, No. 3. Long-term outcomes of early childhood programs* (pp. 25–50). Los Altos, CA: David and Lucile Packard Foundation.

Bloom, B. S. (1964). *Stability and change in human characteristics*. New York: Wiley.

Boocock, S. S. (1995). Early childhood programs in other nations: Goals and outcomes. In *The future of children: Vol. 5, No. 3. Long-term outcomes of early childhood programs* (pp. 94–114). CA: David and Lucile Packard Foundation.

Bridgman, A., & Phillips, D. (Eds.). (1997). *New findings on welfare and children's development: Summary of a research briefing* [National Research Council and Institute of Medicine]. Washington, DC: National Academy Press.

Burchinal, M. R., Roberts, J. E., Nabors, L. A., & Bryant, D. M. (1996). Quality of center child care and infant cognitive and language development. *Child Development, 67*, 606–620.

Caldwell, B. (1991). Educare: New product, new future. *Journal of Developmental and Behavioral Pediatrics, 12*, 199–204.

Carnegie Task Force on Meeting the Needs of Young Children. (1994). *Starting points: Meeting the needs of our youngest children.* New York: Carnegie Corporation.

Child Mental Health Foundations and Agencies Network (FAN). (2000). *A good beginning: Sending America's children to school with the social and emotional competence they need to succeed.* Washington, DC: National Institute of Mental Health [On-line]. Available: http://www.nimh.nih.gov/childhp/fdnconsb.htm.

Children's Defense Fund. (2000). *Yearbook 2000: The state of America's children.* Washington, DC: Author.

Clarke-Stewart, K. A. (1987a). In search of consistencies in child care research. In D. A. Phillips (Ed.), *Quality in child care: What does research tell us?* (pp. 105–120). Washington, DC: National Association for the Education of Young Children.

Clarke-Stewart, K. A. (1987b). Predicting child development from child care forms and features: The Chicago Study. In D. A. Phillips (Ed.), *Quality in child care: What does research tell us?* (pp. 21–42). Washington, DC: National Association for the Education of Young Children.

Cost, Quality and Outcomes Study. (1995). *Cost, quality and child outcomes in child care centers: Public report.* Denver: University of Colorado at Denver.

Cost, Quality and Outcomes Study. (1999). *The children of the cost, quality and outcomes study go to school.* Summary. Chapel Hill, NC: National Center for Early Development and Learning [On-line]. Available: http://www.fpg.unc.edu/~NCEDL/PAGES/cqes.htm.

Fein, G. G., & Clarke-Stewart, K. A. (1973). *Day care in context.* New York: Wiley.

Fuller, B., & Kagan, S. L. (2000). *Remember the children: Mothers balance work and child care under welfare reform* [Growing Up in Poverty Project 2000. Wave 1 Findings—California, Connecticut, Florida]. Berkeley: University of California, Berkeley and Yale University.

Hofferth, S. L., Shauman, K. A., Henke, R. R., & West, J. (1998). *Characteristics of children's early care and education programs: Data from the 1995 National Household Education Survey* (Report No. 989–128). Washington, DC: U.S. Department of Education, National Center for Education Statistics.

Howes, C., & Hamilton, C. E. (1993). Child care for young children. In B. Spodek (Ed.), *Handbook of research on the education of young children* (pp. 322–336). New York: Macmillan.

Howes, C., Phillips, D., & Whitebrook, M. (1992). Thresholds of quality: Implications for the social development of children in center-based child care. *Child Development, 63,* 449–460.

Hunt, J. McV. (1961). *Intelligence and experience.* New York: Ronald Press.

Kagan, S. L., & Cohen, N. E. (1997). *Not by chance: Creating an early care and education system for America's children* (Abridged report. The Quality 2000 Initiative). New Haven, CT: Bush Center in Child Development and Social Policy.

Kammerman, S. B. (1996). Child and family policies: An international overview. In E. F. Zigler, S. L. Kagan, & N. W. Hall (Eds.), *Children, families and government* (pp. 31–48). New York: Cambridge University Press.

Lamb, M. E. (1998). Nonparental child care: Context, quality, correlates, and consequences. In W. Damon (Editor-in-Chief), I. E. Sigel, & K. A. Renninger (Vol. Eds.), *Handbook of child psychology. Vol. 4: Child psychology in practice* (pp. 75–133). New York: Wiley.

Lamb, M. E. (2000). The effects of quality of care on child development. *Applied Developmental Science, 4*(3), 112–115.

Love, J. M., Raikes, H. H., Paulsell, D., & Kisker, E. E. (2000). New directions for studying quality in programs for infants and toddlers. In D. Cryer & T. Harms (Eds.), *Infants and toddlers in out of home care* (pp. 117–162). Baltimore: Brookes.

Love, J. M., Schochet, P. Z., & Meckstroth, A. L. (1996). *Are they in any real danger? What research does—and doesn't—tell us about child care quality and children's well-being.* Princeton, NJ: Mathematica Policy Research.

Mead, L. M. (1996). Welfare reform and children. In E. F. Zigler, S. L. Kagan, & N. W. Hall (Eds.). *Children, families and government* (pp. 51–76). New York: Cambridge University Press.

National Center for Education Statistics. (1996). *Child care and early education program participation of infants, toddlers, and preschoolers* (NCES-98-128). Washington, DC: U.S. Department of Education, National Center for Education Statistics.

National Institute of Child Health and Human Development. (2000a). *Federal Interagency Forum on Child and Family Statistics: Nation's children gain in many areas* [On-line]. Available: http://www.nichd.nih.gov/new/releases/americas.htm.

National Institute on Early Childhood Development and Education. (1998). *Field Initiated Studies Grant Awards for FY 1997* [On-line]. Available: http://www.ed.gov/offices/OERI/FIS/fis-eci.html.

National Institute on Early Childhood Development and Education. (1999). *The Early Childhood Working Group* [Office of Educational Research and Improvement, U.S. Department of Education; On-line]. Available: http://www.ed.gov/offices/OERI/ECI/ecwg.html.

National Research Council. (2001). *Eager to learn: Educating our preschoolers* [Committee on Early Childhood Pedagogy, Commission on Behavioral and Social Sciences and Education], B. T. Bowman, M. S. Donovan, & M. S. Burns (Eds.). Washington, DC: National Academy Press.

National Research Council and Institute of Medicine. (2000). *From Neurons to Neighborhoods: The Science of Early Childhood Development* [Committee on Integrating the Science of Early Childhood Development; Board on Children, Youth and Families; Commission on Behavioral and Social Sciences and Education], J. P. Shonkoff & D. A. Philips (Eds.). Washington, DC: National Academy Press.

NICHD Early Child Care Research Network. (1994). Child care and child development: The NICHD study of early child care. In S. L. Friedman & H. C. Haywood (Eds.), *Developmental follow-up: Concepts, Domains, and methods* (pp. 377–396). New York: Academic Press.

NICHD Early Child Care Research Network. (1998a). Early child care and self-control, compliance, and problem behaviors at twenty-four and thirty-six months. *Child Development, 69*(4), 1145–1170.

NICHD Early Child Care Research Network. (1998b). Relations between family predictors and child outcomes: Are they weaker for children in child care? *Developmental Psychology, 34*(5), 1119–1128.

NICHD Early Child Care Research Network. (1999). Child outcomes when child care center classes meet recommended standards of quality. *American Journal of Public Health, 89*(7), 1072–1077.

NICHD Study of Early Child Care. (2000). *Study summary* [On-line]. Available: http://156.40.88.3/about/crmc/secc/summary.htm.

Newman, S., Brazelton, T. B., Zigler, E., Sherman, L. W., Bratton, W., Sanders, J., & Christeson, W. (2000). *American's child care crisis: A crime prevention strategy. A report from Fight Crime: Invest in Kids* [On-line]. Available: http://www.fightcrime.org

Office of Educational Research and Improvement. (1999). *FY 1999 Field-Initiated Studies (FIS) Grant Awards Abstracts* [On-line]. Available: http://www.ed.gov/offices/OERI/FIS/archive3.html.

Phillips, D., & Howes, C. (1987). Indicators of quality in child care: Review of research. In D. Phillips (Ed.), *Quality in child care: What does research tell us?* (pp. 1–19). Washington, DC: National Association for the Education of Young Children.

Ramey, C. T., & Campbell, F. A. (1991). Poverty, early childhood education and academic competence: The Abecedarian experiment. In A. Juston (Ed.), *Children reared in poverty* (pp. 190–221). New York: Cambridge University Press.

Ramey, C. T., & Campbell, F. A. (1994). Effects of early intervention on intellectual and academic achievement: A follow-up study of children from low-income families. *Child Development, 65,* 684–698.

Ramey, C. T., Campbell, F. A., Burchinal, M., Skinner, M. L., Gardner, D. M., & Ramey, S. L. (2000). Persistent effects of early intervention on high-risk children and their mothers. *Applied Developmental Science, 4*(1), 2–14.

Ruopp, R., Travers, J., Glantz, F., & Coelen, G. (1979). *Children at the center.* Cambridge, MA: Abt Associates.

Sawhill, I. V. (1999, April). Investing in children (Children's Roundtable Report No. 1). Washington, DC: The Brookings Institution [On-line]. Available: http://www.brookings.org/comm/ConferenceReport/cr2/cr2. htm.

Scarr, S. (1998). American child care today. *American Psychologist, 53,* 95–108.

Schumacher, R., & Greenberg, M. (1999). *Child care after leaving welfare: Early evidence from state studies* [Center for Law and Social Policy, Washington, DC; On-line]. Available: http://www.clasp.org/pubs/childcare.

Smith, S. (1998). *The past decade's research on child care quality and children's development: What we are learning, directions for the future* (unpublished paper). Paper prepared for meeting, Child care in the new policy context, sponsored by the Office of the Assistant Secretary for Planning and Evaluation, Washington, DC.

Urban Institute. (2000). *Three out of four young children of employed moms in nonparental child care* [On-line]. Available: http://www.urban.org/news/pressrel/pr000308.html.

U.S. Department of Health and Human Services. (1999). *Inventory of HHS child care research.* Draft [On-line]. Available: http://aspe.hhs.gov/hsp/cyp/ccresinv.htm

U.S. Department of Health and Human Services. (2000). *Introduction to the Office* [Office of the Assistant Secretary for Planning and Evaluation; On-line]. Available: http://www.aspe.hhs.gov.

Vandell, D. L., & Wolfe, B. (2000). *Child care quality: Does it matter and does it need to be improved?* Washington, DC: Office of the Assistant Secretary for Planning and Evaluation, U.S. Department of Health and Human Services [On-line]. Available: http://aspe.hhs.gov/hsp/ccquality00/index.htm.

Wertheimer, R. (1999). *Working poor families with children.* Washington, DC: Child Trends.

West, J., Denton, K., & Germino-Hauskens, E. (2000). *America's kindergartners: Findings from the Early Childhood Longitudinal Study, Kindergarten Class of 1998–99.* Washington, DC: U.S. Department of Education.

Wiltz, N. W., & Klein, E. L. (in press). "What do you do in child care?" Children's perceptions of high and low quality classrooms. *Early Childhood Research Quarterly.*

Zaslow, M. J., McGroder, S. M., & Moore, K. A. (2000). *The national evaluation of welfare-to-work strategies: Impacts on young children and their families two years after enrollment: Findings from the child outcomes study.* Washington, DC: Child Trends [On-line]. Available: http://aspe.hhs.gov/hsp/NEWWS/child-outcomes/summary.htm

Zigler, E. F., & Finn-Stevenson, M. (1996). Funding child care and public education. In *The future of children: Vol. 6, No. 2. Financing child care* (pp. 104–121). Los Altos, CA: David and Lucile Packard Foundation.

Zigler, E. F., & Gilman, E. (1996). Not just any care: Shaping a coherent child care policy. In E. F. Zigler, S. L. Kagan, & N. W. Hall (Eds.), *Children, families and government* (pp. 94–116). New York: Cambridge University Press.

Zigler, E. F., & Styfco, S. S. (1996). Head Start and early childhood intervention: The changing course of social science and social policy. In E. F. Zigler, S. L. Kagan, & N. W. Hall (Eds.), *Children, families and government* (pp. 132–155). New York: Cambridge University Press.

PART V

❧

Conclusions

17

✍

Suppose There Were a Hill in Richmond Hill

GRETA G. FEIN

Most certainly, I have been enjoying this book and the wonderful ideas the contributors offer. But now (whoosh) it's my turn. What can I possibly say that would properly acknowledge the talent, thoughtfulness, and good wishes of these scholars whose work I have admired and whose friendship I have valued? At least, I could follow the festschrift tradition and do what others have done. Working backward, the question then became, "What is the festschrift tradition?" A small survey turned up three models.

In one, the honoree reflects on formative life events. Who am I and how did I get to this splendid celebration? These personal reflections embrace early childhood and beyond. But we scholars are severely trained to write as distantly from ourselves as possible ... about "it" and "them" even more than "he" or "she" ... and infinitely more than "I" and "we." William Kessen's biographical reflections are a superb and moving example of how a scholar writes about "I" and "we" (Kessen, 1991). These reflections are the stories told by parents, sharpened by memory, and sweetened by *imagination*.

In another model, the honoree tries to make sense of what are inevitably diverse chapters about diverse problems. How can we put this diversity together to yield a vision of an integrated theory? In this category, it is almost impossible to compete with Brian Sutton-Smith, whose command of play in all its intricacies and nuances is in a league of its own (Sutton-Smith, 1995). Therefore, I will comment on the contributions, but the scope will be less majestic.

There is a third approach, although I found no examples of it. In the third model, one would simply do a review of one's own work. Something of an annotated bibliography, taking advantage of the opportunity to say what one ought to have said in the first place.

I shall do a little bit of each.

BIOGRAPHY

I was a little Jewish girl from a Queens, New York, neighborhood called Richmond Hill. The name is lovely yet fails to describe this plain, working-class neighborhood of modest, narrow, detached two-story homes, and flat straight streets spreading out from an avenue shaded by an elevated train trestle. The avenue was lined with small shops—butcher, grocer, pharmacy, with "railroad flats" above them. I lived and played in this neighborhood for 20 years.

My parents were immigrants of the 1920s, father from Berlin, Germany, and mother from Prague, Czechoslovakia. My father, who earned an Iron Cross in the service of the Kaiser, left Germany as the country descended into anarchy; youth gangs prowled the streets and the economy was in chaos. Germany's latent antisemitism was emerging as were demagogues willing to exploit it. Hope was westerly, in America. And so he joined the millions of others who left the old for the new.

My mother and three small siblings were orphaned in 1918 when both parents died of typhoid in a refugee camp near the Austro-Hungarian border. After the war, they lived with foster parents in Prague until, at the pleading of relatives in America, my mother (age 17) decided to come to America with her siblings (ages 5, 7, and 9) in tow. Unfortunately, the American relatives were themselves pretty poor, so the girls were farmed out to different aunts and uncles and 2 years later the boy ended up in an orphanage. Eventually, my mother and father met and married, and the day after their honeymoon they traveled to Yonkers to bring my uncle home.

Although my father graduated from an academic high school, college was not a possibility. His dream was a more humble one: to own his own business with no boss over him and the freedom to come and go as he pleased. In reality, the freedom was mostly in coming. He and she worked 6 days a week from 7 in the morning to 11 at night in their very own Army and Navy store on the corner of Jamaica Avenue and Liberty Boulevard in Richmond Hill. Again, their experience was like that of so many others. The mom-and-pop shop, from candy store to grocery store, provided an accessible economic base for the integration of immigrants into American life—the hours were long, the profits meager, but this base offered a degree of blessed autonomy not possible in the old country.

I was born 10 days after Wall Street delivered the Great Depression of 1929. My birth jolted what must have been a quiet, industrious life, mainly because I didn't sleep at night—wall-to-wall screaming from 6 P.M. to midnight. My uncle lived with us and my aunts lived nearby. According to family lore, aunts and uncle sang songs, danced, rocked, jiggled and jangled me until my exhausted parents came home. During the day, I slept in my royal carriage in the store or in its untended fenced yard while my parents worked. When I was old enough, I dug in the dirt, picked weeds, or entertained the customers. No child-care problem for my parents. I was either with them in the store or at home with relatives. And, keep in mind that because we lived in a one-bedroom apartment, it did get a bit crowded at times.

Finally, it was time for kindergarten! Boredom soon replaced excitement. I remember the torture of the primary grades. We sat in rows and each child in turn—30+—read a page in the Dick and Jane basal series. I was a fluent reader and the pace was tortuous; the misery was shared between those who struggled and those who were proficient. My parents protested to the principal, Miss Bell, who dismissed them with an antisemitic remark at which point my outraged parents petitioned to send me to another, larger school. Antisemitism in America? It was my first brush with prejudice.

This incident opened the door to culture and politics. Why does Hitler hate Jews? Why were Negroes enslaved? Why did my Catholic friends go to confession? These were tough questions and my parents did their best. Who will you vote for? This was an easy one. FDR was the answer. Why? Because he's for the little guy. My parents were willing to share their liberal convictions with me and I effortlessly came on board. I suspect that the issues I later studied and wrote about are fairly straight derivatives of these unanswered questions and convictions.

School relief came in fifth grade. The New York Public School System created the IGC classes for intellectually gifted children. And I was chosen to attend the fifth-grade section in Forest Hills. It took a bus, a trolley, and lots of walking to get there, but what a joyous experience it was. Our teacher, Mrs. Goolsby, had no special credentials to take on a class of kids with IQs of 130 or better, but she had exactly the right temperament: motherly, patient, gentle and respectful. In the vacuum, we created our own curriculum. Mrs. Goolsby gave us the less than inspired assignment of writing a research paper about what we wanted to be when we grew up. But, because she was so easygoing, we were able to do our projects in child-organized groups. One boy wanted to be a musicologist—this was Fred Grunfeld who became just that with his own radio program on WQXR. Another was Larry Malcomb, who planned to become a journalist and he did. Among the group was an aspiring chemist, a nurse, and a nun. I do not remember very many of these children, but I remember discovering occupations I had never imagined possible. on a broader theme, this wonderful bit of schooling said quite clearly: School does not have to be as dull and depressing as it had been.

And what about play? By 8 years of age, I became a latchkey child. My mother was at the store when I came home from school and, for an hour or two, I could do whatever I wanted to do. First, I went outside to find friends. Rarely did I leave my block; no need to. We hung out behind the movie theater—double fire escapes, a large concrete platform with two steep driveways down the side—a great play space. one game was jumping, from the platform to the driveway, going as steep as you dared. The game was to go to the end . . . a 12-foot drop. And one day, I made it. I would never have to do it again! And I didn't. We invented other scary challenges. We raided the neighbors' backyards, climbed their trees, and played Ring-a-Lev-eo on their garage roofs. No parents, no supervision, no danger from bad guys other than those we made up.

When neighborhood kids were not around, I played by myself. There was no TV, so I read books and pretended that my funny little dolls were beautiful, sophisticated ladies going to a ball and meeting a handsome prince. My solitary fantasy life enriched the prosaic, often glum world of my working-class neighborhood. My aunts gave me their old party dresses with satin bows and swishy skirts and with these treasures and my mother's old lipstick another kind of make-believe was possible. The glamorous models came from Myrna Loy, Cinderella, Snow White, and especially my chic Aunt Sally, who actually did go to nightclubs in fancy dresses. My dolls' gowns were made out of small pieces of glittering satin, lace, and fur, fastened with a pin. They had boyfriends who were purely imaginary and they danced to music I found on the radio. It was only later that I began to wonder how and why these games were so deeply satisfying. Were they intellectually challenging? Not especially. In my play, I invented a world far more vivid than the drab world in which I lived. In the play world, characters were safe, admired, successful, even powerful. Play made life more lively as it expressed optimistic hopes and desires for the future.

In my junior year of high school, I became editor of the news section of the *Domino*, the school paper. The big adventure of my life happened that year. As reporters for the school paper, my friend Ruthie and I covered a speech by John Roy Carlson who had recently published a book exposing fascist organizations in America. After his speech, we asked for an interview. Over an ice cream soda, he told us the story line of his new book. But he needed help; he needed us to join the Richmond Hill German American Bund and feed him information about what was going on. He already knew that they had a cache of arms and were rehearsing military maneuvers. Ruthie and I went berserk! We were ready to sign up tomorrow. But our uncooperative parents said no . . . absolutely no. We begged, we pleaded, stormed, and cried to no avail. Oh, the hypocrisy of parents! Looking back, I wonder whether the man was a little mad. But the experience paved the way for John Le Carré and Len Deighton.

I applied to Cornell University because I wanted to be a medical doctor; as far as I knew, that was where you studied that. Cornell accepted me, but then my parents found out what it would cost. At that point, we did not know about scholarships or how to apply for one so that ended that. I did go to Queens College, at no cost whatsoever, and majored in psychology, with not much enthusiasm. In those days psychology was dry, behaviorist, and either experimental or clinical. It did not come close to answering the social questions of my childhood. Sociology was no better. Political action was more fun and purposeful, and so I joined rallies opposing the firing of professors accused of being communists and picket lines protesting racial segregation at the local YMCA.

Upon graduation, I got a job teaching 4-year-olds in a day-care center. The job came about as an accidental by-product of summer employment as a camp counselor in Williamsburg, an emerging Brooklyn ghetto. The agency I worked for had a child-care program and I needed a job. To my great surprise, I loved it. Eventually, I went to Bank Street for a master's degree in education. In that era, Bank Street was in a psychodynamic funk. Graduate students discussed at great length among themselves whether we were teachers or therapists. The model of teaching was very Rogerian, personal, sensitive, and responsive. But interleaved with this were Deweyan ideas about curriculum—expose the pipes and let the children walk through the building tracing them from outlet to source; take the children to the docks and watch the ships unload. But stress the "here and now." Except, of course, when it came to favorite books such as *The Carrot Seed* or *Goodnight Moon*. Unfortunately, the transition from field trips to classroom activities was elusive. In some schools, the transition was routinized: second grade ran a school supply store and journeyed downtown to buy from a wholesaler. Yet it happened the same way year after year and the children had little to say about the process. Yes, they learned to count money in a real-life context, but there were no elaborations, such as evaluating alternative suppliers, marking items "on sale," or using graphs to track sales and customers.

Besides, the New York City child-care centers were not friendly to innovation, although, in retrospect, the city sponsored some excellent programs. These centers were sponsored by the welfare department and were aimed at aiding troubled families or disabled parents. The focus was on care rather than education. The problem was more one of teacher fatigue from long hours and frustration from poor pay than curricular policy. Even so, it was possible to raise a duck, plant a garden, or walk to the grocery store to buy the makings of a snack. So, even in a tight system, it was possible to liven things up.

Pretty soon I married, moved to Rockland County, became a public school kindergarten teacher, and 3 years later gave birth to David, the first of three children. From Rockland County, we moved to Salt Lake City. I went back to school and, after Debbie and Josh were born, I became a doctoral student in the Department of Psychology. Thanks to great teachers (Paul Porter, Chuck Uhl, and Lyle Bourne) psychology came to life. But in 1965, we moved again . . . this time to New Haven. I applied to Yale and was admitted with reservations. The director of graduate studies gently transmitted the faculty's concerns: As the mother of three and an older woman, I was considered a poor risk, unlikely to publish and become famous. But because I had the highest test scores of that entry group, they could not in good conscience say no. There it was again . . . all those reasons other than ability for denying respect or admission to one or another group.

Wild bulldogs could not have kept me away. I ran rats for Alan Wagner, was a teaching assistant for Bill Kessen and Michael Kahn, waxed with Joe Glick's enthusiasms, and waned with Edward Zigler's grumbles. It was here that I met Brian Sutton-Smith, Jerry and Dorothy Singer, and Kate Garvey. Soon after, we began our conference symposia on play, and I began to actively study pretend phenomena.

I was having the intellectual time of my life. And it didn't end there. When I graduated in 1969, Bill Kessen hired me to work on a Carnegie project from which grew the study of infant curricula, a collaborative effort with Kessen, Alison Clarke-Stewart, and Susan Starr that comfortably merged my liberal agenda, interest in young children, and curiosity about play. It was a home-based, six-group intervention, with weekly home visits and participants randomly assigned to intervention groups. This intervention was so rigorous that home visitors were randomly assigned to each intervention type and at each of the four assessments (at 12, 18, 24, and 30 months), the children were tested by people who were strangers to them. As you might expect, there were no effects at all. But I had a fistful of play data much of which was published in the 1970s.

In 1975, I moved to Detroit and the Merrill–Palmer Institute as director of child development research. Here I had the great pleasure of working with Douglas R. Powell and Rheta DeVries until the Institute's demise in 1980. From Doug, I learned to appreciate the subtleties of social policy for families; from Rheta, I learned to appreciate how Piaget's grand theory could be pushed to encompass the construction of provocative and humane classrooms. A couple of years later I alit in Maryland where good fortune once again came my way—wonderful colleagues in Nathan Fox, Elisa Klein, and Ken Rubin and totally fantastic students, two of whom, Lois Groth and Lynn Darling, contributed a chapter to this volume. Along the way, I had the good fortune to meet Artin Göncü, Carollee Howes, Inge Bretherton, Keith Sawyer, and Tony Pellegrini; our connection began at the American Educational Research Association or the Society for Research in Child Development conferences and grew into joint presentations and heavy discussions. More recently, I found Rivka and Hananya Glaubman in Israel and Anna Bondioli in Italy along with their superbly thoughtful and original insights regarding children's early pretending. My only regret is that the number of contributors to this volume had to be limited.

PLAY AND STORY:
THE MESSAGES OF AFFECT THEORY

Play as an expressive affect system has received relatively little attention until recently. When we interview children about their memories of pretending, we are struck by the vivid scenes they portray and by the clarity of their accounts. How come at age 71, 1 can remember play episodes that occurred 60-odd years ago? That feat is especially noteworthy as there is so much I cannot remember or remember only vaguely. Yet, I remember pinning a piece of fabric, blue satin with gold sparkles, to a small doll and pretending she dances with a handsome gentleman in a ballroom lit by glittering crystal chandeliers.

Suppose we consider play as a part of the human expressive system. Sutton-Smith suggests that the human nervous system is double layered. Play, especially pretending and storytelling, modulates different levels of emotional response in a process that fine-tunes the balance of internal tensions between primitive, archaic emotions and those more advanced affective structures that flow from higher levels of the brain. Sutton-Smith says, "Play seems to be an attempt to avoid getting out of control while at the same time providing access to the vigor and vitality of the more extreme largely involuntary kinds of emotions." Play is an amazing antidote to boredom as it delivers emotional highs and lows in the context of imagined events.

Certainly, observations in the Cheah, Nelson, and Rubin chapter of this book describe children whose emotional balances are not working. These children seem shut down and lack the vigor, joy, and spontaneous sociability that we so much wish children to have. Play behavior tells a great deal about what children are like, especially those children who seem unable to produce the spontaneous exchanges that characterize "master players" (Fein & Kinney, 1994). Keith Sawyer advances the important idea that social pretend play helps children acquire the improvisational skills essential for ordinary conversation and, perhaps, more grandly, participation in social life.

Would play interventions such as those described by Bondioli or by Glaubman, Kashi, and Koresh make a difference? If individual data can be extracted from these efforts it would be interesting to find out whether low-play children who might be classified by Cheah et al. as socially reticent or solitary–active benefited from these interventions. our case studies of play-inhibited children suggest that a variety of play interventions can turn these children on. Why and how this works constitutes a phenomenon badly in need of a theory. In fact, what is noteworthy in the work of Bondioli and Glaubman et al. is that they take play itself as the intervention target rather than some presumed distal by-product. Careful analyses of what turns play on or off may help us to better understand how play works and, indirectly, what functions it works with.

Herman and Bretherton move the issue to children's original stories and another way of thinking about what these imaginative constructions tell us about children's inner worlds. In analyzing the stories of postdivorce preschoolers, these investigators came up with three provocative categories that tap the emotional tone associated with story characters, namely, benevolent, malevolent, and ambivalent. In our research we use scales that describe the overall events of a story as, for example, representing affection/affiliation, violence/adversity, and the like (see Darling, 2000). These schemes seem to be easier to develop with children's original narratives than with their play, especially when the play involves two or more children.

Finally, we have the Pellegrini and Galda analysis of emotion language in different tasks—one a teacher-directed writing task and the other a toy replica free-play task. Interestingly, the didactic session yielded more metatalk than the play setting. This finding is similar to that reported by Groth (1999). A school condition in which children discussed their original stories with peers yielded a higher level of emergent literacy than a story enactment condition. Although unexpected, that finding is not unreasonable. After all, in the "author's chair" children talk about written text. In enactment, they represent the written text. The theoretical contrast may be between meta-repesentation and representation. My hunch is that measures of originality or emotional expressiveness would give the gold star to enactment.

I was a reviewer for Keith Sawyer's recent book (Sawyer, 1997) and I never regretted my enthusiastic praise for his work. Yes, improvisational theater is an ingenious perspective from which to examine the communicative challenges of children's pretending. Improvisational interchanges during interactive pretending require communications that clarify scenes, characters, and objects because these narrative components may not be as they seem to be (Fein & Schwartz, 1986; Trawick-Smith, 1998). This ambiguity demands strategies to annotate what has and will happen. If pretend play exchanges are improvisations embedded in ambiguity, play partners must tune in to the statements, gestures, and actions of the metaplay in order to keep the exchange moving along. An improvisational perspective moves us away—far away—from the dead end account of pretending as imitation. To the contrary, pretending is owned by the children and in playing children are more likely to distort reality than to imitate it.

CHILD CARE AND ATTACHMENT

One of my great professional satisfactions comes from *Day Care in Context* (Fein & Clarke-Stewart, 1973). In its day, it was a sturdy reminder to the field that child care is amenable to scholarly inquiry. As I thumb through the pages and read snatches of text here and there I am amazed at how well it has survived the past 30 years. of course, the data have changed as has the magnitude of research, but the issues are still with us. Say, Alison, we did a good job.

A major debate in the 1980s was the effects of early-child-care attendance on a young child's attachment to parents. In 1988, Nathan Fox and I coedited two entire issues of the *Early Childhood Research Quarterly* addressed to the crucial issue of whether there is evidence that early child care damages the attachment relationship (Fein & Fox, 1988). Chapters by Clarke-Stewart, Allhusen, and Goossens and by Fox and Bar-Haim in the current volume make it clear that there is little left to argue about. First, there are no group differences when huge numbers enter into the analysis. Second, the differences found for small, narrowly selected groups of children when background variables are not controlled for simply fade away when the appropriate controls are introduced. And third, attachment as measured by our best instruments may simply not be a stable, lifespan variable (Fox & Bar-Haim). Both groups of investigators agree that other measures and other variables need to be investigated if either the child-care experience or multigenerational transmission is to be investigated.

These data will not satisfy those who insist that infant day care necessarily and inevitably intrudes on the depth of the mother–child relationship. If one accepts the early core of attachment theory, this must surely be true: Infants who lack a single, stable caregiver will be emotionally damaged. More likely, emotional and social development depends on the kindliness, stability, and warmth of parental as well as nonparental caregivers. As these chapters note, attachment theory needs to be radically revised or better, replaced by a theory that presupposes a flexible organism able to function in a mobile, fast-paced society. The human infant is far more adaptive than the theory allows; a useful theory must build this adaptability into its very core. Child-care quality and child-care outcomes need to be assessed with different constructs and different measures if we are to learn more about this child's strengths and vulnerabilities.

PARENTS, AND GOVERNMENT, TOO

In 1976, 1 was invited by the Assistant Secretary for Planning and Evaluation (DHEW) to prepare a paper on the Federal Interagency Day Care Requirements, which had come under pressure from child-care providers. I had recently arrived at the Merrill–Palmer Institute and had initiated a series of visits to child-care centers in Detroit. one of my questions was about parents, roles in the centers. In center after center, I was told that parents were free to visit provided they made an appointment first. Further, during my visits, I observed in center after center that children were deposited at the front door and picked up at the front door . . . so that, in effect, most parents rarely saw the inside of the place where their children spent the better part of the day. My reflections on the role of parents in child care was eventually published as *The Informed Parent* (Fein, 1980).

For this reason, Doug Powell's chapter is a happy addition to this volume. Powell tackles the tough problem of how professionals develop sharing relationships with parents. Powell brilliantly sets out the problems. The solutions can only occur on multiple tracks moving by millimeters over many years.

To round out this theme, we have the thoughtful overview of recent federal initiatives by Klein and Tarullo. our national priorities have always favored research, although generosity varies from one administration to another. But generosity at a local level still leaves too many poor-quality programs in the field. The notion that child care might be more accessible as part of the public schools needs stronger support than it has yet received.

RESPONSIVE TEACHERS

In studies we conducted in Italy, we were interested more in infants' adjustment process than in outcomes. For this reason children attending six child-care centers in Pavia were observed over a 6-month period (Fein, 1995; Fein, Gariboldi, & Boni, 1993). This concern with the process whereby young children form attachments to unfamiliar caregivers is addressed in the chapter by Howes and Oldham. The good news is that if caregivers are reasonably attentive, gentle, and responsive, children will become comfortable and at ease in their presence. Research of this type promises to yield constructive strategies for improving and personalizing the child-care experience for young children and their parents.

However, when teachers' behaviors are studied through a fine lens, researchers in a constructivist tradition often find far more didactic, heteronomous behavior than they expected. This is exactly what happened in the finely textured Patt and Göncü study of cooking . . . an activity that presumably provides opportunities for children to develop temporal reasoning, quantification, reading, and cooperation with peers. These results give us pause for reflection. These investigators' conclusions merit emphasis: "Although children participated in choosing a partner and a food to cook, the cooking routine was already established by the teachers, and the recipes, utensils, and ingredients were not a matter of choice but tools that exist in a cultural context beyond the range of children's control." Much like in the Pellegrini and Galda chapter, those of us who seek to understand children's school experiences are obliged to study how sociocultural contexts and the logic of situations controls what people can do and do.

In 1985, 1 published a study that owed much to Nancy King's (1979) classical study of kindergarten children's definitions of play. Those observations were elaborated by Fein and Wiltz (1998), who dealt in part with children's perceptions of play and pretending. The major conclusions of this work is that children are not fooled when teachers introduce learning tasks as games or constrained activities as play. The DeVries chapter offers a sure guide to constructivist practices. I would only add that along with the children, I believe that work can be as much fun as play; the difference is in the degree of choice in what to do and how to do it. In many child-care centers, play is little more than aimless rambling; in others, it is a rich, exploratory adventure. Diverse intervention studies demonstrate the many ways in which teachers can enhance the quality of children's spontaneous play.

Glaubman et al. describe a neat intervention designed to enhance the incidence and quality of play in the classroom. The intervention focuses on the representational object and all the ways a mind can invent it. These sessions occur during circle time, never during free play. The results are striking: Simply asking children to deconstruct and reconstruct ordinary everyday objects carries over into their dramatic play, increasing indices of the intellectual quality of the play itself.

Bondioli records teacher behavior that I observed when I was there and will forever cherish. But it is not what American teachers do. With great humor and joy, these teachers scream, "Did you kill it?" or "A lion! The baby is afraid of the lion. . . . " These teachers intervene with zest and vivid emotions, directly within the play. I assume these are fairly brief sessions, but they nonetheless add affect and empathy to the natural expressiveness of pretend play.

A GRAND RETIREMENT

In this grand retirement of mine, I do not work; in fact, I play an awful lot. My chief intellectual interest began with the pilot study described in this book by Groth and Darling. The question is how an affective theory of narrative representation offers insights into children's social, emotional, and literacy development. The classroom intervention described in that chapter has been elaborated in subsequent studies (Fein, Ardila-Rey, & Groth, 2000; Groth, 1999). When children listen to stories written by peers they do so with rapt attention even though the stories are incomplete and sketchy. How come?

Darling's dissertation (Darling, 2000) described the ways children's original stories mark gender and, more important, can reveal children's understanding of the cultural biases of same and other gender peers. These data support the claim that children's original stories provide a rich corpus for the analysis of expressive forms. This idea launched a seemingly endless study of my own. You see, during the past two decades there has emerged a new and dynamic genre of fiction: the detective story with a female sleuth written by a female author. All told, there are 214 living authors who have published at least 4 series books in this vein. Of these, 6% published their first book in the 1970s or earlier, 34% in the 1980s, and 60% in the 1990s. Of this group, 63 received recognition from professional associations. My sample consists of these 63 women, 4 books from each or a total of 252 books. At this point, I have almost completed the reading—236 novels written by 63 authors.

The scope of characteristics represented by these imaginary sleuths is breathtaking. Their ages range from 20 to 70; the youngest is Stephanie Plum, a bounty hunter from Trenton, New Jersey; the oldest is Angela Benbow and her pal Caledonia Wingate, 70-year-old ladies who live in a retirement home in California. The characters vary in size (5'2" to 6'2"), body (thin to very heavy), ethnicity (Irish, Jewish, Mexican, African American, Polish, or a mix of national origins), and place of residence (Boston to Miami, Baltimore to San Diego, and many places in between). They also differ in independence, with some sleuthing on their own and others having a boyfriend cop to turn to. Their occupations vary as well. Anna Pigeon (created by Nevada Barr) is a National Park Ranger; the series offers an informative guide to our national park system. Bo Bradley (Abigail Padgett) is a manic depressive who works as a social worker with abused children. Abigail Padgett, who herself suffers from a bipolar disorder, offers an informed and moving account of its burdens. The sample of sleuths includes a professor (Kate Fansler created by Amanda Cross), a high school English teacher (Amanda Pepper, by Gillian Roberts), a couple of caterers (e.g., Goldy Bear by Diane Mott Davidson), a forensic anthropologist (Elizabeth McPherson, by Sharon McCrumb), a 19th-century British anthropologist (Amelia Peabody, by Elizabeth Peters), and a generous assortment of lawyers, private eyes, journalists, and plain old housewives.

The feminist side of me is unendingly gleeful to think that our society has become bold enough to imagine so huge an array of personages that women are and can become. I plan to consider what the heroines like and dislike, where they find comfort or fear, how they feel about violence, the identity of bad guys, connections to family and lovers, and moral judgments. These stories integrate a cultural vision of intellectual and personal diversity within a common theme of murder and mayhem. It is this integration that I want to understand.

This project is an extension of my interest in the representation of affect in narratives. But more, these stories are often amazingly gripping, moving, and credible. They describe risks and mastery. And keep in mind that these novels are popular; they sell well. Apparently, adult readers find something valuable in these characters and their experiences. Do children's stories have these elements in some form or another? Is this what makes children so willing to tell and listen? Perhaps an analysis of this single adult genre will provide some clues about the larger functions of narrative forms.

IN SUM

What I am today grew chunk by chunk from blessed, though haphazard, events. No grand scheme, no lifelong ambition, no inherited destiny. I am indebted to the many people who enriched these events, who gave me the opportunity to take risks, jump down 12-foot walls, play as I wished, and cheer causes that I cared about. My parents bequeathed to me an immutable faith in the power of education and schools to make social life more humane and equitable. My children brought me close to the inside of development, and my grandchildren took me to the center.

Among my greatest satisfactions is my contribution to the graduate education of many who are now emerging as leaders in the field: Patricia Kinney, Brent McBride, Shari Castle, Mary Rivkin, Josephine Wilson, Ameetah Shaw, Abbie Griffin, Anastasia Samaras, Shirley Schwartz, June Wright, Mary Fryer, Dora Chen, and Lois A. Groth. Most of these people came to doctoral studies as school-savvy, mature adults and parents. They hit winners for the third generation of opportunity.

Finally, let me say, for sure, there really does not need to be a hill in Richmond Hill, nor a brook in Stony Brook, nor rocks in Rockland County. Human beings whether young or old are able to make conceptual and linguistic distinctions between what is physically apparent and what is mentally apparent. The fruits of this ability are amply evident in the chapters of this book. My gratitude to all of you.

REFERENCES

Darling, L. D. (2000). *Young children's social representations in fictional narratives: Gender identification and prediction.* Unpublished doctoral dissertation, University of Maryland College Park.

Fein, G. G. (1980). The informed parent. In S. Kilmer (Ed.), *Advances in early education and development* (vol. 1, pp. 155–195). Greenwich, CT: JAI Press.

Fein, G. G. (1985). Learning in play: Surfaces of thinking and feeling. In J. L. Frost & S. Sunderlin (Eds.), *When children play* (pp. 71–92). Wheaton, MD: Association of Childhood Education International.

Fein, G. G. (1995). Infants in group care: Despair and detachment. *Early Childhood Research Quarterly, 10,* 121–276.

Fein, G. G., Ardila-Rey, A. E., & Groth, L. A. (2000). The narrative connection: Stories and literacy. In K. A. Roskos & J. F. Christie (Eds.) *Play and literacy in early childhood: Research from multiple perspectives* (pp. 27–44). Mahwah, NJ: Erlbaum.

Fein, G. G., & Clarke-Stewart, A. (1973). *Day care in context*. New York: Wiley

Fein, G. G., & Fox, N. (Eds.). (1988). Infant day care, I and II. *Early Childhood Research Quarterly, 3*(3–4).

Fein, G. G., Gariboldi, A., & Boni, R. (1993) Transitions to group care. *Early Childhood Research Quarterly, 8*, 1–14.

Fein, G. G., & Kinney, P. (1994). He's a nice alligator: Observations on the affective organization of pretense. In A. Slade & D. P. Wolf (Eds.), *Clinical and developmental studies of play* (pp. 181–205). New York: Oxford University Press.

Fein, G. G., & Schwartz, S. S. (1986). The social coordination of pretense in preschool children. In G. G. Fein & M. Rivkin (Eds.), *The young child at play: Reviews of research* (Vol. 4, pp. 91–111). Washington, DC: National Association for the Education of Young Children.

Fein, G. G., & Wiltz, N. (1998). Play as children see it. In D. Fromberg & D. Bergen (Eds.), *Play from birth to twelve* (pp. 31–49). New York: Garland.

Groth, L. (1999). *Sharing original stories: Enactment and discussion in the kindergarten*. Unpublished doctoral dissertation, University of Maryland, College Park.

Kessen, W. (1991). Nearing the end: A lifetime of being 17. In F. Kessel, M. Bornstein, & A. Sameroff (Eds.), *Contemporary constructions of the child* (pp. 281–291). Mahwah, NJ: Erlbaum.

King, N. (1979) Play: The kindergarten perspective. *Elementary School Journal, 80*(2), 81–87.

Sawyer, R. K. (1997). *Pretend play as improvisation: Conversation in the preschool classroom*. Mahwah, NJ: Erlbaum.

Sutton-Smith, B. (1995). Conclusion: The persuasive rhetorics of play. In A. D. Pellegrini (Ed.), *The future of play theory* (pp. 271–296). Albany: State University of New York Press.

Trawick-Smith, J. (1998). A qualitative analysis of metaplay in the preschool years. *Early Childhood Research Quarterly, 13*, 431–452.

Index

Note: A *t* in italics refers to a table.